Fourth edition

Intro[illegible] to marketing

Fourth edition

Introduction to marketing

Prof Johan Strydom, Editor

Ms Natasha da Silva Esclana
Mr Colin Diginis
Prof Flip du Plessis
Mr Richard Machado
Dr Mercy Mpinganjira
Ms Helen McIntee
Prof Sharon Rudansky-Kloppers
Mr Danie Theron

JUTA

IMM africa association of marketers

First published 1998
Second edition 1999
Reprinted 2004
Third edition 2004
Reprinted 2008
Reprinted 2009
Fourth edition 2011
Reprint March 2011

Juta and Company Ltd
1st Floor, Sunclare Building, 21 Dreyer Street, Claremont, 7708

PO Box 14373, Lansdowne, 7779, Cape Town, South Africa

ISBN 978-0-70217-810-8

Project Manager: Sharon Hendrickse
Editor: Stephen Heyns
Proofreader: Ethné Clarke
Typesetter: Wouter Reinders
Indexer: Sanet le Roux
Cover Designer: Waterberry Designs
Printed in South Africa by Academic Press

This book has been independently peer-reviewed by academics who are experts in the field.

Contents

Contributors

Prof Flip du Plessis (Extra-ordinary Professor University of Pretoria and Emeritus Professor University of South Africa)	Chapter 1: Introduction to marketing
Dr Mercy Mpinganjira (University of Johannesburg)	Chapter 2: The marketing environment
Ms Helen McIntee (IMM Graduate School of Marketing)	Chapter 3: Understanding the consumer Chapter 5: Segmentation, targeting and positioning
Prof Sharon Rudansky-Kloppers (University of South Africa – UNISA)	Chapter 4: Marketing information and marketing research Chapter 9: Marketing communication decisions
Mr Danie Theron (UNISA)	Chapter 6: Product decisions
Prof Johan Strydom (UNISA)	Chapter 7: Distribution decisions Chapter 8: Pricing decisions
Mr Colin Digginis (UNISA)	Chapter 10: Developing a marketing mix for service
Mr Ricardo Machado (UNISA)	Chapter 11: Integrated marketing
Ms Natasha da Silva Esclana (UNISA)	Chapter 12: Marketing and the Internet

Preface

One of the most pressing problems in teaching marketing to southern African students remains the lack of a comprehensive marketing textbook for first-year students at tertiary institutions. Most existing texts are published abroad, are aimed at senior undergraduate level, and are extremely expensive. The first edition of this book was launched in 1998, with the objective of making marketing more accessible to the growing number of people involved in everyday marketing activities. This market includes first-time marketing students, budding entrepreneurs who need marketing in the ordinary running of their fledgling businesses, people aspiring to a career in marketing, and those managers who need to brush up on the underlying principles of marketing.

The fourth edition of Introduction to Marketing has been re-developed in response to the encouraging support we received from academics and positive feedback from our students. It is built on the knowledge and know-how of the corps of experienced lecturers in marketing management at the University of South Africa (UNISA), supplemented by authors from other tertiary institutions, such as the University of Johannesburg. Some fresh conceptual knowledge has been provided by Professor Flip du Plessis, previously at the University of Pretoria. We also welcome two new authors from the IMM Graduate School of Marketing (IMM GSM), Ms Helen McIntee, who contributes her hands-on experience of teaching marketing and marketing-related disciplines, and Dr Mercy Mpinganjira from the Marketing Department of the University of Johannesburg.

This edition comprises twelve chapters of which six have been completely rewritten to reflect the most recent changes in marketing thought at the introductory level. The other chapters have been extensively updated.

The new chapters are:

- The introduction (chapter 1), which has been completely rewritten to reflect the most current thought on marketing.
- A new look at the marketing environment (chapter 2).
- Chapter 3 which covers consumer behaviour.
- A new chapter on segmentation, targeting and positioning (chapter 5).
- A new chapter on marketing communication decisions (chapter 9).
- A chapter on integrated marketing (chapter 11), which provides a thorough discussion of the integration process and a look at marketing ethics.

All of the other chapters have been extensively reworked. In order to facilitate the learning process we continued with the mini-case studies at the end of each chapter, as well as a terminology section to help the student master key terms and concepts.

I encourage readers to send their constructive comments and suggestions for possible incorporation in future editions.

Johan Strydom (editor), Strydjw@unisa.ac.za
Pretoria
November 2010

CHAPTER 1

Introduction to marketing

Learning outcomes

After studying this chapter you should be able to:

- define marketing and explain how the 'marketing concept' should guide organisations;
- discuss 'customer centricity' and customer satisfaction;
- identify the management functions of marketing;
- explain the marketing manager's role of planning, co-ordination and integration;
- discuss the concept of marketing planning;
- understand the difference between micro- and macro-marketing; and
- explain how social responsibility and ethics relate to the marketing concept.

Introduction

Welcome to the dynamic world of marketing. In this **book** we will explore the function of marketing, what the marketing function's relationship is with other functions internally, and what its dependence is on the external environment such as technology, and the social-cultural, legal, economic, and political environment. In addition, we will look at what the interface entails with regard to customers,[*] competitors and stakeholders, and how marketing should change or adapt its strategy in transferring value to them.

In this **chapter** a broad view will be given of what marketing is and the processes that are followed to ultimately reach the customer. Customer needs are identified, the organisation[†] develops a product or service which will address those needs, the value it creates is communicated to potential customers, and they are encouraged to buy the product at a certain price to satisfy their need. After the sale is made and the customer is satisfied, a relationship between the customer and the organisation can develop.

---

* In this introductory text, the terminology 'consumer' and 'customer' are deemed to be the same thing, so these terms will be used interchangeably in the text.

† The terms 'organisation', 'firm', 'business', 'enterprise' and 'company' are used interchangeably in this text to mean the same thing.

The organisation and its marketing function need an infrastructure to get information from customers in order to understand their needs, to design customer-driven marketing strategies and programmes, to build relationships with customers, and to capture value for the organisation.[1]

At this point it is useful and practical to look at a few philosophies or orientations of organisations towards marketing.

Marketing orientations

Marketing has two components. It consists of a philosophy and a set of activities (or marketing processes) which are used to implement the philosophy.[2] The marketing process will be discussed later in this chapter.

A first philosophy of an organisation can be a **production orientation** whereby the focus is internally directed towards the capabilities of the organisation and not on the external market requirements of the customers' needs, desires and wants.

A second philosophy can be a **sales orientation** where the emphasis is on aggressive sales techniques. The thinking behind this orientation is that customers will buy more goods and services if this kind of technique is deployed.

The third orientation is a **societal marketing orientation** which has at its core the philosophy that an organisation exists not only to satisfy the needs of customers, but to take the long-term interests of the society and community into consideration. This philosophy is closely related to the ethics of marketing and will be discussed later.

A market orientation, which is similar to the **marketing concept**, is a philosophy that holds that, at the purchase decision stage, a customer will not necessarily respond well to an aggressive sales presentation and pressure from the sales force. Rather, the decision whether or not to buy the product or service is based on a customer's needs. The marketing concept further includes:

- Integration of an organisation's activities so that everyone in the organisation is sensitised to the customer's needs in order that their individual contributions collectively satisfy the customer's needs.
- Achieving the long-term objectives of the organisation.
- Acting in a responsible way in satisfying the needs of customers (societal marketing concept).

Some authors expand on these organisational orientations by adding the idea of the competitor-centred organisation. Here the organisation spends a great deal of time analysing and tracking competitors' actions so that it is able to counter these with appropriate alternative strategies.[3]

Market-oriented organisations should collect and analyse customer- and competitor-related information and use it to design and create value propositions that have a differential advantage over their competitors.

Customer centricity

The world has become 'commoditised' and it is difficult for organisations and their products to be differentiated from competitive products. Customer-centric marketing involves developing mutually beneficial relationships with customers based on focusing on their individual needs.[4] Customer centricity is similar to the market orientation because such an organisation focuses on the needs and behaviours of its customers, rather than focusing inwardly on itself. A general definition of a customer-centric organisation is that it creates meaningful value for customers, leading to sustained competitive advantage for both short- and long-term organisational success.[5]

Customer centricity is pivotal to delivering a unique and distinctive experience in order to acquire, retain and enhance value for target markets in a cost-effective way. The experience and emotions customers experience when using a product or service or when engaging with the organisation can, however, be a differentiator. To remain competitive in most product categories, marketers must design and communicate an experience around every contact point with the customer. A series of positive contact points comprises a customer's total experience of the organisation.[6]

Building a customer-centric organisation requires a change in organisational culture, but that is not easy because it involves changing people's beliefs, their attitudes, and the way they do things at work.[7] Apart from changing the culture, it is also essential for an organisation to align its objectives of sales, marketing and service because these may sometimes have conflicting objectives and strategies, as illustrated in fig. 1.1.

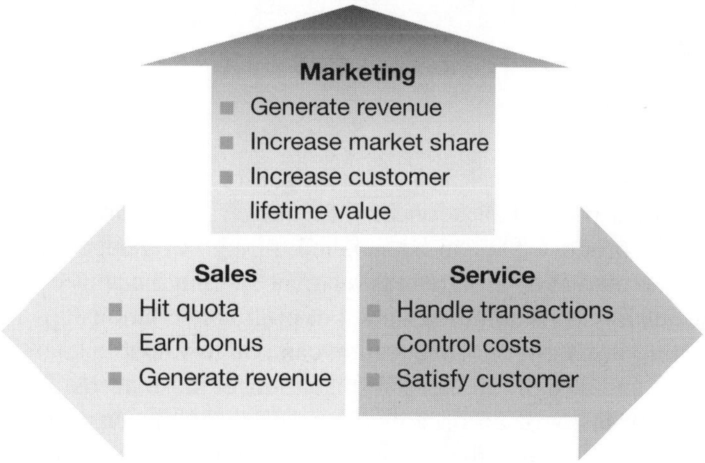

***Figure 1.1** Conflicting objectives of marketing, sales and service*[8]

The customer must be seen as the focal point of these functions and all the objectives (departmental and corporate) must be aligned to satisfy the customers' needs and expectations. The reader will observe that this is similar to the discussion above about the marketing concept and customer-centricity where all customer-facing functions in the organisation should integrate and harmonise their actions in order to satisfy the customer so that the company can achieve profit in the long term.

In the execution of a customer-centric orientation the organisation should be a 'listening organisation' (hear the voice of the customer), respond to information from customers (needs, issues, complaints, suggestions, market changes, negative customer behaviour, negative word-of-mouth, drivers of dissatisfaction, unresolved complaints, and why customers defect).[9] Successfully and proactively designing and delivering a consistent experience across all customer touch points requires employees to be fully engaged with the brand promise and the brand values. This is further discussed in chapter 6. It is now appropriate to look at the elements of a workable definition of marketing.

Marketing defined

It is a cliché, but there are as many definitions of marketing as there are writers on the subject. A synthesis of definitions by some well-known authors and professional marketing associations is summed up below.[10]

> **Definition of marketing**
> Marketing is the process by which organisations create value for customers in the form of ideas, goods and services to facilitate satisfying exchange relationships and to capture value from customers.

From the definition the following concepts can be identified:
- Customer value
- Exchange
- Satisfaction
- Capturing value
- Relationships
- Marketing process

Customer value

Customers are part of the market and a market can be regarded as a set of actual and potential buyers of a product or service. This market has a similar set of needs and expectations of the product that can be satisfied through exchange relationships.[11] The management of the market environment is relatively within the control of the marketing organisation which has as its aim the creation of profitable relationships with customers. Through marketing research, the organisation can obtain valuable knowledge about the customers' needs, and design product offerings to meet those needs.

Two of the main tasks of an organisation are to acquire customers, and to keep those customers. To do this the organisation cannot simply provide a good or service, it must offer customers something that they value. Customer value can be viewed as the ratio of benefits to the sacrifice necessary to obtain those benefits.[12]

Value-driven marketing assumes that customers who are willing and able to make exchanges will do so when the benefits of exchange exceed the costs of exchange and the products or services offer superior value compared to the alternatives.[13] Although value is very subjective, one could venture to define value as the customer's evaluation, adjusted for cost, of how well a good or service meets or exceeds expectations. An important notion underlies this perception of value by customers – as long as they can maximise value, they are not concerned how and whether the organisation maximises cost effectiveness or profit.

Another concept tied to value is the **value proposition**. It can be considered as the market offering (value of whole bundle of benefits or performance) that the customer will receive when buying/using the product or service. An organisation's value propositions should take into account the expectations, needs and wants of the customers. Value propositions are not centred on products and services; rather, they are based on customer criteria. They are a statement about the experience customers will have had from the delivered value offering and their relationship with the supplier.[14]

Customer delivered value is the difference between customer perceptions of benefits from buying and using products and services, and customer perceptions of the costs they incur to acquire and use those products and services.[15] It is thus the ratio between what a customer gets and what he or she gives. *Value is thus better understood through a value equation where customer value equals perceived benefits minus perceived costs*.[16] The marketer can increase the value of the customer offering by increasing the benefits or reducing the costs of the product or services. Benefits can be of a functional or emotional nature, while costs may consist of a monetary value, a time and energy component, and psychic expenditure.

Therefore, the customers will benefit from and be responsive to an extended value proposition by the marketer if it increases the total value they receive, or if it lowers the total costs of the expected result they desire.

The revenues of an organisation represent the value created for the customer as reflected in their willingness to exchange value (e.g. money) for a product or service.

Exchange

Exchange simply means that people give up something of value for something else they value. Examples are: a customer has something of value (money) which he or she wants to exchange for something else of value (a watch or motor car); a person has something of value (expertise, knowledge and experience) which he or she wants to exchange for something else of value which an employer has (money). Exchange does not necessarily require money; two persons may exchange value without money being involved (barter).

Five conditions must be present for an exchange to take place:[17]

- There must be at least two parties.
- Each party must have something of value.
- Each party must be free to accept or reject the exchange offer.
- Each party must be willing to deal with the other party.
- Parties must be capable of communicating with each other.

Exchange takes place within a market. The market consists of people who have needs (discussed in the next section) and the means to pay. They also have the willingness to exchange (either buy or sell). The exchange process is illustrated in fig. 1.2.

Satisfaction

Satisfaction is the third element in the definition of marketing above. Marketing should facilitate satisfying exchange relationships, i.e. both the seller (organisation) and the buyer (customer) must be satisfied by the exchange process.

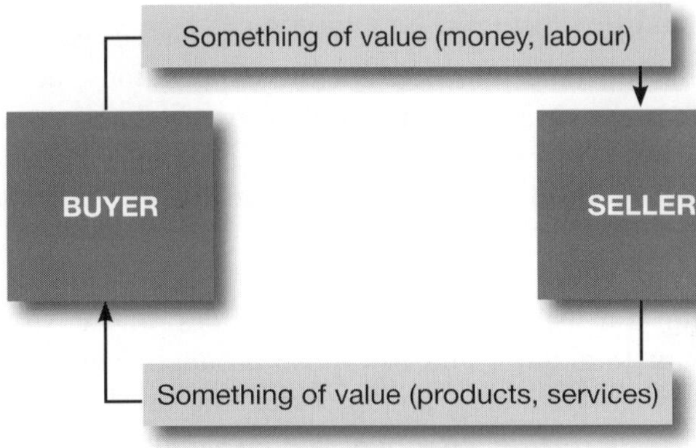

Figure 1.2 *Exchange between buyer and seller*

On the part of the seller, satisfaction would be the result of being able to offer a product or service that satisfies the need of a customer at a profit. The seller's satisfaction will be enhanced if the positive relationship with the customer continues and the customer becomes loyal to the organisation. This would represent an increase in the life-time value of customers.

Customer satisfaction is the result of a customer experiencing that the product or service has met or exceeded his or her expectations. The ideal for an organisation is to satisfy the customer's need at a high level so that the customer becomes a loyal customer who recommends the product to others, who continues to buy the product or service from the same organisation, and who may even expand the quantity or variety of purchases from the organisation. The benefits of strong customer satisfaction and loyalty have a number of benefits for the organisation.

- **Lower acquisition costs**. If an organisation's customers are loyal, then the need to acquire new customers decreases, and total customer acquisition costs will also decrease. Such costs may include advertising, demonstrations of the product, sales calls, and special promotions such as discounts to attract new customers.
- **Lifetime value**. Customers tend to spend more over time and loyal customers increase their spending on other products from the organisation. The amount that a customer spends over a lifetime on that kind of product or service would be captured for the organisation. The combined discounted customer lifetime values of all customers represent the organisation's customer equity.[18]
- **Referrals**. Satisfied customers will recommend an organisation or its products to their friends, colleagues and families. This kind of word-of-mouth recommendation is far more credible than organisation-driven promotion methods such as advertising.
- **Price premium**. Loyal customers are less sensitive to price increases and may even be willing to pay a price premium for an organisation's products because they are satisfied and have a high level of trust in, and commitment towards, the organisation.

The set of activities undertaken by a customer to satisfy his or her needs and wants can be regarded as the customer value chain, and the value-creating factors could be speed, cost, quality and flexibility.[19] The importance of each of these traits depends on the customer's expectations.

Value-driven marketing presupposes that customers have different perceptions of value, and it assumes that different customers may assess the value of the same product in different ways. Some customers may regard an Atos motor vehicle as good value because it provides reliable transportation at a relatively low cost. Others may view a Mercedes SL500 as good value because it is a high-status car that lasts a long time.

The first phase in delivering value to customers is to have a closer look at needs. Needs describe basic human requirements and they become wants when they are directed towards specific products or services that might satisfy those needs.[20] Marketers can influence wants but they cannot create needs. Clothing retailers at the top end of the market might promote the idea that their products will satisfy a buyer's need for social status. However, they cannot create the need for social status.

A customer might have many needs at any given time. Some needs are biogenic; they arise from physiological states of tension such as hunger, thirst, or discomfort. Other needs are psychogenic; they arise from psychological states of tension such as the need for recognition, esteem, or belonging. A need becomes a motive when it is activated to a sufficient level of intensity to drive a person to act in order to satisfy that need. This will be further discussed in chapter 3.

Customer needs give rise to a marketing opportunity and many opportunities can be found by identifying trends. Marketing opportunities must be converted into products or services, which maximise customer value in terms of perceived benefits. The types of benefits include functional, emotional, image, social, service and experiential benefits (this will be discussed further in chapter 10).

Capturing value

The fourth element in the definition of marketing is capturing value from the customer in exchange for the value of the product offering. A customer's value for the organisation is determined by the perceived benefits received, minus the perceived costs. Any for-profit organisation has as its goal the realisation of profit in the long term in order to be sustainable in its raison d'être (reason for existence), obligations to its shareholders, current and future sales, and market share.[21]

The measurement of customer satisfaction must be an ongoing process to enable the organisation to judge whether customers are still satisfied with the product offering or whether their needs are changing. These measurements and feedback from customers are necessary for decisions about possible changes in the marketing mix: product, price, how and where the product can be accessed (distribution), and marketing communication (promotion). Marketing strategies to enhance competitiveness, repositioning the product in terms of the value proposition, or changing processes to accommodate customers' needs can also be implemented when customer satisfaction measurements dictate that any of these factors needs attention.

Although the existence of a relationship between customer loyalty and organisational profits is accepted, it seems customer satisfaction is not enough to ensure ongoing loyalty.[22] Customers want to be completely satisfied; if they have a choice, they can be lured away easily. Research done with Xerox customers found that its totally satisfied customers were six times more likely to repurchase Xerox products over the next 18 months than its satisfied customers.[23] In another study, it was established that between 65% and 85% of customers who defect said that they were satisfied with their former supplier.[24]

Relationships

Some authors regard the concept of relationship as a philosophy of marketing and categorise it as a relationship marketing orientation.[25] These writers argue that customer loyalty is an important consideration in long-term marketing success and regard relationship marketing orientation as the most recent refinement of the marketing concept. This had not been discussed above as a separate philosophy because the authors contend that if the marketing concept as a philosophy is successfully implemented and optimally applied, customer satisfaction will probably result in a high level of customer loyalty and retention. Then relationship-building can be further advanced.

Mention has already been made of the business sense of spending money to attract customers to the product/organisation and to retain them as customers. The transaction with a customer does not end when a sale is made; rather, the transaction should be seen as the beginning of a relationship. An important trend in marketing is customer relationship marketing (CRM) which aims to develop long-term mutually beneficial relationships with customers who are satisfied with the product offering. CRM focuses on using information about customers to develop marketing strategies that enhance relationships with those customers.[26]

The customers that your organisation wants to have relationships with must be identified, and you must establish what is important to them and how they would want the relationship to be. If this is done successfully, the organisation will benefit from increasing business and referrals, and the customer will receive increased value and be more satisfied. The first relationship marketers were probably local storekeepers who knew their customers by name and their grocery lists off by heart.[27] The focus of relationship marketing is on attracting and retaining customers through trust, commitment, and sharing of information. Research has shown that relationship marketing is best implemented in countries where buyer-seller relationships are based on trust, mutual benefits, shared goals, and a harmonious approach to handling disagreements.[28]

Trust and commitment are key elements for retaining customers.

Trust is particularly critical for service-related organisations, since the product is intangible and difficult to evaluate before and after a purchase. Trust can be said to exist when one party has confidence in the reliability and integrity of the exchange partner. The ultimate goal is to establish satisfying relationships between customers and the organisation by gathering information at all customer contact points, in order to better understand their needs and expectations.

Commitment refers to the belief by both parties that the relationship is worth sustaining indefinitely. Customers will be committed to the relationship if they receive a high level of benefits and/or they consider the cost of terminating the relationship to be high. The higher customers' level of commitment, the less likely they are to leave, i.e. the higher the level of customer retention.

Many organisations have embraced relationship marketing with its focus on maximising customer lifetime value. Building relationships is not only confined to customers; the organisation must also 'partner' with its suppliers, distributors, and other stakeholders. Every party's contribution in the supply and value chain has a direct and indirect influence on the ultimate value that the customer will experience. Various authors use the concept of a 'value delivery network' when they discuss the importance of partnering with suppliers.[29]

Other stakeholders can include shareholders, institutional investors, creditors, lenders, customers, regulators, employees, labour unions, the media, analysts, consumers, society in general, communities, auditors and potential investors. The degree and scope of relationship-building with various stakeholders must be determined by each organisation. The criterion for choosing to focus on specific relationships would be that it has high potential for mutually rewarding outcomes.

Successful relationship marketing strategies depend on an organisation having a strong customer orientation; competent staff to support that orientation; front-line employees who have been trained and given the authority and empowerment to make decisions; effective cross-functional collaboration; and teamwork.[30]

The marketing process

The previous discussion of the elements of the definition of marketing can be viewed as part of the marketing process and can be most simply presented as a five-phase model:

1. Understanding customers' needs and their value expectations.
2. Developing a customer-oriented marketing strategy to exchange value.
3. Delivering value-driven product offerings to satisfy customer needs.
4. Capturing value from customers.
5. Building profitable relationships with customers.

Fig. 1.3 describes how the content of this book fits into the model.

What can be marketed?

Broadly speaking, tangible products, intangible products, ideas and causes, persons, experiences and places can be marketed. These can be categorised into: consumer goods and services, and business-to-business products and services.

Consumer goods and services include:

- convenience goods (e.g. newspapers and grocery items);
- semi-durable goods (household appliances – e.g. white goods such as stoves, fridges, microwave ovens and electric kettles);
- speciality or durable goods (e.g. television sets, paintings, motor vehicles and houses and flats);
- services (e.g. banking, auditing, travel, movies, repair services and medical services);

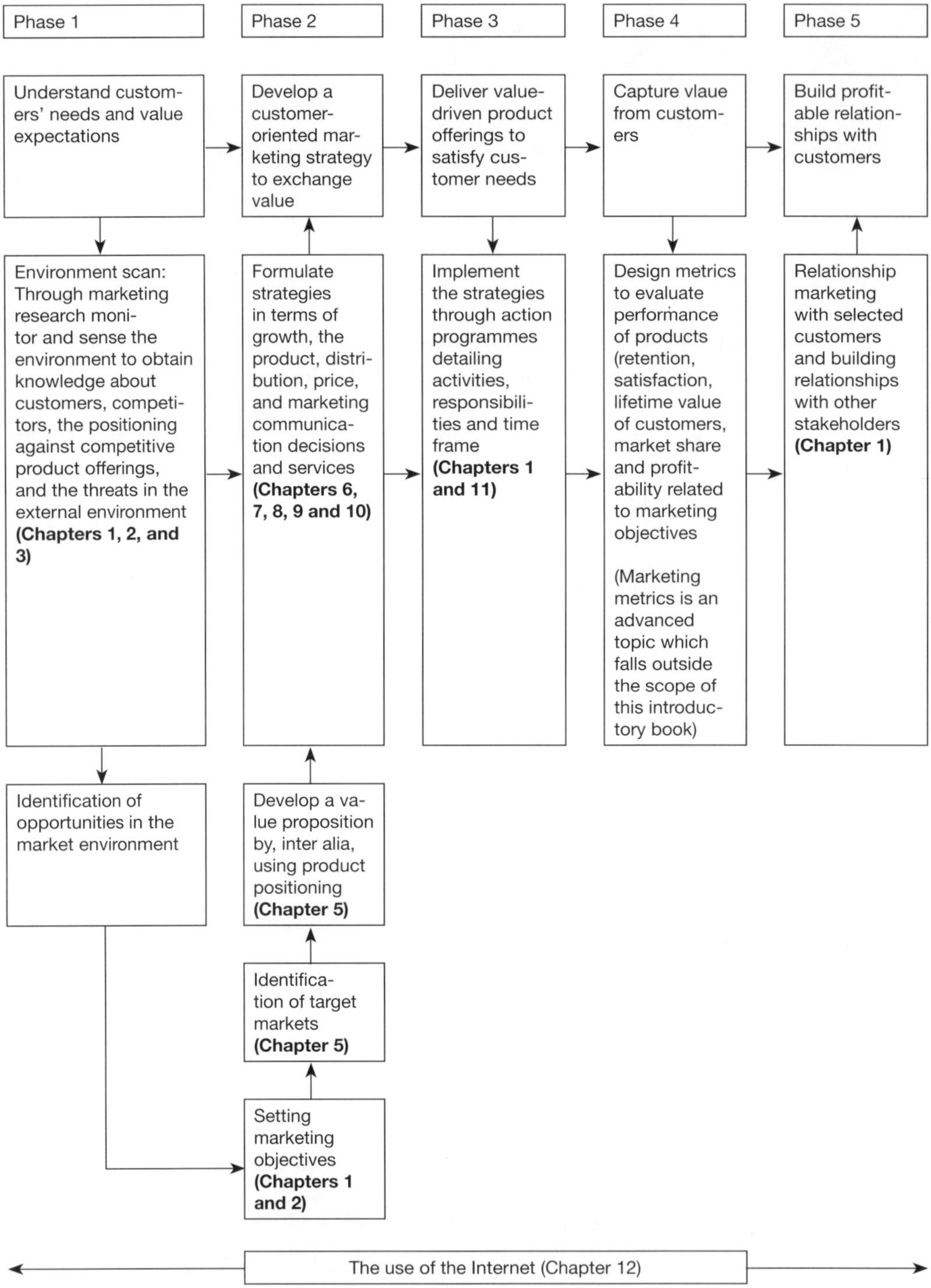

***Figure 1.3** Model of the marketing process*

- ideas and causes (e.g. the work of the Cancer Association of South Africa, the 'don't drink and drive' campaign, and the campaign to encourage the use of seatbelts);
- persons (a political candidate, e.g. Nelson Mandela in 1994);
- experiences (e.g. bungee jumping); and
- places (e.g. the Maldives or the Kruger National Park).

Marketing of goods and services to organisations as inputs to produce other goods or use in their business operations is called business-to-business marketing (B2B), including:
- consumables (maintenance and repair items such as oil, filters, cleaning materials, bolts, nuts and fasteners);
- machinery (e.g. drills, power tools, lathes and computers);
- installations (e.g. buildings, power plants and refineries);
- raw materials (e.g. gold, iron ore, coal, rubber and copper);
- business services (e.g. advertising, fire protection, safety, security and cleaning).

The bundle of benefits, features, information, and experiences must be marketed to satisfy the needs of the customer in a total market offering. A customer might need a 5 mm hole in a wall and the marketer may be offering a drill bit to satisfy that need. A woman buying lipstick needs to be convinced that she is buying beauty, not just a coloured wax object. When an organisation is offering a camera to a certain segment of the market, it is not only marketing the physical product, but it is addressing other needs of a customer, namely the desire for adventure, excitement and memories. This is discussed in more detail in chapter 6.

Managerial functions in an organisation

There are basic managerial functions in every organisation which must report to a General Manager, or a Chief Executive/Chief Executive Officer. These functions must be performed irrespective of the size of the organisation or the industry. If an organisation is small, some or all of these functions will be collapsed into smaller combinations. An organisation can consist of the following managerial functions:
- financial management;
- human resource management;
- operations management;
- purchasing and logistics management;
- information technology; and
- marketing management.

The financial management portfolio is responsible for acquiring funds for the organisation and application of these funds to ensure the organisation is profitable, liquid and can continue to exist.

Human resource (HR) management looks after the well-being of staff. Detailed activities include: recruitment of staff; determining selection processes and criteria; placement of staff; training and development; performance management; remuneration; and dealing with aspects of organisational culture.

Operations management functions include: the utilisation of input materials in the manufacturing of finished goods; maintaining optimal efficiency of equipment; and providing output according to specified specifications. The same general principles of operations management apply in manufacturing and in service organisations.

Purchasing and logistics management involves the acquisition of all supplies, materials, equipment, and ensuring that procedures regarding buying policies and procedures are adhered to.

Information technology spans the boundary between external sources of information and internal deployment of knowledge systems. It normally involves the management of information systems which are very reliant on technology, hardware and software systems.

Marketing management will be discussed in the section dealing with the scope of marketing functions.

It must be noted that the functions mentioned above are generalisations and the functions, structures and even terminology may differ between organisations and industries. For instance, a large manufacturer may also have an engineering function and a large research and development function. Sales and service functions might be regarded as so important in a particular organisation that they are treated as functions in their own right, rather than being part of the typical marketing management function.

Strategic planning

An organisation can be divided into a corporate level and divisional or functional level. At the corporate level, the organisation does strategic planning by establishing a strategic fit between the organisation's objectives and capabilities, and dynamic opportunities in the environment.[31] This strategic planning process starts with the vision, mission, and formulation of objectives and strategies, marketing objectives, marketing strategy and a marketing plan.[32] If the organisation is large, then decisions regarding the portfolio of businesses (strategic business units) must also be taken. Based on these strategies, the corporate level will provide strategic guidelines to people at the functional levels who will in turn develop their own objectives and strategies. These objectives and strategies must of course be congruent with the corporate level's own strategic planning. The hierarchy of planning objectives from the strategic level to marketing management's implementation of relevant strategies is illustrated in fig. 1.4.

To summarise: in order for an organisation to survive and grow in the long term, the managers of the marketing function must make decisions and take actions that are aimed at aligning the objectives and strategies of the marketing function with the achievement of the vision, mission, and strategic objectives of the organisation. There must be congruence between the goals and objectives of the marketing function and the objectives of the other functional areas of the organisation. The internal marketing function must be aligned with the changes in the market and macro environments of the organisation. Marketing management therefore, should support the organisation's strategic planning with more detailed plans for identified marketing opportunities.[33]

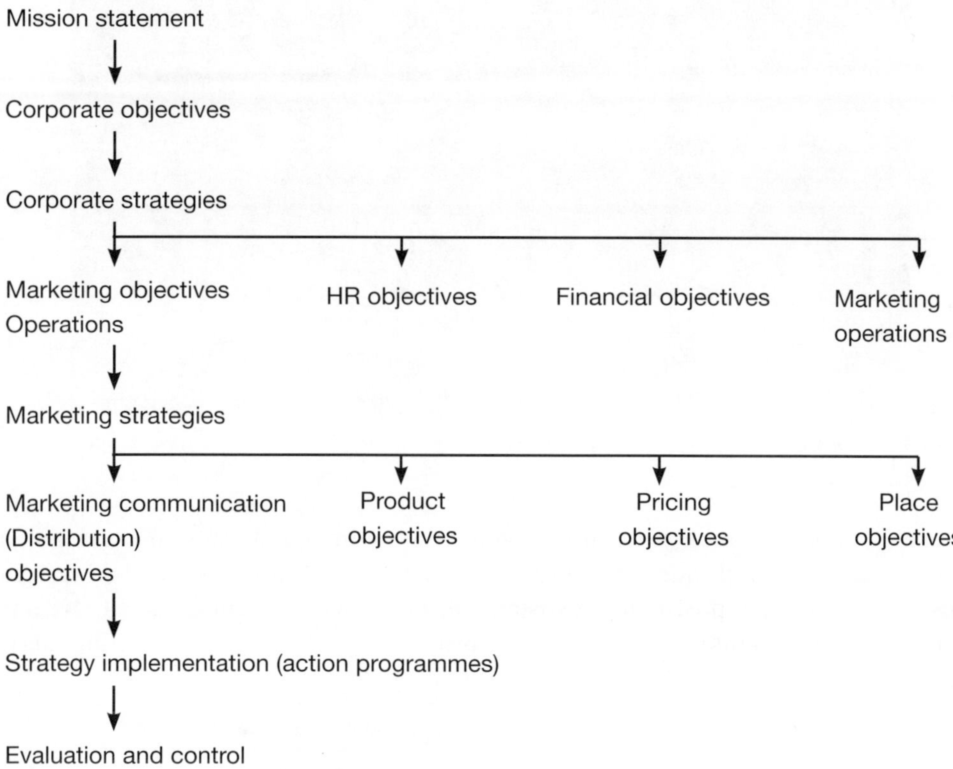

Figure 1.4 *Hierarchy of planning objectives and strategies*

The scope of marketing management functions

As has been said, an organisation develops strategic plans and objectives on the corporate level and provides strategic direction to the various functional levels. The marketing function, for instance, translates it into marketing plans. These marketing plans are the result of the various phases in the marketing process which was illustrated in fig. 1.3. However, this marketing process encapsulates or requires four marketing functions, namely analysis, planning, implementation and control.[34]

Analysis

In this function the organisation can use marketing research (either internally conducted or externally contracted) to obtain the required information. The organisation starts with an analysis of the internal and external environment, as discussed in chapter 2. One tool that can be used is a 'SWOT' analysis in which the organisation's internal strengths and weaknesses are identified, and external opportunities and threats are evaluated (see fig. 1.5).

In addition to a SWOT analysis, the organisation should also explore the market environment to obtain knowledge about customers, potential customers, competitors, the organisation's positioning in respect of competitive market offerings, and intermediaries.

Internal environment	
Strengths	**Weaknesses**
Financial resources Well-known brands Technological skills	Lack of strategic direction High costs Obsolete facilities
External environment	
Opportunities	**Threats**
Potential new markets Potential new products Falling international trade barriers	New competition Slow market growth New regulations

Figure 1.5 *Simplified example of a SWOT analysis*

Once the organisation knows enough about the internal and external environment, then the identified opportunities can be further explored in terms of their viability (markets to be served, profitability, sustainability, growth and compatibility with the organisation's strengths). A useful way of prioritising opportunities (and threats) is by means of an impact/probability matrix (see fig. 1.6).

		Probability of occurrence		
		High	Medium	Low
Impact on the organisation	High	A	B	E
	Medium	C	D	G
	Low	I	H	F

Figure 1.6 *Impact/probability matrix*

Each opportunity must be judged in terms of: (a) what the probability of realising the opportunity is, taking into consideration the strengths of the organisation, competitive advantage, ease of entry into the market, and competitive forces; and (b) what the impact will be on the organisation if the opportunity is realised in terms of growth, profit, sustainability and market share. Using the example in fig. 1.5, only the opportunities listed in cells A, B, C, and D would be further investigated as possible priorities.

At this stage questions must be addressed such as: is this opportunity within the scope of the organisation's mission and aligned to the strategic intent of the organisation, will it add value, and will the product or service have a sustainable competitive advantage?

A sustainable competitive advantage is not easy to develop or to sustain in the long term because it can be copied by competitors. A competitive advantage is an attribute/feature/benefit of a market offering that is valued by customers and which competitors do not have to the same extent. Think of reasons why ABSA bank may be preferred over Standard Bank by some customers, why a large segment of consumers buy at Pick n Pay and not at Woolworths, and why some customers may choose a Lexus over a Mercedes. This could be because they perceive certain products to have specific qualities that they want and which will provide satisfaction and value. Based on its strengths and capabilities, an organisation can develop products or services that will provide a competitive edge. Although there are various ways how this can be effected, the following can be mentioned: service quality, creating customer value, maintaining customer satisfaction, customer-oriented employees, empowerment, teamwork, cost, quality, flexibility, location, safety, image, design[35] and cost leadership, differentiation and focus.[36] An organisation might deliver value that is superior to a competitor's product at the same price as competitors, or the same quality as competitors but at a lower price, or higher value (quality) at a lower price. Topics related to price are addressed in more detail in chapter 8.

After attractive and viable opportunities have been selected, appropriate marketing objectives can be formulated. The marketing objectives must be SMART – simple, measureable, attainable, realistic and timebound. Examples of marketing objectives could be:

- increase market share from 25% in 2010 to 30% in 2011;
- penetrate the youth market in Gauteng to gain market share of 5% in 2011;
- raise awareness level of product Z with 5% within the next six months;
- develop new markets in England for product X to achieve awareness of 15% and 40% trial of the product within three months.

Planning

Marketing planning involves the development of details on who makes up the target market, how value will be created and delivered to the customer, what the value proposition is, and how the marketing mix variables (product, distribution, price and marketing communication) will be optimally utilised to obtain the desired response from the target market. It also consists of the strategic growth strategies of the organisation.

A marketing plan is very similar to the activities which we have identified in the marketing process (fig. 1.3). The marketing plan is a written document formalising the various phases in analysing the environment (internal and external), identification of opportunities, developing marketing objectives, formulating strategies (target market identification, value proposition, differential advantage, and application of sub-strategies of the product, distribution, price, and marketing communication. The marketing plan also contains implementation actions, control measures and time frames. The marketing plan is fully addressed in chapter 11. The contents and stages in a formal marketing plan are set out in table 1.1. A marketing programme is a combination of several marketing plans.[37]

Strategies

Growth strategies must be developed for the organisation and for the marketing plan. The Ansoff matrix[38] can be used in during the decision making phase (fig. 1.7).

***Table 1.1** Phases and descriptions of a marketing plan*[39]

Steps/phases	Description
Executive summary (this appears at the beginning, but can only be compiled once everything else is in place)	Presents an abbreviated overview of the proposed plan, containing assumptions, main thrusts, implementation issues and probable impact on the organisation.
Current marketing situation	Presents relevant background data on the current reality of the market, market drivers, product, competition, and environment.
Opportunities and issues	Assesses the main opportunities/threats, strengths/weaknesses, capabilities and competencies, issues facing the product/s, target markets, market drivers, critical success factors and market attractiveness factors.
Objectives	Defines the objectives of the plan in the areas of sales, volume, market share, customer satisfaction, customer retention and profit.
Marketing strategy	Presents the marketing approach that will be used to reach objectives in terms of: growth strategies, positioning, marketing communication, product, price, distribution and supporting services.
Action programme	Answers the questions what will be done, who will do it, and when will it be done?
Budgets	Summarises the expected financial payoff from the plan.
Evaluation and control	Outlines how the plan will be monitored and when contingency planning must be activated.

		Product	
Market		Present	New
	Present	Market penetration	Product development
	New	Market development	Diversification

***Figure 1.7** Ansoff's competitor strategies*[40]

A marketing strategy contains the marketing objectives, strategies (growth strategies, target market identification, value proposition, differential advantage, and application of sub-strategies of the product, distribution, price, and marketing communication (see table 1.1 [after objectives] and phase 2 in Figure 1.3).

Market segmentation is normally used to identify target markets. It involves the division of the broad market into identifiable segments which display similar responses towards marketing actions. These segments can be chosen on the basis of a variety of variables such as age, income, education level, social class, gender, lifestyle, personality, place of residence, etc. This is fully explored in chapter 5. From the various possible segments, the organisation then chooses one (or more) segments as its target market.

In the analysis function discussed above, the needs and expectations of potential customers were identified as well as the competitors and their competitive positioning of market offerings. Based on this and the target market which were identified, the value proposition can be developed.

The elements of the marketing mix are: product, price, place (distribution) and promotion (marketing communication), commonly known as the 4 Ps. These are covered in more detail in chapters 6 to 9. Some authors argue that the 4 Ps concept is based on the seller's view of the market and not necessarily that of the customer.[41] (See also the discussion above of the production orientation vs. marketing concept.) These writers suggest that the 4 Ps might be replaced by 4 Cs: that product should be 'customer solution'; price should be 'customer cost'; place should be 'convenience'; and promotion should be replaced by 'communication'. Table 1.2 lists some of the components of the 4 Ps.

***Table 1.2** Elements of the marketing mix*

Product • Quality • Design • Features • Brand name • Packaging • Service • Guarantees This is discussed in chapter 6.	**Distribution (place)** • Different channels • Transportation • Locations • Coverage • Logistics • Inventory This is discussed in chapter 7.
Price • List price • Discounts • Credit facilities • Demand • Fixed and variable cost • Cost and profit This is discussed in chapter 8.	**Marketing communication (promotion)** • Advertising • Sales promotion • Direct marketing • Sponsorships • Salespeople • Publicity • Marketing public relations This is discussed in chapter 9.

The 4 Ps all contribute to developing a value proposition that aims to successfully address the needs of the target market (fig. 1.8).

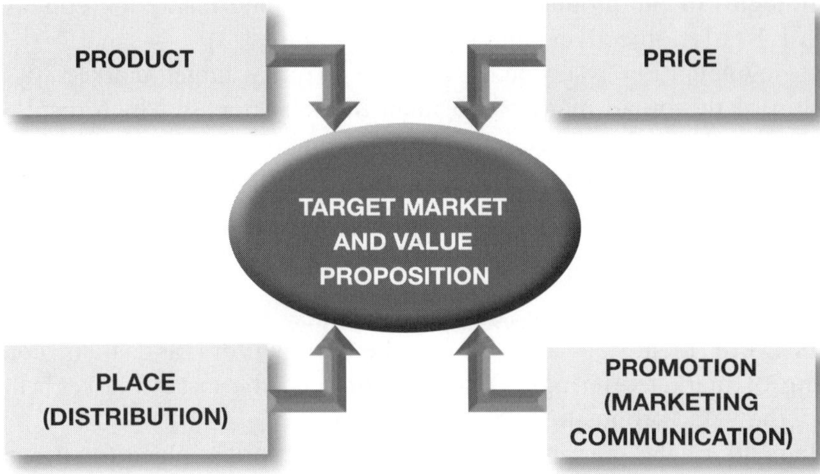

Figure 1.8 *Marketing mix variables*

The notion of the 4 Ps has been extended to 7 Ps, adding in people, processes and physical evidence. This will be further discussed in chapter 10.

Implementation

It can be broadly stated that one of the biggest issues in marketing, and implicitly in marketing planning, is that the planning is not effectively implemented. Marketing planning addresses the 'what' and the 'why' of marketing activities, while marketing implementation is concerned with 'who', 'where', 'when' and 'how'.[42] The strategies should therefore be broken up into manageable activities which can be allocated to people with timelines for completion and it contains measurable criteria for control purposes.

Hypothetical example

An organisation's marketing objective is to raise its market share from the current 25% to 30% within 12 months. The advertising objective is to increase the awareness level from the current 55% to 60% within the next six months. One of the action activities is to place advertisements in daily newspapers during the next three months. The activities associated with this action programme are:

- get advertising rates from media (timeline: 2 weeks);
- develop a profile of readers (timeline: 1 week);
- compare this data to the organisation's target market (timeline: 3 days);
- select media (timeline: 1week);
- place advertisements in selected media (timeline: 1 week);
- after the advertising campaign, do marketing research to determine the current awareness levels of the product (timeline: 3 weeks); and
- compare awareness levels with those before the advertising campaign (3 days).

Responsibilities can be assigned to each activity and those people will be accountable for monitoring and providing feedback on progress.

Chapter 11 will elaborate further on the implementation phase of marketing planning.

Control

Marketing must evaluate the results of all the activities and strategies continuously in order to become aware of any deviations from the plan in good time. If necessary, contingency planning and corrective measures must be instituted to rectify the situation. Normally the ultimate measurement of actual results will be compared to the marketing objectives.

In the control planning process, the organisation should design or develop metrics that are reliable instruments for measuring performance. Today, top management is less willing to approve marketing expenditure, and requires any expenditure to be justified by bottom line results. This makes it even more important to formulate all objectives in measurable terms – preferably also in monetary values which can be used to quantify the return on marketing investment. The discussion above is summarised in fig. 1.9.

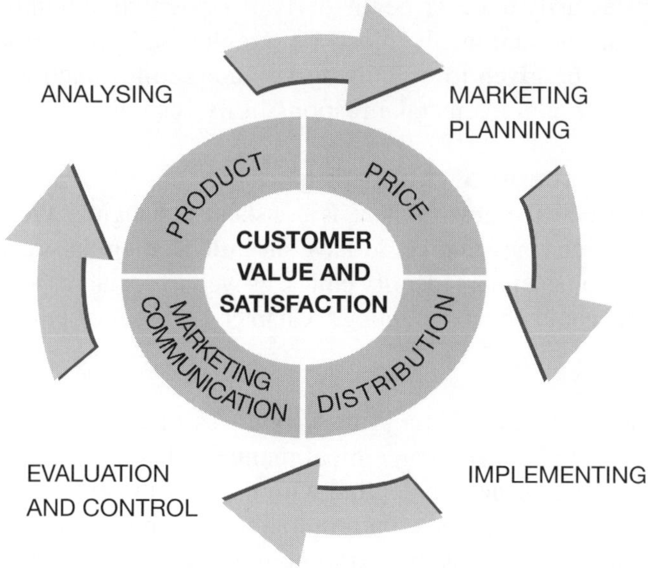

Figure 1.9 *Processes in developing the marketing strategy*

Marketing structures

Conventional wisdom dictates that structure follows strategy. This implies that effective implementation may require making structural changes in the marketing organisational structure. The size and nature of an organisation will determine how the marketing strategies and functions will be organised. In a smaller organisation, for instance, one person may be responsible for all the functions.

Normally a Chief Marketing Officer will head up the marketing functions and will be represented on the organisation's top management team.[43] Different structures can be designed for the marketing organisation and a functional structure arranged according to the activities/processes in the department. For instance: under this type of structure, activities are grouped according to function (advertising, marketing planning, customer service, marketing research, sales, new product development, channel, marketing public relations, and pricing). If the organisation is large enough, each function could operate separately.

If an organisation has many product lines, a product management organisation could be developed in which each product is managed as a separate division with its own marketing functions. In such a scenario, a product manager would be in control of all the strategies for a specific product or a brand. A market or customer management organisation can be designed for specific market or customer segments. Here the manager would be responsible for developing and implementing marketing strategies for that particular market or segment. In some organisations, a combination of these organisational structures can be employed.

It is outside the scope of this book to discuss in detail the wide variety of possible structures to implement marketing strategies in an organisation. Our approach has been to provide a framework within which core marketing functions must be performed, not necessarily to describe the division or department in the organisation responsible for each function. It must be emphasised, however, that serious consideration should be given to organising key marketing functions into projects, and having multifunctional teams take responsibility for implementation.

The changing landscape of marketing

It is common cause that the environment is constantly changing. We are specifically concerned with those changes that could have an influence on an organisation and its marketing function. Some authors identify ethics, as well as social responsibility as some of the key trends that could affect marketing.[44] Chapter 11 discusses ethics in more detail.

Ethics[45]

Ethics is concerned with the rightness or wrongness of human behaviour. Society expects organisations to behave in an ethical manner. This requires that they respect the environment, pursue fairness in dealing with internal and external customers, and strive to improve their communities. Failure to abide by the norms of business ethics has an adverse impact on all stakeholders, including customers, employees and the organisations themselves. Although there is no doubt many top executives continue to engage in unethical conduct, an increasing number are recognising the value of their companies behaving ethically. In South Africa, the Competition Commission fined a number of high profile companies for illegal conduct in a variety of sectors:

- Construction: Aveng paid a fine of R46 million because of non-competitive practices in respect of concrete pipes.[46]
- Bread: Foodcorp paid a fine of R45 million and Tiger Brands R98 million.[47]
- Milk: Lancewood paid a fine of R100 000.[48]
- Chemicals: Sasol paid a fine of R250 million for price-fixing in the fertiliser industry.[49]
- Pharmaceuticals: Adcock Ingram paid a fine of R53 million.[50]
- Motor industry: BMW, Toyota, General Motors, Daimler-Chrysler, Nissan, Volkswagen, Subaru and Citroën paid a total of R52 million in fines.[51]

- Air transport: South African Airlines paid a R55 million fine.[52]
- Steel: ArcelorMittal paid a R145 million.[53]

Business ethics can be described as a concern with good or bad, right and wrong within a business context.[54] Some business ethicists say that the ethics of business is merely the ethics of everyday life applied to business conduct. According to this view, the ethics of business is determined by the moral values and beliefs individuals bring to their business activities.[55] Business itself should play a major role in determining the standards for ethical practices. The subject of ethics in marketing can be viewed as a sub-topic of ethics in business.[56]

Marketing is one of the management fields that is most controversial when the issue of ethics is discussed. Examples of unethical marketing include deceptive advertising, pressure selling, price conspiracies, discriminatory pricing, product packaging littering the environment, poor product safety, and encouraging young people to buy cigarettes and alcohol. A company's marketing activities are highly visible and are therefore subject to a great deal of societal scrutiny. Table 1.3 describes a number of major ethical issues related to marketing.

Table 1.3 *Major ethical issues encountered in marketing communications*[57]

Category	Examples
Children	Many people feel that children should not be targeted for products such as sweetened cereals or violent video games.[58] In its advertising, Gatorade claims to be the 'healthy alternative for thirsty kids'. Nutritionists and other critics assert that Gatorade is unnecessary for children, and is no better than water.[59]
Minorities	A low-priced, high-alcohol beer marketed to young black men in the USA.[60]
The elderly	Telemarketing fraud involving prize promotions, solicitations and investment offers.[61]
Developing countries	USA tobacco organisations used advertising that was banned in the USA in Asia, Eastern Europe and South America.[62]
Sex	Advertisements that exploit women by portraying them as sex objects, and that use underage models in sexually suggestive ways.[63]
Classical conditioning	Prestigious actors or reputable athletes endorsing products or services that have little inherent value.[64]
Business	Bribery: gifts from suppliers, payment of questionable commissions, and 'money under the table'.[65]

Advertising to children under the age of 12 has been banned in Sweden and Quebec, Canada; toy advertising is banned in Greece; in Italy it is illegal to advertise to children under the age of 14.[66]

Social responsibility

During the discussion of organisational orientation above, it was mentioned that the societal concept should be encapsulated in the marketing philosophy. Organisations have a social responsibility towards the environment and stakeholders in general but also to the community. The European Commission's definition of corporate social responsibility (CSR) is:

> A concept whereby companies integrate social and environmental concerns in their business operations and in their interaction with their stakeholders on a voluntary basis.[67]

CSR is a recognition by organisations that they have a responsibility to stakeholder groups, including consumers, employees, suppliers, shareholders, the community, as well as to the environment. The CSR message must be clearly communicated because the organisation will then be able to accrue the benefits of a positive image. At the same time the community will also benefit from organisations' involvement in identified need areas.

Some of the issues dealt with in CSR are corporation's efforts to mitigate their climate change impact as measured by carbon footprint, pollution, recycling, energy efficiency waste management, green power, and ways to engage customers and the public in this dialogue.[68] Some corporations ignore demands by environmental action organisations, but it is advisable that they proactively accept their responsibilities to communities, the environment and even the world around them. The trend is increasing pressure on organisations to take seriously their social and environmental obligations.[69]

South Africa is beset by a host of problems, including severe income inequality. The high level of need in our society creates opportunities for organisations willing to assist through their CSR efforts. For example, Microsoft is actively involved in school projects by providing products and services to underprivileged schools. Senior regional office staff from Sanlam regularly engage face-to-face with communities and take part in municipal conferences, health conferences and teachers' conventions. These meetings provide opportunities for Sanlam to engage with people they might otherwise not meet, and discuss matters like financial planning.[70]

Virgin Active Health Club

Virgin Active recently launched Club-V at select clubs – a fee-based child-minding facility for children aged 6 weeks to 7 years. Here children can enjoy supervised, fun-filled play activities guaranteed to get their hearts and minds racing.

➡

Features: Fee-based childminding facility

- Caters for junior members aged 6 weeks–7 years (i.e. under the age of 8).
- Cotroom and nappy changing area for babies.
- Soft play area with ball pond, wedge, corner combo (for climbing and sliding) and rocker.
- A wide variety of quality toys for boys and girls.
- Basic arts and crafts, board games, foosball, as well as interactive PS2 gaming.
- A variety of children's DVDs.
- Electronic sign-in and sign-out.

Benefits

- Provides an important and 'value for money' offering.
- Provides quality care, security and supervision for children, allowing parents peace of mind whilst they exercise.
- Provides children with unstructured, supervised fun activities allowing for the development of basic motor skills without them even realising it.
- Provides learning experiences through activities that provide fun and creative play in a non-competitive environment.
- Provides children with opportunities for social interaction and to make new friends.
- Provides security and supervision.

Club-V will provide children with the following opportunities:

1. Edutainment (educational and entertaining).
2. Social interaction.
3. Relaxation.
4. Supervised play.
5. Fun.

Source: www.virginactive.co.za

Lexmark South Africa
Cartridge Recycling Initiative for Babies (CRIB)

CRIB forms part of Lexmark's Siyaphambili Initiative, falling under the Corporate Social Investment component. The company aims to minimise landfill waste by recycling where possible, and to avoid using incineration as a waste disposal method. The financial benefits of the company's environmental protection efforts are channelled to poor communities through its Baby Days Fund.

The company encourages customers to return their empty laser and inkjet cartridges for dismantling so that the recyclable components can be reused, and so that the non-recyclable components can be destroyed in a responsible way.

Plastic components are stripped and sorted. These materials are crushed into granules and supplied to companies which manufacture various plastic products such as seedling trays, wire reels and any number of engineering products.

Source: www.lexmark.co.za

Organisation of the book

Chapter 1: Introduction to marketing

This chapter has discussed marketing in terms of the elements that constitute the definition, namely: customer value, exchange, satisfaction, capturing value, relationships and process. The marketing philosophies of organisations can have a sales orientation, a production orientation, a marketing orientation or a societal orientation. The marketing process starts with the identification of customers' needs and their value expectations which can be used as input to develop a value proposition for target customers. The marketing mix (product, price, distribution and marketing communication) is part of the strategy to reach and satisfy customers. Ethics and corporate social responsibility are two of the issues that could affect marketing in the future.

The specific learning aims were to enable the reader to:

- define marketing and explain how the 'marketing concept' should guide organisations;
- discuss 'customer centricity' and customer satisfaction;
- identify the management functions of marketing;
- explain the marketing manager's role of planning, co-ordination and integration;
- discuss the concept of marketing planning;
- understand the difference between micro- and macro-marketing; and
- explain how social responsibility and ethics relate to the marketing concept.

Chapter 2: The marketing environment

In this chapter the micro- and macro-environments are discussed. Certain variables, especially in the micro environment, are within the control of the organisation (and marketing) such as identification of opportunities, strengths/weaknesses of the organisation, and objectives and strategies. Macro-environmental variables such as legislation, climate, economics, technology, sociological changes and political actions are, however, beyond the control of the organisation. The specific learning outcomes of this chapter are for the reader to:

- understand the uncontrollable and controllable variables that impact on the marketer's job;
- conduct macro-environmental analyses using PESTLE analyses;
- explain the meaning of 'competition' and 'competitive advantage' and conduct a thorough competitor analysis;
- describe the competitive forces that determine market attractiveness;
- explain why internal analysis is important;
- explain the meaning of environmental scanning, its importance and how management can execute it; and

- describe SWOT analysis and its relationship to marketing objectives and strategy planning.

It has been emphasised in chapter 1 that the customer is very important to the organisation. Understanding consumers has become a separate science, as discussed in chapter 3.

Chapter 3: Understanding the consumer

In was mentioned in chapter 1 that the organisation should identify the customers' needs and what their value expectations are. Certain variables can influence a customer's decision-making process in terms of how they perceive products and services and what attributes are important to them. The specific learning outcomes of this chapter are for the reader to:

- understand and explain the consumer decision-making process;
- discuss the various influences on consumer buyer behaviour;
- explain the relationship between consumer spending patterns and the stages of the family life cycle and other demographic dimensions;
- understand the consumer adoption process;
- understand business-to-business customers and buyers; and
- explain the purchasing behaviour and the basic e-commerce methods usually employed in business-to-business marketing.

To obtain data from the environment and customers and convert it into useful information for decision making, the function of marketing research can be used. This is discussed in chapter 4.

Chapter 4: Marketing information and marketing research

Marketing research serves as a boundary-spanning unit between the organisation and the external environment. Information such as perceptions of customers, their spending patterns, customer satisfaction levels, changes in needs, competitor activities, economic conditions, demographic trends, and new opportunities can be obtained through marketing research. The specific learning outcomes of this chapter are for the reader to:

- explain the difference between data and information;
- explain how a marketing information system and a marketing decision support system can help marketing managers to make decisions; and
- discuss the marketing research process.

The output of marketing research can be used to refine segments of the total market from which we must choose a target customer group/s in order to effectively position a product or service. This is done in chapter 5.

Chapter 5: Segmentation, targeting and positioning

Armed with an analysis of the environment (chapter 2), and an understanding of what the trends and challenges are in the customer and competitive environment (chapter 3) through formal research systems (chapter 4), marketers can proceed to choose the market they want to serve and convert the needs and expectations of the target customers into a value proposition that can serve as the organisation's competitive advantage. How to segment the market and determine the degree of market coverage are also addressed. The specific learning outcomes of this chapter are for the reader to:

- understand the concept of target market segmentation, and how to segment product markets into submarkets and evaluate each one;
- explain the various market segmentation variables and apply the process of segmenting a market;
- understand the role of the South African Advertising Research Foundation (SAARF) and LSMs (Living Standards Measures) as methods of market segmentation;
- identify and discuss the three different types of market coverage; and
- discuss the role of product positioning and be able to devise appropriate positioning maps.

Chapter 6: Product decisions

Questions about how to design and plan the product or service offering to the target market are crucial. In this chapter the different types of products are categorised, the concept of the product life cycle is explained, as well as how growth strategies can be identified and selected. The specific learning outcomes of this chapter are for the reader to:

- understand what is meant by the term 'product concept';
- demonstrate how products and services are classified;
- contrast product mix and product line decisions;
- explain the importance of branding, packaging and labelling; and
- explain the new product development process and propose changes to the product strategy during the product life cycle.

Chapter 7: Distribution decisions

Decisions regarding the product have already been made as described in chapter 6. In this chapter the question of how and where the product or service must be made available to the target customers must be answered. The specific learning outcomes of this chapter are for the reader to:

- understand the concept of supply chain management and the role of intermediaries in the distribution channel providing value to the customer;
- analyse the distribution activities performed in the distribution channel;
- illustrate with the aid of figures how a product is pulled and pushed through the distribution channel;
- differentiate between the different intermediaries in the various South African distribution channels;
- understand why hybrid channels and vertical marketing systems are used in distribution channels;
- show how the factors involved in selecting a suitable distribution channel are used to develop a distribution channel for a product or service;

- discuss the merits of channel leadership or captaincy and how channel conflict is handled in the distribution channel;
- explain why marketing logistics is such an important factor of the distribution decision; and
- discuss the steps involved in managing a distribution channel.

Chapter 8: Pricing decisions

Price is the only variable in the marketing mix which generates income for the organisation. Aspects which were already discussed in chapters 2 (e.g. economic conditions), 3 and 4 (how will customers perceive and react to different price levels) will be used in this chapter to determine the price of a product. It is important to remember that the price forms only one part of the total offering by the marketer. The specific learning outcomes of this chapter are for the reader to:

- explain the various steps in the determination of the price of a product or service;
- analyse the factors that will influence the determination of the price of a product or service;
- describe the different pricing objectives that may be used by an organisation;
- explain the relationship between cost, volume and profits;
- describe how break-even analysis is used in price determination;
- describe the three methods that may be used to select an approximate price level; and
- write an essay in which the steps followed to determine the price of a real product or service are explained.

Chapter 9: Marketing communication decisions

At this stage the value of the product or the service has been created and in this chapter ways of communicating that value to the target or potential customers will come under the spotlight. The specific learning outcomes of this chapter are for the reader to:

- show how integrated marketing communication (IMC) can help develop the optimal marketing communication mix for the organisation;
- explain the steps in an integrated marketing communication campaign;
- advise on the budgeting techniques that must be used in this process;
- design an advertising campaign;
- explain the role and types of direct marketing;
- describe the personal selling process;
- explain the types of sales promotions; and
- describe the role of public relations and publicity.

Chapter 10: Developing a marketing mix for service products

It has been argued that the classical marketing mix comprising the 4 Ps (product, pricing, place [distribution] and promotion [marketing communication]) should be extended to 7 Ps by including people, process, and physical evidence. The learning outcomes for the reader are to:

- clearly distinguish between a service product and a physical product;

- classify the different types of services that can be provided;
- explain the distinguishing features that are unique to the service product;
- describe the components of the service product; and
- combine the elements of the expanded marketing mix for services into appropriate marketing programmes.

Chapter 11: Integrated marketing

In this chapter the discussions of the previous ten chapters are integrated to provide a holistic view of the marketing process. The specific learning outcomes of this chapter are for the reader to:

- explain how the marketing concept relates to the critical marketing decisions;
- explain how marketing information can be obtained through the marketing information system (MIS);
- explain the effect of the environment on the design of the marketing mix;
- discuss how the determinants of consumer behaviour influence marketing decision making;
- identify how the choice of target market determines the design of the market offering;
- discuss the decisions made for each of the marketing mix elements;
- explain what changes have been made to the marketing mix in terms of a service product; and
- discuss the effect of marketing ethics on a business.

Chapter 12: Marketing and the Internet

The Internet has created new opportunities for the marketer to reach and sell to the customer. Some authors see the role of the Internet as just an additional distribution channel, but it entails much more than that. The specific learning outcomes of this chapter are for the reader to:

- define the concepts of the Internet and the World Wide Web (WWW);
- identify the benefits of the Internet;
- describe the virtual environment in which the Internet operates; and
- identify areas in which the Internet can create value for the marketer.

Summary

Marketing was discussed in terms of the elements that constitute the definition, namely, customer value, exchange, satisfaction, capturing value, relationships and process. The marketing process starts with the identification of customers' needs, and their value expectations. From this a customer-oriented marketing strategy can be developed in order to exchange value. The marketing mix, consisting of the product, price, distribution aspects and marketing communication were mentioned as part of the total offering to a target market using the value proposition as the differential advantage.

In developing the marketing strategy, a process consisting of analysis, marketing planning, implementation, and evaluation and control are applied. Once strategies have been selected, the question of marketing organisational structures must be addressed (structure follows strategy).

Towards the end of the chapter two significant issues that could impact on the marketing landscape in future are discussed, namely ethics and corporate social responsibility. Organisations should proactively plan to incorporate these issues in their strategies because these will have a long term impact on their relationships with their stakeholders. If issues of this nature are not managed properly, the resulting negative perceptions can tarnish the organisation's image, profits and, ultimately, its survival.

Discussion questions

1. If you were an executive of an organisation would you share your experiences on successes and failures in the area of corporate social responsibility? Would it affect your competitive advantage?
2. How can marketers use the marketing mix to enhance customers' perceptions of value?
3. What are the major parts of a marketing strategy and how does it interrelate with strategic/corporate planning?
4. Why is it necessary for organisations to spend money on social responsibility programmes?
5. Does marketing create needs, or does it satisfy them?

Case study: The SAB industrial giant[71]

South African Breweries Ltd (SAB) was founded in 1895 in South Africa and today is the South African subsidiary of SABMiller plc, one of the world's largest beer brewers by volume with more than 200 brands and brewing interests and distribution agreements in over 60 countries across six continents.

SAB is also the second largest listed company on the JSE Securities Exchange, South Africa's leading producer and distributor of alcoholic and non-alcoholic beverages (it is the major distributor of Coca-Cola into Africa) and one of South Africa's largest manufacturing firms.

The company operates seven breweries and 42 depots in South Africa with an annual brewing capacity of 3.1 billion litres. Its portfolio of beer brands meets the needs of a wide range of consumers and includes brands such as Castle Lager, Hansa Pilsener, Carling Black Label and the iconic Dutch beer brand Grolsch.

SAB's soft drinks division is Amalgamated Beverage Industries (ABI), the largest producer and distributor of Coca-Cola brands in Southern Africa. With five manufacturing plants in South Africa, ABI accounts for approximately 60% of Coca-Cola's sales in South Africa.

SAB also owns a hop production company, The South African Breweries Hop Farms (Pty) Ltd; a barley farming company, The South African Breweries Barley Farms (Pty) Ltd; a barley malting company, The South African Breweries Maltings (Pty) Ltd; and a 60% share of the metal crown manufacturer, Coleus Packaging (Pty) Ltd.

SAB employs more than 9 000 people, 75% of whom are from previously disadvantaged groups. In addition SAB's operations support an estimated 48 000 jobs at SAB's primary suppliers. For each job offered by SAB and its primary suppliers, 5,7 additional jobs are supported in the rest of the South African economy. In all, 378 000 full-time jobs in South Africa can directly or indirectly be traced back to the production of SAB's products.

As South Africa's leading brewer, SAB is committed to promoting responsible alcohol behaviour – both inside and outside the company. As a subsidiary of SABMiller plc, it subscribes to the Group's Alcohol Framework and has a comprehensive Code of Commercial Communication in place. SAB also actively seeks to encourage collaboration across the areas of education, access to information, law enforcement and parental involvement to encourage responsible alcohol behaviour.

SAB adopted its first equity strategy as early as 1971 and has been a leading agent for change in South Africa. Through its various corporate social responsibility programmes, SAB annually invests more than R150 million per annum in community partnerships, socio-economic and enterprise development initiatives to build a stronger South Africa.

Exercise

1. Discuss the basic elements of the marketing concept as it is applicable to SAB Miller. Are they using this philosophy? Give examples and explain why.
2. Why is marketing important in our society? Indicate how SAB Miller is using the principles of marketing in its day-to-day operations.
3. In your experience which products and/or services of SAB Miller provide value to you? Give examples.

CHAPTER 2

The marketing environment

Learning outcomes

After studying this chapter you should be able to:

- understand the uncontrollable and controllable variables that impact on the marketer's job;
- conduct macro-environmental analyses using PESTLE analyses;
- explain the meaning of 'competition' and 'competitive advantage' and conduct a thorough competitor analysis;
- describe the competitive forces that determine market attractiveness;
- explain why internal analysis is important;
- explain the meaning of environmental scanning, its importance and how management can execute it; and
- describe SWOT analysis and its relationship to marketing objectives and strategy planning.

Introduction

Chapter 1 emphasised the need for businesses to look outward and identify customer needs before they can decide on the products they should be offering. The ability of organisations to effectively satisfy the needs of their customers and achieve their objectives depends on environmental factors, both internal and external to the organisation. The aim of chapter 2 is to introduce different elements of the marketing environment and discuss how they impact on marketing activities.

Definition of marketing environment

The marketing environment is defined as all actors and forces internal and external to an organisation that affect marketing management's ability to develop and maintain successful transactions with their customers.

The marketing environment is very dynamic – it changes all the time. These changes can be sources of opportunity to an organisation, or they can pose threats. The ability of any organisation to respond to opportunities and threats is critically determined by its strengths and weaknesses. Achieving its goals depends in part on its ability to develop and implement marketing strategies that take into consideration developments in the immediate and wider environment in which it operates. This chapter emphasises the importance of monitoring the marketing environment in order to remain responsive to the changing situation.

Components of the marketing environment

The marketing environment consists of three distinct components. These are:

- **The internal environment**. This consists of actors and forces within an organisation that affect its ability to effectively serve its customers. They include the mission and objectives of the business, its top management, and the various functional groups in the organisation such as finance, human resources management, procurement and manufacturing. It is in this environment that marketing managers develop and implement their marketing plans. The top management of a business has direct control over all aspects relating to the internal environment.
- **The market environment**. This consists of actors and forces immediately outside the business that affect its ability to effectively serve its customers. It includes suppliers, distributors, customers and competitors. Businesses deal directly with most of the actors in the market environment. While organisations have no direct control over these external factors, they may be able to exercise some influence over some of them.
- **The macro-environment**. This consists of broader actors and forces that affect not only the business, but also its suppliers, distributors, customers and competitors. These forces are often grouped as political, economic, social, technological, environmental and legal forces. The macro-environment falls outside any individual organisation's direct sphere of influence.

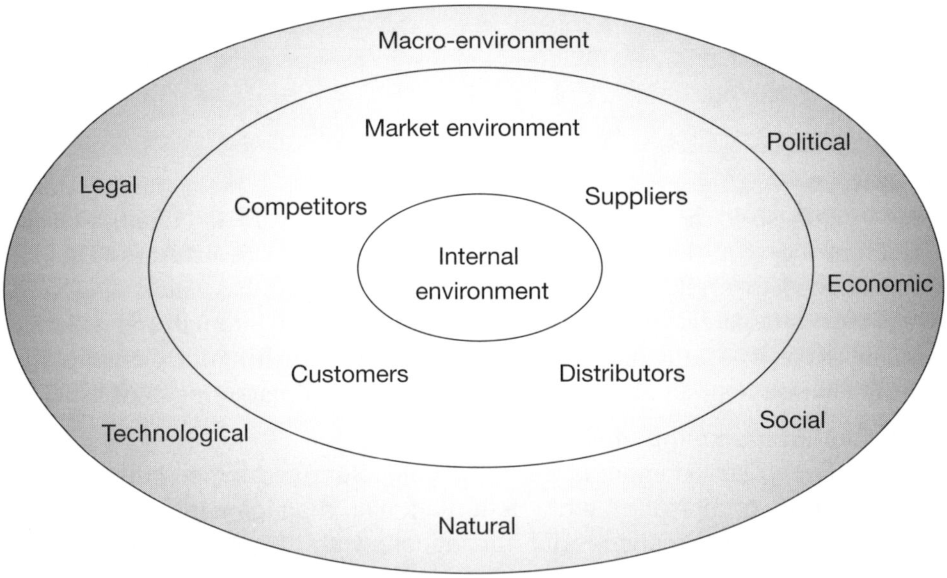

Figure 2.1 *The marketing environment*

The macro-environment

An organisation and actors in its market environment operate within a larger macro-environment (see fig. 2.1). Changes in the macro-environment may not always have an immediate impact on an organisation. For example, changes in population structure are likely to exert little impact on volumes of products demanded in the short term. In the long term, however, the impact in terms of number of potential customers in targeted population groups can be significant. Other changes in the macro-environment result in significant and immediate effect on a business. For example, a change in the rand-dollar exchange rate will have an immediate effect on South African businesses importing or exporting their products.

In any case, changes in the macro-environment are sources of opportunities or threats to businesses and other organisations. Marketing managers need to monitor this environment so that they can identify the opportunities and threats facing the business and find ways to take advantage of opportunities and minimise the potential impact of threats. The macro-environment is commonly subdivided into a number of interdependent sub-environments, namely political, economic, social, technological, legal and environmental, known by the acronym PESTLE.

PESTLE analysis

This is a tool for analysing the macro-environment in which an organisation operates and the opportunities and threats that lie within that environment. There are a number of variations, allowing analysts to emphasise the factors that are most applicable to their situation. These include:

- PEST or STEP analysis (political, economic, social and technological factors);
- SLEPT analysis (social, legal, economic, political and technological factors); and
- PESTLIED analysis (political, economic, social, technological, legal, international, environmental and demographic).

The political environment

The main actors in the political environment include politicians, political parties, governments and pressure groups that seek to influence governments and politicians. In analysing the political environment marketers need to consider a number of factors including:

- **Political stability**. Businesses prefer to operate in environments that are politically stable as political unrest can be disruptive to business activities. In severe cases, political instability can result in loss of assets by businesses without any prospect of compensation. For example, between the years 2000 and 2004, many commercial farmers in Zimbabwe lost their farm land and other assets due to political unrest in the country resulting from the implementation of the government land redistribution programme.
- **Changes in government**. Governments are usually formed by political parties, so it is important for marketers to know the philosophies of the major political parties in a country as these could have an impact on business activities in the event of a change of government.

Governments often exert pressure on business and other organisations through the enactment and enforcement of legislation, and the formulation and implementation of government policies.

In a democratic country, the ruling party is elected to represent the majority of adult citizens of a country. Governments pass legislation and devise regulations aimed at addressing what they consider to be the concerns of the citizens that elected them. These rules and regulations can have significant impact on the cost of running a business and on the way it can market its products. For example, due to public health concerns, the South African government enacted the Tobacco Products Control Act 83 of 1993 which, among other things, prohibits tobacco advertising and sale of cigarettes to anyone under the age of 16.

Government policies influence all areas of the macro-environment. For example, governments use monetary and fiscal policies to influence the economic environment, and this has a direct impact on the amount of money consumers have to spend. Governments may put in place measures aimed at promoting more competition in the marketplace, and controlling imports and exports. In South Africa, these mandates are held by the Department of Trade and Industry (DTI, also known as dti). Import controls can help encourage local production and protect local manufacturers from unfair competition. Export controls are mostly aimed at fulfilling international agreements, e.g. in respect of the export of ammunition and controlled drugs. They may also be used to control the exportation of raw materials required for local manufacturing purposes.

The Motor Industry Development Programme (MIDP)

The motor vehicle industry is of strategic importance to the South African economy. It contributes about 10% to the value of manufacturing in the country and employs about 90 000 people in assembly and component manufacturing.[1] The MIDP was introduced in 1995 to protect and encourage job creation, as well as promote growth in the motor industry. As part of this programme, government has in place an import permit system to restrict the importation of used vehicles. The general principle applied to applications for the importation of such vehicles is to refuse to grant an import permit if the goods concerned or similar/substitute goods are available from local manufacturers.[2]

The economic environment

The state of a country's economy is critical to any business as it affects both supply and demand for goods and services. In assessing the economic environment, marketing managers need to focus on a number of factors.

Levels of economic growth. Economic growth refers to a positive change in the level of production of goods and services by a country over a given period of time. Levels of economic growth tend to rise and fall in tandem with troughs and peaks in the business cycle. During periods of high economic growth, unemployment tends to go down and income tends to increase, bringing with it increased demand for goods and services. A slowdown in economic growth has the opposite effect.

Monetary policy and interest rates. Monetary policy is used by governments to control the supply of money and the rate of interest in an economy. Increased money supply is associated with lower interest rates, while lower money supply is associated with higher interest rates. Governments often delegate the responsibility of managing their monetary policy to a central bank, the South African Reserve Bank in our case. Changes in interest rates often have significant immediate effects on individuals and businesses. Reduced interest rates benefit businesses by reducing the costs associated with servicing business debt and stimulating consumer demand, especially on products normally bought on credit, including cars and houses.

Fiscal policy. This term refers to government policy to influence the direction of the economy through changes in government expenditure and revenue collection.[3] The biggest source of government revenue is tax. Increased government spending can mean increased opportunities for businesses that supply goods or services to government departments. In other sectors, increased government spending on public services may be a threat to private service providers by crowding them out (a kind of competition). Changes in taxation levels can also affect business organisations. For example, changes in personal income tax would increase or decrease the disposable income of consumers, with an obvious impact on the demand for goods and services.

Rate of inflation. Inflation rate refers to the overall general rise in price of goods and services in an economy over a period of time. Very high levels of inflation can cause problems for businesses by reducing consumer spending power, increasing the cost of production, and reducing the overall competitiveness of a country's exports on the international market.

Currency exchange rates. The rate at which the currency of one country is exchanged for the currency of another country has an impact on the price of products traded on international markets. When the local currency appreciates in value against other currencies, imported products become cheaper, making it more difficult for local products to compete. The amount of money that exporters receive for their products will decline at such a time, possibly to below a profitable level. When the local currency loses value, imported goods become more expensive, but the amount of money that exporters receive increases.

Taxi industry protest against introduction of the Bus Rapid Transit (BRT) system

When the government introduced the BRT system in 2009 and 2010, members of the taxi industry felt that their jobs and profits were at risk. This was mainly because commuters paid lower fares on the BRT than minibus taxi fares.[4] The result was widespread strikes by some members of the industry.

The social environment

Consumers do not exist in isolation. They are members of various groups, each with unique characteristics, e.g. in terms of numbers, cultural values and attitudes. It is important for marketers to understand the social environment as it plays a significant role in influencing all the elements of the marketing mix, including the goods and services consumers buy, the effectiveness of promotional programmes, when and where people buy products, as well as what they consider to be an acceptable price to pay for certain goods and services. In analysing the social environment, a marketer needs to look at a host of factors associated with demographic and cultural forces in the light of the impact these may have on the demand for goods and services.

Demographic forces. Analysis of demographic forces includes the study of human populations in terms of size and other characteristics such as geographical distribution, age structure, education levels and income distribution. The rate of HIV/Aids has also become a social issue of concern for businesses. A high prevalence HIV/Aids is a source of threat for most businesses as it impacts negatively on employee productivity and consumer spending. For other businesses such as those in funeral parlours, HIV/Aids counselling services and sales of medication, it can be a source of opportunity.

Some demographic facts about South Africa (2009)[5]

- The population of South Africa grew from 44.8 million in 2001 to 49.3 million in 2009.
- 79% of the population is African, 9% coloured, 2.6% Indian/Asian and 9.1% white.
- The most populated province is Gauteng with 10,5 million people, followed by KwaZulu-Natal with 10.4 million people. The least populated province is Northern Cape with 1.15 million people.
- Nearly one-third (31.4%) of the population is aged younger than 15 years and approximately 7.5% (3.7 million) is 60 years or older.
- The total number of people living with HIV grew from 4.19 million in 2001 to 5.21 million in 2009.

Cultural forces. Culture has been described as a society's personality.[6] Cultural forces include such factors as language, customs, religion, work patterns and artefacts that give society a distinctive character. Cultural forces affect people's values, attitudes and lifestyle. They are critical in determining what is considered important, desirable, right or appropriate. Some of the common consumers' values relate to achievement, equality, patriotism, humanitarianism and sense of morality. Values, attitudes and lifestyle determine demand for specific products and the way people can generally be expected to respond to marketing efforts.

Double income households: Growing the market in South Africa

More and more women have joined the workforce as a result of economic opportunities opening up under government's affirmative action programme. An increased number of households now have two incomes, and this has increased demand for such products and services as child and home care, smart work clothing, labour-saving home appliances and convenience foods. Many business organisations have responded by developing products specifically targeted at this segment of the market, including tailor-made car and financial service packages.

The technological environment

As technology develops, new tools, methods and techniques become available for use production and management processes. Advances in technology and innovation are a result of investments in research and development by businesses, as well as governments. The technological environment influences marketing activities in a variety of ways.

Introduction of new or improved products and services. Products such as computers, body scanners, mobile Internet, cell phones, vehicle tracking systems, robotics and many others have come onto the market during the last century. New or improved products can bring new opportunities, and may drive the demise of others. For example, the typewriter became obsolete once personal computers become widely available.

Improvements in production processes. Advancements in technology have often resulted in automation of design and manufacturing processes, improving quality and reducing the cost of certain products because of productivity gains.

Improvements in the way markets are identified and services provided. Developments in communication and information technology, the Internet in particular, has proved to be an inexpensive way to reach customers. It allows customers to search for and buy goods and services without the need to personally visit service providers or shopping premises, enabling them to buy goods and services across the world. Online social networking technologies such as Twitter and Facebook are increasingly being used by businesses to generate direct sales, attract and stay connected with their customers more cheaply than traditional promotional tools such as television, radio and newspapers. These networks allow individual users to learn about business offers in real time, give feedback on their experiences with the business, as well as offer product ideas.

Changes in the technological environment may be sources of threats to business and other organisations because the cost of acquiring new technologies may significantly increase capital and operating costs. Organisations that are not able to keep pace with changing technology may find themselves unable to compete effectively with their rivals. There may also be social costs associated with changes in technology, e.g. the loss of jobs where people are replaced by machines; as well as damage to the environment, e.g. through production activities and pollution.

Dell generates millions from Twitter and Facebook[7]

Dell reported that in 2009 direct sales of its company products through Facebook and Twitter generated US$9 million. The company urged small and medium businesses in particular to make use of social networks, noting that online social media offers a cheap way to form a 'really personal' relationship with customers.

The legal environment

The legal environment determines the rules by which organisations operate. It is sometimes considered part of the political environment as legislation is debated and passed in Parliament by elected representatives. A number of important pieces of legislation affect marketing activities.

Protecting consumers. Consumer protection laws place obligation on suppliers of goods and services to act in a manner that is fair to the consumer. Examples of such laws include the Consumer Protection Act 68 of 2008, and the National Credit Act 34 of 2005. The Consumer Protection Act gives effect to internationally recognised consumer rights, including the consumer's right to be informed, right to choose, right to be heard, and right to good quality and safe products. Among other things, the National Credit Act prohibits reckless granting of credit and demands that advertisements for credit, or the sale of goods and services on credit, disclose the full costs to customers up front.

Promoting fair competition. Competition is often considered good for everybody because it helps to promote efficiency and provides consumers with a wide range of product choices at competitive prices. An example of legislation aimed at promoting fair competition in South Africa is the Competition Act 89 of 1998. Under this Act, restrictive trading practices that can impact on levels of competition are prohibited. These include fixing of selling or purchase prices, pressuring retailers not to stock competitors' products, or pressuring suppliers not to supply to competitors. Violation of this Act can result in stiff penalties.

Pioneer Foods pays over R1 billion in fines

In February 2010 the Competition Tribunal imposed a R195.7 million fine on Pioneer Foods for its role in a bread price-fixing cartel. The cartel involved Tiger Brands (whose bread brand is Albany), Premier Foods (whose bread brand is Blue Ribbon), Foodcorp (whose bread brand is Sunbake) and Pioneer Foods (whose bread brands are Sasko and Duens). Tiger Brands, Premier Foods and Foodcorp negotiated agreements with the Competition Commission in exchange for leniency, while Pioneer opted to fight the case in court and lost.[8] In November 2010, the Competition Tribunal accepted a Pioneer Foods offer of R855.7 million to settle all outstanding allegations of collusion and price-fixing against the corporation. This comes on top of the fine levied nine months earlier.[9]

Protecting company products. The cost of developing new technologies and products can be exorbitant. Legislation plays a critical role in encouraging investments in research and development by protecting business innovations. South Africa's intellectual property protection laws include the Patent Act, the Copyright Act and the Trademarks Act.

Protecting society in general. Sometimes laws are enacted to protect not only consumers of specific products, but also society in general against marketing activities that may be deemed not to be in the general interest of the public. Examples of such legislation are the Consumer Affairs (Unfair Business Practices) Act 71 of 1988, the Tobacco Products Control Act 83 of 1993, and the Liquor Act 59 of 2003.

Definitions

Patent: A government authority to an individual or organisation conferring the sole right to make, use or sell an invention for a set period of time.[10]

Copyright: This gives the creator of intellectual property an exclusive right to print, distribute and copy the work for a period of time. Copyright owners have the right to control the reproduction of their work.

Trademark: These are the distinctive symbols and branding used by a business to distinguish its products from those of other businesses. A business that has registered its trademark has the exclusive right to use the mark.

The legal environment affects all elements of the marketing mix. Marketers need to be aware of changes taking place in this environment and variations in legislation that may exist at provincial and local level. Failure to comply with regulations may prove too costly for an organisation as it could end up facing the prospect of large fines, court action, and damage to its market reputation.

Natural environment

Environmental problems including global warming, depletion of the ozone layer, depletion of natural resources, and the degradation of air, water and soil quality have become an area of enormous importance to society. Marketers need to be aware of the threats and opportunities associated with changes in this area.

Processes and materials used to produce products. These can cause serious damage to the environment. Some businesses have taken measures to ensure use of biodegradable and natural ingredients in their production processes in an effort to minimise harm to the environment. Public concerns about environmental damage have also created increased demand for products produced in ways that are environment-friendly. Woolworths is an example of a South African company that has proactively capitalised on environmental concerns by pursuing green marketing strategies, resulting in a favourable organisational image.

Woolworths – Helping conserve the environment

Woolworths has a number of initiatives in place aimed at helping conserve the natural environment.[11]

- Farming for the Future programme – this is a holistic farming approach in which Woolworths works with farmers who supply its food products to ensure that food is grown sustainably, in harmony with nature, without compromising quality or adding to costs.
- Animal welfare initiatives – for example, Woolworths does not permit selling of eggs from caged birds in its stores, and it does not permit testing of its health and beauty products on animals.

Scarcity of some natural resources. In many countries environmental degradation has resulted in reduced availability of good farm land and forestry resources, many inland water bodies have dried up, and fish populations have dwindled. As a result industries that rely on such resources face severe production constraints and increased costs of production.

Increased cost of energy. Economic activity is heavily dependent on non-renewable energy sources, especially oil, and increased prices of this diminishing resource has resulted in increased energy costs for both organisations and consumers. Some businesses have seen an opportunity in this and have developed energy-efficient products. In the car manufacturing industry, for example, many have seen a source of competitive advantage in producing fuel-efficient cars, and others have started producing cars that do not use non-renewable energy sources. For example, in 2008, Optical Energy (Pty) Ltd, a Cape Town-based company, unveiled the Joule, South Africa's first electric car. This vehicle is expected to be available in low volumes in mid-2010 and to be in mass manufacture by the end of 2013, for sale in mid-2014.[12]

Increased intervention by government and environmental pressure groups. With increased damage to the environment resulting from business and consumer activities, marketers can expect increased interventions by governments and environmental pressure groups aimed at protecting the environment. One way government intervenes in protecting natural environments is through enactment of laws such as the National Environmental Management Act 107 of 2008. Among other things, the Act promotes the protection of the environment through measures that prevent pollution and ecological degradation on pain of hefty fines. Environmental pressure groups put pressure on governments and industry to take stronger action to saving the natural environment. Such groups are also good at mobilising public opinion, and companies that damage the environment are vulnerable to being exposed and incur reputational damage from negative publicity.

Simple actions to protect the environment

- Do not litter.
- Walk rather than using a car to travel short distances.
- Buy recycled paper.
- Use public transport where possible.
- Print on both sides of paper.
- Switch off all power-consuming devices when not in use.
- Start recycling some of your waste, e.g. collect paper, cans and glass bottles and put these in local recycling bins.

The international environment

The growing interdependence of world economies through increased international trade, foreign direct investment, migration and the spread of technology has increased the potential impact of developments in the international environment on businesses in general. Analysis of the international environment involves examining what is happening outside a country's borders in terms of developments in the political, economic, social, demographic, technological, legal and the natural environment in order to determine impact of changes on a business organisation.

The international environment presents firms with many opportunities, including increased market size, and increased access to new technologies. International markets can also be a source of cheap raw materials and other factors of production, resulting in reduced costs for businesses.

Increased integration of world markets has increased the susceptibility of local businesses to developments in the international environment. This can be a source of threat to businesses. For example:

- Increased global demand for crude oil has resulted in its prices going up on international markets. For a country like South Africa, this has meant increased expenditure of foreign currency reserves on oil imports. It also means increased petrol prices at the local pump and increased transport costs for local businesses and individuals.
- The world economic crisis experienced between 2007 and 2010 resulted in many countries experiencing recession as production levels fell due to reduced international and local demand for goods and services.
- Increased integration of world markets can also be threat to domestic firms through increased competition on the local markets as more and more international companies invest or export their products into the country.

Global recession hits South Africa

In May 2009 it was officially announced that South Africa had joined the long list of countries in recession. The global economic crisis, which started in 2007 and 2008, resulting in massive company failures globally and a sharp drop in international trade. The contractions in South Africa's growth were blamed on a sharp drop in export demand which forced manufactures and miners to cut their production. The impact of the global recession on the local economy was widespread:[13]

- The value of South African exports fell by 24% in the first quarter of 2009.
- Company failures rose by 47% in the first four months of 2009.
- 179,000 jobs were lost in the first quarter of 2009.

The market environment

The market environment consists of suppliers, customers, distributors and competitors to the business. Marketing managers need to closely monitor developments in the market environment since, just like the macro-environment, it can be a source of opportunities and of threats to an organisation.

Suppliers

Suppliers are individuals and businesses that provide resources needed by a business to produce its good and services.[14] Developments in the supplier market can have serious impact on marketing activities in an organisation. For example, increases in the prices of raw materials may force the organisation to increase prices of goods and services, reducing their affordability, thereby impacting on sales volumes and profits.

Marketers need to monitor a number of factors relating to developments in the supply markets. These include price trends, quality of supply, reliability of individual suppliers, flexibility of suppliers to respond to unforeseen demands from the organisation, and the bargaining power of suppliers. The ability of a business to ensure customer satisfaction can be seriously compromised if things are not working well on the supply side.

Toyota's product recall
In 2009 Toyota's image suffered a setback when it recalled some of its car models for repairs due to persistent complaints about sticking accelerator pedals. According to Toyota, the recall only involved models fitted with pedals from one supplier.[15]

To minimise any potential problems that may arise from the supply side, many businesses are now taking steps to develop closer win-win working relationships with their suppliers. These suppliers are viewed as partners with the organisation in a joint effort to deliver value to customers.

Distributors

Large manufacturers that find it impossible to deal with each of their final customers individually use distributors to bridge the gap. Distributors are independent firms that assist in the flow of goods and services from producers to final customers. They include wholesalers, retailers, dealers, agents and physical distribution firms.

Wholesalers and retailers: These firms are also known as resellers. Wholesalers normally purchase goods from manufacturers then resell them to retailers. Retailers operate outlets that trade directly with final customers. Most big retailers in South Africa such as Pick n Pay and Shoprite Checkers get most of their products directly from the manufacturers.

Dealers: Dealers play a similar role to wholesalers and retailers. They differ from normal wholesalers and retailers in that they usually carry a much narrower range of products and are often involved in providing after-sales service to customers on behalf of the producers.

Agents: These are businesses and individuals that sell products and services for a commission, usually a percentage of the sale price.

Physical distribution firms: These assist in storage, handling and movement of goods from their original locations to their destinations. They include warehousing and transportation firms. Warehousing firms store and protect goods before they move to their next destination, while transportation firms move goods from one location to another. A business needs to consider a number of factors when making physical distribution decisions, including safety, cost, and speed of delivery.

It is important for marketers to develop good relationships with their distributors because these play an important role in ensuring that products are available to customers in the right place, the right quantity and at the right time. When an organisation is very dependent on a distributor, the distributor may be a threat, in that it is able to dictate distribution terms such as product delivery schedules, retail profit margins and the need for sales support services. A manufacturer that is unable or unwilling to meet the terms of a powerful supplier may risk the loss of access to important markets.

Customers

Customers are the focal point of any business. They are a key to sales and profits. Marketers need to identify exactly who their customers are, what their needs and wants are, as well as factors that affect their buying behaviour.

A business can operate in five different types of customer markets:

- **Consumer markets**. These consist of individuals and households that buy goods and services for personal use.
- **Business markets**. These are made up of businesses that buy products for further processing or for use in their production processes.
- **Reseller markets**. These are business organisations that buy goods and services and resell them at a profit.
- **Government markets**. These are government units that buy goods and services in order to provide public services.
- **International markets**. These are buyers in other countries and include consumers, producers, resellers, and governments.

Many marketers are taking active steps to develop the kind of relationships with their customers that will lead to increased customer loyalty. One commonly-used method to build a loyal customer base is frequent shopper incentives. Another method is to actively gather information from customers about their levels of satisfaction and to identify areas for improvement.

Competitors

Competitors are a major threat to any organisation. Success in the marketplace depends not only on organisations ensuring customer satisfaction, but doing it better than their competitors. Conducting a thorough competitor analysis and constantly monitoring their activities will help to identify the objectives and strategies, as well as their strengths and weaknesses.

Competitive market structures

The number of sellers, degree of product differentiation, presence of entry and exit barriers help determine the strength of competition in a market. These factors give rise to four general types of competitive market structures: monopoly, oligopoly, monopolistic competition and perfect competition.

- A **monopoly** is a market structure consisting of a single organisation marketing a product with no close substitutes. In South Africa and most other countries, monopolies are discouraged or regulated to prevent those organisations from abusing their power. In the absence of effective regulation, monopolies can charge customers exorbitant prices and give little attention to quality customer service. Examples of monopolies in South Africa include the National Ports Authority and Eskom.
- An **oligopoly** is a market structure consisting of a few firms marketing products that can be either homogenous (e.g. steel and coal are very similar, wherever they come from), or differentiated. An example of oligopoly in South Africa is the cell phone market, which comprises Vodacom, MTN, Cell C and Virgin Mobile.

- **Monopolistic competition** is characterised by a large number of firms marketing similar but differentiated products. Firms use differentiation strategies to help distinguish their products from those of competitors and to help convince customers that their products are the best to buy. Examples include businesses operating in the clothing industry, processed foods such as coffee and tea, as well as those in the home electronics industry selling television sets and other home appliances.
- **Perfect competition** refers to a market characterised by a large number of sellers marketing a homogenous product to buyers who are well informed about the market. In such a market, no single business has any control of price, and every business sells at the prevailing market prices. Entry and exit barriers to such markets are very low. Perfect competition markets are very rare in practice. The closest example is the market for unprocessed agricultural produce such as soya beans and wheat.

***Table 2.1** Characteristics of competitive market structures*

Type of competition	Number of competitors	Type of product	Barriers to market entry	Example
Monopoly	One	Unique – almost no substitutes	Very high/ usually blocked	Eskom
Oligopoly	Few	Homogeneous or differentiated	Major	Cellular phone operators
Monopolistic	Many	Differentiated with many substitutes	Few and not major	Home electronic appliance companies
Perfect competition	Many	Homogeneous	None	Agricultural products such as soya beans

Competitor analysis

Competitor analysis is the process of identifying an organisation's competitors, understanding their objectives and strategies, as well as assessing their strengths, weaknesses and likely responses to what competitors do. The key questions to be addressed in competitor analysis include:

- Who are the organisation's competitors?
- What are their objectives?
- What competitive strategies are they pursuing?

- What are their strengths and weaknesses?
- How are they likely to respond to competitors' actions?

Who are the competitors? There are two common approaches used to identify competitors. These include the industry approach and the marketing approach.[16] The industry approach defines competitors as businesses producing products that are close substitutes. For example Absa, First National Bank, Standard Bank and Nedbank are all competing firms in the banking industry. Coca-Cola and Pepsi are competitors in the soft drink manufacturing industry. The marketing approach defines competitors as all firms providing products that satisfy the same customer needs. This a much broader way of defining competitors, since the same customer need can be satisfied by products which are not always close substitutes. For example, a customer need to quench thirst can be satisfied by a wide range of products that include bottled water, soft drinks, iced tea and fruit juices. The general recommendation is that marketers should avoid defining competitors too narrowly as this can mean they do not pay attention to other important players in the market. Apart from considering current competitors, companies should also consider potential competitors. These are firms that are likely to introduce products that are similar or satisfy the same customer needs and wants.

What are the competitors' objectives? Organisations pursue a mix of different objectives. These objectives often determine the strategies that they take as they compete in the market. Some of the common marketing objectives pursued by business organisations relate to profit, sales, market share and customer orientation. Businesses often have different marketing objectives for different markets or market segments. In doing a competitor analysis, it is important to look at not just overall business objectives, but also objectives at product or market segment level.

What competitive strategies are they pursuing? Businesses often choose to compete on the basis of low prices or product quality. Michael Porter identified three generic competitive strategies used by firms as they compete at individual product/market level.

- **Cost leadership strategy**. A business pursuing this strategy concentrates on producing products at the lowest possible cost in order to sell at prices lower than their competitors to a broad target market. Retailers such as Game and Shoprite emphasise low prices.
- **Differentiation strategy**. A business pursuing this strategy concentrates on producing products that are unique (different to those of its competitors) and selling them to a broader target market. The target market in this case is customers who value differentiated products more than low cost. Woolworths Foods is an example of a company that emphasises differentiation rather than low prices.
- **Focused strategy**. Businesses pursuing a focused strategy chose to target a narrow segment of the market to the exclusion of others. This is sometimes called niche marketing. For example, a clothing retailer may only sell clothing for children between the ages of 3 and 10 years. The focused strategy has two variants, namely focused cost leadership, and focused differentiation. Focused cost leadership is when a business seeks to lower its costs and sell at lower

prices than competitors. Focused differentiation emphasises the uniqueness of the products rather than low prices.

Whatever competitive strategy an organisation chooses, the aim is to gain a competitive advantage over its main competitors.

> **Definition of competitive advantage**
> Competitive advantage refers to an advantage a business has over competitors gained by offering consumers either the same benefits as competitors but at a lower price, or delivering more benefits than competitors.

What are the competitors' strengths and weaknesses? Marketers need to assess the strengths and weaknesses of their competitors to be able to know their capabilities. Through such an assessment, a business will be able to identify those areas of competitive vulnerability that they can capitalise on.

The process of assessing the strengths and weaknesses of competitors requires the collection of as much relevant information as possible. This will include information on: 1) competitors' human resources, including marketing personnel and organisation, the skills of employees and staff development programmes; 2) other resources including financial and technological resources; 3) supplier and customer information, including major customers and suppliers; service quality levels; 4) marketing strategies, planning and control systems including product, pricing, promotion and distribution strategies, as well as the effectiveness of strategies; and 5) operating results over a period of time in terms of sales, market share, profit margins and costs.

This information can be collected from a variety of sources such as annual reports, websites and promotional messages, and personal interviews with the staff, customers and suppliers of competitors. It is always important to make sure that the information is collected in an ethical manner.

Data collected for an assessment of competitor strengths and weaknesses can be used to benchmark a firm against leading firms in the industry, or to compare a number of competing firms against identified key industry success factors.

How are they likely to respond to their competitors' actions? Competitive actions are likely to provoke responses. Some competitors may respond swiftly and aggressively to every competitive move, some may delay their responses, others may choose to respond to some actions and not to others. Each competitor is likely to respond differently.

Understanding competitors' objectives and competitive strategies, how they have behaved in the past, as well as knowing about their strengths and weaknesses is helpful in predicting their likely responses to competitive moves. A competitor that is interested in maintaining a big market share in a strategic market segment is more likely to respond to the actions of competitors if they are trying to make inroads into that strategic market. A business that is following the cost leadership strategy is more likely to respond quickly to price cuts by competitors than it would to competitors increasing their promotional budgets. A company that has responded in a particular way in the past is likely to respond in that way again. A small company may wish to respond to competitors' actions, but lack the wherewithal to do so.

Determining market attractiveness

The different players in the market environment directly affect a company's level of competitiveness. Michael Porter identifies 'five forces of competition' operating in the market environment that affect industry attractiveness and profit potential. The 'five forces' are also widely used to assess a firms' level of competitiveness in a market.[17]

The threat of new entrants. New entrants bring increased competition in a market and can threaten a company's profits and share of the market. For example, when the budget airlines Kulula.com and 1Time came onto the domestic air travel market, South African Airways lost market share. The threat of new entrants is high in industries with low barriers to entry and low where barriers to entry are high. Common barriers to entry include high capital requirements, lack of access to production resources and distribution channels, and effective differentiation resulting in increased customer loyalty. Other barriers to entry include economies of scale and high switching costs. Economies of scale is when the average cost per production unit decreases as the production run gets bigger because the fixed costs are shared over an increased number of goods. Switching costs refers to the once-off costs incurred by customers if they switch to another supplier. For example, a decision to use a different software package in a business will mean that employees will have to be trained it its use. High barriers to entry increase the attractiveness of the market to existing competitors but make the market unattractive to companies wanting to enter the market.

Bargaining power of suppliers. The higher the bargaining power of suppliers in a market, the less attractive that market is. Suppliers have more power in a market if they can increase the cost of their products or lower product quality at will. The power of suppliers in a market is driven by a number of factors, including the number of suppliers relative to the demand, the uniqueness of their products, the quantum of switching costs, and how important the supplier considers a particular client to be. Businesses will find a market unattractive if it has an unfavourable supply situation, i.e. where there are few suppliers offering unique products with no close substitutes. In such a situation, the suppliers have a large amount of bargaining power and can choose who they want to do business with. Switching costs are also likely to be high. For example, African Oxygen (Afrox), the biggest supplier in southern Africa of gasses used in manufacturing soft drinks, often has more demand for its products than it can meet. This means it is in a strong position to bargain with soft drink manufacturers.

Bargaining power of buyers. Customers have more power if they can drive prices down or dictate other terms of sale. In general, the higher the bargaining power of buyers, the less attractive a market is. The power of buyers in a market is driven by a number of factors including the number of buyers relative to the supply, the uniqueness of the product, the quantum of switching costs, and how important a business considers particular buyers to be. Attractive markets to a business are associated with large numbers of unorganised buyers, buying unique products with no close substitutes, with each buyer buying small quantities and facing high switching costs. Many big retailers have so much bargaining power that they can force their suppliers to reduce prices.

Threat of substitute products. Examples of substitute products are margarine and butter, or potatoes and rice. If the price of one product increases, consumers will switch to the other, which tends to limit the potential for price increases. The threat of product substitution increases where switching costs are low, and the quality and performance of the substitute product is equal to or higher than its competitor. For example, the introduction of cell phones to South Africa put Telkom's landline business under pressure.

Intensity of rivalry among competitors. The amount of competitor rivalry in a market is affected by a number of factors, including the number of businesses competing in a market, the level of product differentiation, the size of the market, and whether the market is growing or not. High levels of rivalry are associated with large numbers of competitors, low levels of product differentiation, and slow or declining customer markets.

The internal environment

The internal environment consists of actors and forces within an organisation that affect its ability to effectively serve its customers. It is the only part of the marketing environment that is under the direct control of the organisation's management team. Analysis of the internal environment is important as it helps management to better understand the organisation's strengths and weaknesses. When analysing the internal environment, marketing managers need to look at a number of factors, including the organisation's mission and objectives, and its resources, skills and capabilities.

The mission

An organisation's mission is a statement of its reason for existence, and is a kind of invisible hand to guide the activities of the employees and how its resources are applied. A good mission statement is customer-oriented, because customer satisfaction is the key to success.

Examples of mission statements

The mission of the Institute of Marketing Management Graduate School of Marketing (IMM GSM) is to continually bestow relevant and quality marketing skills, knowledge and competencies to its learners, thus creating professionally qualified and well-equipped marketers, who are fully skilled and able to practise effectively in the business environment. In this manner, IMM GSM graduates will contribute to the overall development of a sound and globally acknowledged economy.[18]

South African Revenue Services (SARS): To optimise revenue yield, facilitate trade and enlist new tax contributors by promoting awareness of the obligation to voluntarily comply with South African tax and customs laws, and to provide a quality and responsive service to the public.[19]

Definition
Business objectives are the things an organisation wants to achieve over a given period of time.

Business objectives

The objectives of a business are directly linked to the mission statement. Together they set out the reason for the existence of the business. If there is nothing to achieve, there is no reason for a business to exist. Objectives are set at various levels of the business including at the corporate level, the strategic business unit level, and functional level. Corporate objectives relate to the whole organisation, e.g. Absa Bank has overall objectives which apply to the entire organisation. Objectives at strategic business unit level relate to specific product markets. They apply only to organisations that are operating in several product markets, each of which may have its own strategies. For example, the home loans section, private banking section and car financing section within Absa will each have its own objectives. Functional-level objectives relate to functional areas of the organisation that support strategic business units and the organisation as a whole. Common functional areas in organisations include marketing, finance, production, procurement and human resource management, each of which will have its own objectives.

Within each level, some objectives apply to specific individuals while others are shared by many (for example, departmental objectives). The managers at each level are ultimately responsible for ensuring that objectives at their level are met.

When formulating business objectives, it is important to ensure that they are SMART, that is:

- **Specific**: Objectives should specify exactly what needs to be achieved. Organisations often have objectives relating to profits, market share, brand awareness, etc.
- **Measurable**: Objectives need to be measurable so that success can be easily tracked. For example, an objective in a specific business may be to increase market share by 10% by the end of the current year.
- **Achievable**: Objectives need to be challenging, but achievable. Managers who set objectives that are too high will cause their staff to become discouraged when they fail to reach their targets.
- **Relevant**: Objectives should add something useful to the organisation. It is important to ensure that lower-level objectives are aligned with overall organisational objectives.
- **Time-bound**: Objectives should be set within a time frame (usually a year, although long-term or short-term plans may have different timeframes).

Corporate objectives

The person commonly referred to as the father of management studies, Peter Drucker, identified eight key result areas for businesses:[20]

- Market standing – products to sell, customers to serve, marketing channels to use and the share of market to capture.
- Productivity – progressively lowering the ratio of inputs to outputs.

- Innovation – often reflected in the form of new products or processes.
- Physical and financial resources – management must ensure an adequate supply of physical and financial resources.
- Profitability – targets should be put in place for this.
- Management performance and development – measures should be in place to assess and promote the performance and development of people at all levels of the organisation.
- Worker performance and attitudes – objectives should include performance standards and building employee relations.
- Public and social responsibility – objectives should be set to ensure the public and social responsibilities of the business are met.

Functional objectives

Functional objectives are set by functional managers in each functional area. The marketing manager will thus be responsible for setting objectives for the marketing department. Functional objectives need to be in line with corporate objectives. Most marketing objectives relate to customer satisfaction; growth in sales and market share; business survival and growth, especially during difficult business times, and achievement of predetermined profit levels. Market managers also set objectives relating to each of the elements of the marketing mix, namely product, price, place (distribution) and promotion.

Examples of marketing instrument objectives

- To grow the range of financial services provided to customers by 15% every year for the next three years (product objective).
- To open five new branches by the end of the year (distribution objective).
- To increase customer brand awareness by 20% by the end of the current year (promotion objective).
- To reduce customer service charges by 5% annually for the following three years (pricing objective).

When analysing the internal environment, the marketing manager should refer to the organisation's mission and objectives and assess how well the business has performed in the past. Through this analysis, managers will know the areas in which they have done well and where they have failed. The next thing is to look for internal factors that can help explain why performance was as it was. This is best done by looking at the resources, skills and capabilities of the business.

Resources, skills and capabilities

The internal resources, skills and capabilities of a business determine whether it will be able to exploit the opportunities in the external environment and counter the threats. The analysis of business resources, skills and capabilities will typically use information from all areas of the business. Table 2.2 provides a list of factors to consider during internal analysis. It is neither possible nor desirable for marketing managers to assess all the variables in the internal environment when they identify strengths and weaknesses; the important thing is to identify the key success factors for a particular business.

Table 2.2 Internal factors

Business area	Key internal factors
Marketing management	• Product portfolio and quality • Success rate of new product launches • Market share relative to major competitors • Customer care strategies • Sales and profit margins for different products • Sales force performance • Promotional campaigns and their success rate • Price competitiveness in relation to competitors' products
Financial management	• Cash flow • Ability to generate internal funds • Borrowing capacity • Cost of capital
Organisational and human resources	• Organisational culture and structure • Communication and information system • Management style and interest • Employee knowledge, skills and experience • Utilisation of human resources • Recruitment and training • Employee morale and turnover
Research and development	• Investments in research and development • Development of new products • Introduction of new production technologies
Production facilities and operations management	• Production capacity • Supplier relationship • Inventory turnover • Location and layout of facilities • Efficiency and cost advantages • Quality control systems

Scanning the marketing environment

The marketing environment is always changing. Marketing managers need to scan for changes in the marketing environment and develop a system for assessing the possible impact of the changes on the ability of the business to achieve its objectives.

Definition
Environmental scanning is the process of identifying, gathering and analysing information on changes in the marketing environment including the macro-, market and internal environments.

The importance of environmental scanning can be summed up as follows:[21]

- It helps the business to capitalise early on opportunities rather than lose to competitors. In other words it helps a business to obtain a 'first-mover' advantage – taking action before the competitors do.
- It provides an early signal of impending problems or threats, which can be diffused if recognised well in advance.
- It sensitises a business to the changing needs and wants of its customers.
- It provides a base of objective information about the internal strengths and weaknesses of a business that determine its ability to counter threats and utilise opportunities.
- It improves the image of the business by showing that it is sensitive and responsive to its environment.

Businesses can engage in environment scanning continuously, periodically (for example, once a year) or irregularly. Continuous scanning allows a business to respond on threats to avoid or mitigate their impact, and to take advantage of opportunities before competitors do.

A variety of information sources are used in environmental scanning including industry reports, information from statistics offices such as Statistics South Africa and other government publications, media reports including newspaper articles, as well as business internal records.

Managers are generally aware of the importance of environmental scanning and analyses. They are also aware of the problems and difficulties involved in monitoring environmental changes, e.g. time constraints. A monitoring system that focuses a manager's attention on relevant key environmental issues that will impact on the business can be very useful. Such an approach is known as strategic environmental issue management and consists of three stages:

- **Stage 1 – environmental scanning**. In this stage, management systematically seeks information about various elements of the environment in order to identify significant new developments.
- **Stage 2 – key environmental issue identification**. Certain new developments in the environment may have a significant impact on some activities of the organisation. These are isolated for further consideration. The key issues are evaluated in terms of the probability that the issue will materialise and the degree of impact it will have on the organisation.
- **Stage 3 – impact evaluation**. Four basic questions must be considered in order to determine the impact of a key environmental issue:
  - Does the issue represent an opportunity or threat to the organisation?
  - How significant will the impact be on the operations and performance of the organisation?

- What is the likely timing of the impact?
- What are the specific marketing areas on which it will impact?

- **Stage 4 – formulation of response strategy**. Given the foreseeable impact of a key environmental issue, managers formulate a response strategy. The response strategy can either be reactive (undertaken in response to a major environmental event) or proactive (formulated in anticipation of a major environmental event).

SWOT analysis

SWOT analysis is a management planning tool commonly used to help understand the internal strength and weaknesses of a business and external opportunities and threats facing it. SWOT stands for strengths, weaknesses, opportunities and threats.

Definitions

- Strengths are areas in which a business does particularly well, that set it apart from competitors.[22]
- Weaknesses are areas that a business needs to improve, should it not want its competitors to gain competitive advantage.[23]
- Opportunities are factors in the external environment that can benefit a business.
- Threats are factors in the external environment that can negatively affect a business.

Examples of strengths include strong financial resources, highly skilled employees, market leadership and strong buyer or supplier relations. Weaknesses are the opposite of strengths. Business strengths and weaknesses exist relative to competitors and the needs of the market which an organisation serves, or expects to serve. In many industries, customer service quality is considered the main factor that gives businesses leverage over competitors. Delivering superior customer service requires that employees have a customer-oriented mindset.

The external environment, consisting of the macro- and market environment, is where an organisation's opportunities and threats lie. The two main lenses through which a marketing manager will view environmental factors are:

- Business objectives – opportunities need to be compatible with business objectives and threats are worthy of much attention if they are likely to impact on the organisation's ability to achieve set objectives.
- Resources, skills and capabilities – these determine the ability of the business to capitalise on opportunities and neutralise threats.

SWOT analysis is based on the assumption that an effective strategy capitalises on strengths and opportunities while minimising the possible impact of weaknesses and threats. In conducting SWOT analysis, managers look at the objectives of the business and identify the internal and external environmental factors that are favourable or unfavourable to achieving those objectives. It is a useful tool for planning and reviewing business objectives as well as strategies. Fig. 2.2 provides a summary of strategic guidelines that flow from the SWOT analysis.

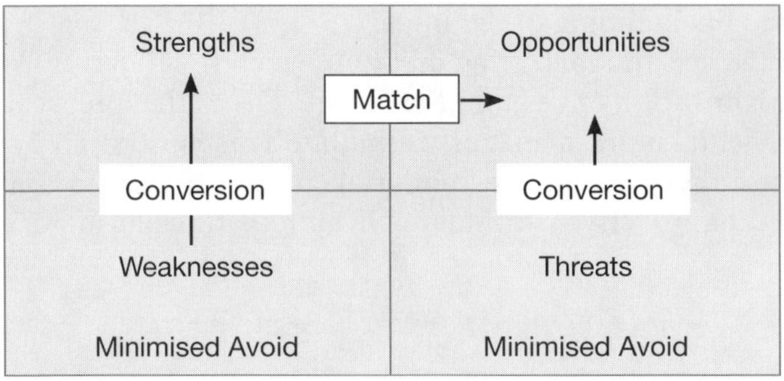

Figure 2.2 *Guidelines for strategic decisions*

Summary

This chapter has discussed the marketing environment in detail. The marketing environment consists of three parts, namely the macro-environment, the market environment and the internal environment. The management of an organisation has control over factors in the internal environment but cannot control factors in the external environment. The external environment is a source of opportunities and threats, while the internal environment is a source of strengths and weaknesses for a business.

It is important for marketing managers to monitor changes in the marketing environment so that they can develop strategies that take advantage of the opportunities and avoid or minimise the potentially negative impact of the threats. The ultimate aim is for a business to effectively serve its customers better than its competitors are able to. Customers are the focal point of any business organisation. Chapter 3 provides a detailed discussion of consumers and the factors that affect consumer behaviour.

Case study: Mr Abram, the independent grocer

The future does not look promising for Mr Abram. His grocery outlet is no longer able to attract as many customers as it used to. Many in the community seem to be enjoying going to the mall and buying their supplies from the chain retailers. What can he do to make sure his business survives?

It all started 30 years ago, when Mr Abram decided to open a grocery store in his remote rural community in Mpumalanga. Back then the store was one of only three grocery outlets in the area, all of which were independently owned by individual members of the local community. Other competitors were located more than 15 km away. Mr Abram's grocery store was a favourite in his area. Most people were attracted to his shop because of his friendly disposition and the fact that he would often allow people to buy on credit.

Things have changed a lot in this rural community over the past 30 years. Most of the major changes have, however, taken place over the last eight years, resulting mainly from government social and economic development projects in the area. Over this period, Government has spent millions building a new hospital, two new high schools and a police station in the area. The population area has grown significantly and many people including professionals have moved in to take up job opportunities in the new government establishments or to open up their own businesses. Two of the country's big banks also opened local branches. Many of the locals have managed to find jobs in public and private establishments. The once remote rural community has quickly become a vibrant commercial area.

The growing economic activities in the area brought a lot of business to Mr Abram. His customer base grew quickly and he was granted a bank loan to expand. Until two years ago, things were looking very promising. Then a mall opened nearby, with a number of chain retailers, including a big national supermarket operator. The supermarket is able to offer far lower prices than any independent retailer because, as part of a national chain, it is able to buy products in bulk straight from the manufacturers, thereby avoiding wholesaler mark-ups. The manufacturers undertake direct deliveries to the supermarket, while independent retailers bear the costs of having to provide their own transportation of goods from wholesalers. The large retail space occupied by the supermarket means it can provide a greater product variety and the added convenience of being able to find most products under one roof.

Independent grocers are finding it very difficult to compete with the supermarket and more than half have had to close. Mr Abram urgently needs to find new competitive strategies that can help ensure the survival of his business.

Exercise

1. Identify and discuss macro-environment factors impacting on Mr Abram's grocery business.
2. Which major actors in the market environment are sources of threats to Mr Abram's grocery business? Justify your answer.
3. What are the major strengths and weaknesses of Mr Abram's grocery business?
4. Mr Abrams needs to find new competitive strategies to ensure the survival of his business.
   (a) Discuss the generic competitive strategies commonly followed by businesses.
   (b) Which generic strategy would you recommend to Mr Abram and why?
   (c) Provide examples of specific competitive actions Mr Abram can take as he pursues your recommended generic strategy.

CHAPTER 3

Understanding the consumer

Learning outcomes

After studying this chapter you should be able to:

- understand and explain the consumer decision-making process;
- discuss the various influences on consumer buyer behaviour;
- explain the relationship between consumer purchasing and the stages of the family life cycle and other demographic dimensions;
- understand the consumer adoption process;
- understand business-to-business customers and buyers; and
- explain the purchasing behaviour and the basic e-commerce methods usually employed in business-to-business marketing.

Introduction

As has been said already, customers are central to the success of any organisation. For this reason, marketers need to understand the needs and wants of their customers, as well as their purchasing behaviour. Marketers must continually gather information about the factors that influence a customer's decision to buy, and the process customers follow when making the purchase.

Broadly speaking, there are four basic views of consumer decision making:

- An **economic** view which assumes that consumers make rational decisions.
- A **passive** view which sees consumers as irrational and impulsive.
- A **cognitive** view which assumes consumers are not able to make perfect decisions, but at least they can try to find enough information to try to make the best decision.
- An **emotional** view which assumes that consumers often make impulsive and slipshod decisions they later regret.[1]

Definition of consumer behaviour

1. The dynamic interaction of affect and cognition, behaviour, and the environment by which human beings conduct the exchange aspects of their lives.
2. The overt actions of consumers.
3. The behaviour of the consumer or decision maker in the market place of products and services. It often is used to describe the interdisciplinary field of scientific study that attempts to understand and describe such behaviour.[2]

Consumer buying decisions vary in accordance with the type of product or service. Purchasing washing powder, a new television, a new house or banking services are all quite different. The higher the risk associated with the purchase and the larger the price, the higher the level of buyer involvement, the more information is required, the more time the purchase is likely to take, and greater the demand will be for alternatives (see fig. 3.1).

CONTINUUM OF CONSUMER BUYING DECISIONS			
Involvement	Low	Low to moderate	High
Time	Short	Short to moderate	Long
Cost	Low	Low to moderate	High
Information search	Internal only	Mostly internal	Internal and external
Number of alternatives	One	Few	Many

Figure 3.1 *The continuum of consumer buying decisions*[3]

Marketers continually need to look for ways to decrease the sense of risk or dissonance that consumers may experience when buying a product. This chapter will describe the consumer buying decision-making process, consumer behaviour and all the factors that influence the consumer purchase decision.

Steps in the consumer decision-making process

By using your own experiences as a consumer of products and services you can easily identify the variety of goods people purchase, the individuality of each purchase event, and the degrees of purchasing complexity that apply to different kinds of buying processes. The steps in the consumer buying decision-making process are depicted in fig. 3.2.

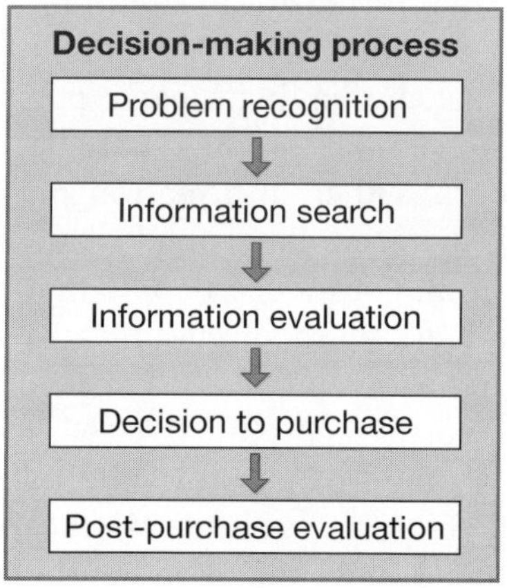

Figure 3.2 *The consumer buying decision-making process*[4]

Problem recognition

This is an awareness of the need and can be explained as the difference between the actual condition and the desired state. The process begins by the recognition of a consumer that there is a 'problem', after which he or she will take steps to solve it. For example, when you feel hungry, or a light indicates your car is running out of fuel, there is a clear problem that needs to be solved by buying food or buying petrol. Other problems are the result of an event, for example the exhaust pipe falls off your car, 'triggering' the need to have it fixed. Other problem situations are not so easy to define. In the case of psychological needs, the recognition of the problem can be a slow realisation or a sudden impulse. For example, having had a long and tiring day, you may stop to buy some bread and milk and end up also purchasing a tub of chocolate ice cream, 'to cheer you up'. The problem here is based on a vague psychological feeling and the imagined 'solution' could have been anything from a bar of chocolate to a glossy magazine or an expensive new coat. Although these examples have come from the consumer recognising a problem that needs to be solved, it is also well known that a marketer can stimulate the recognition of a problem through the use of elements of the marketing mix. In this case the consumer may not have been aware of the need and perhaps only through seeing an advertisement realises that a need exists. For example, if you see an advertisement for a new car that appeals to you, you may start to wonder about replacing your current car and then move on to decide that you wish to buy a new one. In the context of the buying decision-making process, the problem recognition step requires both the consumer's willingness and ability to fulfil the recognised need.

Search for information

Once the need is recognised, and the consumer has both the willingness and the ability to fulfil this need, he or she needs to define what the solution might be. The consumer will do this by gathering relevant information that will assist him or her in making the most appropriate purchase decision. Some information may be gathered passively and is referred to as 'internal search'. This relies mainly on memory. Consumers are exposed to a wide range of communication messages daily and marketers hope that, by having clearly positioned their product in the minds of potential consumers, their product will be remembered as and when the need for purchase occurs. Other information may be actively sought from specialist media, marketing material, labels and retailers. The consumer may also ask experts or influential people, or indeed people that they know have experience and knowledge of the product. Word of mouth is a very important influencer during this step in the purchasing process as the source of the information is usually assumed to be trustworthy and objective. A successful information search leaves the consumer with a range of possible alternatives to solve the problem. This is called the 'evoked set'. For example, if the problem is hunger and the solution is to go out for a meal, the evoked set could be Chinese food, a pizza, a hamburger or curry.

Evaluation of gathered information

The third step in the consumer decision-making process is to evaluate the information that has been gathered. To have criteria for the evaluation, the consumer needs to have a basis of comparison. Relevant comparisons are those benefits or features of the product that the consumer values – e.g. location, speed of purchase, price and after-sales service. Marketers must therefore determine which product attributes are most important to consumers and try to differentiate themselves from competing products. The criteria for selection could be objective, e.g. price or a benchmarked measure of speed, or subjective, e.g. the idea that the product carries enhanced status or better self-image, or that the manufacturer is trustworthy. The consumer can then weigh up the evoked set of alternatives and make a choice. Consumers who are unable to make a choice at this point may resume the search and gather more information.

Decision to purchase

This is the step in the process where the consumer finalises the proposed deal and the actual purchase takes place. This decision could be as simple as placing the chocolate ice cream in the shopping trolley or it may be more complex, involving negotiation and the finalisation of details such as payment, delivery or quantity. This type of purchase complexity is well illustrated in the protracted buying process of a house or property. If the outcome of the negotiation is not satisfactory to a consumer, they may decide to forego the purchase completely or re-evaluate and settle on another option. It is important for marketers to make it as easy as possible for the deal to be concluded as long queues, lack of assistance or bureaucratic procedures could cause consumers to choose another product or decide not to buy at all.

Post-purchase evaluation

Many marketers make the mistake of believing that once payment has been made, then the consumer's involvement with the product ends. This is definitely not the case – the consumer will almost certainly go through a certain degree of post-purchase evaluation during which they will assess whether or not the product has solved the problem and fulfilled expectations. In all cases there is an assessment of the gap between the consumer's expectations of the product and what the product actually delivers. If the performance of the product fell short, then there would be disappointment. If the product met expectations, then the customer would be satisfied. If the product exceeds the expectations of the consumer, then he or she would be delighted.[5]

This is especially true if the purchasing process has been a complex and lengthy one such as buying a car or a house. In these cases the consumer may feel a certain amount of 'cognitive dissonance' – a psychological term meaning a feeling of discomfort caused by holding conflicting ideas simultaneously. In this context the dissonance comes with the possibility of having made the wrong decision, also known as 'buyer's remorse'. It is therefore important that marketers recognise this and embark on some form of dissonance-reducing post-purchase reassurance such as providing guarantees, warranties or after-sales service.

Although the five-step decision-making process seems clear, remember that consumers do not necessarily follow these steps in sequence. They may move in and out of the steps, possibly returning to an earlier stage for more information or to redefine the problem. The consumer may also end the process at any stage and choose not to purchase, or the problem is solved by other means.

Influences on the consumer decision-making process

Fig. 3.3 shows a number of influences that may exert pressure on the consumer at any stage during the purchasing decision-making process. These can be grouped into individual, group, situational and marketing mix elements.

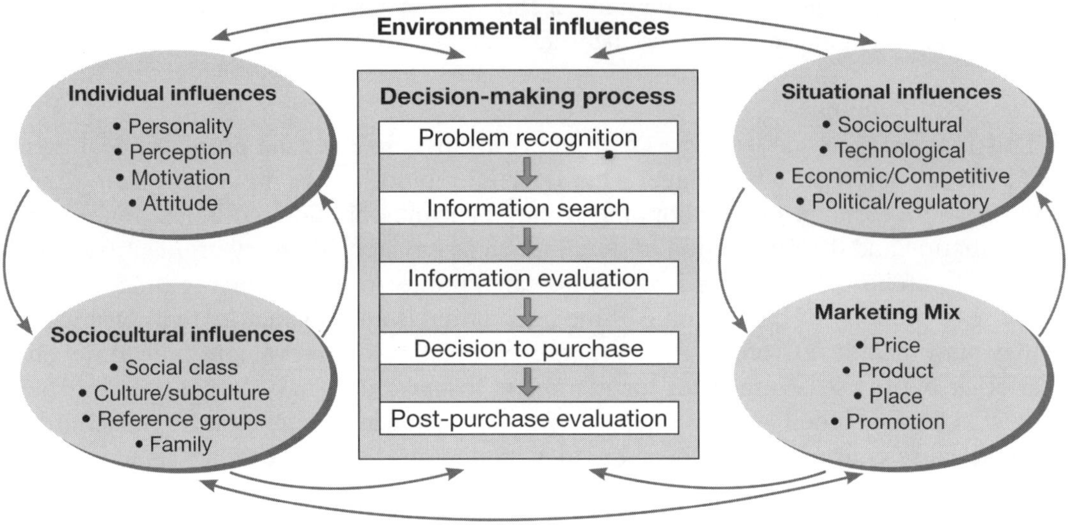

Figure 3.3 *Influences on the consumer decision-making process*[6]

Individual influences

Through the process of market segmentation discussed in a chapter 5, marketers attempt to group individuals together on the basis of similar characteristics. However valid certain generalisations may be, the unique personality, perceptions, motivations and attitudes of every individual in the segment determine what happens in the buying process.

Personality

Distinctive personality traits, behaviours and experiences and their potential ability to influence purchasing decisions have long been a topic of research and discussion and no definite links have been proven. However, it may be safe to assume that if the purchasing decision relates to a high involvement product where there are strong emotional and psychological needs to fulfil, then a consumer's personality traits would exert relatively more influence on the decision. When buying clothing, for example, an extroverted, confident person may select high style, brightly coloured or off-beat fashion items, while a shy, retiring individual might prefer more conservative, less conspicuous, more traditional outfits. Other personality traits that may affect the buying process include compulsiveness, adaptability, ambitiousness, dogmatism, introversion, aggressiveness, competitiveness and friendliness.

Perception

Perception is the process of selecting, analysing and interpreting stimuli to produce meaning and assign relevance. Faced with a plethora of marketing communication stimuli (e.g. advertising, packaging and merchandising displays) consumers make decisions and act on what they perceive to be reality. Marketers should obviously develop messages that have a greater chance of being noticed and remembered. There are three key issues regarding perception which are relevant to marketers, namely selective exposure, selective distortion and selective retention.

Selective exposure

Consumers usually only perceive and interpret stimuli that hold some form of meaning to them or that they choose to be exposed to. Consumers may leave the room when television commercials begin. For this reason marketers continually attempt to 'break through' the clutter and find new and unconventional ways of attracting consumers to notice their communication messages. Restroom advertising, building wraps and street pole advertising are all fairly new and innovative ways of ensuring the target segment is exposed to the message and that the message gets more attention than competitors' messages do.

Selective distortion

Perception is affected by previous experience and individual attitudes. People interpret stimuli in a way that best suits their perceptions. Negative associations with particular products or companies are likely to create negative attitudes towards certain products or services.

Example of selective distortion

When a consumer has had serious problems with a service provider such as Telkom, its advertisements for new products or special savings on services will probably not have the desired effect. Such a consumer will remember the dissatisfaction and will probably be more receptive to ordering a landline telephone service from a competing company.

Selective retention

Because they are faced with very large numbers of stimuli, consumers tend to filter out stimuli that do not support their beliefs and/or they do not wish to remember. Repeating adverts and reminding consumers about products through familiar and easily remembered stimuli such as logos, packaging colours and brand names is one way of overcoming this problem. The now famous Klipdrift brandy advertisements which have been shown in various forms over a long period are a good example of how to effectively jog consumers' memories about a product.

Motivation

Motives are energising or driving forces that drive people to fulfil their needs and wants. Individual actions are affected by a complex set of motives and often individuals themselves cannot identify what it is that motivates them to behave in a certain way at a certain time. For example, a couple travelling by car from Johannesburg to Durban may initially be relaxed and intend to have a pleasant drive, take in the scenery on the way, have a leisurely lunch, arrive at their destination in the afternoon, and find a comfortable place to spend the night. If on the way they experience lengthy delays due to road construction, they may arrive in Durban at 9 pm, no longer wanting to find a comfortable hotel, but simply wanting to find any place that is still open and has accommodation available. Marketers take motivational influences such as these into account when designing a marketing mix. A well-lit hotel sign with messages like 'vacancies' and 'open 24 hours' would certainly appeal to tired and frustrated travellers.

Classifying motives can help the marketer to better understand human and thus consumer behaviour. Maslow's hierarchy of needs (fig. 3.4) has long been used to classify basic individual motivations. Marketers need to determine at what level of the motivation hierarchy their target consumers are in order to determine what kind of message would most effectively motivate their purchase of a particular product or service.

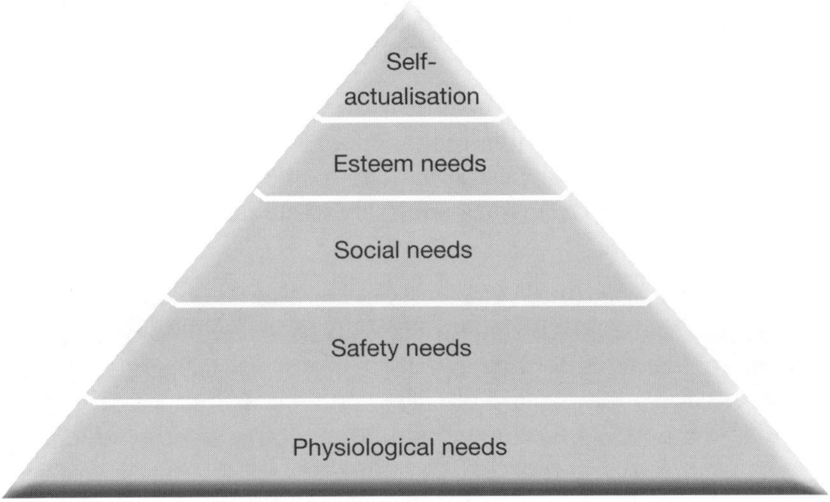

***Figure 3.4** Maslow's hierarchy of needs*[7]

Abraham Maslow identified a set of human motives and classified them in a hierarchy, with the largest and most fundamental needs at the bottom, and the need for self-actualisation at the top. Starting at the bottom of the pyramid, each need must be met before the next level of need arises.

Physiological: The most basic needs are the physiological requirements necessary for survival. These include food, water, sex and sleep. When consumers become hungry and thirsty, they will be motivated to purchase food and drink.

Safety: Once the needs for the basic requirements for survival have been met, the next level of motivation arises, driven by the need for safety, health, shelter and security. The need for security may drive a consumer to install a burglar alarm or purchase membership of a medical aid scheme.

Social: After physiological and safety needs have met, middle order social motivations arise, e.g. the need for belonging, love, friendship and social acceptance. Consumers buy fashionable clothing, cosmetics, toiletries and grooming services to meet social needs.

Esteem: Esteem motives arise once the bottom three needs have been met. The desire for status, prestige, respect and social standing drive the purchase of such products as jewellery, perfumes and expensive branded clothing.

Self-actualisation: The need for self-fulfilment is the highest order motivation. Self-actualisation means different things to different people. One person may feel self-actualised by becoming CEO of an international company, another may reach fulfilment by raising a healthy and happy family. Only the individual will know whether he or she has achieved a state of self-actualisation.

Attitude

Attitudes comprise positive or negative feelings and beliefs about an object, an activity or an organisation. Consumers develop attitudes towards products through learned knowledge gained from experience and interaction. These attitudes greatly influence the extent to which a company's marketing strategies succeed or fail. Consumers tend to filter out information that conflicts with their attitudes and they may distort information or selectively retain certain aspects so that the information reinforces their existing attitudes.

Certain attitudes change along with personal and lifestyle changes and may be susceptible to the influence of marketing, but other attitudes may be so firmly embedded that they are extremely difficult to change. Even if a consumer has a positive attitude towards a product or service, he or she may not buy it for a variety of reasons. Perhaps the product is unaffordable. Perhaps the consumer likes the brand, but prefers to buy another one. In order to influence consumer behaviour, marketers must understand the beliefs that underpin prevailing attitudes and the reasons for those attitudes.

Ways in which marketers can influence consumer attitudes include:

- Increasing the emphasis on an important brand attribute.
- Selecting a new differentiating attribute and trying to influence consumers to attach a higher significance to that attribute.
- Emphasising additional benefits received from a new attribute.
- Changing the perception of a competing product though comparison to the competitive product's attributes. Direct comparative advertising is common in countries such as the US, but is not allowed in South Africa.

Sociocultural influences

Group

Individuals form part of many diverse social groupings. These can be recognised units within society such as the family or informal groupings such as reference groups. Purchasing decisions are usually influenced by membership of social groupings, since these can affect how individual consumers differentiate between what is essential and what is not. Socio-cultural group influences influence final decision making when limited resources demand that consumers prioritise their spending.

Social class

Social class can be viewed as a group of individuals who share a similar rank in society. It is a form of dividing society up into layers, e.g. upper class, upper middle class, middle class, lower middle class and working class. There is an argument against using social class to distinguish between individuals in modern egalitarian societies. In the UK, class is largely determined by occupation. In South Africa class is largely defined by income so the demographic variable that influences the buying decision is seen as the 'ability to purchase'.

Certain theorists continue to argue that people in different classes seek out products to enhance their standing in that segment of society. Middle and upper-middle class people, may, for example look for goods that will increase their self-esteem and social status, whilst the working class may be seen to be more motivated by family values and less materialistic than other classes. People tend to see the world through the eyes of their own social class, so marketers must make themselves aware of what may be important to people from other social classes.

Culture and subculture

A culture can be described as a set of values, norms, mores and attitudes that determine the 'personality' of the society in which a person lives. Culture is passed on from generation to generation and may have a strong influence on the way of life of groups of individuals, including implicit standards and rules for the group.[8] Culture affects what people buy, how they buy and when they buy. A product with benefits that are in line with what a specific culture values as important has a better chance of being successful in that market. Cultures manifest themselves in many ways, e.g. what and when we eat. Breakfast for most people living in the UK and some people in South Africa may consist of cereal, toast, bacon, eggs and juice whilst in continental Europe it could be cold meats, cheeses, croissants and coffee. In Spain, lunch generally begins at 4 pm and supper served after 10 pm. In Central Europe many restaurants close for the night at around 5 pm. It is important for marketers to understand the values and belief system of their target market because the marketing strategy will fail unless it addresses the needs of that cultural group.

Any culture can be divided into subcultures, and certain subcultures transcend cultural groupings. Individuals belonging to a subculture are members of a broader cultural group but also show specific characteristics common to a smaller group. Subcultures can be identified in many ways, e.g. ethnic origin, language, religious belief or lifestyle orientation. For example a South African marketer may see South African as the dominant culture but with significant subcultures such as Asian South Africans (ethnic origin), Afrikaans teenagers (age, language and ethnic background) or Christian motorcyclists (religious beliefs and lifestyle orientation).

Reference groups

Reference groups are groups that individuals identify with (either groups they belong to already, or groups they aspire to belong to), and the extent to which those individuals take on many of the values and behaviours common to group members. Reference groups can be 'membership groups' such as professional bodies, social or activity-based associations. They may be 'automatic groups' to which individuals belong due to age, gender or occupation, e.g. teenagers, teachers, etc. Reference groups can also be 'aspirant groups'. These are groups to which individuals aspire to belong, such as a group with a higher status among peers, or the group surrounding a celebrity. Finally there are 'dissociative groups' – groups to which an individual does not want to belong. Marketers must be aware of the target customer's frame of reference in respect of groups, since this exerts a strong influence on the buying process. A consumer often purchases a product to obtain or retain membership of a group. Peer pressure, especially among younger consumers, is a powerful factor in buying decisions.

Family

Even with changes in the modern family structure and behaviour, the family still remains a major influence of the how, why and what people purchase. The marketing family life cycle devised in 1966 was updated in 1979 (table 3.1).[9]

Table 3.1 *The nine-stage family life cycle*[10]

1	Young, single
2	Young, married without children
3a	Young, divorced without children
3b	Young, married with children, infant, 4–12 years old, adolescent
3c	Young, divorced with children, infant, 4–12 years old, adolescent
4a	Middle-aged, married without children
4b	Middle-aged, divorced without children
4c	Middle-aged, married with children, young, adolescent
4d	Middle-aged, divorced with children, young, adolescent
4e	Middle-aged, married without dependent children
4f	Middle-aged divorced without dependent children
5a	Older, married
5b	Older, unmarried, divorced, widowed
6	Others

Whatever the family structure, members of the family can participate in the purchasing decisions of the others, and the purchasing behaviour of most individuals is copied from their parents. In certain cases, individual members will make decisions that will affect the entire household, but they are influenced by other members of the family. The roles of each family member will change from purchase decision to purchase decision. At different times different family members may play the role of initiator, user, influencer, decider or purchaser. Take the example of a child wanting a new bicycle. The child is the initiator and will be the user of the purchase. (Never underestimate the 'pester power' of children, parents will often make great sacrifices to fulfil their children's needs.) In this example, perhaps the mother agrees that it would be a good idea for a birthday present and becomes an influencer in the purchasing decisions. Both parents may agree to the purchase and are therefore both the deciders. Perhaps the father goes alone to buy the bicycle and is therefore the purchaser.

Environmental influences

Socio-cultural

Consumers are influenced by societal trends. For example there has been a trend towards sustainability as an economic and moral imperative and consumers are increasingly demanding 'green' and environmentally friendly products. Indeed in South Africa, with the recent release of the King III report on corporate governance, it has become advisable for organisations to formally report on their 'triple bottom line', i.e. their social, environmental and financial status. Recent trends are indicating that consumers are moving towards responsible consumption, and companies would be well advised to respond by adopting ethical marketing and manufacturing practices. Socio-cultural influences on the buying process includes levels of literacy, the impact of HIV/Aids on society and the use of children in advertising. Marketers must identify what issues in the social environment may be influencing the consumer buying process in respect of their products and services.

Technological

Advances in technology influence both the consumer's buying behaviour and also the marketer's ability to formulate increasingly appropriate marketing strategies. Database technology, for example, can track the movements of an individual consumer on a website and allow marketers to tailor what that individual sees on the website next time he or she visits the site. Technology also allows for innovations in product development and distribution.

Economic/competitive

It is obvious that the world-wide recession has had a major impact on consumer purchasing trends. As consumers have had to tighten their belts, they have postponed certain purchases, altered their criteria for making purchase decisions, and may have stopped buying certain products entirely. Price and value for money have come to the fore in many target markets as the strongest influence on the purchase decision. Some of the largest retailing groups in South Africa have reported that there is a permanent shift in the buying behaviour of their customers towards more frequent shopping trips with less being spent on each trip.

Most consumers do not buy without at least some consideration of competitive offerings, so marketers must fully analyse what their competitors are doing. Direct competitors may be easy to identify – e.g. a tyre manufacturer's competitors are the other tyre manufacturers active in the market. However, more lifestyle-oriented products such as movie theatres are competing not only with other movie theatres, but also with other leisure activities that consumers may choose to spend their money on, e.g. restaurants, ice skating and going on a picnic. Marketers must ensure that the benefits of their products are easily comparable to those of their competitors to make the consumer's buying decision easier.

Political/regulatory

Political and regulatory influences may exert a heavy influence on the consumer's behaviour in the purchasing process. Safety regulations, packaging laws, consumer privacy and consumer rights are all beneficial to the consumer as they help reduce the inherent perceived risks in the purchase and give some level of reassurance. Lowering risk for the consumer is especially important when dealing with high involvement products where making the wrong decision could seriously affect the consumer's well-being. Education and day care facilities and financial services are good examples of high-risk products.

The perception of political stability in a country may also have an influence on buying decisions, e.g. decisions around buying fixed property. When Nelson Mandela was still president of South Africa, the media reported seeing an ambulance outside his residence, and the consequence was a major selloff of shares on the stock exchange.

The marketing mix

When marketing a tangible good, marketers use the 4 Ps to make up their marketing mix – product, price, place and promotion. Marketers offering an intangible product or service use the extended marketing mix – the 7 Ps, namely product, price, place, promotion, physical evidence, process and people. The marketing mix that consumers are exposed to also make up part of the external environment.

The consumer adoption process

When a consumer is purchasing a product for the first time the level of perceived risk is high. Perceived risks can fall into any one or more of the following categories:

- Financial risk (the money spent will be wasted if the product does not fullfil the need).
- Functional risk (the product will not perform according to expectation).
- Social risk (the product may lower the individual's standing among contemporaries).
- Physical risk (the product may cause harm to the individual's health).

In making the decision about whether or not to purchase a specific product or service, the consumer will usually move through five stages.

1. **Awareness**: The consumer becomes aware of the product or service but as yet has no information about it.

2. **Interest**: The consumer becomes interested in the product or service and starts to gather information about it.
3. **Evaluation**: Based on the information the consumer has gathered he or she considers whether or not to try the product.
4. **Trial**: The consumer decides to try the product on a limited first buy basis in order to improve his or her information about the product based on experience.
5. **Adoption/rejection**: The consumer either makes a full commitment to adopting the product and uses it regularly or decides to reject and continue the search.

Based on the information regarding the consumer's perception of risk and the stages of adoption/rejection, marketers must ensure that they formulate a marketing mix which will lessen the perceived risk as much as possible, or at least make the risk appear less severe than the risks associated with competitors' offerings.

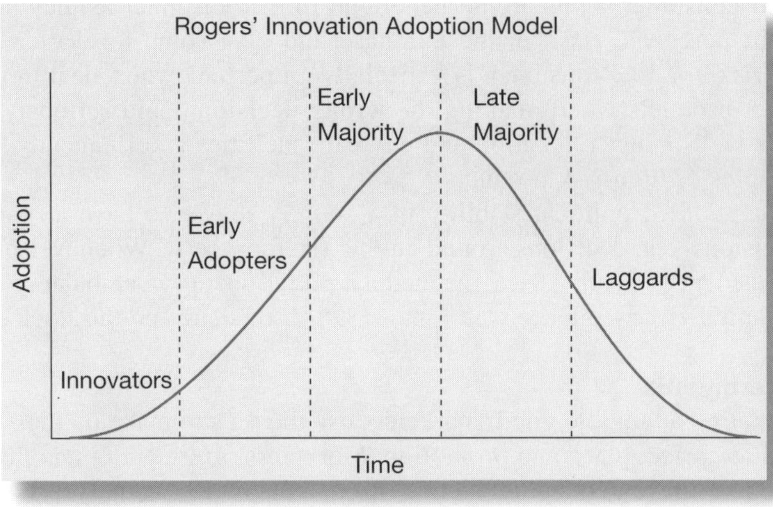

***Figure 3.5** Rogers' innovation adoption model*[11]

Rogers' Innovation Adoption Process as depicted in fig. 3.5 suggests that consumers differ greatly in their readiness to try a new product or innovation.

- **Innovators**: These consumers are adventurous and eager to try something new. Innovators tend to be younger and better educated.
- **Early adopters**: They are also well educated and are often opinion leaders within their communities. They are happy to adopt early but are generally careful in their decision and take calculated risks.
- **Early majority**: These people are more cautious consumers, preferring to adopt an innovation after the product has proven successful.
- **Late majority**: This group is sceptical and will only adopt the product after the majority has purchased it. These consumers tend to be older and often only adopt the product because of external pressures.
- **Laggards**: They do not like change; they are conservative, traditional and suspicious of new things. These people will only adopt the product once it is seen to have developed its own traditional status.

The organisational buying process

Marketers have the same broad objective when addressing individual consumers and business/organisational consumers. However, the buying process that organisations follow is somewhat different to the process followed by individual consumers.

- Business customers usually purchase products and services to fit a specific business need with the emphasis on economic benefits, and they follow a rational decision-making process. Consumers usually buy products to meet individual or family needs and the emphasis is largely on meeting psychological needs. The buying decisions of individuals tend to be more emotionally based.
- The purchasing process within organisations tends to be far lengthier, more technical, tends to involve a team of people, and usually purchases involve larger quantities than is the case in the individual consumer market.
- Individual consumers may experience some irritation if a product fails or the suppliers run out of stock, and they generally find it easy to substitute or switch brands and/or suppliers. The impact of a product failing or of a supply disruption may be more severe in an organisational context, and switching to another supplier may be more difficult and time-consuming.

Organisations usually engage in three types of buying.

- **Straight/routine rebuy**: Here the purchasing department regularly reorders low risk, frequently purchased items such as office supplies, cleaning materials or computer consumables. There is often an approved list of suppliers, the decision-making process is simple, and few people are involved.
- **Modified rebuy**: This arises when there has been some prior experience with the product but a need exists for a review or modification. Perhaps there has been a change in product specifications, pricing or the terms and conditions of the service level agreement. A modified rebuy situation is more complex and costly than a routine rebuy, and more people are involved. Proposals may be invited from more than one supplier, which will require a thorough evaluation of what the various suppliers are offering.
- **New task buying**: This is when the organisation purchases a product for the first time. Because the organisation has no previous experience with the product, the number of people involved is likely to be greater, and more information will need to be gathered. The amount of effort that goes into new task buying will be proportional to the level of risk and cost, and it may take months to finalise.

Fig. 3.6 shows that the additional complexities of the organisational buying process mean that there are eight steps in the decision-making process. Compare this to the five steps that make up the individual consumer decision-making process (fig. 3.2).

The term 'buying centre' refers to the group of people who participate in the organisational buying process.

- **Initiators/users** are the people in the organisation who recognise the need for the product or service and initiate the buying process. They may also be users of the product.

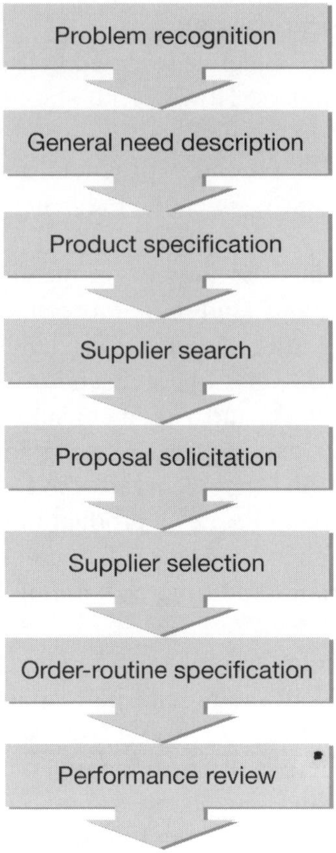

Figure 3.6 *Steps in the organisational buying process*[12]

- **Influencers** are those people who have any kind of influence on the outcome of the decision-making process. This influence could be based on skills or expertise, e.g. an accountant who works out the break-even point on the expenditure. The influence could also be more informal, e.g. the personal preferences of an individual staff member.
- **Deciders** are the people who have the formal or informal authority to decide on the product specifications or on the final approved suppliers.
- **Buyers** have the formal authority to select suppliers, negotiate with them, and conclude transactions. Junior buyers may be able to authorise straight rebuys, and more senior staff may have to be involved in new task purchases.
- **Gatekeepers** exert control over purchasing decisions, or some aspect of purchasing decisions. They have the potential to adversely influence the outcome of such a decision. For example, a gatekeeper may be in a position to interfere with the flow of important information, or to restrict access to a key decision maker.

Organisational buying decisions are also influenced by external influences such as environmental factors; internal factors such as organisational goals, policies and procedures; interpersonal relationships; and the factors which apply to buyers as individuals.

Summary
This chapter describes the consumer buying decision-making process, and the various factors that influence these decisions. It then briefly describes how the organisational buying process differs from the process that applies to individual consumers.

CHAPTER 4

Marketing information and marketing research

Learning outcomes

After studying this chapter you should be able to:

- explain the difference between data and information;
- explain how a marketing information system and a marketing decision support system can help marketing managers to make decisions; and
- discuss the marketing research process.

Introduction

In order to implement marketing decisions, marketers require information about the characteristics, needs and purchasing patterns of their target markets. Given the intense competition in today's marketplace, information is often the key to a successful marketing strategy. Marketing research and information systems provide information that can help business and other organisations avoid assumptions and misunderstandings that could result in poor marketing performance.

The real value of marketing research and marketing information systems is measured by improvements in a marketer's ability to make decisions. Marketers treat information as they do other resources utilised by businesses. They weigh the costs of obtaining information against the benefits gained. Information is worthwhile if it results in marketing activities that lead to increased sales and profits or help the business to achieve some other goal, such as building customer relationships. The efficient management of marketing information and marketing research is currently considered a strategic priority of a business, as it can provide insight into possible future events.

The need for marketing information

Marketing managers should be future-oriented. They should anticipate environmental changes, forecast the direction and the impact these changes will have on their businesses, and plan accordingly. In order to implement these tasks, management requires information regarding the various internal and external environmental variables which may affect the business. Information about the business micro-environment (internal environment) can be obtained from sources such as the financial, production, human resources, purchasing and marketing departments. External information can be collected from both the market and macro-environments in which the business operates. For example, consumers could be directly contacted for information about the market. Information on the economic, technological and political-legal environments, and competitors and suppliers can be obtained by consulting secondary sources.

Examples of information required by marketing managers

- Socio-cultural changes, such as the increasing urbanisation of the South African population, in so far as these may have an impact on demand and consumption patterns.
- Technological trends, such as the increasing use of cellphone technology heightening consumer pressures for product information, guarantees and service.
- Competitive activities, which may be intensifying in the face of globalisation, and in environments where there is privatisation and deregulation of government enterprises.
- Increasing complexity of marketing decision making, such as shorter product life cycles and the associated need for more product development, expansion to new markets and the management of multiple distribution channels.

Fast-changing environmental conditions mean that every business has to manage its marketing information as efficiently as possible. Marketing managers often discover that their information problems are a result of too much data being available, rather than too little. Data and information are not the same thing. **Data** refers to all facts or recorded measures of certain phenomena, while **information** is a body of facts in a format suitable to support decision making or to define the relationship between two pieces of data.[1] Progress in communication media and data processing technology has resulted in a tremendous increase in the volume of available data.

Data vs. information[2]

Edgars records thousands of unsummarised facts. A store clerk enters data into the computer system every time a customer purchases a product. Simultaneously, the data is also entered into a computerised inventory system. This data lacks any meaning, however, until managers request the information system to translate the data into product sales totals by store, province or by city so that they can undertake sales forecasts.

In addition, the complexity of data has further increased owing to new data collection and presentation methods. This development has made it even more difficult to make the distinction between relevant data (in other words, information) and irrelevant data. The popular term for this phenomenon is 'the information explosion'.

Marketing information is useful only if it can help a marketing manager make a decision. In order to be useful, information should be of high quality, relevant, timely and complete.[3] To be considered **high quality**, information should provide a good reflection of reality and it should therefore be accurate, valid and reliable. The information should also be **relevant**, in other words, it should clarify the questions that face the decision maker. Marketing information should also be **timely**, as outdated information could lead to poor decisions. If, for example, the business intends to launch a new product in winter, all the research regarding the price, packaging, name, logo, and so forth should be conducted well in advance. Finally, it is also important that the information is **complete**.

The efficiency of a marketing information system is a key factor contributing to the speed and accuracy of marketing decision making. An efficient marketing information system is one that filters the massive inflow of data and provides information for decision making to the appropriate decision makers, when and where they need it, and in a form in which they can use it.

Information management

Marketing information systems

Definition[4]
A marketing information system (MIS) is a set of procedures and methods for the regular planning, collection, analyses and presentation of information for use in making marketing decisions.

In a marketing context, information management refers to planning, organising, co-ordinating, controlling and providing leadership in respect of marketing information so that the information requirements of marketing decision makers are optimally satisfied. Information requirements have to be continually monitored and data sources must be up to date and accessible. Data reduction has to take place efficiently and the supply of the resulting information to decision makers has to be timeous and in a useful format. The most common way of undertaking this process is to set up a marketing information system.

Example of a marketing information system[5]
The Agricultural Marketing Information System is part of AGIS (the Agricultural Geo-Referenced Information System) of South Africa's Department of Agriculture, Forestry and Fisheries. It aims to provide a variety of stakeholders including policy makers and land users with the information they need to make the best choices about using available resources. The larger objective is to achieve sustainable levels of food production and development in an increasingly complex operating environment.

The system provides marketing information relevant to each province, town and market type. The elements of the package are geo-referenced land, climate, plant nutrient, production and water information, integrated with infrastructural and socio-economic factors. An agricultural atlas provides potential buyers and sellers with visual information about towns, agricultural areas, borders and markets. In addition, clients can get information from experts in their field and agricultural organisations.

The marketing manager starts by defining a problem or opportunity and decides whether additional data should be collected. If the cost of collecting additional data exceeds its potential value, available data will be used. However, if a decision is made to gather additional data, external and internal data is collected. All data is then processed, analysed and transferred into information for marketing decision-making. Fig. 4.1 illustrates the process of developing a marketing information system.

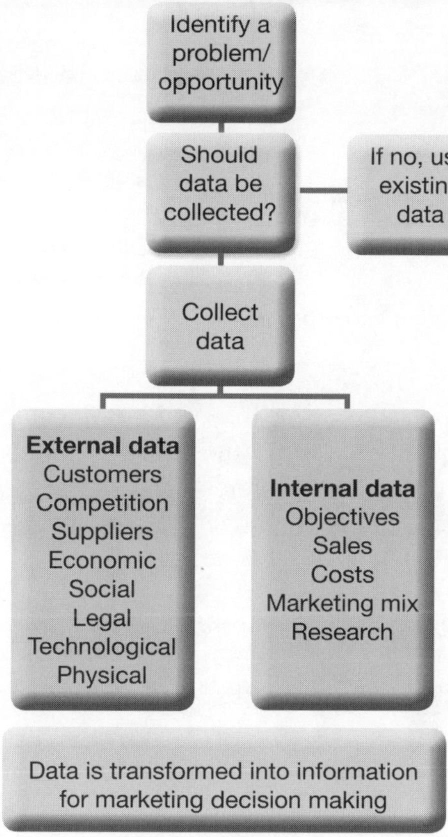

Figure 4.1 *Components of a marketing information system*

A management information system comprises a routine data component and a special purpose data component (fig. 4.2).

For a local independent retailer, the routine data component could comprise information from internal sources on key elements of the business such as sales, stocks, debtors and creditors. Information such as local population growth, competitive activities and trade association statistics can be collected from external sources on a regular basis.

The special purpose component of the MIS is marketing research. The retailer, for example, could employ a marketing research agency to determine the feasibility of a particular retail space in a new shopping centre. This is external marketing research. Other retailers may choose to do internal marketing research, e.g. by conducting a survey among existing customers to determine their degree of satisfaction. This constitutes internal marketing research, as it is launched from internal sources. The marketing research component of the MIS is discussed in detail on the following page.

Collecting information about competitors, also known as competitive intelligence, has become extremely important.

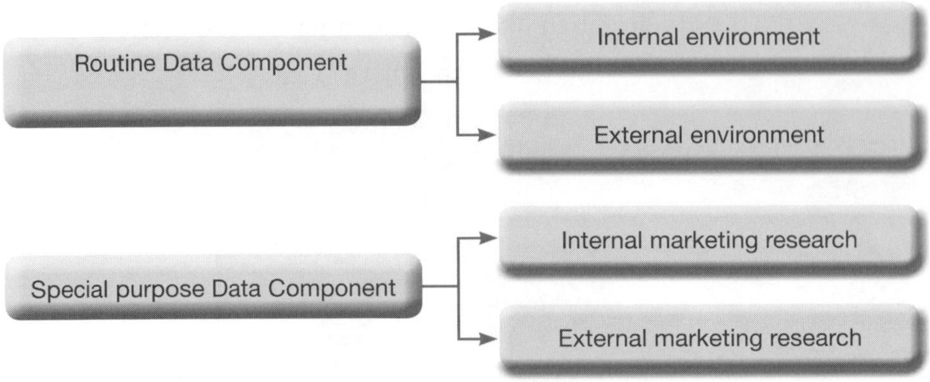

Figure 4.2 *Steps in developing a marketing information system*

Using competitive intelligence (CI)[6]

Competitive intelligence is the purposeful and co-ordinated monitoring of competitor(s), wherever and whoever they may be, within a specific marketplace. A Fortune 500 company survey showed 55% make use of competitive information in composing business strategy. Each firm is a leader in its industry and each firm knows its enemies.

The goal of a competitor analysis is to develop a profile of the nature of strategy changes each competitor might make, each competitor's possible response to the range of likely strategic moves other firms could make, and each competitor's likely reaction to industry changes and environmental shifts that might take place.

A company which does not rigorously monitor and analyse key competitors is poorly equipped to compose and deploy effective competitive strategy, leaving itself and its markets vulnerable to attack. CI revolves around decisions made by managers about the positioning of a business to maximise the value of the capabilities that distinguish it from its competitors. Failure to collect, analyse and act upon information about competitors in an organised fashion can lead to the failure of the firm itself.

The Chinese military strategist Sun Tzu emphasised the need for CI as follows: 'Now the reason the enlightened prince and the wise general conquer the enemy whenever they move, and their achievements surpass those of ordinary men, is foreknowledge'.

The focus of market research tends to be on the problems associated with the profitable marketing of a firm's products and services. The scope of competitive intelligence is far broader. CI is a value-added concept that sits over the top of business development, market research and strategic planning.

Examples of research objectives of a competitive intelligence project could be: the manufacturing capabilities of the competitor; analysis of alliances and/or joint ventures entered into by competitors; the future plans of competitors and their strategies for specific markets, or product lines; and reasons behind changes in their corporate or business unit strategy.

➡

➡

Many business schools offer courses in CI. Training is difficult as students (and managers) are obviously reluctant to divulge corporate strengths, weaknesses and plans. Computer programs are not readily available to deal with and manage the information gathered in the marketplace. Most training in CI is therefore done internally and information usually is considered highly confidential. Obviously unethical methods of obtaining information about the activities of competitors (like industrial espionage) cannot be condoned.

Many large companies in South Africa are using CI, e.g. Sasol, Iscor, Kumba, African Bank and Nestlé in order to gain a competitive advantage over the opposition in a highly competitive and fluid environment.

Marketing decision support systems

Definition[7]

A computer-based system that helps marketing decision makers confront problems through direct interaction with databases and analytical software programs.

In contrast to an MIS, which is mainly concerned with the preparation of routine reports, a marketing decision support system (MDSS) includes software to assist marketers to make difficult decisions.

Differences between an MDSS and an MIS[8]

- An MDSS is aimed at the less well-structured, under-specified problems that managers face rather than at problems that can be investigated using a relatively standard set of procedures and comparisons.
- An MDSS combines the use of models and analytical techniques and procedures with the more traditional data access and retrieval functions of an MIS.
- An MDSS specifically incorporates features that make it easy to use and interactive.
- An MDSS emphasises flexibility and adaptability. It can accommodate different decision-making styles and changing environmental conditions.

An MDSS helps to transform raw data, such as product sales for the previous day, into more useful information. For example, it may draw graphs to compare elements of the data set and show relationships between these elements. An MDSS could, for example, compare one day's sales with another over a similar period. An MDSS might allow managers to see the potential outcome of changing an element in the situation. For example, a manager may want to estimate whether the likely percentage change in sales if the business expands into a new market area. The MDSS could require the manager to estimate what percentage of business could possibly be won from each competitor in the market. Using this input and drawing on data in the database, the system would make an informed estimate of likely sales. An effective MDSS puts a manager in a better position to study available data and make better marketing decisions more quickly.

The need for marketing research

According to the marketing concept, marketing managers should be able to meet the needs of customers and anticipate new needs. However, many marketing managers are isolated in business offices, far from potential customers.

> **Definition**[9]
> Marketing research is the systematic design, collection, analysis and reporting of data relevant to a specific marketing situation facing an organisation.

It is simply not possible to keep up with all the changes taking place in the market. This means that marketing managers have to rely on help from marketing research. Marketing research refers to procedures used to develop and analyse new information which helps marketing managers to make decisions.

Marketing research is conducted on a special-project basis, with the research methods being chosen and adapted to the problem, and taking changes in the environment into account. It is usually characterised by an in-depth analysis of major problems or issues. Often the information needed is available only from sources outside the formal channels of information of a business. For example, a business may want to know something about its competitors or to gain an unbiased understanding of its own customers. Such information needs may require an independent investigation through marketing research.

Example of how research can produce results

A local award-winning marketing tool, the brand value index, is enabling manufacturers to have their products assessed by a sample of people, and from the results, predict market share.[10]

The index was used in determining the value and ideal positioning of the Jetta brand when a new model was introduced two years ago. A new model Jetta was flown in from Germany prior to the South African launch. People were invited to a 'car clinic' to view the car, which was stripped of identifying marks. No test drives were permitted but the subjects were able to sit in the vehicle and view it from all sides, and then, by questionnaire, rated the car.

The index provided feedback from customers as well as non-customers. To increase market share effectively, it was essential to understand and address the shortcomings of the brand from the perspective of people who were not buying it. The feedback also revealed where in the purchasing process the brand was eliminated.

The results indicated that most people (85%) buy cars for emotional reasons like appeal and image. Only 15% make a purely rational decision buying a specific car because it will get them from A to B reliably and economically.

➡

The prelaunch market share forecast for the Jetta was very accurate, with a 0.1 percentage point difference between actual and predicted market penetration.

- A construction company in San Francisco in the United States was trying to gain a competitive edge. They decided to do marketing research, and asked their customers about their competitors' worst habits. The customers told them about some of these, which included being impolite, uncaring about the dirt they brought into a house, and staff and equipment that looked shoddy. This was not acceptable to the majority of their customers, who were fairly wealthy.[11]

  This information convinced the construction company to improve their image. They bought new equipment, which they kept spotless, trained their workers to be polite and dressed them well to project a good image. The research and changes paid off. In less than two years, they increased their annual sales by 500%.
- NutraSweet's patent on the artificial sweetener aspartame was due to expire. The company faced disaster as chemical and sugar companies planned to enter the market. NutraSweet analysed competitor's prices, customer relations, expansion plans and advertising campaigns. The company used this information to cut costs, improve service and preserve most of their market. They managed to maintain an 80% market share.[12]

The use of the Internet has had a major impact on the marketing research industry.[13] It can virtually replace libraries and various printed materials as sources of secondary data; it serves as a vehicle for data collection; it aids in project management; it can be used to distribute reports; and team members working on a project can use it to communicate with one another. Research reports can be published on the Internet in a wide variety of electronic forms, making them available all over the world instantly. Using search engines like Google, full text searching is available not only of website pages, but also of documents, spreadsheets and presentations.

Examples of marketing research information needs[14]

- Sales personnel rely on research to provide them with feedback on sales performance or to identify likely purchasers.
- Media planners need information to tell them which specific magazines or television shows are most likely to be seen by a targeted market segment.
- Advertising agencies need feedback to 'flesh out' a picture of what the needs and wants of target consumers are.
- Brand managers want to know how their product is perceived in the marketplace, especially in comparison with competing brands.

Some marketers conduct limited, low-cost research projects by searching their MIS databases to find data that can be turned into the information they need. More often, a marketer requires very specific information to solve a problem and relies on marketing research to systematically gather relevant data.

Large companies like Coca-Cola have extensive marketing research capabilities to conduct their own research. Other companies may hire research companies to conduct some or all of the research they need to answer their marketing questions.

Finding marketing research companies on the Internet[15]
The websites of good research companies provide an opportunity for doing a preliminary review of potential service providers. In addition to the usual contact information, some companies have facilities for potential clients to fill in requests for proposal forms.

The marketing research process[16]

To maintain the control needed for obtaining accurate information, marketers approach marketing research by using four key steps (fig. 4.3).

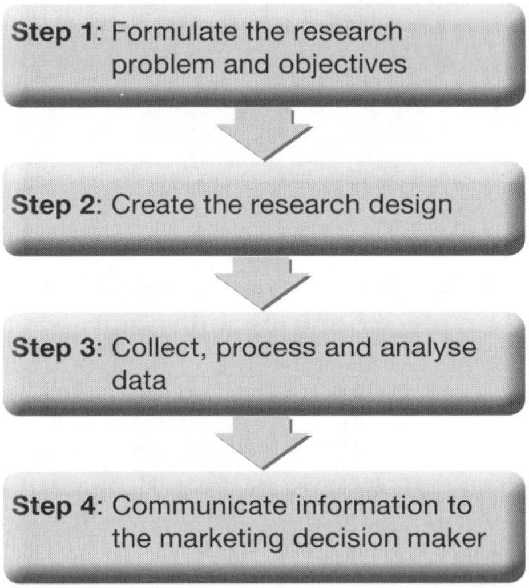

Figure 4.3 *Steps in the marketing research process*

Step 1: Formulate the research problem and objectives

No research project should be attempted before the marketing manager has clearly defined the problem and the research objectives. The old adage which says 'A problem well-defined is half solved' applies well to marketing research. Problem formulation refers to those situations that might represent real problems to the marketing decision maker, as well as to those situations that might be better described as opportunities.[17] A problem in the environment may, for example, be an increase in competition, a change in consumer preferences, or the withdrawal of retailers from the distribution system of the manufacturer. These may be symptoms of larger problems which have to be clearly defined. A weak diagnosis may lead to an inefficient solution.

Identifying the true problem

A common flaw in marketing research is to confuse a symptom with the true problem. For example, decreased sales may present as a problem, but may in fact be a symptom of a larger problem. To identify the real issue, the owner of the business must list all the possible factors that may have caused the problem. Useful questions for marketers to ask are: Is there new competition? Are the company's sales representatives impolite or not knowledgeable enough? Have customer tastes changed? Is the product line too narrow? Do customers have trouble finding what they want?

After the marketing manager has explained how he or she sees the problem, the researcher would conduct an investigation into the real situation. The confirmation or rejection of the problem as stated by the decision maker is a critical phase of the research project. The researcher conducts this investigation by consulting with relevant experts, especially those who are directly involved. Once the research problem has been confirmed and clearly defined or redefined, the research objectives should be established. If the objectives are successfully achieved, the marketing decision maker will have the information he or she needs to solve the problem.[18]

Redefinition of a problem

The sales manager of a local potato crisp manufacturer notices that the sales of a specific brand have been declining for two months in a row. He or she interprets the problem as 'ineffective advertising'. The manager instructs the marketing researcher to investigate the efficacy of the company's advertising campaign. The researcher conducts interviews with sales representatives, wholesalers and retailers, and discovers that retailer support has declined because of a new competitive product that provides higher profit margins on sales. Retailers are therefore making more profit by selling the competitive product. This information makes it clear to the researcher that an investigation of advertising efficacy will not solve the problem. This means the problem needs to be redefined, in conjunction with the sales manager, as 'competitive pricing and profit margin tactics'.

Step 2: Create the research design

The research design is the plan according to which the research investigation will be conducted. It specifies the data that will be required and the broad framework of procedures for the collection, processing and analysis of the data. From the research design, an estimate can be made of the costs of the investigation. The marketer can then assess the desirability and feasibility of the research in relation to its potential value. There are various research designs which a researcher can employ, depending on the specific research objectives.

- **Exploratory research**. This research design is used when more information about a problem, opportunity or phenomenon is needed. Exploratory research is usually undertaken where more than one hypothesis (or reason) for a problem has been generated through discussions.

- **Descriptive research** is necessary when knowledge about a particular market or other marketing aspect is vague. For example, an entrepreneur who is considering entering the hotel industry may have described the 'conference market' as one of his or her targets, but does not yet know enough about the market to take the next step. Descriptive research may also be necessary where the nature of the competition in a particular industry is vague.
- **Causal research** is done to determine cause-and-effect relationships. For example, increased advertising expenditure (cause) should lead to an increase in sales (effect). With descriptive research, a possible relationship between certain variables is often revealed, while causal research confirms that this relationship exists and how it operates, or concludes that there is no causal relationship.
- **Predictive research** is conducted to forecast future values, for example, sales income, market shares and retail orders. Political pollsters use predictive research to forecast how many people will vote for a particular candidate in an upcoming election. Businesses engage in sales forecasting to predict sales of the products during a specific period, e.g. a financial year. Predictive research helps to anticipate the opportunities and threats that are likely to arise in the future.

The basic activities in research design creation are: 1) determining data needs; 2) determining data sources; 3) determining the primary information collection method; 4) designing the research instrument; and 5) designing the sampling plan.

Determining data needs

Marketing research objectives must be translated into specific data needs, and a distinction must be made between primary and secondary data.

- **Primary data** is data that does not yet exist, so it has to be generated through original research. Primary data collection is relatively expensive and slow, but the data is usually more relevant to the research objectives than secondary data. This type of data usually requires some form of survey or another.
- **Secondary data** already exists, for example, historical data that has been collected before, either by the business itself or by outsiders. Secondary data is usually cheaper and faster to obtain than primary data, but the researcher always has to consider its relevance, accuracy, reliability and timeousness. In the last few years, the rapid development of information sources on the Internet has eliminated much of the drudgery associated with the collection of secondary data.

There are a number of advantages of using the Internet for marketing research.[19]

- It enables the researcher to be one of the first to know. Information is often published on a website before it becomes available through other media.
- It helps the researcher to exert more control of the information flow. Instead of receiving information in a pre-packaged form, e.g. in a daily newspaper column written to a specific word limit, the online researcher can find more detailed information in a less filtered form. The researcher therefore has a greater opportunity to draw his or her own conclusions about, e.g. trends and the value of information, and can consider a wider range of opinions.

Specific data needs: The South African Police Service (SAPS)[20]

Suppose the SAPS wants to find out what steps it can take to improve the quality of recruits. The information necessary to satisfy this research objective might include:

- a detailed description of recruiting incentives currently being offered by the SAPS;
- young people's attitudes toward existing recruiting incentives;
- the demographic and lifestyle characteristics of current high achiever police recruits;
- a detailed description of recruiting activities currently in use at recruiting centres; and
- a forecast of unemployment rates for the next decade.

- It saves valuable staff time and cuts research and associated costs. The Internet is available at any time of the night or day from any computer anywhere in the world. Researchers may not have to travel to trade shows or conferences, struggle to contact people or listen to the grapevine. Internet access is cheap and the information is often free. It is usually an excellent source of background information and many topics are covered in detail.

Researching on the Internet

The Internet is a worldwide network of computers that allows users access to information and documents from distant sources. It can be viewed as the world's largest public library. The World Wide Web is a term referring to a range of websites and website pages, which can include textual information, documents, graphic images, video and sound clips.[21]

There are few subjects on which information cannot be found on the Internet. Examples of information useful to marketers are product information, public relations material, sales material, collaborative scientific, economic and social reports, government information, article reprints, mission statements of companies, library catalogues, current news and information about different countries.[22]

A researcher who finds a particular site or document on the Internet or is just looking for a resource list on a particular subject can use one of the many Internet search engines, the most well known of which is Google. A search engine is a tool that allows the researcher to enter words as search criteria. The search engine then sifts through the millions of websites for matching words, ranking the results by various criteria, including the degree of relevance and how frequently the site has been visited.[23]

Major international search engines include www.google.com, www.alltheweb.com, www.altavista.com, www.excite.com, www.hotbot.com, www.lycos.com, www.northernlight.com, http://webcrawler.com, and www.yahoo.com.[24] A list of 23 websites relevant to South Africa can be found at www.philb.com/cse/southafrica.htm.[25]

Well over 1.9 billion people in the world use the Internet (table 4.1).

Table 4.1 *World Internet usage and population statistics as at 30 June 2010*[26]

World regions	Population (2010 Est.)	Internet Users Dec. 31, 2000	Internet Users Latest Data	Penetration (% Population)	Growth 2000–2010	Users % of Table
Africa	1 013 779 050	4 514 400	110 931 700	10.9%	2 357.3%	5.6%
Asia	3 834 792 852	114 304 000	825 094 396	21.5%	621.8%	42.0%
Europe	813 319 511	105 096 093	475 069 448	58.4%	352.0%	24.2%
Middle East	212 336 924	3 284 800	63 240 946	29.8%	1 825.3%	3.2%
North America	344 124 450	108 096 800	266 224 500	77.4%	146.3%	13.5%
Latin America/ Caribbean	592 556 972	18 068 919	204 689 836	34.5%	1 032.8%	10.4%
Oceania/ Australia	34 700 201	7 620 480	21 263 990	61.3%	179.0%	1.1%
WORLD TOTAL	6 845 609 960	360 985 492	1 966 514 816	28.7%	444.8%	100.0%

Determining data sources

Both primary and secondary data can be obtained from internal company and/or external sources, as can be seen in fig. 4.4.

Determining the primary data collection method

The collection of secondary data is usually more straightforward, because the assistance of librarians and relevant government bodies, among others, could be used. Primary data can be collected by four methods, namely observational research, experimental research, focus groups and survey research.

Observational research is conducted by watching people and situations. It is the systematic process of witnessing and recording the behavioural patterns of objects, through human or artificial observation methods. Human observation is conducted when researchers, for example, personally monitor the number and behaviour of consumers in a supermarket. Researchers then register the data on predesigned forms. Artificial observation takes place through the use of mechanical or electronic equipment. For example, electronic television meters are used to determine the number of viewers of specific television programmes.

Experimental research involves testing something in controlled conditions and using the results to draw conclusions about the wider environment. For example, a supermarket chain store group may conduct an experiment in one of its stores to test the effects of a new display technique. The results shape decisions about whether the technique will be applied in the whole chain.

A **focus group** is a small group of people, usually between 8 and 12, brought together and guided by a moderator through an unstructured, spontaneous discussion about some topic. It is called a 'focus' group because the moderator serves to focus the discussion of the topic and does not let the group move off onto

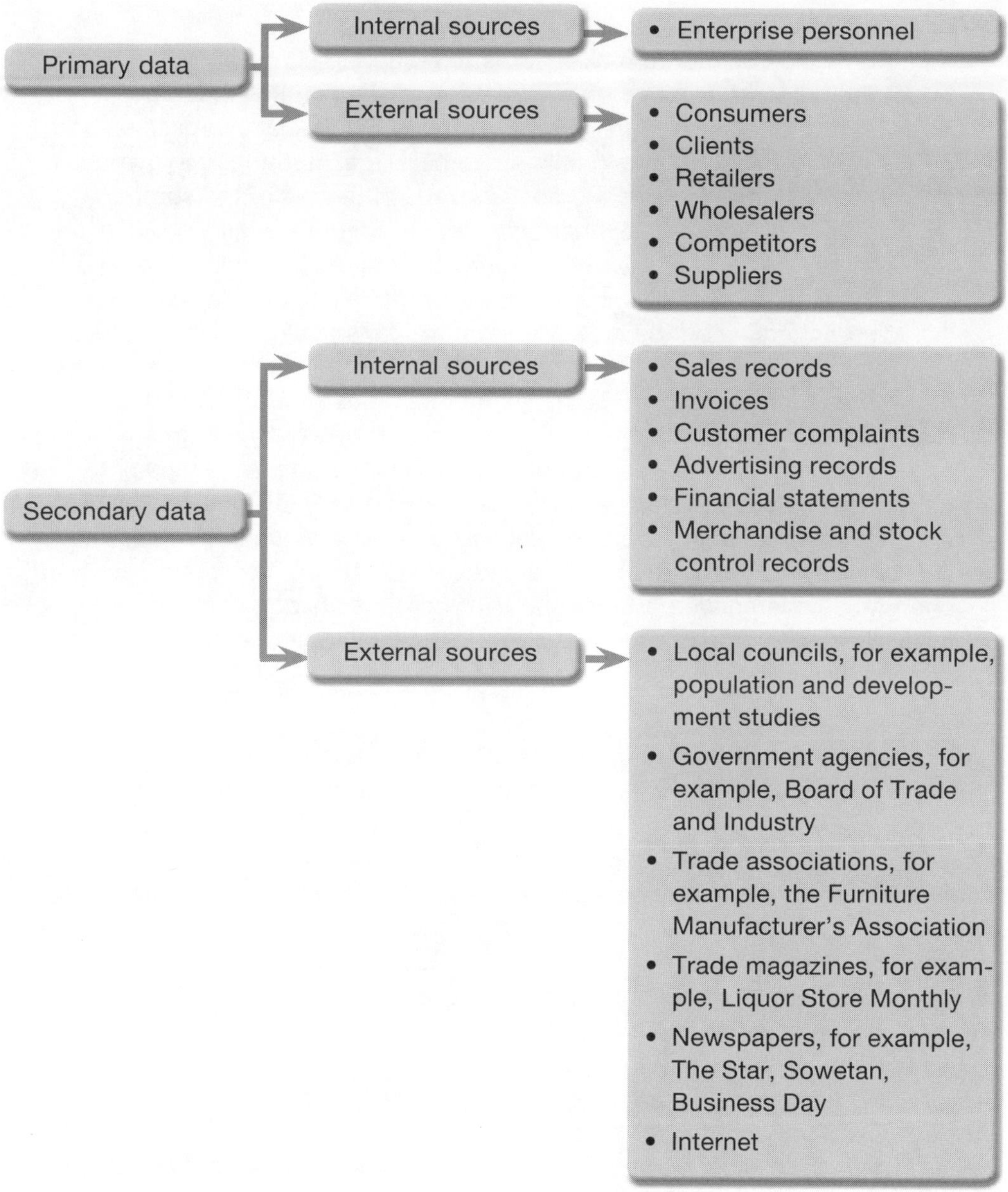

Figure 4.4 *Internal and external sources of primary and secondary data*

tangents or irrelevant points. The goal of a focus group is to draw out ideas, feelings and experiences about a certain issue that would be obscured or stifled by more structured methods of data collection. The use of a small group allows the operation of a group dynamic and aids in making the participants feel comfortable in a strange environment.

Focus groups have been useful in understanding basic shifts in consumer lifestyles, values and purchase patterns. Usually the focus group members share homogeneous characteristics such as similarities in age (they may all be in their

Practical examples of observational research[27]

- A fast-growing chain of furniture stores hired a market research firm to videotape customers in one of its outlets. Analyses of the videotapes revealed that people shop for furniture in twos. The facial expressions and other body language of many male customers indicated that they were ill at ease amid fluffed pillows and floral duvets. The head of the company realised that sales were lost when spouses or boyfriends felt uncomfortable, wanting their partners to leave the stores as soon as possible. As a result of the observation research, the company remodelled its 23 stores by including entertainment centres where sports fans could watch live events on television. This allowed the women to shop at their leisure because the men were doing something they enjoyed in a different part of the shop.
- A shopping centre developer wondered whether one of his centres was attracting customers from all surrounding areas. He hired a company to record the registration numbers of cars in the parking lot. By using the registration information, the addresses of all shoppers were then obtained and plotted on a map. The research indicated that very few customers from one particular area were visiting the centre. The developer then aimed direct mail advertising at that targeted area and was able to generate a great deal of new business.

A practical example of experimental research

Marketing managers for the Mars chocolate bar company used the experimental method to help solve a problem. They were losing customers to other sweet and snack companies and wanted to identify the reason. Surveys showed that many customers thought that the Mars bar, which was now being sold in a smaller size, was too small. They also did not want to pay more for a larger bar. The managers of Mars wanted to know if making their chocolate bar bigger would increase sales enough to offset the higher cost. To decide, they needed more information.

The company carefully varied the size of candy bars sold in different markets. Otherwise, the marketing mix stayed the same. Researchers then tracked sales in each market area to determine the effect of the different sizes. They saw a big difference immediately. It was clear that the added sales would more than offset the cost of a bigger candy bar. Marketing managers at Mars therefore made a decision that took them in the opposite direction from other candy companies. This experimental research proved to be a 'sweet' success.

early 30s), job situations (they may all be sales managers), family composition (they may all have pre-school children), or even leisure pursuits (they may all play tennis). The intention of convening a homogeneous group is to minimise the risk of differences in the group confounding the conclusions that the researcher will draw after reviewing the data from the discussion.

For example, a focus group of housewives may be invited to talk about their desires, preferences and buying behaviour with respect to various brands of cheese. The group will be chosen to be as homogeneous as possible with respect to demographic and other characteristics. The focus group discussion can furnish qualitative data about these consumers on such matters as language; emotional and behavioural responses to advertising; lifestyle; relationships; responses to the product category and specific brand; unconscious consumer responses around the product category and specific brand; and unconscious consumer responses to product design, packaging, promotion or any other facet of the marketing programme under study. When evaluating the results of a focus group discussion, it must always be borne in mind that focus group results are qualitative, not quantitative, and that a focus group is not large enough to really represent the larger population of people with those characteristics.

A practical example of focus group research[28]
BMW made use of focus groups to design its Z3 model. They conducted focus groups in Japan, the United States, the United Kingdom and Germany to determine the needs of these consumers. The influence of American interviewees is, for instance, visible in the car's dual cupholders, the coinholder and the third brake light.

The newest development in group interviews is the on-line or cyber focus group.[29] A number of organisations are currently offering this new means of conducting focus group interviews on the Internet. The research firm builds a database of respondents via a screening questionnaire on its website. When a client approaches the company with a need for research reflecting the views of a particular focus group, researchers are able to identify individuals in the database who appear to fit the criteria and send them an e-mail to request them to log on to a particular website at a particular time scheduled for the group. A moderator runs the group by typing in questions on-line for all those logged on to see. The group operates in a chat-room-type environment so that all participants see all questions and responses. The complete text of the focus group discussion is therefore already captured and available for review after the group session. An on-line environment allows respondents to interact voluntarily and therefore encourages them to respond honestly and spontaneously.

A practical example of focus group research[30]
A soft-drinks company made use of on-line focus groups to test teenager opinions of its new packaging ideas. The 10–15 minute Internet survey included dozens of questions as well as 765 different images of labels and bottle shapes. About 600 teenagers participated over a three to four day period. Detailed analysis of the survey was completed and available just five days after all the responses had been received.

Survey research is the gathering of primary data from respondents by mail, by fax, by telephone, by computer or in person. Survey research can be highly structured or highly unstructured. In a structured survey, all respondents are asked the same list of questions in the same way. In an unstructured survey, interviewers are free to ask their own questions to encourage respondents to open up. Three types of data are usually sought in survey research: facts, opinions and motives.

Types of data in survey research

- In a factual survey, respondents are asked questions such as 'What type of car do you drive?'
- In an opinion survey respondents are asked to give opinions, although they believe they are reporting facts. An example of an opinion survey question is 'What type of toothpaste tastes better?'
- In a motivational survey, respondents are asked to interpret and report their motives. These surveys ask 'why' questions such as 'Why do you holiday in Cape Town every year?'

Computer-assisted surveys have become very popular for collecting marketing research data. Researchers make use of two types of computer-assisted surveys, namely e-mail surveys and Internet surveys. An e-mail survey is a self-administered data collection technique in which the survey is delivered to and returned from the respondent by e-mail. The Internet survey is a self-administered questionnaire that is placed on a website for prospective subjects to read and complete.[31]

Computer-assisted surveys have many advantages. 'Branding' can, for instance, be incorporated so that respondents do not have to answer questions that are not applicable to them. Data collection may be much faster with electronic media and response times can be measured and recorded. Graphics can also be incorporated into questions and encoding and other errors associated with manual labour are reduced, if not completely eliminated.

Designing the data collection instrument

Two types of research instruments are used for the collection of primary data: 1) mechanical and electronic instruments; and 2) questionnaires.

Mechanical and electronic devices are instruments such as galvanometers (instruments that detect and measure small electrical currents), tachistoscopes (instruments that measure brief exposures of objects to the eye), cameras, and other electronic and mechanical meters. These instruments range from simple counting meters, for example, the number of people passing through a turnstile, to sophisticated reaction measurement instruments, for example, gauging the level of emotional reaction to a specific advertisement.

The questionnaire is the most common instrument used to collect primary data. Careful consideration must be given to the type of questions, their format, wording and sequence. The nature of questions should be relevant and easily understood by the respondent. Questions can either be open, where respondents reply in their own words, or closed, where respondents select options from a list. The major problem with open-ended questions is that the clarity of response depends to a large extent on how articulate the respondent is, and how willing he or she is to compile a written answer. Examples of open-ended questions would be 'What is your opinion of the Toyota Fortuner?' or 'When I choose a new car, the most important consideration is…'. Table 4.2 contrasts open- and closed-ended questions.

The wording of the questions and instructions has to be simple, clear and direct. Leading questions (those that give the respondent a clue as to how he or she should answer) should be avoided. The sequence of the questions also has to be considered when structuring the questions. A 'funnel' approach which uses a wide-to-narrow or general-to-specific flow of questions works well. For example, the introductory questions should arouse interest and ensure co-operation, while the difficult and/or more personal questions should be asked towards the end of the questionnaire.

Before finalising the questionnaire, a final evaluation should be conducted on the entire instrument. A pretest involves testing the survey on a small, representative set of respondents in order to reveal questionnaire errors and weaknesses so that these can be addressed before the survey is launched.

Table 4.2 *Open- and closed-ended questions*

Open-ended questions	Closed-ended questions
1 Totally open What do you think of the Renault Scenic?	1 Dichotomous (two choices) Do you think air bags should be standard in all new cars? Yes No
2 Sentence completion When buying a new car, the most important thing to keep in mind is	2 Multiple choice What age group are you in? 20 or under ...... 40–49 ...... 21–29 ...... 50–59 ...... 30–39 ...... 60 or over ......
3 Word association Domestic cars Foreign cars Auto dealership Renault	3 Semantic differential What words would you use to describe the Renault Scenic? Large ...... Small ...... Modern ...... Old-fashioned ......
4 Picture completion 	4 Rating scale Customer service at Renault dealers is .... 1. ...... Excellent 2. ...... Very good 3. ...... Good 4. ...... Fair 5. ...... Poor

Designing the sampling plan

In this step of the research process the elements from which the information will be collected must be selected. There are two ways in which to do this – a census or a sample. A census involves an investigation of all the individual elements or members of a defined target population.

Examples of a census[32]

- A study on the marketing knowledge of supermarket retailers who are members of NAFCOC [the National African Federated Chamber of Commerce], revealed that only 200 members were supermarket retailers. Since this population was relatively small, all of the members were studied, so it was a census.
- Suppose Toyota South Africa want to survey people in the country who bought a new Yaris over the previous three years to assess their opinions about the car. The marketing manager could easily obtain a list of the names of these people. Then each buyer could be surveyed – most likely by mail. Since this particular survey would include all people in the population of Yaris owners, it would be a complete enumeration, or census of the population.

When the population is very large, it might only be possible to use a sample. A sample is a segment of the population selected to represent the population as a whole. The sample should be representative so that the researcher can make accurate estimates of the thoughts and behaviours of the larger population.[33] Sampling can save the researcher both time and money. It would, for instance, be much more expensive and time-consuming to collect information about one million people (a census) than to gather information about one thousand people (a sample) from the group of one million.

Examples of a sample

- If the expenditure of households in Soweto is being researched, the researcher may include all the households, which would be a census. However, the researcher may also decide to interview only a number of households, for example, 10% of the households, which is a sample.
- A shoe manufacturer who wanted to study the brand preferences of all teenagers between 13 and 16 years found it almost impossible to research all these teenagers and decided to draw a sample of 2 500 teenagers on the assumption that the findings could be generalised to the wider population.

In the sampling process the target population first has to be defined by answering the question 'who do we want to study?' The target population is therefore the complete set of elements identified for investigation. An element is a person or object from which data and information are sought. The sampling unit, on the other hand, is a single element or group of elements subject to selection in the sample. If South African Airways, for instance, wants to sample its passengers, it may take the name

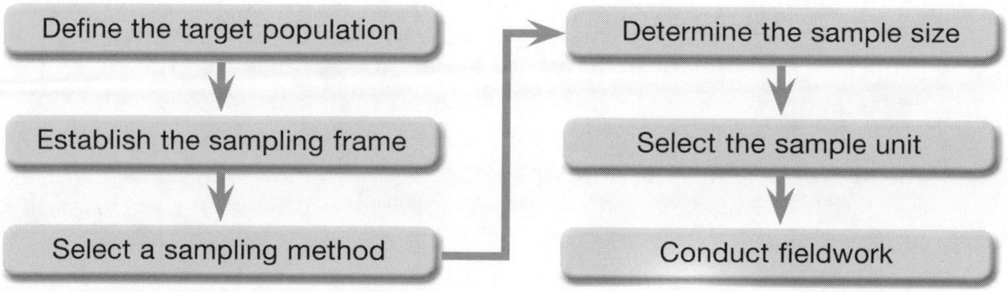

Figure 4.5 *The sampling process*[35]

of every 30th passengers to compile the sample. In this case the sampling unit is the same as the elements. However, if the airline first selects certain flights as the sampling unit, then selects certain passengers on each flight, the sampling unit will contain many elements.[36]

After the target population has been defined, the researcher has to establish the sampling frame. This means that the researcher has to assemble a list of all eligible sampling units. Examples of sampling frames would be a list of all members or agencies of the Estate Agency Affairs Board of South Africa or a list of all registered voters.

Once a sampling frame has been established, a sampling method must be selected. A good sampling plan will produce a sample that is representative of the characteristics of the population from which it is drawn. Two basic sampling methods are probability (random) samples and non-probability (non-random) samples.

A probability (or random) sample is a selection in which each item in a population has a known chance of being included through strict statistical procedures. It is the best way to ensure a representative sample. Methods of probability sampling include simple random sampling, stratified random sampling and systematic sampling.

Probability sampling methods

- **Simple random sampling:** Simple random sampling is the same principle as taking numbers at random from a hat. To draw a random sample of ten flats from a block of flats, the researcher would list the entire population (compile a list of every flat). Flat numbers will then be drawn at random until the prescribed sample size has been reached (ten).
- **Stratified random sampling:** Here the population is divided into mutually exclusive groups (for example streets), and random samples are drawn from each group.
- In **systematic sampling**, a starting point is selected by a random process and then every nth number on the list (e.g. every 10th number) is selected.

A non-probability (or non-random) sample is a selection in which not every item in a population has a known chance of being included because researcher judgement enters into the selection. The sample's level of representivity depends on the judgement of the researcher. Non-probability sampling can take three forms, namely convenience sampling, quota sampling and judgement sampling.

Non-probability sampling methods

- In the case of **convenience sampling**, the sampling units are chosen simply on the basis of convenience. Examples are on-the-street interviews, asking people in a supermarket their opinions about a new brand of detergent, and conducting taste tests with supermarket customers. Only the people who are in the same place and time as the researcher is present have a chance of being included in the sample.[37]
- With **quota sampling** the researcher finds and interviews a prescribed number of people in several categories. A research company that wants to interview 20 first year students of both sexes might interview the first ten men who walk past and then interview the first ten women who walk past, based on the knowledge that the male:female ratio in the population is about 50:50.
- In the case of **judgement sampling**, units are chosen on the basis of the researcher's opinion as to their representivity. Examples of judgement sampling include selecting a sample of salespeople for their opinions as input to preparing a sales forecast and selecting cities in which to test the market's new products.

The determination of sample size follows after the sampling method has been selected. The sample size is the number of units that are included in the investigation. There are no fixed rules about the number of units to be included, but some general norms and guidelines apply. Samples used in consumer research can often be less than 1% of the population, on condition that a probability sample and statistical formulae are used. In the case of industrial research, however, larger samples are used. This is for the simple reason that there are fewer industrial clients than individual consumers, making a larger sample feasible. Once the sample size has been determined, the operational procedures of selecting the sampling units and conducting fieldwork must be executed.

Step 3: Collect, process and analyse the data

Data collection is often the most expensive aspect of the research process and the possibility of gathering inaccurate data is high. The researcher has an important control task to perform. If respondents are not at home when the interviewer visits or telephones, substitutes have to be found. Some respondents may refuse to co-operate, while others may provide dishonest answers or misinterpret the questions. The field worker may also make mistakes when asking questions or recording responses. Interviewer cheating may also occur – this refers to a situation when interviewers make no contact with respondents and fill in fake answers on questionnaires. Some interviewers fake part of a questionnaire to make it acceptable to a field supervisor, while others fake answers when they find questions embarrassing or difficult to ask because of sensitive issues. Clear instructions and relevant motivational and training methods have to be used to ensure that respondents and field workers are co-operative and honest.

Processing has to take place after the data has been collected. The collected data must be edited and codified to facilitate processing and analysis. Editing[38] involves checking the data collection forms for omissions, legibility and consistency in classification. Through editing, problems such as interviewer errors (e.g. an answer recorded on the wrong portion of the questionnaire) are corrected before the data is transferred to the computer. Coding refers to meaningful categories and character symbols that are established for groups of responses before the data can be tabulated.

Data processing is followed by analysis of the results. The researcher has to study the processed data and transform it into relevant information for decision makers. Analysis is the application of reasoning to understand the data that has been collected. Various data analysis methods exist. They range from the very simple, for example, working out averages and measures of dispersion of data, to the highly sophisticated, for example, using multi-variable techniques, such as cluster analysis. Various computer programs exist to aid data processing and analysis, for example, SPSS (Statistical Package for the Social Sciences), Statgraphics and STATFORM.

Example of applying the results of research

A fast-food outlet asked 50 of its customers what new food they would like the outlet to provide. The results were as follows:

Food type	Number of responses	Percentage
Pizza	12	24
Fried chicken	24	48
Self-help salads	8	16
Garlic bread	20	40

The owner of the fast-food outlet decided that she would add both fried chicken and garlic bread to her menu and would send a pamphlet to all her existing customers informing them of this.

Step 4: Communicate information to the marketing decision maker

The last step in the marketing research process involves the interpretation of information for decision-making purposes. It also involves communicating this information to the relevant decision maker, usually in the form of a report. It is important that the decision-making context is thoroughly grasped and that the communication takes place in an appropriate manner. This is because communication problems between researchers and line managers often arise owing to their different backgrounds and work environments.

The research report should be of a high standard and criteria such as understandability, relevance, clarity, organisation, punctuality, accuracy and comprehensiveness should be applied. In addition to the written report, an oral presentation is often made, which has to be planned and delivered according to the requirements of the decision makers.

In the research report, the problem situation is defined, and the information from secondary and primary sources is analysed and interpreted. Conclusions and recommendations are made. It is not the researcher's task to make decisions or to implement these.

Case study: Researching the male consumer[39]

Discovery Networks, the company responsible for the Discovery channel on DSTV, decided to do a comprehensive study in order to shed light on the global male consumer and how to communicate with him.

Researchers surveyed over 12 000 men between the ages of 25 and 39 in 15 countries. Participants in the study were made to complete lifestyle diaries, segmentation analysis, telephone interviews and in-depth lifestyle interviews at their homes. Over 50 experts were consulted during the process, including academics (professors of gender studies, psychology and sociology), economists, marketers, journalists and social commentators.

The groundbreaking research revealed that 21st century pressures have caused men to enter a new stage in their evolution. The findings suggest that the lives of men seem to be more complex than in the past, and as a result men are under increased pressure to deal with their changing role.

The report's findings suggest that there are four types of modern man:

1. 'Pressured Provider' – 26% are traditional family men with a conservative view of his role in family and society.
2. 'Modern and in Control' – 34% are men who have a modern view of gender roles and are able to juggle numerous commitments.
3. 'All About Me' – 26% of young men prioritise themselves over relationships and are less family-oriented.
4. 'Non-Committal' – 14% live for the day and shy away from serious commitment or responsibility.

The report also found that there are significant themes that young men share in their lives.

- Young men are delaying and reordering the traditional milestones of growing up.
- Greater equality for men and women means relationships between them have never been as complex.
- Young men are delaying becoming dads, but not because they don't care about having kids.
- Young men are spending more time and money on their looks, but being aware of their image can bring anxiety as well as pride.
- Safer sex and potency pills, binge drinking and superfoods. The more hype about what makes a healthy life, the harder it is to live.

The study has significant relevance for the local marketing and advertising industry as it shows how modern young males view various life issues such as relationships, success, money, grooming, health, etc.

Exercise

1. What was the objective of Discovery Network's marketing research?
2. What type of data was collected during the research?
3. Explain the type of research that was conducted by Discovery Network.
4. Did the research make use of a sample or a census?
5. Suggest possible ways in which marketing decision makers would be able to use the results of the research.

CHAPTER 5

Segmentation, targeting and positioning

Learning outcomes

After studying this chapter you should be able to:

- understand the concept of target market segmentation, and how to segment product markets into submarkets and evaluate each one;
- explain the various market segmentation variables and apply the process of segmenting a market;
- understand the role of the South African Advertising Research Foundation (SAARF) LSMs (Living Standards Measures) as methods of market segmentation;
- identify and discuss the three different types of market coverage; and
- discuss the role of product positioning and be able to devise appropriate positioning maps.

Introduction

All organisations have constraints with resources and available capacity and it is therefore critical to 'cut the cloth to suit the need'. Marketing is all about matching scarce available resources such as human skills and financial means to the best possible opportunities, which in turn enables the company to make the most profit. Marketers need to find those people who are most likely to have an affinity to their specific product/s. As we learn more and more about consumers and their unique and individual needs, wants and expectations, it becomes obvious that it is almost impossible to satisfy everyone's needs and wants with one product. One size usually does not fit all, so marketers must target sections of the population that have similar (or homogeneous) needs.

Market segmentation entails a company dividing the market into smaller groups of consumers with similar needs so that the company can focus its products and marketing to achieve the best possible results. In this chapter we will define the process of segmentation, targeting and positioning (also known by the acronym STP). We will discuss the four basic levels of market segmentation: mass marketing (broadly defined targets), segment marketing (segments defined around specific dimensions), niche marketing (smaller, premium target segments), and micro-markets (extremely specific target markets with a very particular and defined need). This chapter will also identify and discuss the various dimensions upon which segmentation can be conducted, such as the variables of demographics, geographic, behaviour and psychographics.

Once the market has been divided into segments, marketers need to evaluate the potential within each segment and ensure that they select the target market or markets that are most likely to find functional or social benefits in the product offering. This is done through a detailed segment assessment process also covered in this chapter.

In addition we will present the aspect of target market coverage and discuss the issues that need to be identified in order to assist the marketer in making the decision of whether or not the marketer should select undifferentiated, differentiated or concentrated marketing coverage. Finally this chapter will lead the reader through the steps of market positioning.

Definition of market segmentation

Market segmentation is the necessary process of dividing a very broad heterogeneous (dissimilar) group of individuals into smaller cluster groups of people exhibiting similar (homogeneous) needs, wants, and desires for a specific product and/or its performance attributes.[1]

Why segment the market?[2]

Marketers segment the consumer market for a number of reasons:

- It is costly and time consuming to attempt to address the diverse needs and wants of a broad and large market (the mass marketing approach) – most organisations selling to a mass market have a 'one size fits' all approach and thus it becomes necessary and more cost effective to find that group of customers that is 'most likely' to have the need for the product.
- Smaller unserved markets may be identified through the segmentation process which if targeted with an appropriate marketing mix, could lead to increased profitable opportunities.
- Limited marketing resources can be used more efficiently and achieve a more appropriate return on marketing investment. Instead of using the 'shotgun' approach where all consumers receive a general communication on the basis that at least someone will see it, marketers can now use the segmentation process to develop a 'rifle shot' approach, meaning that a more specific marketing mix is communicated to those most likely to have the need, ability and authority to purchase the product, thus reducing advertising and communication wastage.

Example of different segments for a single product

Cotton wool provides a good example of differing needs occurring in different clusters of a market. Remember that each need requires a different marketing mix. One group of cotton wool purchasers are new mothers who buy cotton wool to care for their newborns – wiping faces, cleaning noses and ears and so on. This group of customers may seek softness or naturalness as the criteria on which to base their purchase decision. Another group of cotton wool customers are women who use cotton wool to remove eye make-up – these women may be swayed by the product's attribute of being 'fibreless', because their concern is knowing they will not get stray fibres in their eyes. A

➡

further group of cotton wool customers are those in the medical field who would use the product to cleanse the skin prior to injections or to apply an antiseptic treatment; in this case the decision to purchase may be based on price or the ability to buy in bulk, on the understanding that all cotton wool products are absorbent enough to do the job.

We will now examine the four levels of marketing segmentation beginning with the broadest form of mass marketing and narrowing it down to the most specific form – micro-marketing (fig. 5.1).

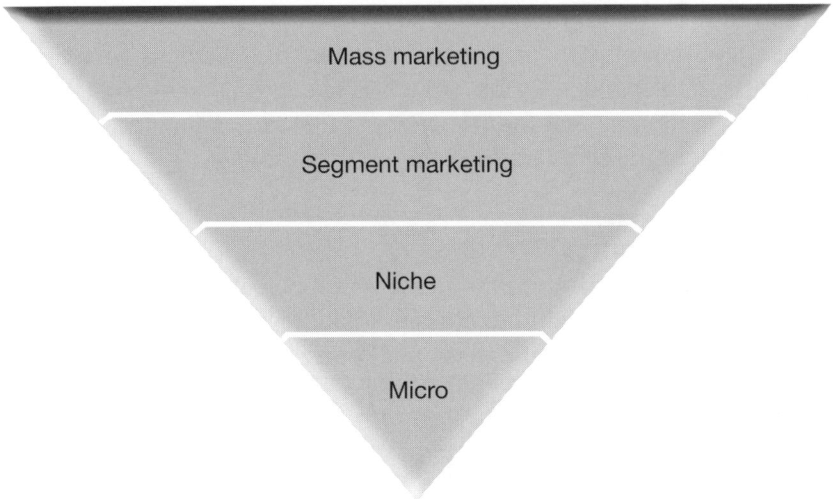

***Figure 5.1** The four levels of marketing segmentation*

The four levels of marketing segmentation[3]

Mass marketing

This type of marketing requires the very lowest form of segmentation and is usually based on the basic segmentation variables of geography and demography. This was the historical way of marketing, when an organisation produces a non-customised product and has a broad and large generic mass market; the product has few differentiating factors and thus can be targeted at a very large potential consumer base with common needs. The organisation manufactures the product en masse and therefore can achieve lower costs of sales and production. Nowadays, however, with various modern channels of distribution, the increased available media and a greater understanding of consumer needs and wants means it is not so easy to succeed with a mass marketed product.

Examples of mass marketed products are matches and table salt, although now some salt manufacturers are differentiating their product from that of their competitors based on source, e.g. Maldon sea salt.

Segment marketing

Nowadays most FMCG (fast-moving consumer goods) organisations embark on a certain level of segment marketing. In these instances a product is directed towards a particular group of people who have been identified as having similar needs and desires. One of the clear advantages of segment marketing is that the firm can use its marketing resources more efficiently by targeting that segment of the population that has been identified as most likely to buy what the company has to offer.

Niche marketing

Niche marketing refers to the identification of a small group of potential consumers with a very specific need. Because there are fewer consumers, the unit cost per potential customer is high. However because of the specificity of the need or requirement, it is usually possible to charge a premium for a more customised niche product. Private banking is an example. It is highly service-intensive because the banks need to provide a personalised complete banking service to high net-worth individuals but the very nature of the clientele means they can afford to pay for a high level of service. All the major banks in South Africa (ABSA, First National Bank, Nedbank and Standard Bank) have private bankers and a clientele of high net worth clients.

Micro-marketing

Whilst some people believe that micro-marketing is an alternative term for niche marketing, it is in fact a separate marketing strategy which involves the more precise and focused targeting of an even smaller market, usually in smaller service-based businesses. Micro-marketing has become more viable as computers, the Internet and databases now allow marketers to identify customers with very specific needs for which a service can be customised. This segmentation exercise has also been called the market-of-one, meaning that each individual customer is regarded as a special segment in the marketplace. For example, every yacht built for the Americas Cup is customised for a single customer's requirements.

Having established the desired level of marketing segmentation, the marketer then moves to the segmentation, targeting and positioning process.

The STP process[4]

The segmentation, targeting and positioning 'go-to-market' process comprises six steps (fig. 5.2).

1. Identify the segmentation variables and segment the market.
2. Develop profiles of the segments.
3. Evaluate the attractiveness of each segment.
4. Select the target segments.
5. Identify possible positioning concepts for each target segment.
6. Select, develop and communicate the chosen positioning concept.

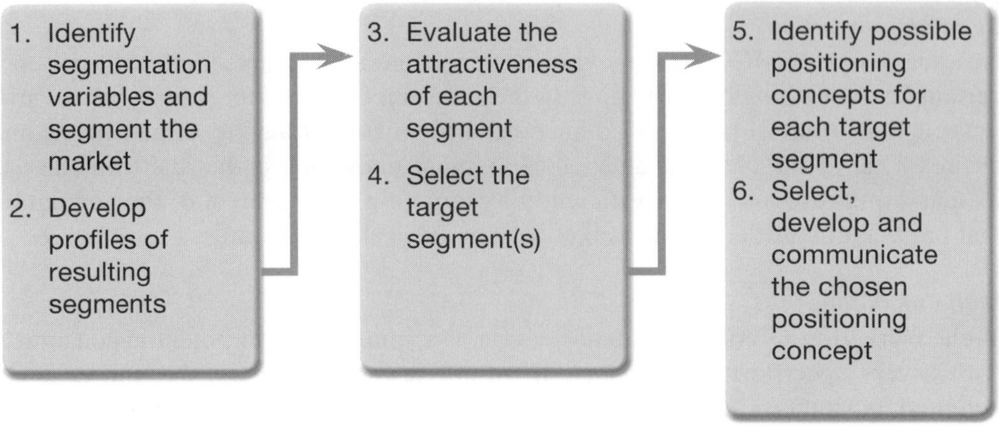

***Figure 5.2** The STP process*

- **Segmentation**: As described above, the process of segmentation is dividing up or grouping individuals within a broad mass market into smaller groups of people with similar characteristics, who are expected to have similar expectations, and who are seeking similar benefits from a specific product.
- **Targeting** involves a careful profiling and evaluation of each subsequent segment (revealed by the segmentation process), and then, on the basis of specified assessment criteria, deciding which segment or segments the company should target for its products. This guides the development of a marketing mix appropriate for each target group.
- **Positioning** can be described as the 'position' a product holds in the mind of the consumer, relative to the offerings of competitors. Positioning is not what marketers tell consumers about the product, it refers to consumer perceptions about the product. The efforts of marketers to position products are based on various product attributes that consumers consider to be of value.

Deciding on a basis for segmentation

The first step is to consider the segmentation variables. There are five sets of variables that can be selected for use in the marketing segmentation process, the most basic of which are geographic variables (clustering people on the basis of location). Among the most popular choice of variables for grouping the market are those of demography, based on measurable and easily identifiable attributes. It must be noted, however, that these only give a basic, one-dimensional description of the customer. Further segmentation can be based on behavioural variables (i.e. benefits sought).

The more a company wants to know about its target customer, the more it will invest in the segmentation process. A marketer wanting to develop an intensive relationship with a customer would need to know as much about that customer as possible. This requires conducting in-depth segmentation aimed at identifying a psychographic profile of the target customer. An additional set of variables, namely geo-demographic, aims to profile the target customer based on geographic, demographic and lifestyle attributes (see table 5.1).

Table 5.1 *Bases of market segmentation*[5]

Bases of segmentation	Variables
Geographic segmentation	Region, size of city, density and climate
Demographic segmentation	Age, gender, family size, income, occupation, religion, race and education
Psychographic segmentation	Lifestyle, personality and social class
Benefits segmentation	Specific benefits sought by consumers
Market-value-based segmentation	Performance or social value of a product

Geographic segmentation

Examples of geographic variables are rural/urban, provinces/municipalities, cities/towns/villages and local climate. Although this is a very basic way of grouping people together, it is still very relevant for the marketing of mass market and undifferentiated products in which segments are easily developed on the basis of location. Depending on the type of product, a firm may decide that it will concentrate on a specific geographic area. Many freely available statistics can assist marketers to find out about where their target customers live, what the dominant language in the area is and a host of other demographic variables.

Table 5.2 *Provincial distribution of South Africa's population*[6]

Province	Population	%
KwaZulu-Natal	9 426 017	21.0
Gauteng	8 837 178	19.7
Eastern Cape	6 436 763	14.4
Limpopo	5 273 642	11.8
Western Cape	4 524 335	10.1
North West	3 669 349	8.2
Mpumalanga	3 122 990	7.0
Free State	2 706 775	6.0
Northern Cape	822 727	1.8
Total	44 819 778	100.0

***Table 5.3** Dominant language by province*[7]

Province	Provincial capital	Major languages by number of speakers
KwaZulu-Natal	Durban	isiZulu (80.6%) English isiXhosa Afrikaans
Gauteng	Johannesburg	isiZulu (21.5%) Afrikaans Sesotho English
Eastern Cape	Bhisho	isiXhosa (83%) Afrikaans English
Limpopo	Polokwane	Sepedi (57%) Xitsonga Tshivenda
Western Cape	Cape Town	Afrikaans (55.5%) English isiXhosa
North West	Mafikeng	Setswana (65.4%) Afrikaans
Mpumalanga	Nelspruit	isiSwati (30.8%) isiZulu isiNdebele
Free State	Bloemfontein	Sesotho (62%) Afrikaans Xhosa
Northern Cape	Kimberley	Afrikaans (68%) Setswana
South Africa	Pretoria (administrative) Bloemfontein (judicial) Cape Town (legislative)	Afrikaans English isiNdebele isiXhosa isiZulu Sepedi Sesotho Setswana siSwati Tshivenda Xitsonga

Demographic segmentation

Demographic variables include: age, gender, education level, race, income level, family life-cycle stage, nationality, ethnicity, family size, religious affinity, occupation, literacy level and social class. Because they are easy to identify and are based on existing statistics, demographic variables are often the most popular initial basis of segmentation. A marketer aiming one product at men and another at women, would easily be able to ascertain just how many men and how many women live in South Africa. A marketer aiming at a certain age group would be able to determine how many people of that age live in various places in the country. Although basic demographic data is a useful starting point, it provides no more than a single dimensional view of the potential customer.

Through using age, gender or other demographic variables, the marketer's job is immediately made a little easier as it quickly defines the type of distribution channels and media that could be employed to reach the specific target audience.

Using demographic variables to identify a suitable advertising channel

If the identified target segment is young people between the ages of 18 and 35 who live in urban Gauteng then perhaps 94.7 Highveld Stereo radio station could be the most appropriate channel of communication. If, however, the target segment consists of young educated mothers living in metropolitan areas, then perhaps placing an advert in Baby magazine would be the most effective way to communicate with them.

Keeping an eye on demographic trends is also extremely important. Table 5.4 shows quite clearly that the population is skewed towards the younger generation with 68.9% of the population falling below 35 years of age.

Table 5.4 *South African population by age group*[8]

Age group	% of South African population
Ageing 65+ years	4.9
Mature adulthood 35–64 years	26.1
Youth 14–34 years	39.1
Childhood 5–13 years	19.9
Infancy 0–4 years	9.9

Another demographic trend is the changing role of women in society. A growing proportion of the female population are working women, many of them single, and many of them mothers. The larger percentage of economically active women means that women are making purchase decisions that were in the past viewed to be the domain of men (e.g. motor vehicles and insurance policies). Time-strapped working mothers also have an increasing need for convenience products such as microwave ovens and other household appliances, childcare services, and foods that are quick and easy to prepare.

The male market has also changed over the past years. With so many women in the workplace, men are playing an ever increasing role in assisting with childcare and are now often involved in grocery purchasing decisions. These changes in gender roles mean that gender is no longer the best way to cluster individual consumers in certain product categories.

***Table 5.5** South African population by gender and race*[9]

Population group	% of total population		
	Male	Female	Total
African	79.2	79.5	79.3
Coloured	9.0	9.0	9.0
Indian/Asian	2.6	2.5	2.6
White	9.2	9.0	9.1
Total	100.0	100.0	100.0

Geo-demographic segmentation

The concept of using geo-demographic variables is fairly new, and refers to the grouping of people who are located together in neighbourhoods with similar demographics (e.g. young married professionals with a young family living on a golfing estate). The basic premise being that similar individuals who live in a specific location are likely to share similar basic interests and needs.

Behaviour/'benefits sought' segmentation

If an in-depth knowledge of the customer is necessary for marketing purposes and the segmentation needs to go further than what is possible using location and demographic variables, then the market could be divided up on the basis of benefits sought or behavioural variables. Many organisations conduct ongoing usage and attitude (U & A) research studies for this kind of segmentation. People can be grouped on the basis of having similar behaviours, such as their product selection behaviour or how they spend their leisure time. Benefits sought segmentation helps to identify groups of consumers who may buy the same product for different reasons – see the cotton wool example above and the Milton example below.

Example of benefits sought segmentation

Because Milton bleach has multiple uses its market can be segmented by means of benefits sought. One market segment utilises Milton to disinfect baby bottles, another adds bleach to the water in a vase to prolong the life of flowers, and a third segment uses Milton as a general household disinfectant.

Psychographic segmentation

Determining the variables on which to divide up the potential market into segments is greatly dependent on the type of product you offer. If your product is aimed at the mass market, e.g. matches, you probably do not need more than the two most basic sets of segmentation variables – demographics and geographic attributes. If you wish to build a stronger relationship with your customers, e.g. the kind of relationship a financial services organisation is looking for, you will need to develop a deeper understanding of your customers.

Psychographic and behavioural variables will help the marketer understand more about the potential customer's behaviour and the reasoning behind why and how consumers decide to purchase certain products. Psychographic segmentation is based on variables such as consumer lifestyles, personality traits and other characteristics such as class and cultural attributes. The internationally used VALS (values and lifestyle) segmentation model uses the activities, interests and opinions of consumers to determine their resources (financial and personal) and key psychological motivations for behaving as they do.

Living Standards Measures

During the late 1980s the South African Advertising Research Foundation (SAARF) began devising a way of segmenting the entire South African population into subgroups. This groundbreaking research has divided the South African population into ten basic groups (or 12 if the high- and low sub-categories are included) using a combination of non-personal variables called the Living Standards Measures (LSMs). LSM groups are defined by their living standards using a combination of non-personal variables such as level of urbanisation or the ownership of certain durables. Although income levels emerge during the analysis, income is never used as a distinct criterion for segmentation. After a number of extensive reviews, the most recent of which was completed in 2004, the current SAARF Universal LSM index uses the descriptors listed in table 5.6.

Table 5.7 shows the current South African LSM groupings and references the dominant living standards measures and characteristics.

Table 5.6 *SAARF Universal LSM variables*[10]

1	Hot running water	16	Less than 2 radio sets in household
2	Fridge/freezer	17	Hi-fi/music centre
3	Microwave oven	18	Rural outside Gauteng/W.Cape
4	Flush toilet in/outside house	19	Built-in kitchen sink
5	No domestic in household	20	Home security service
6	VCR	21	Deep freezer
7	Vacuum cleaner/floor polisher	22	Water in home/on plot
8	No cell phone in household	23	M-Net/DStv subscription
9	Traditional hut	24	Dishwasher
10	Washing machine	25	Electricity
11	PC in home	26	Sewing machine
12	Electric stove	27	Gauteng
13	TV set	28	Western Cape
14	Tumble dryer	29	Motor vehicle in household
15	Home telephone		

Table 5.7 *LSM characteristics*[11]

LSM 1 (3.5% of population) **Demographics** Female 50+ Some primary education level achieved Rural Traditional hut R1 269 average household income per month **Media** Radio main channel of media communication, commercial radio mainly African language services (ALS) **General** Minimal access to services Minimal ownership of durables except radios	**LSM 2 (7.3% of population)** **Demographics** Female 16–24 years old, 50+ Some high school Rural Traditional hut R1 475 average household income per month **Media** Radio: commercial mainly ALS **General** Water on plot Minimal ownership of durables except radios and stoves

Minimal participation in activities, mostly cooking for pleasure and gardening	Minimal participation in activities
LSM 3 (7.8% of population) **Demographics** Male 16–24, 35–49 Up to some high school Rural House/townhouse/cluster house R2 267 average household income per month **Media** Radio, commercial mainly ALS TV: SABC1 Outdoor **General** Electricity, water on plot Minimal ownership of durables except radios and stoves Activities: cook for pleasure, watch videos/DVDs, knitting	**LSM 4 (14.2% of population)** **Demographics** Female 16–34 Education up to some high school Rural R2 424 average household income per month **Media** Radio: commercial, Limpopo combo, mainly ALS Outdoor **General** Electricity, water on plot, flush toilet TV sets, hi-fi/radio set, electric hotplates, fridge Activities: read a newspaper with local news that's for sale in town, cook for pleasure, watch videos/DVDs, attend church/synagogue
LSM 5 (15.5% of population) **Demographics** Male 16–34 Up to matric Rural R3 122 average household income per month **Media** Radio: commercial mainly ALS, Metro fm TV: SABC 1, 2, 3, e-tv Daily/weekly newspapers, magazines Outdoor **General** Electricity, water, flush toilet TV set, hi-fi/radio, stove, fridge Activities: read a newspaper with local news bought in town, watch	**LSM 6 (19.5% of population)** **Demographics** Female 25–49 Matric and higher Urban R5 755 average household income per month **Media** Wide range of commercial and community radio TV: SABC 1, 2, 3, e-tv Daily/weekly newspapers, magazines Cinema and outdoor **General** Electricity, hot running water, flush toilet Ownership of a number of durables plus cell phone

DVDs/videos, read a free newspaper delivered to home, read books, cook for pleasure, buy lottery tickets	Participates in a number of activities
LSM 7 LOW (5.2% of population) **Demographics** Male 16–24, 35–49, 50+ Matric and higher Urban R9 242 average household income per month **Media** Wide range of commercial and community radio TV: SABC 1, 2, 3, e-tv, MNet Daily/weekly newspapers, magazines Accessed Internet in past 4 weeks Cinema and outdoor **General** Full access to services Increased ownership of durables plus motor vehicle Participation in all activities	**LSM 7 HIGH (5% of population)** **Demographics** Male 35–49 Matric and higher Urban R10 044 average household income per month **Media** Wide range of commercial and community radio TV: SABC 1, 2, 3, e-tv, MNet, DSTV Daily/weekly newspapers, magazines Accessed Internet in past 4 weeks Cinema and outdoor **General** Full access to services Increased ownership of durables plus motor vehicle Participation in all activities
LSM 8 LOW (3.5% of population) **Demographics** Male 35+ Matric and higher Urban R12 068 average household income per month **Media** Wide range of commercial and community radio TV: SABC 1, 2, 3, e-tv, MNet, DSTV Daily/weekly newspapers, magazines Accessed Internet in past 4 weeks Cinema and outdoor **General** Full access to services Full ownership of durables including DVD, PC and satellite dish	**LSM 8 HIGH (3.4% of population)** **Demographics** Male 35+ Matric and higher Urban R14 017 average household income per month **Media** Wide range of commercial and community radio TV: SABC 1, 2, 3, e-tv, MNet, DSTV Daily/weekly newspapers, magazines Accessed Internet in past 4 weeks Cinema and outdoor **General** Full access to services Full ownership of durables including DVD, PC and satellite dish

Increased participation in activities	Increased participation in activities
LSM 9 LOW (4.2% of population) **Demographics** Male 35+ Matric and higher Urban R15 853 average household income per month **Media** Wide range of commercial and community radio TV: SABC 2, 3, e-tv, MNet, DSTV Daily/weekly newspapers, magazines Accessed Internet in past 4 weeks Cinema and outdoor **General** Full access to services Full ownership of durables including DVD, PC and satellite dish Increased participation in activities, excluding stokvel meetings	**LSM 9 HIGH (4.2% of population)** **Demographics** Male 35+ Matric and higher Urban R19 453 average household income per month **Media** Wide range of commercial and community radio TV: SABC 2, 3, e-tv, MNet, DSTV Daily/weekly newspapers, magazines Accessed Internet in past 4 weeks Cinema and outdoor **General** Full access to services Full ownership of durables including DVD, PC and satellite dish Increased participation in activities, excluding stokvel meetings
LSM 10 LOW (3.2% of population) **Demographics** Male 35+ Matric and higher Urban R22 043 average household income per month **Media** Wide range of commercial and community radio TV: SABC 2, 3, e-tv, MNet, DSTV Daily/weekly newspapers, magazines Accessed Internet in past 4 weeks Cinema and outdoor **General** Full access to services Full ownership of durables including DVD, PC and satellite dish Increased participation in activities, excluding stokvel meetings	**LSM 10 HIGH (3.1% of population)** **Demographics** Male 35+ Matric and higher Urban R28 467 average household income per month **Media** Wide range of commercial and community radio TV: SABC 2, 3, e-tv, MNet, DSTV Daily/weekly newspapers, magazines Accessed Internet in past 4 weeks Cinema and outdoor **General** Full access to services Full ownership of durables including DVD, PC and satellite dish Increased participation in activities, excluding stokvel meetings

Developing and evaluating segment profiles

Once segments have been identified, then the marketer must develop profiles of the segments. Profiles provide descriptions of each segment in order to help the marketer to identify which of the segments are the best ones to target. A profile may look like this:

- **Segment A**: A group of employed male consumers, with tertiary education, living in an urban environment, aged 18–24 years, single, enjoy sports and clubs.
- **Segment B**: A group of black women living outside the metropolitan areas, unemployed with families of two or more children, aged 35–45 years, grade 10 education but no individual income.

Marketers of condoms may be very interested in targeting the first group described in Segment A, and marketers of handwash powder such as Omo might be more than a little interested in the second detailed profile, Segment B.

Segment assessment

Once one or more segments have been identified it is then necessary to evaluate or assess each of the segments in terms of its attractiveness as a target market. This evaluation should be conducted by rating each segment according to the following criteria:

- **Accessibility**: The selected target segment should be available to both distribute to and also to communicate with.
- **Defendability**: It is very important that the company's product has a distinct differential advantage over the competitors so that its position within the target segment can be defended.
- **Tangibility**: It is essential that the target segment is of a sufficient size to make it profitable for a good return on investment.
- **Distinctiveness**: The segment should be different enough from other target segments so that a clear product differential can be obtained.

Other aspects to be considered include:

- The growth rate of the segment.
- The brand loyalty of the potential target customer.
- Attainable market share in terms of money available for promotional expenditure compared to what competitors can spend.

Market coverage[12]

The organisation then needs to decide which and how many of the segments it will serve with its product range. This is called target market selection, where a target market can be defined as a group of consumers with similar characteristics and thus share similar needs. There are three basic strategies that can be employed in determining target market coverage (tables 5.8 to 5.10).

Undifferentiated marketing

The strategy of undifferentiated or mass marketing is employed by companies that do not differentiate between the needs of their potential consumers. They focus rather on the common needs and quantity, and therefore target the whole market with one product. The product and its marketing plan thus focus on appealing the largest possible number of consumers (all segments – S1, S2 and S3, and all targets – T1, T2 and T3). This strategy necessarily involves mass distribution and also utilises mass communication channels.

Table 5.8 *Undifferentiated marketing*

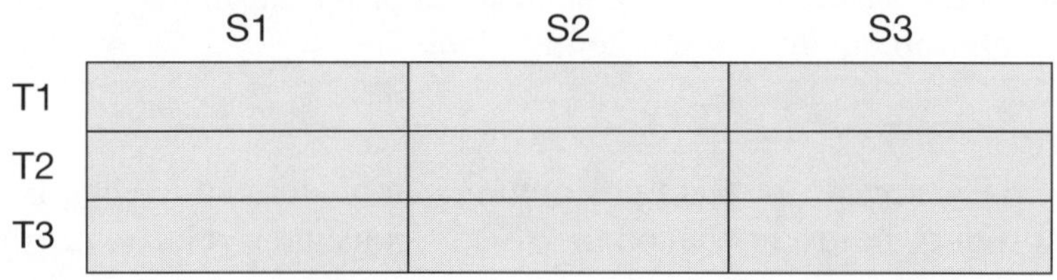

Differentiated marketing

This strategy requires the organisation to target different market segments with different products. By targeting groups of people with different needs with specifically designed products, the company can then reach more than one group of customers with more than one product and can then hope to achieve a higher return on the resource investment. It should be noted, however, that having a range of products with vastly differing marketing mixes may also increase the costs. For this reason, segment marketing is regarded as more expensive than mass marketing.

Table 5.9 *Differentiated marketing*

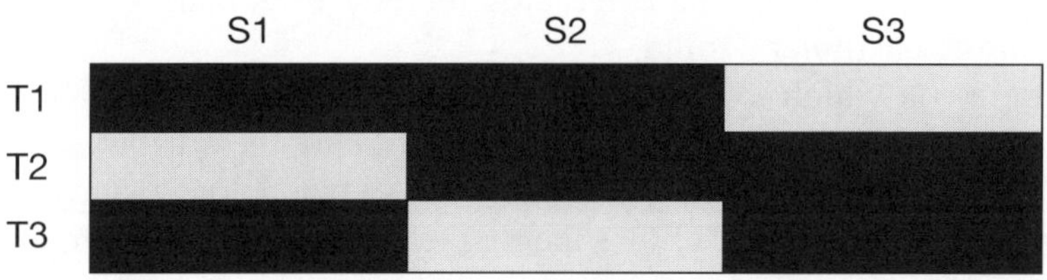

Concentrated marketing

This form of market coverage involves targeting a product at a specific need within the larger segment. It provides a company with a chance to develop a strong market presence based on an in-depth knowledge of the segment. This could give smaller companies a competitive edge over other players. If a company employs this strategy then they need to recognise that there is a higher risk involved, as their turnover is dependent on only one target segment.

Table 5.10 Concentrated marketing

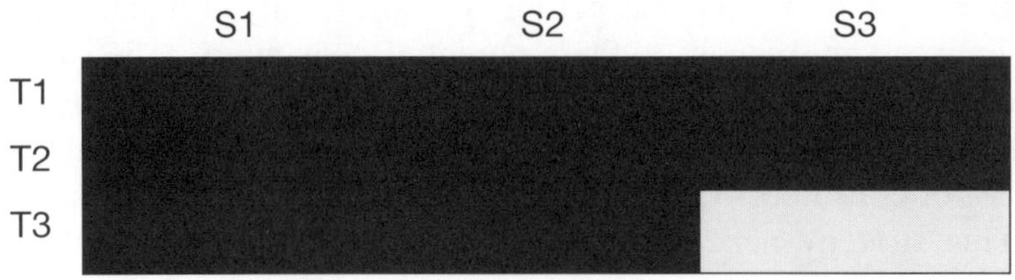

Once the selection of the most appropriate target market/s has been conducted, i.e. those groups that are most likely to allow maximum return on the resource investment, then a marketer will need to formulate an appropriate marketing mix (the 4 Ps) and develop an implementable marketing plan.

Product positioning

As the last step in the STP process, product positioning can be defined as the place or position that the product holds in the minds of the consumer relative to the competitors' offerings. It is really the descriptor or image that an organisation wants its consumers to think of when the product is mentioned.

Examples of product positioning

Volvos are strongly positioned on safety whilst Audi's positioning is on technical expertise ('Vorsprung durch Technik'). Nedbank has positioned itself as the 'green' bank thus taking advantage of the hot topic of sustainability, whilst Standard Bank has positioned itself on a 'moving forward' platform, suggesting a future, planning approach.

Through successful market positioning and the subsequent establishment of a set of valued product attributes and benefits, marketers can influence their products' demand by setting out these specific characteristics thereby establishing a clear image of the product in the customer's mind.

There are various bases on which to position a product. It is useful to draw up a series of 'positioning maps' (see for example table 5.11) utilising the attributes that the potential customer values most. A two by two matrix as shown below, using axes or relevant benefits or product attributes, allows the marketer to position the product as well as plotting the competitors products so that they can ascertain a 'gap' where the product can be differentiated from the competitors' offerings. These bases of positioning include:

- **Product attribute** where the company uses a distinctive attribute on which to position its product. An example is the dryness of Savanna Cider: 'it's dry, but you can drink it'.
- **Product benefit** where the company selects a unique product benefit. For example, Mitchum deodorant lasts longer: 'you can even miss a day'.
- **Price vs. quality**: Here the positioning strategy focuses on superior quality or the best value for money/lowest price. For example, Woolworths is known for being pricey whilst Pick n Pay positions itself on best value, lowest price.

- **Use or application positioning:** This method is based on usage or application.
- **Product user**: This method of positioning is based on the consumer/end user. Private banking is usually positioned as a professional, full-service offering for time-strapped business executives.
- **Competitor**: Here the company positions its product offering directly against its competitor. A good example is the highly competitive Pepsi/Coca-Cola positioning.
- **Origin**: Here the positioning focuses on where the product came from. A good example would be mineral water which is often positioned as being pure spring water from the heart of a mountain range.

Table 5.11 *Example of a positioning map*

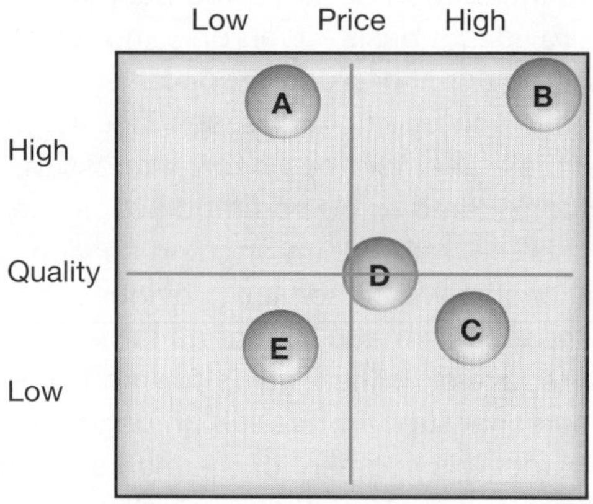

If a product is copied by a competitor or in some way loses its relevance or clear differentiating factor, then a marketer may have to undertake the process of repositioning. This is the process of altering the image and brand personality so that it appeals to a new or different target segment.

Summary

Marketers realise that with the limited financial and human resources at their disposal, fulfilling the needs and wants of the entire market is not likely to be successful. They call the process of identifying the consumers who are most likely to purchase the product 'segmentation', using variables which will deliver the amount of information they require. Once the segmentation step is complete, it is necessary to evaluate each emerging segment against a set of business criteria to choose the best target segment or segments. The final step in the process involves mapping the product against those of the competitors and developing a clear and communicative image and bundle of attributes for the customer. This positioning is the foundation for developing the marketing mix of product, price, promotion and place.

Case study: Capitec – Simplicity is the ultimate sophistication[13]

Capitec, South Africa's youngest retail bank, has become the only African brand to be recognised as a 'Great Brand of Tomorrow' by Swiss financial service group Credit Suisse. These are brands considered to have the ability to significantly outperform their markets and competitors over a three to five year period. Capitec's success can be attributed to its innovative business model and unique approach to market segmentation. By simplifying banking processes through pioneering use of technology, Capitec has established itself as the bank for the wider South African population.

Capitec has adopted the notion that everyday money management is required for clients to manage their daily lives. This can be achieved through constant interaction between the bank and clients' needs which, in turn, provides a basis for an ongoing relationship between the two parties. Traditional banking products such as home loans are often regarded as cumbersome processes initially, with little or no interaction after the agreement has been processed. Banking products of this kind are considered to be commodities, since price often dictates the consumer's choice, rather than ongoing service quality and an established relationship with a service provider.

In contrast, Capitec has made it clear its target is the individual – consumers who require simplified, value-for-money essential banking and are looking for personal support through an ongoing banking relationship. To successfully target this segment of the market, Capitec has designed innovative products and systems that are built specifically to address their market's unique needs for easy-to-use, low-cost banking. It has significantly more cash dispensing facilities at till points in major retailers across South Africa than automatic teller machines (ATMs). This allows clients easy access to their money (a service that is currently provided free of charge). By using this unconventional distribution channel, Capitec is able to save clients time and money, an attractive feature for the target market. Another innovative approach is the use of a standard flat fee pricing structure instead of the sliding scales used by traditional banks. Because service fees do not depend on the amount being withdrawn, customers are clear about the cost of any transaction.

Recent statistics indicate that the current formal banking industry in South Africa (which comprises banking, insurance and retail credit), was utilised by 64% of the adult population. However, during the 2010 financial year this decreased to 60%, something which was attributed to the decline in economic conditions and continued job losses in 2009. Consumers in lower income groups often become inactive bank users when they lose employment and tend to manage their money in a 'hand-to-mouth' way. It is encouraging for the banking industry and wider economy that the most banked individuals fall in the age group 18 to 29 years.

Capitec currently has 11% of the total banked individuals in South Africa – 2.5 million active clients. Of these clients, 11% primarily use a debit card and a much lower percentage makes use of electronic transaction services (as is the case for the South African banking industry as a whole). Capitec's other segments are distributed as follows: saving plans – 10%; lending – 37%; and salaried clients – 26%. Client growth is at an all-time high. Capitec is encouraging existing clients to make use of all of the transacting, saving and lending facilities. Its product offering is a single solution accessed via a single application which offers saving and lending solutions that can be defined by the client. All the bank's processes are characterised by simplicity.

South Africans are well known for low levels of saving, with only 38% of individuals indicating some saving behaviour. Most individuals who save make use of products at formal institutions other than traditional banks (16.6%) or save their money at home (12.7%). Only 8.5% of individuals prefer to save using bank products. Capitec is targeting the savings segment as brand confidence grows and increased brand awareness has led existing clients to open savings accounts. To date it has managed to secure 3% of South Africa's bank saving clients.

Capitec is also targeting the lending market, and has managed to attract 21.4% of the unsecured credit market. Although the bank is a relatively small player within the mortgage bond segment (3.4% of total market share), other lending segments such as retail credit and secure credit are showing good opportunities for growth at 12.6% and 5.6% respectively, against the background of the difficult market conditions after the 2009 economic crisis. Capitec's current focus in this segment is to attract short-term credit clients in the form of store cards, credit cards and lower value vehicle finance.

The bad debt ratio for the group declined to 1.5%, a figure that continues to fall, indicating that Capitec is effectively targeting clients who are able to pay back their loans. A further segment Capitec is targeting within the lending market is loans to small informal businesses such as spaza shops to assist them to purchase weekly supplies. These loans are designed for spaza shops and may be accessed weekly, provided that the loan is repaid before it becomes available again. Currently about 600 spaza shops are participating in this venture, allowing Capitec to test the market's ability to repay loans and also to fine tune its product for this market. Another product aimed at this market is an electronic payment card that would lower the chances of robberies significantly.

According to Capitec, the biggest contribution to its success is the ability to provide targeted segments with lower-cost products, as well as accessibility, a feature which is becoming increasingly important to consumers. The bank has designed systems for the lowest possible cost infrastructure which allows it to compete with bigger banks which must address the needs of a wider range of customers. This enables Capitec to compete with banks with significantly more market share.

Key facts:

- Capitec was established on 1 March 2001 and listed on the Johannesburg Stock Exchange on 18 February 2002.
- Over 2.5 clients are served in over 400 branches by 4 154 employees.
- Capitec owns 1 200 ATMs and 20 000 point of sale machines
- The bank has R1.7 billion in shareholder funds.
- Capitec's Global One Banking facility addresses most savings, lending and transacting needs and is the most affordable money management facility. Cash withdrawals cost only R1 per transaction.
- Communication is structured in a way that allows clients to clearly understand what is being delivered and at what cost.
- Advanced technology such as fingerprint biometrics and photo verification is used to provide clients with easy access to their accounts and prevent illegal or unauthorised activity.
- Capitec staff are employed for potential and provided with skills training to ensure consistent quality at the service interface.
- Capitec is able to offer clients an average of 48 more banking hours a month than traditional banks (standard weekday operating hours are from 08h00 to 17h00).

Exercise

1. When selecting their target market, which variables do you think Capitec bank used to segment the South African market? Explain the appropriateness of these variables.
2. Describe the profile of Capitec's target market consumer.
3. Explain which strategy of market coverage Capitec has used and give reasons for your answers.
4. Upon which specific attributes has Capitec Bank positioned itself relative to traditional banking institutions?

CHAPTER 6

Product decisions

Learning outcomes

After studying this chapter you should be able to:

- understand what is meant by the term 'product concept';
- demonstrate how products and services are classified;
- contrast product mix and product line decisions;
- explain the importance of branding, packaging and labelling; and
- explain the new product development process and propose changes to the product strategy during the product life cycle.

Introduction

The product decision is the first of the four decision-making areas, also called instruments of the marketing mix. Products are usually purchased less for their real physical features and more on the basis of the customer's perception of the package of need-satisfying attributes that the product possesses. Marketing incorporates all these physical and non-physical, and real and perceptual attributes into the four elements of the marketing mix:

- **Product**. This refers to the product and/or service the company offers. A product can be a physical object, an intangible service, an idea, a campaign or even a personality.
- **Price**. The price of a product should reflect its value to the consumer. This also entails the relative price versus quality level that the product maintains against the competitors.
- **Place**. This refers to the place where the product is to be sold (distribution).
- **Promotion**. Promotion refers to the marketing communication methods used to inform, persuade and remind the target market of the product or service.

Marketing management uses all four of these instruments to deliver its 'need-satisfying package' to the consumer. This unique combination of the four instruments or decision areas is also called the marketing mix.

In line with what we said about the 'need-satisfying package', it is obvious that marketing managers must have a clear idea of what the essence of the product is that is being marketed to the target market. The product concept is made up of the four levels depicted in fig. 6.1, which together deliver value to the customer.

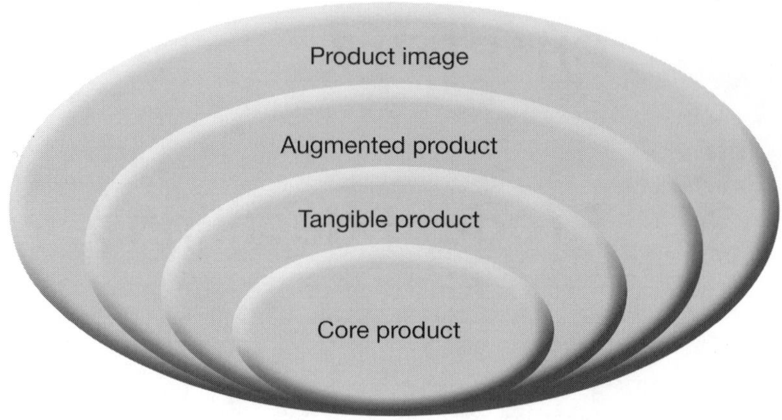

Figure 6.1 *The product concept*

- **Core product**. At the basic level of the product or service is the core product. It answers the question 'What is the buyer really buying?' It represents the main benefit or benefits consumers look for in a product to satisfy their needs. For example, one car buyer may see this benefit as a quick method of transport between points A and B. Another car buyer may see this benefit as safety, another as high performance or prestige. Remember, any one consumer may require all of these benefits in a single product.
- **Tangible product**. The desired benefits the consumer sees in the core product must now be turned into product attributes. Product attributes represent the tangible product. The product attributes can be placed into five categories: a quality level, features (or physical characteristics), styling (or design), a brand name and packaging.
- **Augmented product**. The third element of the product concept is sales support features, such as delivery, installation, warranties and services. Examples are free advanced driver lessons for BMW car buyers, an information help-line and quick repair services. This level of the product concept is known as the augmented product. For example, part of Toyota's augmented product is a five-year or 100 000 km warranty.
- **Product image**. The fourth dimension of a product arises from the tangible and augmented features present in the product, as well as from the other marketing activities performed by the company. For example, the promotion message, the retail outlets chosen and the price level convey a certain 'message' to the consumer. This 'message' is called the product image and ties in with the product positioning concept that will be discussed later on. Marketers operating in a very competitive market sometimes rely more on the image they have created for the product than on its real attributes, in an attempt to counteract the actions of their competitors. For example, BMW uses product image extensively in the marketing of its range of products.

LG – a company image on the rise

The South Korean manufacturer Goldstar originally entered the South African market with products such as microwaves, radios, televisions and compact disc players aimed at the lower end of the market. The company then changed its name to LG and improved their quality levels, accompanied by a promotion campaign emphasising the unique features of their products, for example, the sound of their television sets, their easy-to-use microwave ovens and their excellent washing machines. LG hopes that these promotion campaigns will enhance the general image of the product range. Its aim is for these products to be regarded as being of similar or better quality than the Panasonic, Sony, Telefunken and Philips products on the market.

The product concept represents the product value package of the business, which encapsulates all the physical, intangible and emotional (image) attributes of the product being offered to consumers.[1] The extent to which the product of the business satisfies consumer needs should be compared with those of competitors. If better value is offered to consumers over the long term, a strong relationship can be established with consumers and would ensure that the organisation makes a profit. This relationship is graphically presented in fig. 6.2.

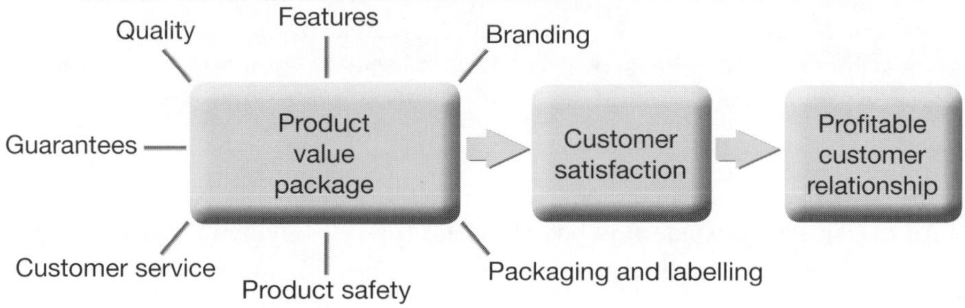

***Figure 6.2** The product value package*[2]

Classifying products and services

Products can be classified in four different ways: by durability, by buying behaviour, by buyer type and by tangibility.

Classifying by durability

Classifying products in terms of durability means that differentiation is based on how durable they are: durable products, non-durable products and service products. Keep in mind that, although service products are mainly intangible, they may also have physical features. For example, a man or a woman who visits a hair salon uses a service (intangible) through which he or she may acquire a new hairstyle (tangible).

Durable vs. non-durable

- A bicycle is a durable product because it could be used for years.
- Milk is a non-durable product which must be used within a day or two of being bought or thrown away.

Classifying by buying behaviour

From a marketing point of view, the most important way of classifying products is by the buying behaviour of consumers. The four categories are convenience products, shopping products, speciality products and unsought products.

Examples of products classified by buying behaviour

- **Convenience products.** These are products that the consumer wants to buy with the minimum of effort and must therefore be sold in many places, e.g. milk, bread, cigarettes and beer.
- **Shopping products.** These are products that the consumer will go to some trouble to find. For example, a woman who wants to buy a new dress may take time to visit a range of stores. This is called 'shopping around' which is where the term 'shopping products' comes from.
- **Speciality products.** These are products that the consumer will go to a lot of trouble to find. Examples include a Carducci suit, a Benetton shirt, a Ferrari sports car or Bally shoes.
- **Unsought products.** These are products a consumer usually does not want, but is sometimes forced to buy. Examples include life insurance, a funeral policy or timeshare.

Classifying by buyer type

The third classification system is based on the type of buyer who buys the product, further subdivided into final consumers and business consumers.

The marketing of products by one business to another is called business-to-business marketing. Business consumers buy computers, office furniture, airline tickets, motor vehicles, raw materials and machinery. These consumers are not only manufacturing businesses, but also government departments and private institutions such as hospitals, universities, churches, clubs and trade unions.

Final consumers are individuals buying products for individual or household consumption, such as clothes, white goods (such as fridges and microwave ovens), groceries, sporting goods and haircuts. These types of product are called consumer products. This chapter is mainly concerned with the marketing issues involved in marketing consumer products to the final consumer.

Classifying by tangibility

When we think about products, we usually imagine a physical product, e.g. a car, suit or washing machine. However, many products are intangible, that is they cannot be seen, smelled or tasted. An intangible product can also be called a service or a service product.

When we analyse services, we must distinguish between services attached to a product on the one hand (the service attributes attached to a physical product) and service as a product (where the product itself is a service). Services as products constitute nearly half of all consumer products bought and proportion is increasing. In fact, the term 'service economy' is widely used. Chapter 10 describes service products in more detail.

Examples of services

- **A university degree.** When you enrol for a BCom degree or a national business diploma you are buying a service product. The tangible attributes of this service are the textbooks and study material and, if you are successful, the degree or diploma at the end. The main product attribute, however, is knowledge, which is intangible.
- **Curing an ailment.** A medical practitioner renders a service to a patient by doing a medical inspection (with physical actions), making a diagnosis of the ailment (intangible), and then prescribing treatment, usually in the form of medication (physical). The ailment and whether it is cured are both physical phenomena, but the overall product is a service.

Products in each category are marketed differently. The approach to marketing a newspaper (a non-durable, convenience, consumer and tangible product) is quite different from marketing a piece of production machinery (a durable, tangible and business product), or marketing an overseas trip (an intangible, speciality and service product). In the next few chapters on the other elements of the marketing mix you will see how the unique features of a product have a marked influence on decisions about price, promotion and distribution.

Product mix and product line decisions

Very few organisations manufacture and market only a single product item, most offer a range. The **product mix**, also called the product assortment of a business, refers to all the product items it has on the market. Some of these products may be related to one another in terms of usage or application, for example, razor blades and shaving cream. They may be related to one another in terms of basic technology, for example, the motors of a fridge and a freezer. Or they may be related to one another in terms of the market segments they serve, for example, luxury four-wheel drive off-road vehicles and luxury sports cars are sold to the same market segment. Related products are called a **product line**. The product mix of a company may consist of a number of product lines. For example, a company such as Johnson & Johnson may have a nappy line, a toothpaste line, a soap bar line, a deodorant line, and so on. The number of product lines an organisation carries refers to its **product line width**.

The **length** of a product line refers to the average number of items the company carries in each product line. Large supermarkets in South Africa carry more than 1 000 products, whereas General Electric in the USA manufactures as many as 250 000 product items.[3]

The **depth** of a product line refers to how many versions are offered of each product item or brand within a product line. For example, the Nescafé instant coffee brand comprises a number of versions, namely Classic, Gold and Decaffeinated. The company may also have other coffee brands in its coffee line. By dividing the product line depth by the number of product lines the company holds, the average depth of the company's product mix can be calculated.

The **consistency** of the product mix refers to how closely related the different product lines are in terms of end users, production systems, distribution channels or raw materials. For instance, smaller speciality shops and small supermarkets like Spar hold products that are highly related, or are highly consistent. On the other hand large supermarkets such as Makro and hypermarkets carry product lines that are diverse, from foodstuffs to hardware products.

These four product mix elements – width, length, depth and consistency – represent all the possible product strategy options. The organisation can add new product lines, thus increasing the product mix width. It can add more product items to a specific product line, for example, a new brand of children's toothpaste to the toothpaste line, thus increasing the product mix length. It can add more versions to a brand, for instance a canned kiwifruit to its canned fruit line, thus deepening the product line. Finally, the organisation can decide to pursue greater consistency by sticking to its existing approach when product launches are considered.

Product mix and product line decisions are critically important to retailers, such as convenience stores at petrol filling stations, and supermarkets like Spar and Pick n Pay. The convenience stores concentrate to some extent on the 'urgent needs' of consumers, while supermarkets and hypermarkets aim for the 'total shopping experience', catering for the longer term requirements of the household.

Sony Corporation: Operating in new markets

Product mix and product line extensions are largely influenced by technological advancements. Sony Corporation has not competed in the still-picture market until recently. However, advancements in the electronics field have opened up a market for digital cameras, with computer-linked attributes. Sony has strongly entered this market, competing against well-established brands in the still camera field like Nikon, Canon and Pentax.

Branding, packaging and labelling

In consumer and business markets, branding, packaging and labelling are crucial 'weapons' in the marketer's arsenal. They give identity to a product in the same way that a name and face and identity book give identity to a person. A brand is a sign, symbol or name or a combination of these that identifies the product or service in the eyes of the customer. However, brands are much more than just the names and symbols attached to a product or service. In essence, a brand reflects the customer's perceptions about the product or service and the performance that person expects. We can say that a brand exists in the mind of the customer and the **brand equity** is defined by what the customer thinks about the product or service. The most powerful brands in the world have high brand equity.

Coca-Cola: A name like no other

Coca-Cola is the world's best-known brand name by far. The company has attained this position by spending huge amounts of money on promotion over many decades. Part of the promotion budget is spent on outdoor advertising, for example, billboards, neon-lit signs and window displays usually at cafés, stalls and caravans at sporting events. These displays always use the well-known red and white corporate colours. Next time you are on the road, count how many times you are exposed to the promotion of the Coca-Cola brand. You will realise that it is so common, you hardly notice it. Subconsciously, however, each of these exposures leaves an imprint on your mind.

Branding decisions about an organisation are whether the product or service is a manufacturer's brand or a private brand, a licensed brand, or a co-brand.

- **Manufacturers' brands** are manufactured by the manufacturer and are usually distributed throughout the country. In the past, through its brand the manufacturer could dominate the market and set the rules about how its range of products should be sold. In the past few decades some retailers have clawed back their power in the 'battle of the brands' through launching **private brands** (also called store brands).
- **Licensed brands** are taken over under a licensing agreement from famous people like Elizabeth Taylor who allow their names to be attached to products such as perfume in return for royalty payments on sales.
- **Co-branding** is when two organisations join forces to create a joint or composite brand. Mercedes Benz and AMG are well known for their limited edition, high-performance vehicles. Another example is the co-branding between New Zealand's All Blacks rugby team and Adidas of Germany. Co-branding arrangements use the appeal of both brands to appeal to a larger segment of the market.

Packaging is the way in which the product or service is presented, e.g. the box, tin, or bottle in which a product is sold. Initially the focus of packaging was to protect the product but in more recent times it forms an invaluable part of the perceptions of consumers. Innovative packaging could be the competitive advantage for a product. Think, for example, of the way the traditional aluminium toothpaste container was replaced by the more durable plastic container, which was later changed to a standalone plastic tube.

A label forms an integral part of the product and helps to sell the product. It identifies the product, provides information, and can help to promote the product, making it an invaluable marketing tool.

Surprisingly, branding, packaging and labelling are often more important to the marketer than the physical features of the product itself. This is because, in many cases, competing products are fairly similar in terms of their inherent features. The marketer must therefore use something else to help consumers to differentiate the product from others. Branding, packaging and labelling are used to establish intangible product differences. For this reason, you should regard these three aspects as important product-related instruments through which a company's products are given a distinctive identity.

The label says 'buy me'
The label of a product may also serve to market it. Running shoes often have a label attached to them highlighting the qualities of the product, for example, the research that went into the product prior to manufacturing, the unique features of the shoes, and the extended warranty offered on the product. In other cases, the label serves only to describe the product better, such as the size of a garment and what fabric was used to make it.

Changes in the use of branding as a marketing tool[4]

Businesses that manufacture well-known branded products and services currently face a serious challenge. Over and above the effects of the global economic downturn which started in 2009 and resulted in a drastic decline in sales, customers are less loyal to and appreciative of the tried and trusted brands of the past. While the value of a handful of brands such as Google, Apple and Nike is increasing, the value of most brands all over the world has been steadily falling. Successful brands such as Adidas, iPhone, Pixar and Wikipedia are succeeding in getting the attention of customers by communicating excitement, dynamism and creativity in ways that the vast majority of brands are failing to do. By focusing on these positives, these businesses are keeping their brands in the public eye and improving brand equity.

Brand equity comprises four measures: trust, awareness, regard and esteem. High scores on these four measures provide an indication that consumers are likely to continue purchasing the specific brand and remain brand loyal. The burning issue for most brands is why customers lost their trust in, and respect for, these brands and what the businesses can do to increase brand performance and increases in sales.

- **Excess capacity** is a global problem with too many brands chasing the attention of customers, and those customers finding it increasingly difficult to distinguish between competing brands. More and more research finds that, despite increasing promotional budgets, customers find it difficult to tell the difference between brands.
- **A lack of creativity** means that many businesses are struggling to attract the attention of customers in a market that is characterised by high levels of innovation and new ideas.
- There has been a **loss of trust** among consumers towards brands, institutions and leaders.

Developing new products

Reasons for developing new products[5]

- Any business exists because it has products and/or services to sell to customers. It must therefore continually consider improving existing products and developing new ones. Microsoft, for example, launches a new version of Office every few years and continually develops new products and services.

- Mature products are usually subject to internal competition, which restricts profit margins. However, successful innovative new products usually enjoy bigger profit margins, which can offset the lack of profits of older products in the market.
- Technological innovation is taking place at an increasing rate in most industries. It is a matter of keeping up or falling by the wayside. For instance, the emergence of DVD technology rendered videotapes obsolete, and DVD technology is now being challenged by the emergence of high-definition formats like Blue Ray. Motor car manufacturers spend millions on improving the safety, performance and convenience of their products to ensure their products remain competitive. The entire industry is facing a revolution as engines powered by fossil fuel technology are phased out.
- Certain environmental variables stimulate product development. A substantial improvement in the living standards of certain groups of people in the world means they have higher levels of disposable income. This is stimulating demand for certain kinds of products. The preferences of consumers are changing. For example, 'green' environmental considerations are playing an ever-increasing role in the choices that consumers are making.

'Green' strategy pays off for Pretoria Portland Cement (PPC)[6]

A common expression in the cement industry is 'cement is cement', i.e. there is no real difference between competing brands. PPC is in the process of turning this idea on its head by using new green technologies in the hope of creating a sustainable competitive advantage for the company and its products. Since 1990 PPC's cement, dolomite and lime factories have reduced their carbon emissions by 15%, and over the past nine years energy consumed declined by 17%. PPC's cement and lime plants are ISO14001 certified, an international standard based on three pillars, namely preventing pollution, complying with legal and other requirements, and continuous improvements in performance.

- The growing tendency towards one-stop shopping and the concentration in retail competition in the three retail giants (Pick n Pay, Shoprite Checkers and Spar) have led to a shortage in retail shelf space. Old products find it increasingly difficult to compete for shelf space against new, innovative products for which there is a growing demand.
- The organisation usually has to consider launching more than one new product at a time, because of the high rate of new product failures. An American study of new product launches found that 40% of new consumer products, 20% of new industrial products and 18% of new service products fail. Another study found that, of 700 consumer and industrial products manufactured in the USA, only 65% are successful. Still another study estimates that of the 2 500 new products introduced in the USA each year, 90% do not survive past the first three years.[7]

New product options

New product development can be done by modifying the existing product, extending the product line, developing related products, or entering a new field with a product or service that is totally unrelated to what went before.

Examples of new product options

- **Product modification.** The computer industry is well known for its upgrading of existing products. The power of personal computers doubles every two years while the price falls dramatically (Moore's Law).
- **Product line development.** Clothing manufacturers often climb on the 'special event' bandwagon. The 2010 Soccer World Cup in South Africa created opportunities for manufacturers, subject to licensing conditions, to produce hats, scarves, t-shirts, tracksuits and other clothing in team colours, flags of competing countries, and the Zakumi mascot.
- **Entry into related field of products.** Many of the world's leading electronic companies, such as Sony, Panasonic, Motorola and Philips, ventured into the lucrative cellular telephone market on the back of their experience in related electronic fields.
- **Entry into an entirely new field.** With the possibility of electricity generation being opened up to competition, Eskom, the sole supplier of electricity in South Africa, has considered entering the telecommunication industry.

Deciding which of the new product options should be pursued represents a crucial strategic commitment by the business. The size of the business and its world-wide market share are important considerations. A small business would probably opt for a less ambitious approach due to its capital constraints. The options range from the well known to the entirely new, for example, imitative products, adaptive innovations and breakthrough innovations. Every option would place different demands on the marketing division.

Any consideration of whether to develop products that are new to the company and to consumers would require substantial research about the requirements of consumers and what the target market might be. Such products might require aggressive marketing to establish a position in the marketplace.

New product development

To **identify new product opportunities**, the marketing department uses its knowledge of consumer needs and characteristics and competitor actions to look for possible profitable gaps in the market (fig. 6.3). These two elements of the marketing environment are probably the richest sources of new product areas available to the company. Other sources of new product ideas are participants in the distribution channel, the research and development department, the sales force, top management and employees. The business should aim to identify as many new product ideas as possible – even ones that might seem ridiculous as some of the most fundamental technology changes originate from so-called ridiculous ideas.

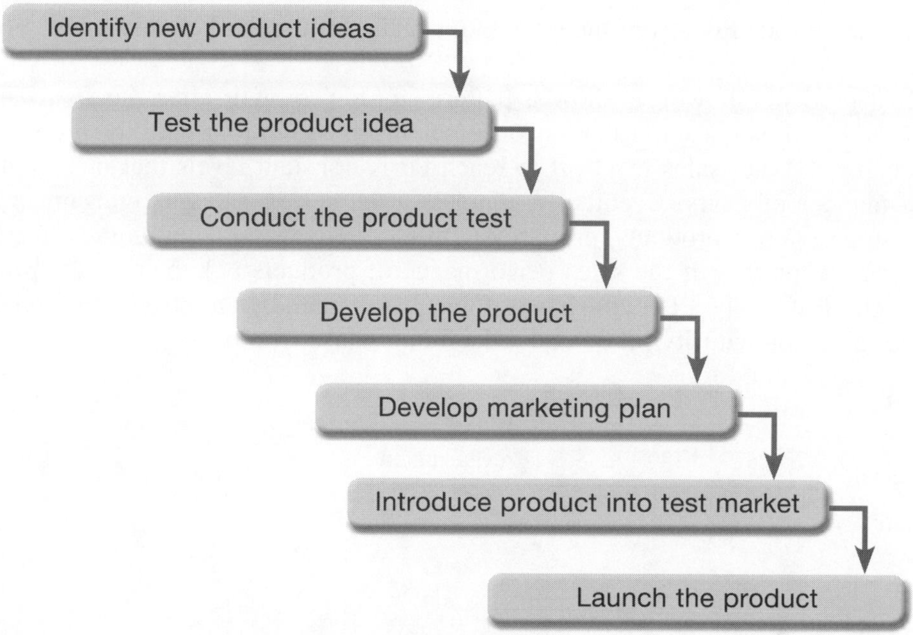

Figure 6.3 *The new product development process*[8]

The next step is to **test new product ideas**. Each idea must be evaluated in terms of its general viability, marketability and its manufacturing and financial viability. 'Venture teams', consisting of a number of employees from different departments in the business, are often used for **developing and testing the product**. Large businesses may have a separate Research and Development (R&D) department for this purpose. During this phase, the marketing department should ensure that the specific requirements expressed by consumers are incorporated in the prototype and that they are then thoroughly evaluated by potential consumers. Marketing should work closely with the operations/manufacturing division to ensure that the attributes of the product remain focused on the specific customer needs identified earlier in the marketplace.

Test marketing is part of the phase during which the product is launched in a limited geographical market. The marketing strategy should be aimed only at that market to see whether the product will be successful and whether the planned marketing strategy for a national launch needs to be adapted. Once all the marketing and production problems have been resolved, the product can be **launched** nationally (or internationally) with the aid of a detailed marketing plan.

Product life cycle

Once a product has been launched on the market (this is also called the commercialisation of the product), any one of a number of things can happen to it. It may be an instant success with sales growing rapidly to high levels, but eventually declining again as new competing products or revitalised products start competing strongly with it. The product may also be only moderately successful after its launch, but may continue to be profitable for a number of years. Another possibility is that the product fails from the start and is taken off the market only a few months after its launch.

Most products, however, show a pattern of slow growth after the first launch, followed by an increase in sales as consumers become familiar with the product and start using it. Later sales level off to reach fairly constant levels that may continue for a number of years. Eventually, there is a decline in sales as consumers start switching to newer products, probably with more advanced technological features. This general pattern of the sales performance of products is known as the product life cycle (PLC). The PLC consists of four phases: namely an introductory phase, a growth phase, a maturity phase and a declining phase (fig. 6.4).

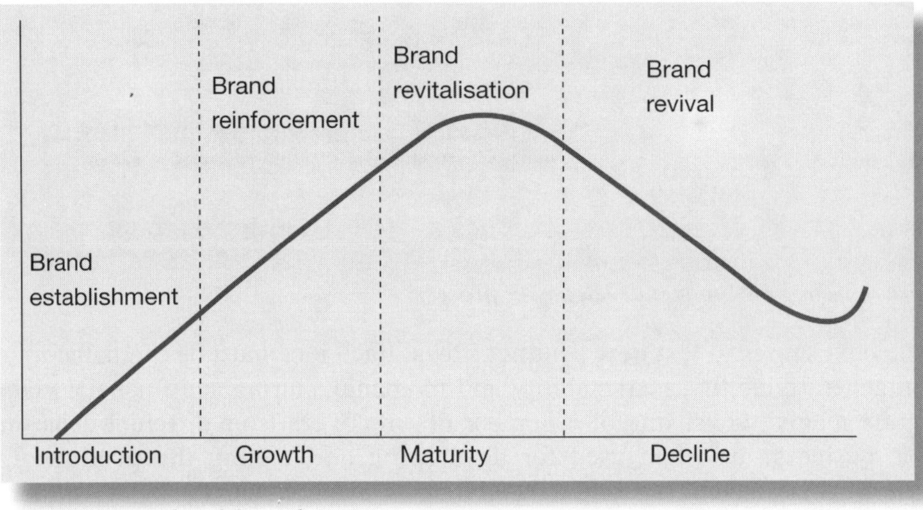

***Figure 6.4** The product life cycle*

Each of these phases shows unique characteristics in terms of consumer requirements and buying behaviour, competitive intensity and levels of profitability. Consequently, each phase requires specific marketing action in terms of the provision of product features, distribution activities, promotion programmes and the setting of price levels. Let us now look at each of these phases.

Introductory phase

When a product is introduced to the market, the key question is whether this type of product is known to consumers, for example, a new brand of soap. The product may be totally unknown to consumers, for example, a new invention such as a hand-held device that cooks food with concentrated microwaves. In the case of the known product, the marketer would immediately embark on establishing brand awareness for the product. With entirely new products, the emphasis falls on introducing the new technology to potential consumers. In both cases the main aim remains to encourage use of the product by emphasising its unique attributes. Problems with quality and availability of the product at the retail level are common during this stage and should be resolved as soon as they appear as this will improve the sales, profitability and eventual length of the life cycle of the product.

Growth phase

During the growth phase, the product becomes well known to most potential consumers and competitors enter the market or begin to compete for market share. New market segments can be identified and the product can be adapted to satisfy the unique needs of these segments. Owing to increased competition, prices might be lowered during this phase.

Maturity phase

Sales eventually level out during the maturity phase. Now marketing managers must decide whether they are satisfied with its present position, or whether new actions should be taken to establish renewed growth in sales. Product adaptations are made during this phase and additional incentives are provided to intermediaries and consumers to ensure that high sales levels are maintained or even increased.

Declining phase

When sales start declining on a fairly consistent basis, marketing managers should make a decision about the future of the product. They can decide to revive the product by introducing a new and aggressive marketing campaign. They can also decide to harvest the remaining benefits of the product by allowing it to decline slowly while spending as little on keeping it in the market as possible. Or they could decide to withdraw it from the market completely.

Life-cycle analysis

Marketing management must not only know in which phase of the PLC their product or service is, but also what actions to take during each phase. Obviously each business wants the sales of its product to keep on growing. The aim should be to maintain a high level of sales for as long as possible. If sales start to decline, the business usually hopes it can implement strategies to remedy the situation, that is to renew the product or marketing campaign. If it seems that nothing will extend the product's life, the business would aim to withdraw the product from the market without damaging the image of the business and those products remaining in the market. In all phases it is extremely important to differentiate the product from those of competitors. This can be done by pushing the brand name, package, logo, price and/or its unique features in the promotion campaign.

The life-cycle analysis therefore has two implications for marketing management:

1. It should be aware of the characteristics of each life-cycle phase and compare the performance of its product with these characteristics, so that the product can be placed in its applicable life-cycle phase.
2. On the basis of this analysis, an appropriate marketing campaign can be developed.

The secret differentiates the product[9]

The secret formula for Coca-Cola, called 7X, is contained in five yellowing scraps of paper locked in a New York bank vault. In 1885, Frank Robinson invented the drink and devised a name, written in the distinctive script that became the company's internationally recognised logo. He also masterminded the company's early advertising and marketing campaigns. Over decades, Coca-Cola has maintained its market position (and even improved it), although hundreds of new non-alcoholic and light alcoholic drinks have been launched. While some have been successful, most have come and gone.

Summary

This chapter deals with product decisions, new product development and the product life cycle. It is now clear that new, mature and even declining products must be made readily available to potential consumers through appropriate distribution channels. The next chapter deals with the task of the intermediaries in the distribution process.

Case study: Woolworths goes green[10]

Woolworths originated from humble beginnings in 1931 in the old Royal Hotel in Cape Town. The bleak economy following the recession of the 1930s had most consumers doubting the prospect of long-term success, but with an imaginative store policy, the company has managed to do very well. It its 74 years of existence, Woolworths has become synonymous with innovation, quality and value for money and the group has grown to comprise 149 corporate stores, 51 international franchise stores and 69 local franchise stores.

One of its recent product innovations caters to emerging consumer preferences for greener living. The Woolworths 'good business journey' aims to reduce the company's impact on the environment, create sustainable green products, and become more active in local community development.

In 2008 the Earth Friendly range of 60 household cleaning and personal care products, including products for babies, was launched. These products are all made out of naturally derived, plant-based, biodegradable ingredients and contain no petrochemicals, animal ingredients or artificial colours. Every product is endorsed by Beauty Without Cruelty to show it has not been tested on animals. Packaging is made out of a minimum of 30% recycled material. This range offers consumers an environmentally friendly alternative to traditional products.

Shortly afterwards, Woolworths reached another key milestone in its good business journey by switching the packaging of its 'to go' range of products from plastic to cardboard derived from sustainable and well-managed forests. The company took this a step further by making the transparent window of the packaging from maize, a renewable resource, instead of plastic. The new sandwich packaging carries the stamp of approval of the Forest Stewardship Council, an internationally recognised body backed by a large number of leading conservation groups, providing consumers with the reassurance that this green initiative is indeed green. The new packaging had no impact on the prices of the sandwiches and the cleverly designed box 'unzips' into a handy, self-contained and disposable tray. The packaging is colour-coded for consumers to identify the main ingredient – orange for chicken, red for pork, blue for fish, yellow for egg, brown for beef and green for vegetarian food.

Another key success is the introduction of more than 100 new organic grocery products. As the third largest consumer of organic cotton in the world, Woolworths has contributed significantly to encouraging cleaner farming practices that are better for the environment. The special range of organic cotton linens and homeware is farmed without synthetic chemicals that could contaminate the environment and safeguards consumers against pesticide residues. The organic food item range is also free of synthetic pesticides. Instead, farmers protect their crops by using natural pest repellents and companion planting (planting plants together that help protect one another against disease and insects). Woolworths buys only from farmers who do not treat their cows and hens with routine antibiotics that end up in the final produce. It also sells free-range meat and chicken.

Woolworths also ensures the best quality fruit and vegetables by not supporting the use of processes that artificially extend the growing season. Its organic farmers subscribe to the ideals of building soil fertility, minimising damage to the environment, working with rather than against natural systems, and respecting animal welfare. Its organic dairy products come from animals fed an organic diet, with no hormones, no gelatine, no added preservatives, and reduced sugar contents.

The Woolworths 'farming for the future' initiative supports holistic farming approaches that maximise production while minimising the negative impact on the environment. Here the focus is on caring for the soil, adding only necessary conventional chemicals (unlike organic farming where no chemicals are used), supporting biodiversity conservation, and conserving water resources. This approach to farming has resulted in initial savings of up to 25% in the use of water, pesticides and chemical fertilisers. By 2012, all of the locally produced produce sold by Woolworths will be grown this way.

Another product initiative is the Home Lifestyle Project which promotes the work of local designers in selected stores in Johannesburg and Cape Town and includes the following new product lines:

- Wonki Ware studio (distinctive crockery).
- Clayton-Emil Couturiers (a 'green' range of scatter cushions).
- Inini Glass (eco-friendly glass products such as plates, salad bowls and platters).

- Siblings Linen (finest quality bed and table linen produced by previously disadvantaged women).
- Design Team (table linen and scatter cushions with a quirky take on local icons).

These product lines focus on locally sourced, environmentally friendly products, and the involvement and upliftment of the local community.

The company's 'green' approach has influenced its suppliers to become more environmentally aware. In 2008, three suppliers won Woolworths Eco-Efficiency Awards. La Motte, which produces red wines for Woolworths, reduced their water usage per litre wine by 41% and their relative energy usage by 17%. Kimberly-Clark, a tissue paper product supplier, achieved the ISO 14001 certification, reduced its total water usage by 10% and implemented various projects to update facilities and train employees. Westfalia, which provides avocado to all Woolworths stores, managed to offset its carbon footprint of 2 453 tons of carbon dioxide emissions by planting enough orchards to transform 41 250 tons of carbon dioxide into oxygen.

Woolworths was the first company in South Africa to introduce yoghurts with only natural flavours and colours, fresh baby food, sell-by dates on food packaging, and children's shoes that have been approved by experts. It is one of the leaders in eco-friendly products in South Africa by being the third biggest consumers of organic cotton, the first South African provider of organic Merino wool, and having all its beauty products endorsed by Beauty Without Cruelty. The company is supporting predator-friendly farming, planting trees, recycling plastic used during operations, and promoting sustainable wine production. Woolworths also believes in contributing to local communities by offering a fair price for coffee and tea, using organic farming to ensure sustainable farms for the local community, employing previously disadvantaged people to produce its biltong range, and ensuring its tea estate provides job opportunities for the local people. Woolworths is also committed to building sustainable schools and helping schools grow food for their learners.

It is clear that Woolworths has gone 'green' by incorporating sustainable product ranges into its product lines and modifying its business practices.

Exercise

1. By applying the principles of the product concept, identify the different dimensions of Woolworths' new Earth Friendly bathroom wipes making up the 'total product' as discussed in this chapter.
2. How does Woolworths target market influence its product mix?
3. What actions is Woolworths taking to extend the life cycle of its products?

CHAPTER 7

Distribution decisions

Learning outcomes

After studying this chapter you should be able to:

- understand the concept of supply chain management and the role of intermediaries in the distribution channel providing value to the customer;
- analyse the distribution activities performed in the distribution channel;
- illustrate with the aid of figures how a product is pulled and pushed through the distribution channel;
- differentiate between the different intermediaries in the various South African distribution channels;
- understand why hybrid channels and vertical marketing systems are used in distribution channels;
- show how the factors involved in selecting a suitable distribution channel are used to develop a distribution channel for a product or service;
- discuss the merits of channel leadership or captaincy and how channel conflict is handled in the distribution channel;
- explain why marketing logistics is such an important factor of the distribution decision; and
- discuss the steps involved in managing a distribution channel.

Introduction

To manufacture a product or service and then to deliver it to the consumer is a comprehensive process that requires building relationships with a number of roleplayers in the marketplace. Those roleplayers collectively make up the supply chain of that organisation. Broadly speaking, we can say that the supply chain consists of organisations involved upstream or downstream from the manufacturer, each of which plays a role in eventually creating value for the customer.

Upstream activities include all those activities performed by suppliers of raw material, capital equipment supplies such as manufacturing equipment, component manufacturers such as we find in the motor industry, and financing. These organisations are actively involved in helping to create the product that the customer wants. **Downstream activities** include the role played by the well-known intermediaries such as wholesalers and retailers that deliver the product to the final customer. There are also **reverse logistics** in the supply chain which refers to returning all the unwanted, damaged and outdated returns of material products and services back to the source of supply.

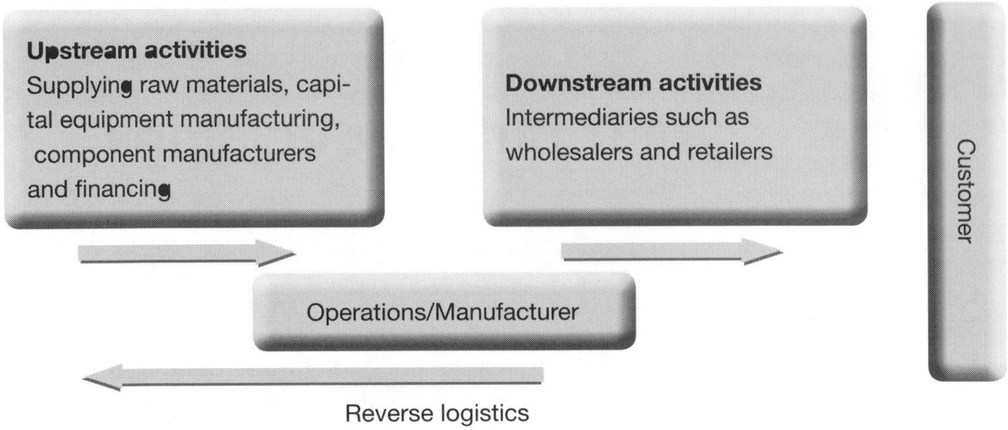

Figure 7.1 The supply chain of an organisation[1]

The supply chain of a cereal manufacturer like Bokomo or Tiger Oats might look like fig. 7.2.

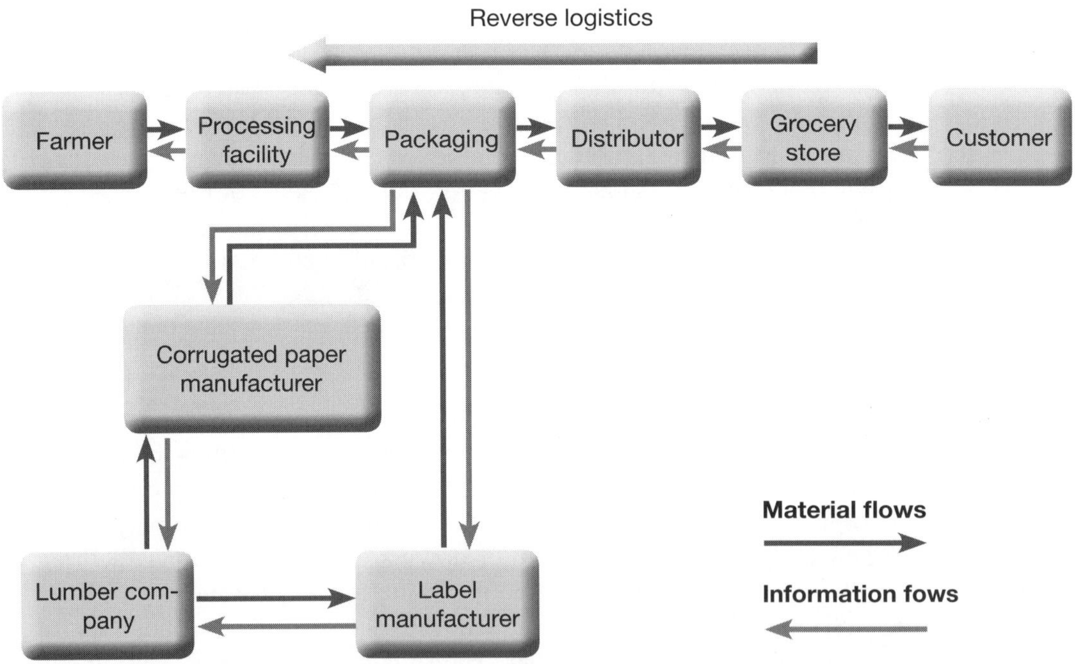

Figure 7.2 The supply chain of an organisation

As can be seen from this practical example, the upstream activity consists of the farmer and the suppliers further upstream, namely the banks, co-operatives, etc. and the processing facility, which usually is a miller. The activities involved in the packaging includes support activities delivered by the lumber organisation that feeds raw material (wood) to the corrugated paper manufacturer which provides the paper boxes in which the cereal is packaged. The manufacturer of the labels is also involved in a supporting role. Once the cereal boxes leave the factory, the product is distributed through a wholesaler to a retailer and then sold to the customer. Reverse logistics refers to the flow back from any of the roleplayers in the supply chain back to a supplier. If, for example, the boxes are defective, they would be returned to the supplier.

Traditionally marketing literature has focused more on the downstream activities of the supply chain. The distribution channel, also called the marketing channel, delivers the product or service to the final consumer. In this process, wholesalers, retailers and other intermediaries are used to present a product, service or idea to the final consumer. A gap usually exists between the provider of a product or service and the final consumer. Distribution activities are therefore the method through which the gap is closed and through which the product or service is made available to the final consumer.

Practical examples of distribution

- Convenience stores at petrol filling stations (called forecourts) sell groceries such as bread and milk to their customers.
- A university such as UNISA distributes study guides and related materials to its students.
- Manufacturers sell to stores such as Checkers, which sell and distribute goods to final customers.
- News media such as etv, MNet, SAfm and *Cape Times* distribute media items to their readers, listeners and viewers.
- Non-profit groups such as the Society for the Prevention of Cruelty to Animals (SPCA) and churches distribute a service to their supporters or congregations.

The basic distribution decisions

Distribution decisions centre on two broad activities of equal importance, namely channel management and physical distribution management.[2]

Channel management concentrates on the transaction flow of the product or service through the channel. The most optimal channels have to be used to make the product available to the consumer and include the buying and selling activities and how many organisations are involved in distributing the product. For example, Coca-Cola uses supermarkets, wholesalers, cafés and convenience shops as distribution outlets to make its soft drinks available to the consumer. By using these and other outlets, Coca-Cola is delivered virtually to the consumer's doorstep. It requires very little effort for the consumer to buy this product, making Coca-Cola a convenience product due to its extensive distribution coverage.

Physical distribution management also called **marketing logistics**, focuses on the physical flow of the product from the factory to the distribution outlet or to the final consumer. For example, Coca-Cola uses road transport (delivery vehicles) to move cases containing 24 Coke tins 340 ml in size in a truck that carries thousands of tins at a time. This truck leaves from the Amalgamated Bottling Industries (ABI) bottling plant in Olifantsfontein and covers a fixed route to all the hypermarkets, supermarkets, cafés, schools and restaurants in the southern area of Pretoria and Kempton Park.

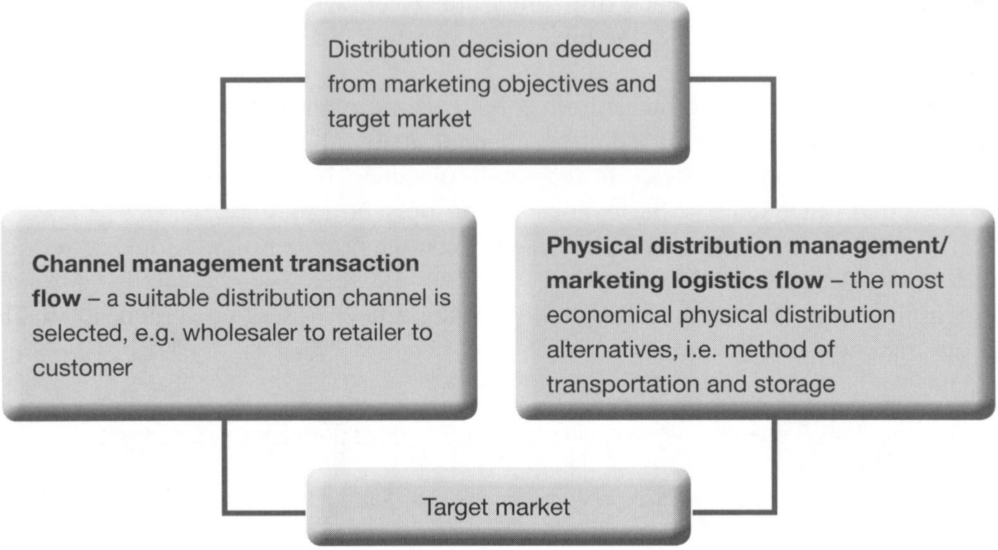

Figure 7.3 *The basic distribution decisions*[3]

Activities performed in the distribution channel

Buying and selling

The organisations ('members') involved in the distribution channel usually have to buy the products, thereby taking ownership of the product, for reselling further down the supply chain.

Risk taking

Any distribution channel member involved in buying and selling is taking on a risk, because the product could be damaged or stolen, or it could become obsolete, lowering the value of the product and resulting in a loss for the title holder.

Transportation

By transporting a product, place value is added, making it possible for customers to buy that product at the local grocery shop, even if the factory is thousands of kilometres away.

Storage

Storage of the product creates time value by making storage at warehouses possible which means that the product is always available. For example, the demand for maize meal in South Africa is fairly consistent throughout the year. However, maize is only harvested in the period May to August and must be stored in various forms by the distribution channel members. Members involved in the storage of this product include farmers, co-operatives, millers, wholesalers and retailers.

Rearrangement
Maize meal is one of thousands of products stocked by a supermarket. Different products must be accumulated and different assortments must be developed to fit the tastes of the consumer. Cake flour is packed into 50 kg bags but the ordinary consumer does not want more than a 2 kg or 5 kg bag. Distribution channel members such as wholesalers and retailers bridge the quantity and ownership gap between the manufacturer and the consumer by, for example, repackaging cake flour.

Creating possession value for the consumer
A growing trend in South Africa is for the customer to use credit facilities such as a bank overdraft or credit card. By providing this service, the financial institution is making it easier for the customer to buy the product and is therefore creating value for the customer. Another kind of financing is when the retailer provides a shopping card to consumers to buy food and clothing from stores such as Woolworths and Edgars. This credit facility adds value to the process of buying or selling of products and services. Banks and specialised finance companies like Wesbank help consumers buy more expensive products such as cars.

Providing information to the consumer
Facilitating the decision-making process through information provides information value to the potential buyer. Members of the distribution channel help to identify the target market and to communicate information about the product/service to the customer. Motor car magazines such as *Car* and *Drive* carry advertisements placed by manufacturers, and do their own reviews of new models.

Ensuring a uniform quality standard of product
Ensuring that the product sold is of a uniform quality reduces the risk to the consumer. This distribution activity creates value by, for example, giving after-sales service to the consumer in the form of guarantees or warranties. The consumer benefits by having greater peace of mind and less cognitive dissonance about the product purchase. These distribution channel activities can be grouped together into three broad categories, namely, transactional activities, logistical activities and facilitating activities (fig. 7.4).

Basic distribution channels
A basic distribution channel can be described as a set of organisations working together to make the product or service available to the final customer. Once a distribution channel has been developed and implemented it takes on a life of its own as the creation of the channel requires a long-term commitment from the roleplayers. This is why it is so important to select the right intermediaries as the wrong selection could have disastrous consequences for the distribution channel and all the upstream roleplayers. An intermediary is either an organisation such as a

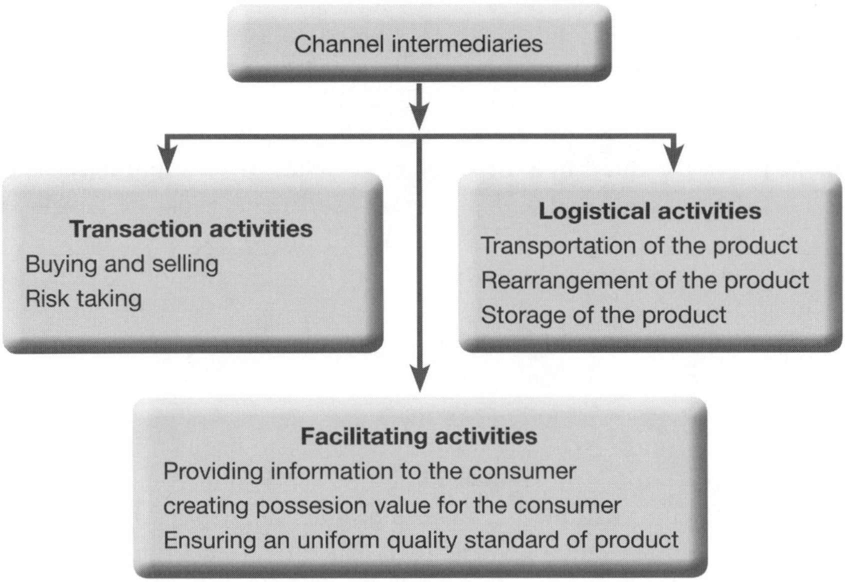

Figure 7.4 *Activities performed in the distribution channel*[4]

wholesaler or retailer or it can be an agent that operates between the manufacturer and the final buyer of a product. They are all members of the basic distribution channel. Intermediaries that form the distribution channel can be divided into two broad categories, namely sales intermediaries and resellers (fig. 7.5).

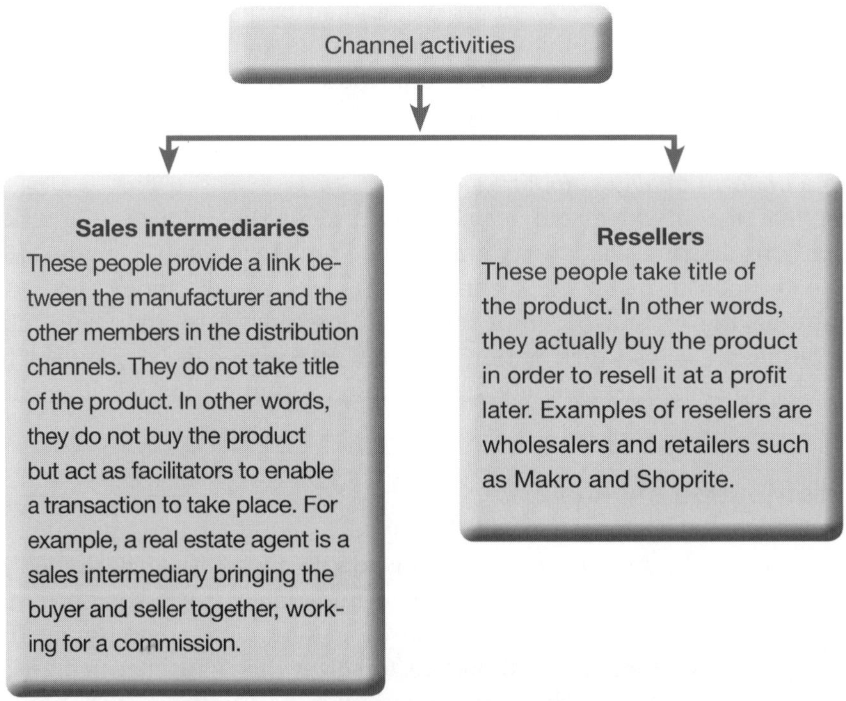

Figure 7.5 *Different types of intermediaries*

A wide range of products and services use distribution channels to distribute their goods. Distribution channels for consumer goods and services are different to those for industrial or business products.

Distribution channels for consumer goods

The different distribution channels used to sell consumer products are shown in fig. 7.6.

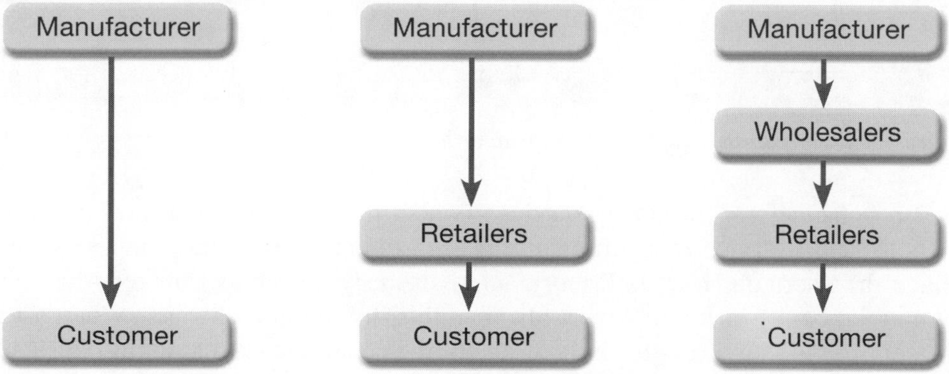

Figure 7.6 *Distribution channels for consumer goods*

The first channel is called the direct channel because the manufacturer or producer sells directly to the final consumer. For example, should you buy directly from a fruit farm stall you may even be allowed to pick your own peaches. In such a case, a direct channel of distribution is used.

The second distribution channel alternative includes a retailer or group of retailers and is widely used in South Africa. The large retailers in South Africa include Pick n Pay and the Shoprite group which have a major share of sales to the final customer.

The third channel includes a wholesaler and a retailer and was, for almost a century, the most widely-used distribution mechanism in South Africa. It remains the most used channel for smaller retailers. Small businesses such as the Spar Group, a voluntary trade association, buy their groceries from WG Brown, a wholesaler which provides most of their products. This enables Spar retailers to compete with large retailing groups such as Pick n Pay. Other examples include the independent retailers like the café on the corner, the rural retailer, and township spaza shops. They buy from wholesalers such as Makro and Metro Cash and Carry, both of which are indirect distribution channels because there is no direct contact between manufacturer and the final customer.

Distribution channels for consumer services

As is the case with consumer goods, consumer services are also distributed using distribution channels (see fig. 7.7). Services range from purely intangible goods such as the consultation provided by a psychologist to a situation where the service is partly intangible, like a doctor's appointment that may involve a tangible product such as an injection and a prescription for medicine.

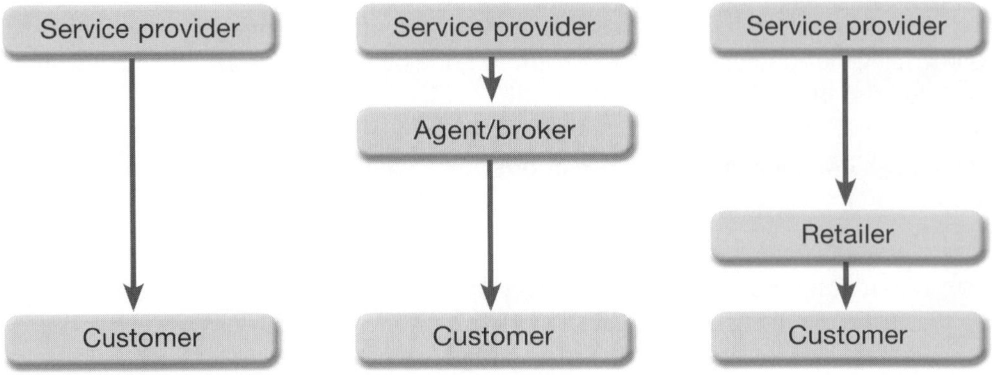

Figure 7.7 *Distribution channels for consumer services*

The first channel for consumer services is also the direct channel and is used by hotels to sell a service (accommodation) on a direct basis to the client. Examples include the Sheraton Hotel in Pretoria and hairdressers such as Hair for Africa. The commercial banks in South Africa also use this distribution channel. When a bank sells services to you through a branch, the branch could be seen as a kind of retailer.

The second channel includes an agent/broker who provides the service to the consumer. Airline and hotel reservations can be obtained through travel agents who provide a service to the client and work on a commission basis. Another example is estate agents in South Africa who obtain 'stock' (the right to sell a house or a flat) and try to match a certain house with a prospective buyer.

The third channel is used where the consumer service is product-related, for example, providing after-sales service on a physical product (for example, a Toyota Land Cruiser). Middelburg Toyota provides the pre-delivery service on the car and the follow-up services.

Distribution channels for industrial products

Industrial/business-to-business (commonly known as B2B) markets use fairly similar distribution channels to consumer products (see fig. 7.8).

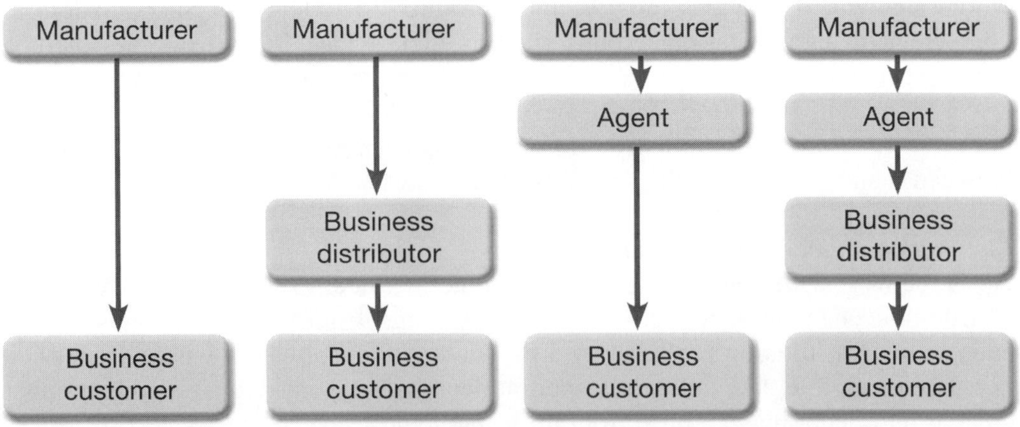

Figure 7.8 *B2B (industrial) distribution channels*

There is also a direct channel where the manufacturer sells directly to the industrial user, for example, Dell, the computer company, which sells directly to the South African government, or to any large company. The second channel is used when a local manufacturer of industrial equipment appoints business (industrial) distributors throughout South Africa. Examples of products sold through this channel include electric water pumps for the mines and for irrigation on farms. The third channel is when the industrial manufacturer is small and does not have the capital to develop its own distribution network. An agent is, therefore, appointed to distribute the product. This agent also provides after-sales service. The last channel is also used by small manufacturers who introduce a product to the market and use the distribution network of an agent to promote the product to the industrial distributor. Another example of this type of distribution channel is the international industrial manufacturer that appoints a local agent to promote the industrial product inside South Africa.

Hybrid channels/multiple channels

Until now the discussion of the development of a distribution channel focused on the selection of the single best distribution channel to distribute the product or service. The reliance on a single channel strategy allows the organisation to focus all their management efforts in building a more homogeneous and coordinated distribution system. What is also of importance is that the organisation limits channel conflict and can provide a better level of customer support.[5]

In a real-life situation we see that a manufacturer may use quite a number of distribution channels to distribute the product or service. To use more than one distribution channel is to use hybrid channels or multiple channels. A hybrid distribution system can be defined as a multi-channel arrangement in which distribution tasks are performed by a combination of different channels.[6] The distribution channels are designed to satisfy the needs of diverse market segments by delivering a variety of product/service offerings.[7] Hybrid channels (also called multiple channels) are developed when a manufacturer or supplier of a consumer product, industrial product or a consumer service uses more than one channel at a time to sell a product.[8] Multiple channels may be a response to shifts in customer shopping behaviour so as to increase market share, the widening horizon of international markets which necessitates the use of additional distribution channels, and the advent of e-commerce (selling over the Internet) as a new, cost-effective distribution alternative.

There are obvious benefits from using hybrid distribution strategies. Firstly it means that the organisation can adapt better to changing customer needs and shopping patterns. Secondly organisations with a wide number of product lines benefit because they carry a range of products that are too broad to be marketed through a single distribution channel. It is unlikely that a single channel type will be optimal for all products in its product range. Finally, the availability of additional channels enables the organisation to focus more precisely on specific niche target markets, thereby improving competitiveness and penetration in the market.

Multiple distribution channels may place conflicting demands on the organisational resources such as capital, personnel, products, and technology. Smaller manufacturers may find it difficult to supply enough personnel and money to ensure the smooth functioning of every distribution channel. This may result in conflicts which may reduce the customer satisfaction levels.

An example of multiple distribution channels
The manufacturer of Panado, a general painkiller, uses more than one channel to distribute the product. The product can be bought in Pick n Pay and it is also distributed through a wholesaler to any retail pharmacy and to Spar. The product can also be directly dispensed by a dispensing doctor.

Vertical marketing systems (VMS)

Until now we have discussed the distribution channels and the intermediaries operating in these channels as individuals operating independently in the system. Obviously working for your own interest could be detrimental towards the smooth functioning of the whole distribution channel. This is why vertical marketing systems were developed. A vertical marketing system can be described as a special kind of distribution channel where the various channel members are working closely together so as to obtain the best operating efficiencies for the whole channel.[9] The optimum degree of co-ordination and control in the VMS is obtained through one of three mechanisms:

1. Ownership of the different levels of the distribution channel.
2. Contractual agreements between channel members.
3. The market power of one or more of the channel members.

Ownership of different levels in a distribution channel implies that a channel member owns the other members of the channel. This is called a corporate VMS which can be useful in a situation where the manufacturer also owns the retailing outlets through which its products are sold. This ties in with another strategic management aspect, namely that of vertical integration. When the manufacturer owns the wholesaler and retailer through which it sells its product, then it is called **forward vertical integration**. The opposite is also true, if the retailers owns the manufacturer and the manufacturer delivers products exclusively for the retailer then it is called **backward vertical integration**.

Contractual agreements between independent members imply that the different levels of intermediaries in the distribution channel work together on a contractual agreement basis to obtain economies of scale. One of the most common examples of a contractual agreement VMS is a franchising agreement. Franchising is a distribution system that enables the franchisor to reach a very wide target market through the efforts of the contracted business. It provides profitable opportunities for small and medium enterprises (SMEs), where the owner (franchisee) is prepared to work under the guidance of a franchisor.

Franchising is a business arrangement whereby a company or individual (the franchisor) grants an independent party (the franchisee) the right to sell the products or services of the business according to guidelines set down by the franchisor. The franchisee uses the company's name, goodwill, products and services, marketing procedures, expertise, systems and support facilities to sell the product or service. In exchange, the franchisee pays the business an up-front fee and ongoing management service fees (or royalties) as set out in the franchise agreement.

Franchising in South Africa

Franchising started in the USA. The first franchise in South Africa started in the mid 1960s with the opening of the first Steers restaurant. The majority of local franchises used ideas developed by South African entrepreneurs during the long period of economic isolation under sanctions. The result is that, unlike in most other countries, most South African franchises are adapted to the demands of local consumers. Petrol stations account for the biggest proportion of franchise turnover in South Africa, followed by fast-food franchises (e.g. Wimpy, McDonald's, Steers and KFC) and retail convenience stores, e.g. Pick n Pay Family Stores.

The three basic types of franchises operating in South Africa are:

- **Manufacturer franchises** in which a manufacturer such as Toyota SA gives the right (licensing agreement) to an independent dealer to sell its range of cars subject to certain conditions.
- **Manufacturer to wholesaler franchise** such as Amalgamated Beverage Industries (ABI) selling Coca-Cola under licence from Coca-Cola in the USA.
- **Service sponsor franchise** where the service enterprise licenses a retailer to provide a specific package such as a delivery system for fast food, e.g. Wimpy, Steers, Nando's and McDonald's.

The market power VMS, also called administered VMS depends on the sheer authority of one of the members and their buying power to ensure co-operation in the distribution channel. The large retailers such as Shoprite and Pick n Pay are examples of the power of administered VMS at work in South Africa. This also ties in with the concept of channel leadership which is discussed below.

Channel conflict

Channel conflict is described as the situation where one intermediary perceives another intermediary that sells the same product as trying to injure or thwart the original intermediary.[10] If we look at multiple channels we see that channel conflict occurs when one channel group sees another channel group as engaging in behaviour that prevents the first group from achieving its objectives (usually sales or market share). Scrutinising this definition, we see that hybrid channel conflict occurs when one distribution group believes that another group is seeking to take away scarce resources such as capital, expertise, etc at its expense. It can therefore be expected that hybrid channel conflict is a common occurrence when organisations make use of multiple channels and resources are limited.[11]

One of the most common reasons for channel conflict is when an intermediary sells a product as a loss leader, that is, sells a product below cost to try to buy market share. When a manufacturer wants to protect the image of the product and the retailer starts discounting the product, the scene is set for channel conflict.

Each of the roleplayers in the distribution channel has a degree of authority and power over other channel members. The more powerful channel members will therefore exert pressure on the less powerful members to conform to their wishes. These powerful channel members are called channel leaders. The authority and power wielded by these powerful members could therefore also provide conflict. There are five sources of power in the distribution channel.[12]

- **Legitimate power** refers to the dominant position of the member in the distribution channel. Through sheer size this channel member can force other members to conform to its wishes. In the past manufacturers had this kind of power, but this situation has been reversed with large retailing groups now being the legitimate powerhouses dominating the distribution channel. Ultimately, the customer should have the most power by virtue of his or her decision regarding which distribution channel member to buy from.
- **Reward power** refers to the ability of a channel member to help other members attain their objectives. The manufacturer, for instance, could reward the retailers selling its products by giving discounts. Customers could be rewarded by giving them a present for buying the specific product.
- **Coercive power** is the opposite of reward power and intends to take positive results away from certain channel members or to inflict punishment on those members. The manufacturer may, for example, slow down deliveries of a certain product to a certain retailer when it has wilfully decided to ignore manufacturer instructions. The retailer could do the same by giving the manufacturers' product poor exposure on the supermarket shelves, thus slowing down sales of the product.
- **Information power** refers to the old adage that knowledge is power. Keeping information away from certain retailers can derail their sales volumes. Information regarding sales potential, market trends and usage rates could be vital for the intermediary. On the other hand, the retailers, being nearer to the customer, could be in a position to prevent important information from flowing back to the manufacturer.
- **Referent power** refers to the personal relationship that develops between members of the distribution channel. Salespeople who interact well on a personal level with retailers may help to push up sales volumes. If the relationship is not good, sales might suffer.

Traditional marketing channels have for decades been dependent on the use of legitimate, reward and coercive power to get the channel moving the necessary products and services from supplier to customer. However, this situation has changed in recent years.

Currently the focus is on developing collaborative distribution channels of supply chains where everyone is working together (a win-win situation) with reward and reference power coming more to the fore as methods of persuasion to get the distribution channel working. This also ties in with the supply chain concepts as discussed at the beginning of this chapter.

Factors determining the design of the distribution channel

Certain characteristics can influence the design of a distribution channel and must be carefully considered by the marketer.[13]

Customer characteristics

The design of a specific channel has as the point of departure the needs and wants of the consumer. In the case of an industrial user, it makes sense to deal directly with the manufacturer, so a short distribution channel is needed. If the target market for a consumer product is widely dispersed, the manufacturer would need help in reaching all the customers, for example, by using national retailers with a footprint all over the country. If small quantities are bought fairly frequently, then a longer channel is needed, probably involving wholesalers and retailers.

Product characteristics

The specific characteristics of the product also play a dominant role in the design of the specific distribution channel:

- **Perishability**. Perishable products, for example flowers, require a distribution channel that is fairly short, perhaps with only one intermediary, whereas non-perishable products could have a longer distribution channel which could include wholesalers and retailers.
- **Bulky products**. Low-value bulky products, such as cement, follow a shorter channel than more expensive products such as jewellery which is a high-value product.
- **Fashion products**. A short channel is used because fashion products are only in demand for a short time. Other clothing follows a much longer distribution channel.
- **Specialised products**. Specialised products, for example Dell computers, move through a short channel which requires aftersales service. Dell is well-known for its approach – customers can order computers with unique specifications over the Internet.
- **Standardised products**. Standardised products follow a longer distribution channel than customised products. Standardised products such as canned food could be sold using a long distribution channel. On the other hand a customised product such as the development of a new beach house will use a short channel of distribution.

Characteristics of the manufacturer

The size of the manufacturer will also have a determining input in the development of the distribution channel. The stronger the manufacturer, the better the chance of selling directly to a large retailer or to the final consumer. Small manufacturers do not have the resources to be able to dictate where and how their products must be sold and so they are totally dependent on intermediaries.

Characteristics of the existing distribution system

The availability and quality of existing intermediaries in the distribution system are also crucial factors in the channel development process. Some intermediaries will not carry an unproven or a new product, others do not want to carry stock at all.

Sometimes the poor quality of existing intermediaries or the lack of intermediaries forces manufacturers to develop their own distribution channel. A good example is the formal agreements between established car manufacturers and their dealers. This creates a barrier for entry to new car manufacturers such as Kia. Kia had to develop a new dealership system throughout the country to sell its cars in South Africa. The same happened when Honda broke off its dealer relationship with Mercedes Benz. The intermediaries on the downstream side of the supply chain are divided into two basic groups, namely wholesalers and retailers.

Different types of wholesalers

Per definition, wholesalers earn more than 50% of their total sales income from other businesses or organisations. Four types of wholesalers can be identified:

- **Cash-and-carry wholesalers**, for example, Makro and Metro, where retailers or private customers buy for cash.
- **Rack-jobbers** who manage shelf space in retail stores, and usually specialise in certain areas, for example, supplying batteries to motor spares shops, where the retailer obtains a certain income (a percentage) from the sale of the product.
- **Truck-jobbers**, who deliver perishable products, for example, vegetables and bread, to retailers.
- **Mail-order wholesalers**, who use the postal service or the telephone for orders and then dispatch these products, usually on a cash or cash-on-delivery (COD) basis.

Different types of retailers

Retailers earn more than 50% of their total sales from the general public for private consumption.

- **General dealers** are found in rural areas such as Lichtenburg (North West) and Tulbagh (Western Cape). They sell a wide and diverse range of products, from bicycles to maize meal, women's dresses to headache tablets.
- **Department stores** are large stores, arranged in definite departments, such as lingerie, perfumes and men's clothing. Examples are Stuttafords and Edgars.
- **Speciality stores** have fewer product lines but a wide variety is carried in each product line. Examples include jewellery stores, such as American Swiss and Sterns, and boutique curry shops in Durban.
- **Chain stores** are similar to speciality stores, although they have several branches operating from various places and controlled by a head office, for example, American Swiss jewellery stores. All chain stores are under the control of the head office.
- **Discount houses** usually sell at a low price markup and achieve a high turnover. Well-known examples are Dion and Game discount stores.
- **Supermarkets** sell mostly food-related products on a self-service basis. Shoprite Checkers supermarkets are examples of this type of retailer.
- **Hypermarkets** are a larger version of a supermarket and sell a larger range of products. They also sell more non-food products such as fridges, sports equipment and hardware. Examples include Checkers Hypers and Pick n Pay Hypermarkets.
- **Spaza shops** are small informal shops that usually operate in townships. They

sell basic foodstuffs in small quantities, such as bread, salt, washing powder, and so on.

- **Convenience stores** include corner cafés selling items such as bread, magazines, milk and sweets during extended shopping hours, for example from 6 am to 9 pm. A more recent development is convenience stores at petrol filling stations, called forecourts, which contribute a sizeable percentage of the total sales and are in direct competition with the original convenience store concept of cafés.
- **Mail-order stores** sell products by mail, using a catalogue and advertisements. Well-known examples include Woolworths Leading Concepts that sells novel products, and Verimark that sells upmarket products, for example, leather briefcases and executive equipment, such as notepads.
- **Internet retailers** sell through a cyber mall. Here a whole range of products is sold through a website rather than a physical store and distribution (delivery of the product) takes place from a warehouse and the final product is delivered by mail or courier. Internet retailers (also called e-tailers) which are currently doing well in South Africa are those that combine an existing bricks-and-mortar store with Internet sales. One example is the e-tailing arm of Pick n Pay (Picknpay.co.za) that combines the successful hypermarket stores concept with selling groceries on the Internet. Kalahari.com is a successful e-tailer which, among other things, sells textbooks to UNISA students.

Managing physical distribution activities (marketing logistics)[14]

Management must make decisions to ensure that their range of products and services are stored and moved in such a way that they are available to the customer in the right quantity, at the right place and at the right time. Marketing logistics therefore involves the process of planning, implementing and controlling the physical flow of products, services and information in such a manner that the customer receives the greatest value and the organisation incurs the lowest cost to do so. Marketing logistics includes both the basic upstream and downstream activities of the supply chain (see figure 7.1), as well as reverse logistics which entails the movement back of broken, unwanted and outdated products and services to the suppliers.

Marketing logistics in practice

An example of a marketing logistics objective would be to deliver 95% of all products of a manufacturer in South Africa within 48 hours, or to prevent out-of-stock situations occurring altogether. This type of objective makes sense if we look at the current inventory management system of just-in-time (JIT) used by motor manufacturers like Toyota, Nissan and others. With this kind of system an out-of-stock situation would mean that hundreds of workers would not be able to assemble cars, with a resulting loss for the manufacturer's workers and the country.

Marketing logistics are receiving more attention nowadays as it is seen as the most obvious place where cost and efficiency savings can be effected for the organisation whilst also being used to improve service to the customer.

The functions of marketing logistics are warehousing, transportation, inventory management and logistics information management.

Warehousing

How many and where precisely warehouses are to be situated is an important issue because the manufacturing and consumption cycles of products and services rarely match. This is why it is so important that the right decisions be made to fulfil the stated objectives of being able to deliver the needed products within a specified time limit. Some large manufacturers based in Gauteng have warehouses in the Western Cape and in the Free State. With these locations or warehouses, they can deliver a service in line with the set objectives of the organisation.

Transportation

The choice of transportation has a direct effect on the pricing of the product or service, the delivery performance and the condition of goods on delivery. The modes of transport include air, road, rail, pipelines and water. Intermodal transport systems combine two or more modes of transport, e.g. imported goods arriving in the country by air and then being transported by road to the customer. The same factors mentioned in fig. 7.3 should be considered when decisions are made about what mode of transport to use. Transnet is a major player in this field with strategic business units like South African Airways, Spoornet (railways) and Portnet (harbours) heavily involved in the transportation of products and services.

Inventory management

There is usually a trade-off between cost, space, risk and required levels of customer satisfaction. The cost of carrying inventory must be balanced with the space necessary for doing so. This must furthermore be balanced with the risk of an out-of-stock situation which could result in lost sales and long-term buyer relationship problems. If, for example, products a customer is looking for are not on the shelves of the supermarket group when he or she needs it, that customer would not be satisfied.

Logistics information management

Information is a critical component of any supply chain. The trend is to share information between members of the supply chain to assist all the members of the distribution channel to play their parts as well as possible. This information includes customer orders, inventory levels, billing for payment, etc. One of the methods for sharing information is electronic data interchange (EDI) on the Internet. Sharing information facilitates the smooth functioning of the supply chain.

Distribution management[15]

Once the organisation has evaluated all the alternatives and decided on the best supply chain, it must implement and manage the chain. Distribution management concentrates on managing the two major distribution activities, namely managing the distribution channel and managing the marketing logistic activities.

Managing the distribution channel

Planning, implementation and control are part of the management of a distribution channel.

Planning

The first step in the planning process is to determine the distribution objectives. The distribution objective is dependent on the organisation's objective and the marketing objectives. An example of a distribution objective is for McCarthy to open to new multi-franchising dealerships in South Africa through which 10 000 units of Peugeot and Citroen cars will be sold by December 2012.

The second step is to decide on the channel to be used. The question is if a single channel will be used or would it be better to use a hybrid channel?

The third step is to determine the number of intermediaries needed. Here the manufacturer must decide on the intensity of distribution. Three alternatives are available, namely:

- **Intensive distribution**. Here the manufacturer uses all the available outlets. Products such as Coca-Cola are distributed on an intensive distribution basis to all types of outlets in South Africa and neighbouring countries.
- **Selective distribution**. Here, fewer outlets are selected. Shopping products such as fridges, furniture and clothing are distributed in this way. For example, Defy washing machines are distributed through Furniture City, Game and various furniture stores throughout South Africa.
- **Exclusive distribution**. Here only one or two selected intermediaries carry the product. Franchises follow this route of distribution, providing a franchisee with exclusive rights to a certain geographical area, for example, KFC.

The fourth step is to select suitable intermediaries. Obviously the best wholesalers or retailers must be selected if they are available. The financial position, quality of management and location of these intermediaries are important to the manufacturer in the selection process.

The fifth step is to motivate the intermediaries. Incentives such as 'push money' are used to make it financially attractive for the intermediary to sell the product. 'Push money' implies giving the retailer and his or her salespeople financial incentives to sell the product.

Implementation

The key issues include solving problems, resolving conflict and controlling the distribution channel.

- **Solving problems**. Problems regarding conflicting objectives, pricing decisions, duties and responsibilities of channel members must be solved to the satisfaction of all participants.
- **Resolving conflict**. Conflict between members of the channel will be to the disadvantage of all members, as well as to the final consumer. Conflict must therefore be avoided and close co-operation should be encouraged.

Controlling the distribution channel

- The channel leader of a distribution channel must control the activities of the whole channel to ensure the satisfaction of the final consumer. The leader in the channel can either be the manufacturer or the retailer. The leader is often referred to as the **channel 'captain'**. A channel leader is the person or member who can control the distribution channel. In the past, manufacturers were usually strong enough, in other words, they had the capital, knowledge and/or infrastructure, to be the channel leader. The manufacturer decided on the distribution structure and the channel members had a well-known brand name to sell and proven guarantees on the product. The balance of power has changed now towards intermediaries, and especially retailers.

The shift in power towards retailers has occurred for the following reasons:

- The major retail groups in South Africa have surpassed the manufacturers in size and scope. An example is the Shoprite Checkers group with its massive turnover and large number of outlets. See also the case study at the end of this chapter.
- The development and growth of retailers' own label products. These own label products are sometimes perceived to be of a higher quality than some of the manufacturers' labels.
- Market information is now in the hands of the intermediaries. Store scanning equipment provides so much information that manufacturers are now dependent on retailers for information regarding the customer.

Summary

This chapter dealt with the supply chain and the distribution decisions that are made in managing distribution channels. Products and services must be made available when, where and in enough quantity to the customers. The physical distribution activities like transport and warehousing are becoming more important for the smooth functioning of the supply chain.

Case study: The use of the supply chain by the Shoprite Group in South Africa[16]

History

The Shoprite Group of Companies started from small beginnings in 1979 with the purchase of a chain of eight Cape-based supermarkets for R1 million. In 1983 the Group opened its first branch outside the Western Cape – in Hartswater in the Northern Cape. At the end of that year, Shoprite opened its 21st outlet in Worcester and celebrated an increase in turnover of almost 600% over the four years of its existence. A year later Shoprite sped up its growth by buying six food stores from Ackermans. In 1986 the Group expanded to the Free State, opening a store in Bloemfontein and was listed on the JSE Securities Exchange South Africa with a market capitalisation of R29 million. It then owned 33 outlets. Two years later Shoprite ventured northwards and opened two stores, the first of which is situated in Polokwane in Limpopo.

In 1990 Shoprite opened in Namibia. Within four years of listing on the JSE, Shoprite increased its outlets four-fold by acquiring Grand Bazaars. In 1991 it grew almost six-fold with the acquisition of the national Checkers chain of supermarkets. Overnight Shoprite trebled in size to a chain of 241 outlets with a staff of 22 600.

With these acquisitions Shoprite gained country-wide representation. Expansion plans for the rest of the continent were put into place and by 1995 the Group was able to open its first store in Central Africa – Shoprite Lusaka in Zambia.

That same year Shoprite increased its distribution substantially by acquiring the central buying organisation then known as Sentra, which acted as a buying group for 550 owner-manager supermarket members. Shoprite thus entered into the franchising field, enabling it to compete in smaller markets where the emphasis is on convenience.

In 1997 Shoprite acquired the ailing OK Bazaars Group from SAB in the now legendary 'R1 deal'. This strategic expansion move added 157 super- and hyper-sized supermarkets and 146 furniture stores to the Group. The Group also invested in a development in Mozambique and opened its first store in Maputo. All the OK stores in Swaziland were converted into Shoprite stores and a year later the same process was followed in Botswana.

In 2000 the group opened its first supermarkets in Zimbabwe and Uganda. A year later in 2001 the first of seven supermarkets opened in Egypt, taking Shoprite into the North African market. The group also started operating in Malawi and Lesotho.

October 2002 saw the acquisition of the French-owned Champion supermarket group in Madagascar in an agreement that enabled Shoprite to take control of five supermarkets now trading under the Shoprite banner, and one distribution centre.

The November 2002 opening of the group's first outlet in Mauritius – the first Shoprite Hyper beyond South African borders – made group history by achieving the highest turnover ever recorded for a single opening day of trade.

Shoprite ended the year 2002 on a high note with the acquisition of Score Supermarkets' Tanzanian operation – three supermarkets and a small distribution centre – which became effective on 31 December of that year.

After listing on the Namibian Stock Exchange towards the end of 2002, the first highlight of the year 2003 was the Company's listing of 2.7 million shares on the Lusaka Stock Exchange at an initial listing price of 4 200 Kwacha per share. The group's main listing remains on the Johannesburg Stock Exchange. In 2004 Shoprite started trading as a wholesale operation in India and franchised its first Shoprite Hyper in that country, in a modern shopping centre in Mumbai.

In 2005 the Shoprite Group acquired both Foodworld, with 13 stores, and Computicket, as well as opening the first Shoprite Liquor Shop. In December of the same year, Shoprite entered Nigeria, the world's fifth largest oil producer by opening a supermarket in a new shopping centre in Lagos. During 2006 the Group divested from Egypt due to ongoing restrictions on retailing. Its seven stores were closed, resulting in a loss of R19.9 million.

In December 2007 Shoprite announced an investment of US$80 million into the Democratic Republic of Congo for the development of two world class supermarkets in the major cities of Lubumbashi and Kinshasa. During 2009 the company acquired Transfarm, a pharmaceutical wholesale company.

In 2010, the Shoprite Group comprises 1 137 corporate and 276 franchise outlets in 17 countries across Africa, bringing the total number of stores in the Group to 1 413.

Shopper profile

The Shoprite Group has a broad customer base which closely mirrors the demographic profile of the country and 60 million customers visit its stores per month. The various store formats within the Group cater for all income groups with the Checkers, Checkers Hyper and House & Home stores focusing on the higher income groups, and Shoprite and OK Furniture, focusing on the broad middle to lower market. The latest format introduced by the Group, Shoprite Usave, focuses on the lower-end of the market.

Positioning

The primary business of the Shoprite Group of Companies is food retailing to consumers of all income levels. Management's goal is to provide all communities in Africa with food and household items in a first-world shopping environment, at the lowest prices. At the same time the Group, inextricably linked to Africa, contributes to the nurturing of stable economies and the social upliftment of its people.

Store formats

In 2010, Shoprite Holdings Ltd comprises the following entities: the Shoprite Checkers supermarket group, which consists of 394 Shoprite supermarkets; 141 Checkers supermarkets; 25 Checkers Hypers; 183 Usave stores; 20 distribution centres supplying group stores with groceries, non-foods and perishable lines; 209 OK Furniture outlets; 15 OK Power Express stores; 47 House & Home stores; and 129 Hungry Lion fast food outlets. Through its OK Franchise Division, the Group procures and distributes stock to 26 OK MiniMark convenience stores; 21 OK Foods supermarkets; 78 OK Grocer stores; 35 Megasave wholesale stores; 32 OK Value stores and 73 Sentra stores and buying partners.

Store formats	Positioning	Target customer	Shopping experience
SHOPRITE	The biggest business unit and the brand used predominantly outside the borders of South Africa, spearheading the Group's growth into new markets.	Middle to lower-income consumers in the living standards measurement 4 to 7.	To provide customers with everyday low prices while offering the lowest prices on basic foods.
Checkers	Acquired in 1991, the major brand after Shoprite. It operates throughout South Africa and in some neighbouring countries. It focuses more strongly on fresh produce and offers a wider range of choice food items to a more affluent clientele.	Repositioned to cater for customers in the upper-income groups and targets living standards measurement 7 to 10.	The shopping destination for time-pressed consumers. It has strongly developed lifestyle departments such as for wine, cheese and meat.
Checkers Hyper	Located in high population density areas, the positioning is very similar to that of the main Checkers brand. Carry a much larger	Target customer is the same as for Checkers: living standards measurement 7 to 10.	These stores offer the customer low prices on a wide range of foods and non-food products in a pleasant environment.

	product range, especially non-foods, and encourage bulk rather than convenience shopping.		
SHOPRITE Usave	A no-frills discounter initially focused on the lower-income consumer but becoming a preferred shopping destination in its own right. The ideal vehicle for the Group's expansion into Africa but also greater penetration on the lower end of the domestic market.	Target customers are: living standards measurement 1 to 5.	A limited range of essential fast-moving products offered in a functional environment at the lowest possible prices.
OK Furniture No Problem	Wide geographic spread of stores, offers a range of furniture, electrical appliances and home entertainment products at discounted prices, for cash or on credit.	Target customers are: living standards measurement 5 to 8.	Essential products offered in a standardised in-store environment on easy payment conditions. Also online, selecting from an extensive catalogue.

House & Home Making Your House a Home	Offers a larger selection of contemporary quality furniture, white goods and home entertainment products for more affluent consumers.	Target customers are: living standards measurement 7 to 10.	Amenable shopping environment with well-displayed products. Customers can also buy online, selecting from an extensive catalogue.
OK Power Express More for you	A new chain of small-format stores located mainly in high-density areas sell a reduced range of white goods and home entertainment products in addition to bedding and carpeting.	Target customers are: living standards measurement 5 to 8.	Offers a pleasing ambience coupled with compact stores and personalised service.
OK FRANCHISE DIVISION	The OK Franchise Group is focused on the smaller, convenience-oriented markets. There are four retail formats – OK Foods, OK Grocer, OK MiniMark and OK Value apart from its wholesale format Megasave.	Satisfying the needs of the community in which it is located.	Conveniently located stores offering timesaving shopping at competitive prices.

The Shoprite supply chain

Shoprite is the largest distributor of fast-moving consumer goods in South Africa. The focus of the Supply Chain Management Division is to ensure that the Group's consumers have uninterrupted access to the products of their choice at the lowest possible prices. To achieve this it actively controls the distribution of products from the time of manufacture to the time when the customer purchases the product. This is done by means of an effective and cost-efficient distribution network that stretches from the supplier via distribution centres to the individual stores.

The Shoprite Group has more than 220 000 m^2 of distribution space, with the largest centres being 50 000 m^2 in Cape Town and 65 000 m^2 in Gauteng. The Group's investment in supply chain-related infrastructure, combined with the learning-curve it has developed by operating some of the continent's most sophisticated centres, provides a distinct competitive advantage to the Shoprite Group. The expansion into Africa has increased the distribution infrastructure and it can now deliver products to some of the most remote areas within 17 countries outside South Africa. Multiple modes of transportation are used, crossing numerous borders. It is also active in the distribution of temperature sensitive goods ranging from fresh fruit and vegetables to perishable and frozen food. These centres can control both the temperature and the humidity levels in order to enhance the quality of products, thereby maintaining the cold chain.

Shoprite distributes product by road, rail, air and sea to all the countries it operates in with each country's language, import regulations and lead-time adding to the complexity of supply. The challenge is to satisfy customer demand even in the most remote locations in Africa. During 2009 Shoprite became the first retailer on the continent to achieve the internationally recognised ISO 9002 certification for its freight forwarding and clearing processes. This ability to trade internationally utilising its in-house infrastructure provides the group with yet one more distinct competitive advantage.

The move away from direct-to-store delivery by vendors towards a centralised distribution model ensured the smooth flow of merchandise to stores, countering the risk of erratic supplier deliveries. The centres also provided the mechanism to stockpile merchandise during a time of rising prices, thereby assisting in maintaining lower prices for longer periods of time. The Group's inventory management team achieved inventory turns and service levels at distribution centres in excess of the industry average which contributed to the group gaining market share by improving on product availability in-store. The Shoprite Group's infrastructure also assists small to medium-sized suppliers to compete more effectively by being able to deliver directly into its distribution centres instead of to individual stores. Small suppliers are able to invest their capital in production where their strength lies, instead of capital-intensive transportation and warehousing infrastructure.

This empowerment option not only increases market participation, it also provides the foundation to enhance the group's competitiveness, while offering the consumer more choice in locally manufactured products.

The sound growth that the Shoprite Group enjoyed saw its own transportation fleet of trucks and trailers expand to more than 860 moving units. The investment in expert-based route planning and scheduling solutions continued to deliver further benefits, adding efficiency in the execution of night deliveries and primary transport. This reduces traffic congestion on the country's roads and at the receiving bays at retail outlets and reduces the carbon footprint and operating costs – making it possible to offer lowest prices on basic food stuffs on a daily basis. This initiative will enable the Group to extend its distribution services to more vendors, managing almost 90% of ambient product flow on a centralised basis. This will add to the existing benefits derived through economies of scale. The development will also accommodate transport facilities and a reclamation centre where international best practices will be used to recycle waste and manage equipment used in the distribution process.

Exercise

1. What type of supply chain activities are described in the case study of the Shoprite Group?
2. What type of distribution activities are described in the case study regarding the Shoprite Group?
3. Is the Shoprite Group using any type of vertical marketing systems? Explain your answer.
4. What type of power is the Shoprite Group exerting on the market in which it operates?
5. Look at the eight store formats that are described in the Shoprite Group case study. Classify each of the formats looking specifically at the retailing classification system discussed in this chapter.
6. Provide examples of marketing logistics employed by the Shoprite Group.
7. Review the section on the intensity of distribution and evaluate the level of intensity being used by the eight store formats of the Shoprite group.

CHAPTER 8

Pricing decisions

Learning outcomes

After studying this chapter you should be able to:

- explain the various steps in the determination of the price of a product or service;
- analyse the factors that will influence the determination of the price of a product or service;
- describe the different pricing objectives that may be used by an organisation;
- explain the relationship between cost, volume and profits;
- describe how break-even analysis is used in price determination;
- describe the three methods that may be used to select approximate price level; and
- write an essay in which the steps followed to determine the price of a real product or service are explained.

Introduction

The price that is determined for the product or service is the only way that the business can generate an income to pay for all the costs incurred in the development and distribution of the product or service. The costs involved in developing new products are prohibitive. It is estimated that to manufacture a new pharmaceutical drug and to obtain permission to market it could cost up to US$500 million and take an average of 12 to 15 years.[1] The price that is paid by the consumer represents the income generated for the business. If the price is set too low, the business will have difficulty surviving and if this situation continues for a long period, the business will go bankrupt.

As far as the consumer is concerned, the price that he or she pays must provide some form of value, i.e. be commensurate with what the product or service can do for him or her. If, for example, the consumer pays R140 000 for a Toyota Yaris, then he/she is buying not only the car but the value that the car can provide, i.e. the utility value of transportation, that is moving you from point A to point B, as well as the image value of being the owner of a new car.

The nature of pricing

Price is not only the amount of money paid to a manufacturer for a product or service. It can also be in the form of payment in kind, e.g. when products are

Definition[2]

Price is the amount of money charged for a product or service. More broadly, price is the sum of the values consumers exchange for the benefits of having or using the product or service of the manufacturer or service provider.

bartered (exchanged). South Africa has overcome the constraints of a lack of foreign exchange by exchanging maize for minerals. A person-to-person barter exchange may be accepting payment for work in the form of cellphone airtime.

Example of pricing terminology in everyday life

- The price you pay for the modules that you enrol for at university or college is called a **tuition fee**.
- The price you pay borrowing money from the bank is called **interest**.
- The price you pay for hiring industrial equipment, such as a portable power generator, is called **rent**.
- The **toll fee** you pay when travelling on the N1 highway to Polokwane is the price of using this road.
- The price you pay for using the services of an attorney or a doctor is called a **fee** or a **retainer.**
- The price of a taxi ride is called a **fare**.
- The price you are paid by a company you work for is often called your **salary**.

The steps in determining the price for a product or service are depicted in fig. 8.1.

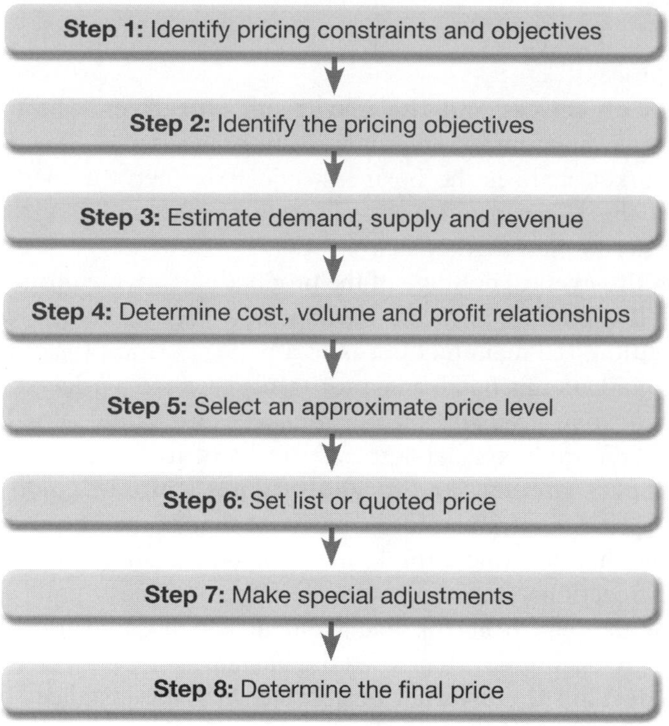

Figure 8.1 *Steps in determining the price of a product or service*

Step 1: Identify pricing constraints

Factors that influence the determination of a price

Various factors or constraints influence the determination of the price of a product or service. These factors can be grouped into two groups, namely organisational (internal) factors and environmental (external) factors.[3] These factors are depicted in fig. 8.2.

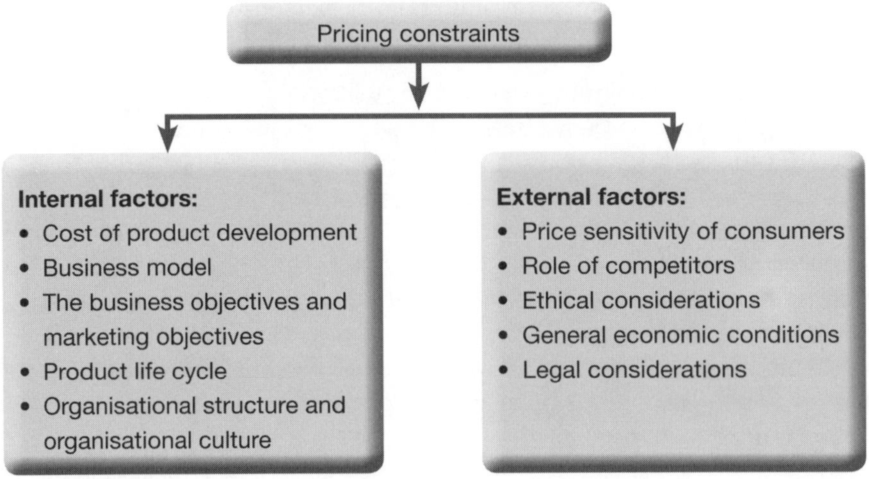

***Figure 8.2** Steps in determining the price of a product or service*

Internal factors

A number of factors inside the organisation have an influence on the price determination process.

- **The business objectives and the marketing objectives**. The overall business objectives must be considered when setting the price. For example, when increasing market share is the business objective, then the marketing objective must support this. The business may decide to start reducing the price of the product in order to gain market share.
- **The product life cycle**. The stage of the product's life cycle influences the setting of the price. If a product is in the introductory stage of its life cycle with little or no competition, the manufacturer is in a better position to set a price that will recover costs and attain a handsome profit (this is called a price-skimming pricing strategy). Innovative products such as a cancer cure could actually demand any price during the introductory and growth stages of its life cycle.
- **Organisational structure and organisational culture** could also have an influence on price determination. A business that is market-oriented takes into consideration what customers think, the competitive situation in the market and the potential reactions from competitors. Other business units in the business would follow the lead from top management which could reflect into different pricing strategies being developed for the business.
- **The cost to develop the product or service**. In some instances tens of millions of Rands may have to be spent to develop a product or service. For example, the

long development process that new medicines must proceed through to eventually be marketed to doctors and pharmacies as mentioned above. This invested capital must be recouped and the price charged would obviously reflect this fact.

- **The business model**. For example, understanding Pick n Pay's business model explains how it is making a profit and keeping itself relevant in a cut-throat market with low profit margins.

Pick n Pay's business model: The slim margin[4]

Definition of terms

- Gross margin = The difference between total revenue and the cost of goods sold, as a percentage of revenue.
- Trading margin = Gross margin, less expenses, as a percentage of revenue.
- Net margin = Profitability after all costs, expenses and taxes have been paid, as a percentage of revenue.

At Pick n Pay:

- Gross margin for 2009 was 18.97%.
- Other income contribution to the gross margin was 0.4%.
- Trading margin: (gross margin less expenses of 15.99%, including labour cost) was 3.38%.
- The net margin after tax: 2.1%.

For the 2009 financial year, Pick n Pay made 2.1 (2.1%) cents profit for every rand spent in its stores. This 2.1 cents was used to pay dividends to shareholders and some was retained for growing the business. This margin is paper-thin and shows that the smallest financial mishap could be disastrous for Pick n Pay. What is interesting is that Pick n Pay and similar retailers generate a hefty part of their profit through prudent cash management. Profit margins for food retailers in South Africa are extremely thin – 4% is seen as extremely good for pure grocery stores. The 2.1% profit that Pick n Pay turns is good for a product mix that also includes white goods and other non-grocery items. The key issue is about the number of customers visiting and buying at Pick n Pay. Also important is the stock turn rate (that is how fast goods are sold), and how the cash generated is managed. Large grocery retailers all over the world operate like banks, in a certain sense. They bank the cash received from customers on a daily basis and receive daily interest until the end of the month when they pay their suppliers. Trade payables exceed trade receivables by a degree and therefore creditor funding is a key part of the Pick n Pay business model.

External factors

Price sensitivity of consumers

Establishing the price for a product or service depends on how price-sensitive the consumer is about that product or service. Consumers who are very knowledgeable about a product are likely to be very price-sensitive. For example, the price of tickets for the 2010 FIFA Soccer World Cup was well-known to soccer supporters and high prices were seen as a contributing factor for slow tickets sales. The more price sensitive the consumer, the less leeway the business has to increase the price for the product or service. The price of the product could be low but the product could be of such importance to the customer that any price increase could spark a national debate. The price of bread is one example.

The demand for arms is not price-sensitive[5]
Even in the worst economic decline in the past few decades the amounts spent on weapons has remained the same or increased slightly. The strong demand for weapons of war means they are relatively price-insensitive.

The role of competitors
The amount of rivalry in the marketplace will obviously influence the price that could be charged for the product or service. The more rivalry between businesses selling the same product or service the more keen the price competition is likely to be. This ties in with the concept of demand and supply which is covered in more detail below. Briefly it must be stated that the final price for a product or service is directly influenced by the demand from the consumer's side, as well as the supply of the product. If there is a strong demand for a product and a limited supply, then the price will probably increase. The opposite is also true. When there is slow demand from the consumer and an oversupply from the manufacturer, the price will probably come down or be fixed at a lower point. However, the responsiveness of prices to demand and supply is distorted under certain market conditions. For example, Eskom has a monopoly to generate and sell electricity in South Africa.

Competition in the marketplace[6]
Economists distinguish between different types of market conditions, namely perfect competition, monopolistic competition, oligopoly and monopoly.

1. **Perfect competition** refers to market conditions where there are many sellers of identical products and no one buyer or seller has control over the determination of the final price. It is furthermore easy to enter the market and resources needed to manufacture the product are freely available.
2. **Monopolistic competition** occurs when there are many manufacturers of a product that are not similar to each other (e.g. additional services and guarantees are added making it difficult for the customer to compare the products from different manufacturers). This is called the product differentiation process. Entry into the market is still easy and there is no collusion between the different suppliers. Prices charged may vary between suppliers.
3. **Oligopoly** is a market structure where there are only a few suppliers of a product that could be identical or differentiated. There could be millions of consumers asking for the product. There is not much price competition in such a market place.
4. **Monopoly** is a market structure where there is only one supplier of a product or service with millions of consumers asking for the product. Prices are usually set quite high making it a very profitable situation for the supplier.

Ethical considerations
Ethics also play an important role. The question here is whether the price should truly reflect the cost of the product and its value for the consumer. During the 2010 Soccer World Cup there were dramatic increases in prices for accommodation and transport. Airlines started selling flight tickets to the highest bidder, raising the prices by up to 400% on a normal domestic ticket during the time that the World Cup was to be hosted in South Africa. Bed and Breakfast operations and lower graded hotels tried to charge up to R1 000 a night for a standard room and metered-taxi drivers were contemplating raising their fares ten-fold for a short distance trip.[7] The attitude of some small businesses was that it is acceptable to charge foreign supporters high prices because the government said the World Cup would be an opportunity for small businesses to make big money. The soccer and tourism authorities were concerned about the greedy and irrational practices and called on businesses to exercise restraint, saying their high prices could scare potential visitors away and undermine international tourism to South Africa in the long run.

General economic conditions
The general economic conditions are a very important constraint, depending on the type of product or service being sold. For example, for some basic commodities such as petrol, the demand was largely insensitive to general economic conditions (although this started to change during the global economic crisis that started in 2009 and continued to have an impact in 2010). The extended period of recession in the 1980s and early 1990s did not dampen the demand for petrol or beer. Luxury goods such as jewellery, diamonds and fur coats are more sensitive to economic fluctuations and the level of disposable income. Some of the smaller jewellery stores in Johannesburg closed down during the recession because of the lack of disposable income among customers. On the manufacturing side, poor economic conditions usually lead to a 'wait-and-see' attitude and a lack of capital investment. A characteristic of such a period of economic decline is the increase in price sensitivity on the part of the consumer. Price becomes a major concern and price wars between retailers are prevalent.

Another economic factor that needs to be considered is the inflation rate. In December 2009, the inflation rate fell within the Reserve Bank's target band of 3 to 6%, which is relatively low by South African standards as 2008 and the first part of 2009 showed drastic increases in the inflation rate. The South African consumer grew accustomed to single-digit inflation figures in the first half of the decade. An extended period of low inflation dampens inflation expectations and results in a more discerning customer who will actually demand more value for money and also better after-sales service. The opposite is also true with higher inflation expectations and less competition as was the case in the period between 1985 and 1990.

Legal considerations
These are an important issue for most people buying certain types of products such as a property or a car. Legislation promulgated by government exerts an influence on the final price you pay for your car, through the car deposit that is

required and the payback period. The banks can charge the consumer a maximum interest rate (previously governed under the Usury Act, and now regulated under the National Credit Act of 2007). Value Added Tax (VAT) is another factor that must be considered in the pricing decision. Some basic foodstuffs such as milk and a standard loaf of bread are exempt from VAT. For other products and services, a 14% VAT rate applies. The price that the customer pays normally includes VAT of 14%.

Step 2: Identify pricing objectives

Three types of pricing objectives can be identified (see fig. 8.3). These objectives are derived from the overall objectives set by the business.

> **Definition**
> A pricing objective is a general goal that describes what a business hopes to achieve through its pricing activities. Pricing objectives should be measurable so that they can be evaluated.

Profit-oriented objectives

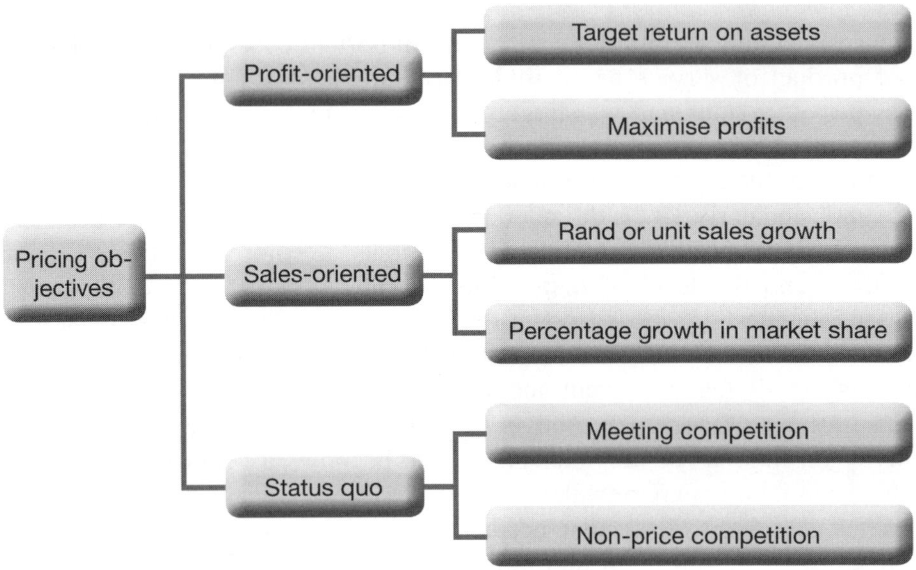

Figure 8.3 *Possible pricing objectives*[8]

A business may also strive to achieve maximum profits. This means that a price is selected that results in the highest profit possible as in the case of an innovative product which is first launched in the market. One such an example is that Volkswagen intends to sell its new small car concept the VW Up for 9 000 Euros in Europe whilst the manufacturing costs in the Indian factory are calculated at 900 Euros, meaning a markup of 1 000%. There are obviously logistical costs involved as well as import taxes, but the net result should still be a hefty profit for VW seeing that they estimate the size of the market for the car to be 1.4 million units.[9]

Return on assets (ROA) explained

Underlying calculation

- Income (e.g. sales, commission, fees, retainer) minus costs (all cost, such as the telephone bill and wages, etc.) = profit.
- Profit minus tax = net profit
- Rate of return on total assets = $\frac{\text{net profit after tax} \times 100}{\text{Total assets}}$

Practical example

The net profit, after a tax deduction of 35% of Bakers, an industrial organisation that manufactures flanges, is R144 000. Total investment in equipment, tools and office furniture is R900 000.

Therefore: ROA = $\frac{\text{R144 000} \times 100}{\text{R90 000}}$ =16%

Bakers should ask itself: is this return good enough to make it worth continuing with this kind of business?

Sales-oriented objectives

Rand sales or units sold is a sales-oriented objective and can be quantified. The same applies to a percentage growth in market share.

Hyundai's aggressive sales objectives[10]

Hyundai is now the world's fourth largest motor manufacturer after overtaking the Ford Motor Company of America as the fastest-growing manufacturer in the world. Its reputation for aggressive sales objectives are both good and bad for this company. It was expected to manufacture 5.2 million cars in 2009 and aimed to increase the sales objective to 6.5 million by the end of 2011. This type of drastic increase has in the past resulted in compromising manufacturing quality and eventually leading to a dilution in the brand equity of this manufacturer.

In 1986 Hyundai entered the US market with a single model, the Excel which sold at $4 995, which was so cheap that 126 000 cars were sold in that year. The following year, sales increased to 264 000. In its haste to increase sales Hyundai made two great errors – it made below-quality cars and sold them to customers with a poor credit record. When the cars were repossessed, the resale value was so poor that they sold for less than the outstanding loan on each car. This impacted negatively on the brand equity of the company for a number of years.

Toyota: Market share as an objective

Toyota South Africa's chief executive Dr Johan van Zyl stated in an interview that he wanted to keep their objectives quite simple. For the 2003 financial year they wanted to grow their market share in the South African automobile market to 25%. This was duly obtained.

Status quo objectives

The question of using status quo pricing is linked to a basic decision that the business must take, regarding whether to compete on price in the market or to follow the route of non-price competition.

Meeting a competitor's prices implies that the business is satisfied with its current market position. The business can decide to meet a competitor's prices, that is, to be a price follower. This is illustrated in the South African motor vehicle market where a price increase by one manufacturer, for example, Toyota, is quickly followed by similar increases in the prices of competing manufacturers such as Nissan, Mazda and Ford. In this example, Toyota is the price leader and the other manufacturers are the price followers.

Another form of status quo pricing occurs when the business in a certain industry follows a strategy of price stability. This implies that there is little difference between the prices of a competitor's products and services. By doing this, price competition is limited and price stability in the market prevails. Cinema tickets in South Africa are priced by following a strategy of price stability. Price competition, on the other hand, degenerates into destructive price wars which adversely affect the long-term profitability of all the competitors. A South African example was the price war in the early 1970s between the 'late' Inter-Continental Breweries, which sold products such as Kronenbrau and Luyt Lager beer, and South African Breweries. Both companies had weaker financial year-end results because of a destructive price war.

Pricing cigarettes in South Africa[11]

During the decade until 2001, cigarette consumption in South Africa had fallen by more than 30% because of the prohibition of advertising and the steep increase in the price of a packet of cigarettes (an increase of about 600%).

Non-price competition is an active strategy followed by a business to add value to its range of products and services. The objective is to differentiate the product or service to such an extent that the consumer is prepared to pay more for the product or service, instead of buying the cheaper competitor's offering. Usually heavy promotional spending is needed to help ensure the differentiation of the product or service in the mind of the consumer. For example, the Apple range of products does not try to compete on price with other computer manufacturers.[12] (See information box on next page.)

Step 3: Estimate demand, supply and revenue

The third step in the process of determining the price of a product or service is to estimate the demand and supply for it. This issue is linked to market research, where information is gathered to ascertain the price range that the customer is prepared to pay for a product or service (demand) and the competitors who are producing similar products (supply). Too many competitors may result in an over-supply and this will cause the price to drop.

Apple follows the route of non-price competition

It is accepted in the marketplace that Apple is a premium brand that demands and earns a price premium against its competitors. This price premium spans the entire Apple product line-up encompassing the Macintosh, iPod, iPhone, software, and accessories. Apple's positioning is aligned with its targeting of a less price-sensitive customer. As a result, Apple's culture and internal activities are focused to meet the needs of these customers, so-called needs-based positioning approach. Apple has thus created a culture and a set of activities to differentiate itself from rivals in order to meet the needs of their target customers (who are niche customers). If Apple were to focus on competing in all customer segments, it would have to reduce product prices. The problem with such an approach is that it would not only dilute the company's premium brand image, but it would also undermine the company's culture of innovation and internal activities focused on being at the forefront of technology. This short-gain approach could eventually destroy the company.

How demand and supply is set

When a customer makes a decision about what to purchase, he or she forms part of the process of how demand for a product or service is determined. The producers of fruit or the manufacturers of a product such as canned food provides (supply) the product to the customer. Supply therefore refers to quantity of a product or service that a business is willing and able to supply. The following example illustrates the point how the demand and supply for a product is recorded.

Thabang Foods is a small company that owns a few farms in North West upon which they grow farm produce. This produce is shipped to the Housewife's Market. After doing research the chief executive of the company developed the following demand and supply schedule for sales of fresh produce (tomatoes) to the Housewife's Market. Thabang Foods has an exclusive supply agreement with Housewife's Market.

Table 8.1 *Supply and demand schedule for tomatoes for the Housewife's Market*

Price per package of tomatoes	Packages demanded by Housewife's Market (×)	Packages supplied by Thabang Foods (*)
R15.00	100	600
R12.50	200	500
R10.00	300	400
R7.50	400	300
R5.00	500	200
R2.50	600	100

The demand and supply schedule can now be depicted graphically in fig. 8.4.

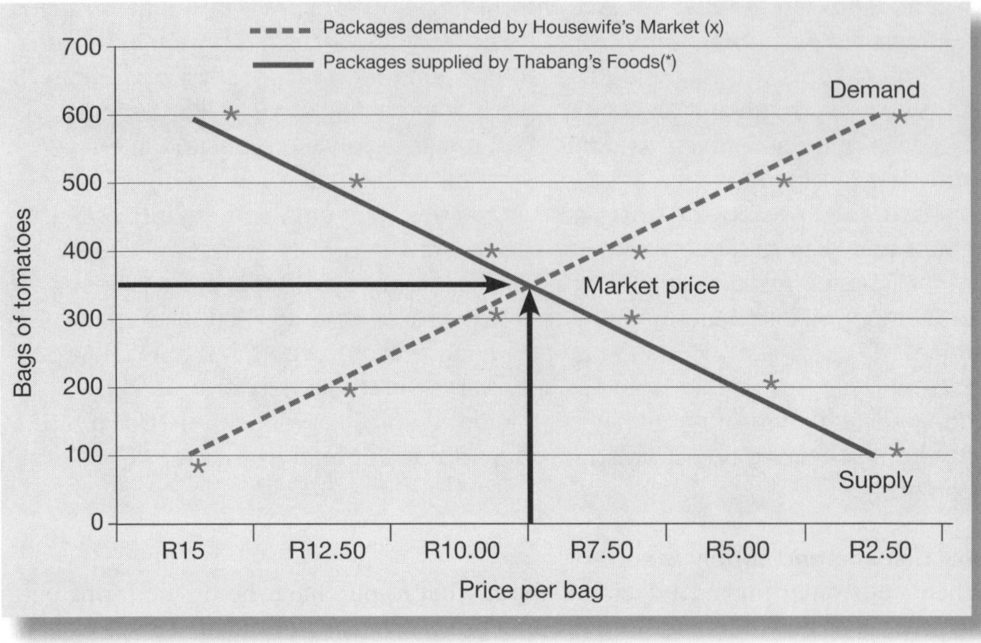

Figure 8.4 *Supply and demand and the price of tomatoes*

At a low price (say R2.50) the Housewife's Market will want to obtain the biggest supply of tomatoes (600), whilst Thabang would like to sell the smallest quantity of its tomatoes (100). As can further be seen from the above figure there is a point where the demand and supply curves meet, that is at a price of R8.75 and a supply of 350 bags. The market price is therefore the point where the supply and demand for a product is equal. In the above example this point is reached at a price of R8.75 and a supply of 350 bags.

What is also important to understand is the price elasticity of demand for products and services by customers. The price elasticity of a customer is defined as the responsiveness to the quantity demanded when the price changes. The responsiveness is determined as a percentage change in the quantity demanded by the customer relative to the change in the price for the product.[13] Businesses must understand how price changes would impact on the demand for the product. Two price concepts must be understood, namely **elastic demand** and **inelastic demand**.

If the demand for a product hardly changes when there is small change in the price it is defined as inelastic demand. If demand changes considerably with the small change in price the demand is elastic. Demand for a product is usually experienced as less elastic under the following circumstances:

1. In a monopoly situation (a single supplier) or where there are no substitutes for the product.
2. When customers do not respond to small price increases on the products and services.
3. When customers are so comfortable with the product they are slow to react to

changes in price by looking for lower priced products elsewhere. Over the short term there might be no change in demand, but this could eventually change over the long term.
4. When the customer acknowledges that a higher price is justified.

For many years a commodity product such as petrol was seen as being subject to inelastic demand. However, things have changed in recent years. At the time when the price increased at a rate of about R1 per litre per month, demand did decline.

By analysing likely supply and demand, a business is able to estimate price levels for its products and services, and therefore project what its total revenue is likely to be.

Step 4: Determine cost, volume and profit relationships

The next step in determining the price of a product or service is to establish the cost, volume and profit relationships. Costs to the business can broadly be classified into two categories, namely fixed costs (FC) and variable costs (VC).

Definitions

- **Fixed costs** are expenses to the business that are stable and do not change according to the quantity of a product or service that is manufactured and sold (within a certain production capacity range). Examples of fixed costs are rent on the building, executive salaries and insurance.
- **Variable costs** are costs that change according to the quantity of products or goods that are produced. Examples of variable costs are the cost of labour, materials and overheads such as electricity.
- **Total costs** (TC) are the total expenses incurred by the business in manufacturing and selling the product. Total costs are the sum of fixed costs and variable costs. The equation is therefore: Total Cost (TC) = FC + VC.

In Step 3 total expected revenue (TR) at different price levels was determined. Now we have also defined the total costs (TC) for the product. The next step is to calculate the profit. The profit of the business can be determined by using the following equation: Profit = TR – TC

Calculating profit and loss for Four Jacks Milling

Four Jacks Milling is a small miller and manufacturer of maize meal in Lichtenburg, North West. The current situation is as follows:

- Probable price per kg = R10.
- Variable costs percent (UVC) per kg = R7.
- Fixed costs (FC) = R1 000 000 (invested in machines and equipment).
- Four Jacks sells 1 000 000 kg of maize meal (Q) per year.

Calculation of the profit of Four Jacks Milling:

Profit = TR (Q x Price) – [FC + (UVC x Q)]
= (1 000 000 x R10) – [R1 000 000 + (R7 x 1 000 000)]
= R10 000 000 – R8 000 000
= R2 000 000

Four Jacks Milling should now decide whether the profit of R2 million per year is acceptable. Should the price per kilogram perhaps be increased or decreased?

Step 5: Select an approximate price level

In this step all the background information regarding demand, supply and break-even point discussed above are now gathered. The business now has a good idea of the actual costs to manufacture and sell a product or service. At this stage, three basic methods of selecting an approximate price level must be considered (fig. 8.5).[14] (See also table 8.2 page 173 for a summary of the unique characteristics of each of these methods.)

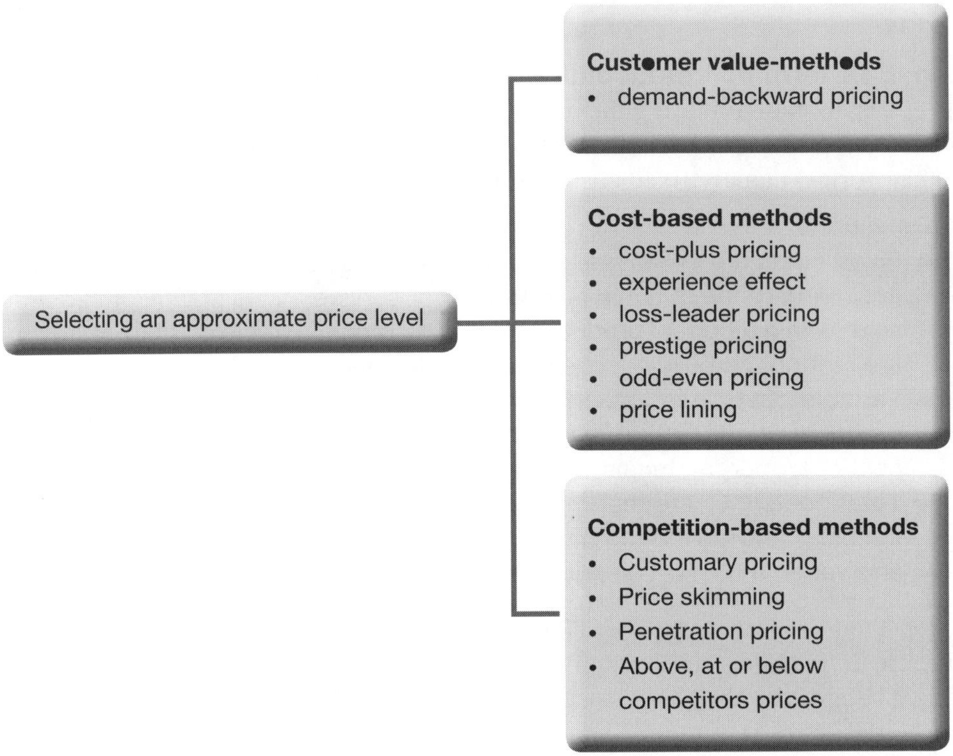

Figure 8.5 *Methods of selecting an approximate price level*

Customer value-based methods

The customer value-based method of pricing implies that the price for a product or service is determined from the customer's viewpoint.

Demand-backward pricing

This is an excellent way of determining the price of a product or service. By doing some market research, the business determines what the final consumer perceived to be the value of the product or service and what he or she is prepared to pay for this product or service. By starting at the final price, the business can now work backwards and determine the mark-up percentages for the intermediaries and determine the cost price for the business. This will provide the business with information to determine if it would be possible to manufacture this product or deliver this service and still make a profit.

However, it is difficult to communicate value to the customer because he or she is subjected to a great number of promotional messages. Three levels of communicating value to a customer may be considered.[15]

- **Communicating product features** is the traditional way of informing the customer of the value of the product, for example the strength of a car engine measured in kilowatts. In most cases the customer does not care very much about these features.
- **Communicating customer value benefits** is a more positive experience for customers because they are interested in hearing about the benefits of the product, e.g. the low road noise of the car in question.
- **Communicating benefits that meet customer needs**. Here the customer is more likely to hear and remember the message because they are strongly interested in having their needs met. The kind of promotional message for a car that may reach the customer in this way is how safe the car is for carrying babies and toddlers.

Cost-based methods

Cost-based pricing methods use the information supplied by the management accounting system of the business to determine the price. This means that, among other things, the fixed and variable components of the product or service must be determined. The following cost-based methods are used in basing the price of a product or service on cost information available:

- **Cost-plus pricing**. This is one of the most popular methods used to determine the price of a product or service. The cost of the product is determined and a set percentage is added to the cost price as the profit margin. If this percentage is too high, the product becomes expensive and may not sell well. The opposite is also true. If the markup is too low, the product or service could be selling at a loss, which could harm the sustainability of the business.
- **The experience effect**. The cost price declines as a business accumulates experience in manufacturing and delivering products. Cost savings can lead to lower prices. The most famous example is that of the Model T Ford which was the first mass-manufactured car in the world. The price of the car dropped by more than 50% in the 20 odd years that it was manufactured.
- **Loss-leader pricing**. This method is used when a product or service is priced at or below cost in order to attract customers. In such a situation, the business hopes that customers will also buy high-margin products and so increase the sales volume and profits of the organisation. This type of pricing is familiar to the average South African consumer. One of the best examples is in the speciality goods market. Promotions gain consumers' attention with messages such as 'Incredible sale' and 'Prices below cost'. Usually three or four products are advertised at really low prices. The less obvious condition is that these products are available in very limited quantities. This is a favourite ploy used when a new store is opened. The objective is to encourage customers to visit the store and to assume that all the products are cheap.

- **Prestige pricing**. Here price is used to indicate the quality or prestige of your product or service. Your business could follow a high-margin high-price strategy if your customers think that a high price indicates high quality. This strategy works quite well in the high-income or high-status segment of the market. For example, if you start a dry-cleaning business, your prices could be higher than those of the rest of your competitors.
- **Odd-even pricing**. This refers to the use of prices that end in odd numbers. A good example is the now traditional R99.99 because it appears to be much less than R100. This type of pricing is extensively applied in South African supermarkets.
- **Price lining**. A limited number of prices are set for a group of merchandise or a certain product line. For example, should you want to buy running shoes, price lines are set at R499; R599; R699; R799 and R999. In each of the price lines, you will find branded running shoes of Nike, Reebok and Adidas.

Consumers often maintain a price-quality association. The higher the price of a product, the better it is perceived to be. Cost savings can be used to pay for extra promotion and consequently a higher demand. This means the marketing manager must consider the cost-based price very carefully. However, the price cannot be allowed to drop below cost for a significant period of time, for obvious reasons.

Competition-based methods

When using competition-based pricing, a business sets prices based on its competitor's prices rather than using information regarding own costs and revenue. The following methods can be used:

- **Price skimming**. This method is normally used when a new, unique product is launched onto the market, such as a treatment for cancer. The pharmaceutical organisation selects a high price to recover the costs of research and development as soon as possible – i.e. skimming the cream of rich profits. The problem with this method is that it could attract new competitors to the market because it is so lucrative. Entry barriers, easily allowing competition, are usually quite low when price skimming is used. Patents can, however, protect organisations for a certain period from direction competition. The fashion house Chanel uses the price skimming strategy. It would rather destroy branded goods than discount them.
- **Penetration pricing**. This is the opposite of price skimming. Here the organisation decides to introduce the product at a low price, which just covers the cost of manufacturing the product. The reason for keeping the price level low is to make it more difficult for competitors to enter the market. We therefore say that the entry barriers are higher because the profit margin is much lower, making it more difficult (less profitable) for a competitor to consider entering the market. The business will have more time to penetrate this market at a time when it is difficult for competitors to enter the market because of the low profit margin.
- **Customary pricing**. Products and services are priced based on tradition and the prices of competitors are also the same. This is usually found with vending machines where snacks and beverages are sold. For example, a cold drink bought at a vending machine will cost R6.00 and all the brands cost the same amount.

Table 8.2 *Alternative approaches to setting the price*[16]

Aspect	Cost-based methods	Competition-based methods	Customer value-based methods
Definition	Cost-based approach determines prices primarily with inputs from the management accounting section	Competition-based pricing uses anticipated or observed price levels of competitors as a primary source for setting prices	Use the value a product or service delivers to an identified segment in the market as the main factor for setting prices
Examples	Cost-plus pricing, mark-up pricing, target-return pricing	Penetration and skim pricing, parallel pricing, umbrella pricing	Demand backward pricing
Main strength	Historical data always available	Data from competitors available	Take the customer in account when setting prices
Main weaknesses	Do not take competition in account Do not take the customer in account	Do not take the customer into account	Research data difficult to get and understand May lead to high prices, need to take long-term profitability into account Customer value is not a well-known aspect but must be promoted to the customer
Overall evaluation	Weakest of the three approaches	Not the ideal option, can work for commodities where the product or service cannot be differentiated	Best approach, linked to the customer needs and will eventually result in improved bottom-line for the business

- **Above, at or below competitors' prices**. With this approach, the business is trying to establish the price level, taking competitors' pricing structures into consideration. To set a **price above the market price** requires justifying the higher price in the customer's mind by means of better after-sales service, better quality or a better location. **Pricing at the market price** suggests that you do not have a competitive advantage over the competitors' products or you want to avoid competing on price. **Pricing below the market price** is a way of increasing sales volumes in the hope that higher sales will compensate for lower margins.

Step 6: Set list or quoted price

After all the factors mentioned in the previous sections have been considered, it is now necessary to determine the list price. In other words, this is the price at which the product or service will be sold to the intermediary or the final consumer.

> **The price of a loaf of bread**
> Expenses make up 40% of the total cost of a bread (this includes production cost of 15%, distribution cost of 15% and administration cost of 7%). The raw materials used to produce a bread cost 60% (this includes flour which constitutes 48% of the cost, additional ingredients such as yeast, salt, etc which costs 8% and packaging costs account for 4%).

Step 7: Make special adjustments

After the list price has been determined, the final fine-tuning or adjustments can be made. These adjustments are described below.

Allowances

To encourage intermediaries such as wholesalers and retailers to perform the functions mentioned earlier in this chapter, various allowances are extended to wholesalers and retailers, as well as the end-users who form part of the distribution channel. One allowance is a trade-in allowance, which is familiar to those who have had contact with vehicle, cellular telephone and industrial machinery businesses in South Africa. Many consumers have had the experience of having traded-in a well-kept car, where the price they receive is far below their expectations. Another form of allowance is a promotional allowance. This kind of allowance is used by the manufacturer to encourage intermediaries to carry and sell more products. The intermediary could also be given a cash allowance for advertising the product in the market in the specific location where it is operating.

Discounts

A common practice in the industrial and consumer product market is to offer a discount. The following types of discounts are used:[17]

- **Quantity discounts**. This is one way of encouraging customers to buy larger volumes. The popular method in South Africa is 'buy one and get one absolutely free' or 'buy two suits and get the cheaper one free'.
- **Cash discounts**. Cash discounts are a straightforward encouragement to the customer to pay cash. This is a method used to improve the cash-flow of the business. For example, the buyer who pays within 14 days may be offered a 5% cash discount.

- **Trade discounts**. These are discounts offered to the intermediaries to promote higher sales or to move slow-selling products.
- **Seasonal discounts**. These are given to retailers to encourage them to stock up on certain items before the season starts. A good example is collapsible Christmas trees that are seasonally discounted in September and October.

The cherry-picking customer[18]

Cherry pickers are defined as those consumers who are extremely price sensitive and visit different retail stores to pick the best-priced items. Research found that these cherry-picking consumers not only save money but that the savings are enough to offset the time it takes to do the extra shopping. There were also a substantial number of shoppers who were intelligent and diligent enough to make cherry picking pay off.

This research has implications for retailers who are the targets of cherry pickers. The message is to not try and prevent cherry pickers from buying from the store and risk alienating customers; instead, try to entice cherry pickers into buying higher margin items. An interesting fact is that cherry pickers visit more stores per day than other customers.

The rationale for cherry picking is explained by the researchers in the following manner: 'When people go cherry picking, two things happen: They double the number of discount opportunities that will be available to them because they go to two stores. And, because stores have deals on more than one item, that expands the opportunities for cherry pickers to save money. But even this in itself would not necessarily make cherry picking worth the effort of driving to more than one store. The second thing, the thing that really makes cherry picking worth it, is that these shoppers buy more items than other shoppers. To make cherry picking pay off, you have to buy a lot of stuff. Cherry pickers understand that they need to increase economies of scale to take advantage of the discounts available. They plan in advance to buy a lot.'

Geographical adjustments

Prices may differ based on geographical distance. In Durban, for example, the price of unleaded petrol is a few cents lower than in the Gauteng area. The price of the same petrol in North West is even higher than in the Gauteng area.

Step 8: Determine the final price

Once the list price has been adjusted to accommodate allowances, discounts and geographical allowances, the final price for the product or service has been determined.

Summary

The four decision-making areas that have influenced marketing decisions have been discussed in isolation. All four marketing instruments must now be combined in a single strategy so that one decision supports and reinforces the others. It would serve no purpose, for example, to decide on a price that potential customers are willing to pay, that covers costs and delivers a handsome profit, if the product is not available in the stores, or if the marketing communication message gives incorrect details. In Chapter 11 the combination of the four marketing instruments into a marketing strategy that must be planned implemented and controlled is discussed.

Case study: The impact of cartels on the price of bread[19]

The Competition Tribunal levied a fine of R195.7 million on Pioneer Foods which was the last remaining member of the bread cartel. The initial four members of this cartel were:

- Tiger Brands which uses the brand name Albany.
- Foodcorp which uses the brand name Sunbake.
- Premier which uses the brand name Blue Ribbon.
- Pioneer which has two brands namely Sasko and Duens.

These four members controlled 60% of the total bread market in South Africa. Premier was the first member of the cartel to ask for leniency. Premier divulged additional information that implicated Tiger, Foodcorp and Pioneer. For this information Premier was exempted from penalties in 2007. Tiger also secured an amnesty and acknowledged its role in the cartel and paid a fine of R98.9 million. In January 2009 Foodcorp followed the same route and paid a fine of R45 million.

Pioneer was therefore the only member prepared to argue the case in court. Pioneer lost the case and was fined the maximum fine, namely 10% of turnover, resulting in a fine of R195.7 million.

The Competition Board's opinion was that this cartel was responsible for higher prices of this staple food, resulting in less consumer freedom of choice and inferior customer service.

In November 2010, the Competition Tribunal accepted a Pioneer Foods offer of R855.7 million to settle all outstanding allegations of collusion and price-fixing against the corporation, meaning that Pioneer paid almost R1 billion in fines.[20]

Exercise

1. Read the section in this chapter on pricing constraints and state the factors that should have played a role in determining the price of bread if the cartel was not in operation.
2. What type of competitive situation was occurring during the time of the bread cartel in South Africa? Consult the section dealing with the role of competitors to answer this question.
3. Explain the cost-volume and profit relationship for the bread market under the cartel set-up.
4. Was there any effect on the demand and supply situation in the market during the period discussed above? Explain your answer.
5. Did the manufacturers of bread embark on a strategy to ensure price stability in the market?

CHAPTER 9

Marketing communication decisions

Learning outcomes

After studying this chapter you should be able to:

- show how integrated marketing communication (IMC) can help develop the optimal marketing communication mix for the organisation;
- explain the steps in the integrated marketing communication campaign;
- advise on the budgeting techniques that must be used in this process;
- design an advertising campaign;
- explain the role and types of direct marketing;
- describe the personal selling process;
- explain the types of sales promotions; and
- describe public relations and publicity.

Introduction

We live in a society where communication is of the utmost importance and where dramatic changes are occurring in communications technology. In our daily life we see the influence of the communication revolution – we have cell phones, the Internet and television which connect us to the world. This communication equipment links us with the global village where something is happening every minute of the day. A war in the Middle East, famine in Africa and World Cup Soccer at stadiums all over South Africa can be seen in our living rooms and we can share in the tragedies and triumphs of the world. The business world also communicates with its external markets – which in most cases is the ordinary consumer. This is called its promotion or marketing communication and can be defined as the communication by marketers that informs, persuades, and reminds potential buyers of a product or service in order to positively influence their opinion and to get them to respond.[1]

Let's take a closer look at the key words of this definition.

- Marketers must **inform** the potential customer about the availability of the product or service. Most of us have viewed with interest the promotional material used to promote the use of the DVD 'home theatre' system that replaced the old video player. This promotional material that is presented can be seen as effort by the manufacturers to inform us (the potential target market) about the advantages of this technology and also to tell us where the product can be bought. To illustrate the point about informing the customer an example is the launch of the

Virgin Money credit card in South Africa where, inter alia, television and printed advertisements were used.

- **Persuasion** is a vital component of most marketing communication with the customer or target markets. Even the most basic advertisement for the Virgin Money credit card was an elaborate cover page in the *Sunday Times Lifestyle Supplement* with a message that basically said, 'Why are you still paying your bank for the privilege of using a credit card?' and the solution: 'Now get your Virgin Money Credit Card for free'. This initial campaign did so well that the website www.virginmoney.co.za was blocked for new subscribers for a time.
- Customers tend to forget marketing communication messages. This is why marketers must **remind** potential customers about their products and services. Do you remember the last Berocca advertisement? Berocca, a Vitamin-B Complex product, was advertised with the following message: 'Be ready, be sharp, be somebody – Berocca.' The advertisement has had different role players, one of the most memorable being the 'businessman cum athlete staying ahead of a train' shown on TV to remind customers to continue buying and using Berocca.

Integrated marketing communication

In order to develop the optimal marketing communication message to the organisation's customers, the organisation must optimise the various communication instruments at its disposal. To this end, it is important to obtain integrated marketing communication (IMC). Integrated marketing communications can be described as the process of planning marketing communications, which acknowledges the importance of a comprehensive plan that evaluates the strategic use of the variety of communication disciplines. For our purposes, these disciplines include: advertising, direct marketing, personal selling, sales promotion, public relations and publicity. These disciplines are combined to obtain clarity, consistency and maximum communications impact.[2] The IMC process, depicted in fig. 9.1, is necessary to obtain synergy in the effort to communicate with the customer.

Review the marketing plan and objectives

The marketing plan will give an indication as to where the company has been, its current market position, where it intends to go and how it plans to get there. This information is vital for developing an integrated marketing communication programme.

As can be seen in fig. 9.1, the whole IMC process starts with the review of the marketing plan and objectives. To illustrate the point, we can use the Virgin Money credit card example again. At the launch of this product in July 2006, Virgin said it wanted to have 150 000 customers using their credit cards by the end of 2006.

Setting of marketing communication objectives

The marketing communication objectives should support the marketing objectives set above. They should be clear, specific and achievable. Objectives could be aimed at inter alia, creating awareness of a product, building positive images of products in people's minds or at keeping customers.

Figure 9.1 *The IMC process*

The marketing communication objectives of Virgin Money were to persuade the target audience to change its behaviour and to subscribe to this new credit card. The marketing communication objectives could be formulated as 'To increase the preference for the Virgin Credit Card as preferred credit card of LSM groups 7 to 10 (age groups 25 to 40 and earning above R120 000 per year)'.

Identify the target audience

In order to design an effective marketing communication campaign, the marketer should have a definite target audience in mind. The target market selected will influence decisions regarding what will be said in the marketing communication elements, how it will be said, when it will be said, where it will be said and who will say it.[3]

Determine the marketing communications budget

The budget to attain the set objectives is a very important part of the IMC process. There are two basic sets of budgeting techniques that can be used, the one is judgement-based and the other is data-driven. Table 9.1 summarises these two categories of budgeting.

The judgement-based techniques include the following:

- The **percentage-of-sales** method is one of the easiest to use. It is based on a certain fixed percentage of sales of the previous year. The argument is that communication is a cost and should be directly related to the turnover/sales of the business for the previous period.

Table 9.1 Different types of IMC budgeting techniques[4]

Judgement-based techniques	Data-driven techniques
1. Percentage-of-sales method	1. Objective-and-task method
2. Units-sold method	2. Competitive-parity method
3. All-that-we-can-afford method	3. Experimentation-and-testing method
4. Arbitrary allocation	4. Modelling-and-simulation method

- The **units-sold** method uses experience and historical figures to determine the amount of communication money that is needed to sell one unit of product. For instance, if you have sold 1 000 units of the product the previous year and you spent R10 000 on promoting the product, you can deduce that an average of R10 is spent on promoting and selling one unit. Therefore, should you want to sell 20 000 units in the current year, you would need to spend R200 000 on marketing communications.
- The **all-that-we-can-afford** method is used by top management which decides what the organisation can afford to spend on promotion per year. This is based upon historical figures.
- **Arbitrary allocation** is similar to the all-we-can-afford method in that top management decides, without any information, or without any reason why, an amount is budgeted for.

The data-driven budget techniques include the following:

- The **objective-and-task** method starts with the communication objectives. If the objective is to increase sales by 10% in the 65+ year old category of people living in homes for the elderly, then you must ascertain what communication media will get you exposure to this group of people. It could be that personal selling is the best communication method, which means that the organisation must employ a sales force of 10 people, which will cost you an average of R200 000 per salesperson per year. This means that your communication budget would be R2 million for the year.
- The **competitive-parity** method uses data obtained from sources about what the competition is spending on promotion and the organisation then follows with the same budgeted amount.
- The **experimentation-and-testing** method is where the organisation experiments in the market and monitors the results. If, for instance, the company spends R500 000 and gets sales of 1 000 units, they know that they must spend more in the next period to increase sales.
- The **modelling-and-simulation** method uses sophisticated computer programming to predict 'what-if' scenarios. This kind of method is used by larger organisations in South Africa.

Select the marketing communication elements

The company must distribute the marketing communication budget among the marketing communication elements chosen. The elements which the company can use for its promotion are advertising, sales promotion, direct marketing, personal selling and publicity/public relations.

Companies can choose one of two marketing communication mix strategies – a **push** strategy or a **pull** strategy.[5] These two strategies are illustrated in fig. 9.2. With a push strategy the product is pushed through the distribution channel to final consumers. The manufacturer directs its marketing activities at channel members to induce them to carry the product and to promote it to final consumers. When using a pull strategy the manufacturer directs its marketing activities at final consumers to convince them to purchase the product. If the strategy is effective, consumers will demand the product from distribution channel members and they will demand it from the manufacturers. Consumer demand will therefore 'pull' the product through the channel.

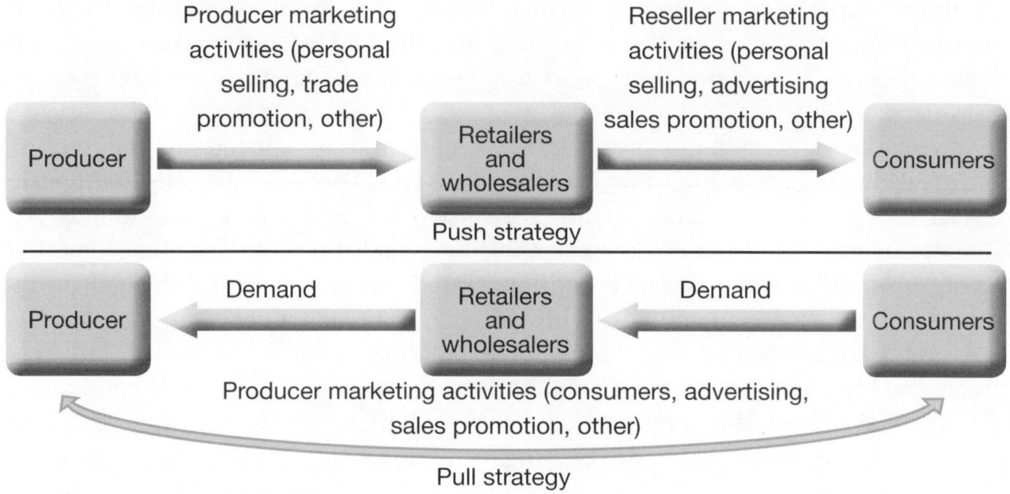

Figure 9.2 *Push and pull strategies*[6]

The particular marketing communication mix chosen by a company depends on a number of factors.

Nature of the product

Personal selling is used more than the other marketing communication elements for industrial products because salespeople must explain and demonstrate the operation of products and answer the questions of the customers. Because consumer products are not custom-made, they do not require the selling efforts of a salesperson and advertising is thus used mainly for consumer products to create brand familiarity. Personal selling is generally used more for expensive products and products which involve more perceived risk.

Product life-cycle stage

Marketers also have to consider the product's life-cycle stage when deciding on the marketing communication mix. In the introduction stage, advertising and public relations are used for making consumers aware of the product, while sales promotion is used to convince consumers to try the product. Personal selling is used to induce the trade to carry the product. In the growth stage, advertising and public relations should still be used, but sales can be reduced because fewer incentives are needed. During the maturity stage sales promotion becomes more important than advertising, since consumers already know the brand and need only be reminded about it through advertising. During the decline stage of the product life cycle, advertising should be reduced, but personal selling and sales promotion can be continued at retail level.

The target market

Companies marketing to household consumers should use different marketing communication methods to those marketing to organisational consumers. Where household consumers are concerned, advertising is more important since these consumers do not go through a formal buying process, it is relatively easy to identify the decision maker for a product and because of the self-service nature of the products. Personal selling plays a larger role when selling to organisational customers.[7]

The marketing communication elements chosen also depend on the type of consumer buying decision. For routine decisions, such as buying toothpaste, advertising and sales promotion are used to draw attention to the brand (e.g. Colgate) or to remind the consumer about the brand. For complex decisions, like buying a motor vehicle, personal selling is used, since consumers depend on the salesperson to provide them with information and to reach a decision.

A target audience with widely scattered potential consumers, highly informed buyers and brand loyal customers requires more advertising and sales promotion and less personal selling. When products are sold in markets where potential customers are difficult to locate, print advertising can be used to reach them. Potential customers can be invited to call for more information, and salespeople are then sent to visit them.[8]

Budget factors

The money available for marketing communication will obviously greatly determine the marketing communication elements selected for a campaign. A company that is not strong financially will have to concentrate only on certain marketing communication elements, for example free publicity. Television advertising is very expensive and will therefore not be an option for a smaller company.

Implement the marketing communication campaign

The specifics of the campaign now have to be spelt out, such as the media to use, the expenditure and time schedules. All these specifics must then be assigned to specific people who will take responsibility for the different tasks, for example an advertising agency or a public relations consultant. The campaign can then be implemented.

Monitoring, evaluation and control

In the final stage of the integrated marketing communication process, it is essential to establish how well the campaign is meeting the marketing communication objectives and helping the company to accomplish its overall marketing objectives. It is important to not only determine how well the campaign is doing, but to also determine why it is doing well or not well. The reasons for the results are important in order to be able to take corrective steps.

In the following sections we will look at the different marketing communication elements.

Advertising

Advertising is the most visible part of marketing communication and is seen as the communication instrument which can deliver the communication message to the largest number of customers (i.e. a mass communication method).

Advertising can be defined as the non-personal presentation and promotion of ideas, products and services by a sponsor that can be identified and who has paid for this communication. Looking at this definition, we see the following key characteristics of advertising:

1. **Non-personal presentation** implies that advertising is not one-on-one, personal communication. It is a mass-media communication method. Examples of mass-media communication can be seen on television and in newspapers and heard on the radio.
2. The second key aspect that is mentioned is the **promotion of ideas, services and products**. Advertising can be used to promote more than just physical products. It can, for example, be used to promote the buying of South African products, e.g. the Buy South Africa Campaign. Advertising can also be used, for example, to promote the services of a dry cleaner in the local newspaper or to promote the sale of KWV wines on television.
3. The third aspect is **the identifiable sponsor**. Advertising is tied to a person or organisation that is sponsoring the advertisement. In most cases this makes sense. Why would you advertise without telling the customer where he or she can buy the product?
4. The last aspect of the definition is **payment**. There is always a sponsor who is prepared to pay money to promote a product or service.

Types of advertising

There are different types of advertising that can be used by a company. **Product advertising** promotes the benefits of a specific branded product or service. Every time we see a television advertisement promoting the Nissan Hardbody Bakkie or the 2010 Soccer World Cup, we see product advertising in action. The product or service's stage in the life cycle will influence the specific type of product or service advertising that will be used. We know that traditionally a product or service moves through four phases in the life cycle, namely the introductory, the growth, the maturity and the decline phase. For each phase a different form of advertising can be used, for example in the introduction phase – pioneering advertising, in the growth phase – competitive advertising and in the maturity phase – comparative advertising.

- **Pioneer advertising** is used to promote the use of a new product or service. When cell phones were first introduced in South Africa, this form of advertising was used to promote the use of this product and the services related to it.
- **Competitive advertising** is used when the product or service enters the growth phase in its life cycle and competitors enter the market. When the organisation realises that there is now a threat to its product, it starts building demand for its own brand.The main objective is to get brand recall for the brand, e.g. Kia Picanto cars, not just cars in general. Look at the Virgin Mobile cell phone advertisement below, which is a good example of competitive advertising. Virgin was a late entrant in the cell-phone market and has to compete for subscriptions against established competitors such as Vodacom, MTN and Cell C.

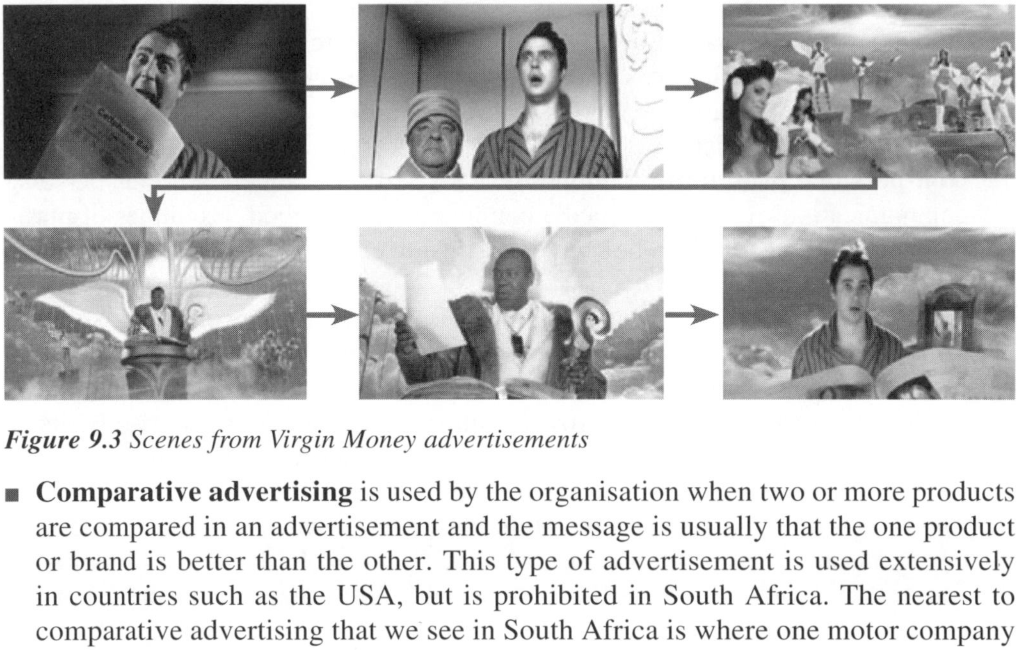

Figure 9.3 *Scenes from Virgin Money advertisements*

- **Comparative advertising** is used by the organisation when two or more products are compared in an advertisement and the message is usually that the one product or brand is better than the other. This type of advertisement is used extensively in countries such as the USA, but is prohibited in South Africa. The nearest to comparative advertising that we see in South Africa is where one motor company will compare its product with its major counterparts. The brand names of the two competitors are not spelt out but the audience can draw their own conclusions as to which competitors are being referred to. Factors such as price, engine capacity and added features such as assisted braking, airbags, etc. are compared in the advertisement.
- One other form of advertising also used in the maturity phase of the product is **reminder advertisin**g. This type of advertising is used on a regular basis by the organisation to remind the customer that the product is still available. One of the best examples of reminder advertising is the Cremora advertisement that was flighted for several years with the same message: 'Cremora – it's not inside, it's on top'.
- **Institutional advertising** is used to promote an idea or the corporation as a whole. When the South African Blood Transfusion Service urges people to donate blood

it is seen as institutional advertising. It is promoting the idea that people must donate blood because of the decline in reserves during the holiday season. Another form of institutional advertising is where the corporation advertises to enhance their corporate image. The Pick n Pay group of supermarkets did this after it had a poisoned goods scare some years ago. This was done to thank the customers who had stayed loyal to them and to promote the overall image of Pick n Pay.

Steps in the advertising campaign

There are nine steps that must be followed in the management of an advertising campaign. Fig. 9.4 provides a schematic presentation of the management of the advertising campaign.

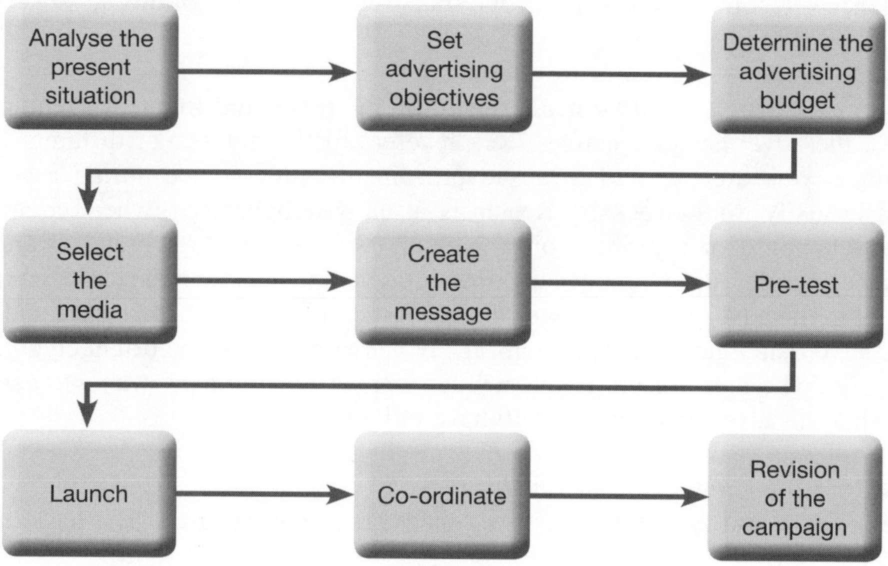

***Figure 9.4** Managing an advertising campaign*

Analyse the present situation

Analysing the situation in which the organisation operates forms part of the environmental scanning process that must be done continously. In this analysis, the broad market environment must be scanned and specific attention must be focused on competitors. What is of real importance is to understand who the customers are that use the product, their preferences, reasons for buying or for not buying the product, etc. Competitors must also be scrutinised. The organisation must examine their products and services and their advertising campaigns. The organisation's products or services must also be investigated to see where the weaknesses are and to identify the competitive advantage(s).

Set the advertising objectives

An advertising objective must have a specific communication task, that is, it must be aimed at a specific target market for a specific time period. The advertising objective may be to increase awareness of the organisation's product from the present 10% to 20% by the end of the financial year. This could mean a situation where a product is currently unknown, and success could be one in five people in the designated target market knowing about the product.

Set the advertising budget

As mentioned above, various methods may be used to determine the amount of money that will be spent on the advertising campaign. A variety of budgeting methods are described above.

Select the media

In order to select the advertising media, four steps should be followed.[9]

1. Decide on the reach, frequency and impact

Decisions must first of all be made regarding the reach and frequency required to achieve the advertising objectives. Reach refers to the number of different target consumers who are exposed to an advertisement at least once during a specific period, usually four weeks.[10] Reach is usually emphasised when companies are introducing a new product or when they want to increase brand awareness. Frequency is a measure of how many times the average person in the target market is exposed to the advertising message. Impact is the impression made on the audience by the advertising message. High impact can be reached by using bright colours and large sizes. The more reach, frequency and impact the company wants to achieve, the higher the advertising budget will have to be.

2. Choose among the major media types

There are different types of advertising media that may be used. The basic media alternatives are:

- **Printed media**. Examples of printed media are newspapers, magazines and billboards.
- **Audio-visual media**. An example of this is television which is used by a number of large organisations. Radio and cinema are other examples of this type of media and are usually used by small and medium-sized organisations. Radio is used specifically by small and medium organisations where the regional stations provide enough focus to reach its potential audience. Another example of audio-visual media is the Internet which has a more limited market reach because fewer people can access it.

The advantages and disadvantages of the major media types are indicated in table 9.2. The type of media which the target market prefers, the nature of the product, the cost of the medium and the type of message will greatly determine the media chosen.

Table 9.2 Advantages and disadvantages of different types of media[11]

Media	Advantages	Disadvantages
Television	Mass coverage High reach Impact of sight, sound, motion High prestige Low cost per exposure Attention getting Favourable image	Low selectivity Short message life High absolute cost High production costs Clutter
Radio	Local coverage Low cost High frequency Flexible Low production costs Well-segmented audience	Audio only Clutter Low attention getting Fleeting message
Magazines	Segmentation potential Quality reproduction High information content Longevity Multiple readers	Long lead time for ad placement Visuals only Lack of flexibility
Newspapers	High coverage Low cost Short lead time for placing ads Ads can be placed in interest sections Timely/current Reader controls exposure Can be used for coupons	Short life Clutter Low attention-getting capabilities Poor reproduction quality Selective reader exposure
Outdoor	Location specific High repetition Easily noticed	Short exposure time requires short ad Local restrictions
Internet and interactive media	User selects product information User attention and involvement Interactive relationship Direct selling potential Flexible message platform	Crowded access Technology limitations Few valid measurement techniques Limited reach

3. Select specific media vehicles

Once the major media type has been chosen the advertiser must choose specific media within each general media type, for example, a specific radio programme, television show or magazine. If, for example, a clothing company has chosen women's magazines as a medium for their advertisement, they must choose a specific magazine, such as *Fair Lady* or *Femina*. Companies should determine the cost per thousand persons reached by the different vehicles and select those with the lower cost per thousand for reaching the target market.

4. Decide on media scheduling

The next step is for advertisers to draw up a media schedule. A media schedule indicates the medium to be used (e.g. magazine or television), the specific vehicle chosen (e.g. *Car* magazine or *Carte Blanche* television show), and the dates on which the advertisements will appear in these vehicles. The following different types of media schedules can be drawn up.[12]

- **Continuous media schedule**, where the advertisement runs steadily throughout the advertising period. This usually applies to reminder advertising, for example advertisements for Coca-Cola.
- **Flighted media schedule**, where the advertiser must schedule the advertisements heavily every other month or every two weeks to achieve more impact with an increased frequency and reach at those times.
- **Pulsing media schedule**, which combines the continuous and flighted media schedules. Here advertising is heavier during the best sales periods. For instance, Waltons might advertise their stationery right throughout the year, but advertise more heavily during the holidays, just before school starts again.
- **Seasonal media schedule**, where products are advertised only during certain seasons. Nivea sun screens are for instance advertised during the summer.

Create the message

Different approaches are used by advertisers to create a message which will relate to the target market and be memorable enough to overcome the many barriers that consumers nowadays employ to screen out advertising messages. Some of these approaches are:

- **Rational approach**. This approach uses facts so that the consumer can obtain an objective and factual account of what the product or service can do for them. An advertisement for the Toyota Fortuner in which it is stated that this specific model is an investment and that the resale value is guaranteed to be the same after a three year period, is an example of a rational approach.
- **Emotional approach**. A mood is created for an emotional appeal, such as a romantic setting with candlelight and roses for a jewellery advertisement.
- **Humorous approach**. This type of approach is a favourite of many advertisers. 'Red Bull gives you wings' is an example of a humorous approach. Another organisation that follows this approach is kulula.com, the no-frills airline. Their pay-off line is, 'Now anyone can fly'.

- **Fear-inducing approach**. This approach is used to show customers what the negative effects are of using certain products. The Road Safety campaign used scare-tactics to drive home the message that you must not drink-and-drive, that you must take rest-breaks and be careful to avoid pedestrians on South African roads. Another example of the fear-inducing approach is the anti-smoking campaign where advertisements are used which show the negative effects of smoking.
- **A slice-of-life approach**. This type of advertisement makes an appeal to which everybody in the same situation can relate. The advertisement where the little girl helps her mom prepare dinner, but the dinner lands up a complete mess on the floor is a good example here. Her mom then saves the day by buying Kentucky and saying that she bought the food because she needed the night off.
- **A fantasy approach**. This approach uses extreme exaggeration. Story-book characters, people from outer space and monsters are used to create a fantasy approach. The advertisement draws attention, but sometimes falls outside the background of the receiver. It can thus be interpreted incorrectly. The Mr Muscle advertisement in fig. 9.5 is a good example:

Figure 9.5 *Mr Muscle – a fictional hero*

- **Testimonial approach**. An important personality is used to deliver the message. An ordinary person can be used at a lower cost, as long as the receiver perceives this person to be an expert on a specific topic. An example of such an expert could be a doctor who testifies about the positive results of a well-known headache tablet.
- **Slogans and jingles** are unique approaches with high impact. The word 'slogan' means 'battle cry'. A slogan sums up the approach in a single sentence, giving the reason why a product is better than its competitors. Successful and innovative slogans become common knowledge. If possible, the name of the product or service must be part of the slogan. A slogan is often set to music, resulting in a jingle which will allow potential customers to sing along. Well-known examples are 'Everything keeps going right, Toyota' and 'Them Stones, them Stones, them Firestones'.

Pre-test the advertising campaign

In most cases, advertisements must be pre-tested to determine if the message is clearly understood and will result in getting the anticipated results. A panel of potential customers is selected and their reaction toward the advertisement is evaluated.

Different types of pre-tests can be used.[13] In a portfolio test, participants are given a portfolio which contains the advertisement and other advertisements. They are then asked questions such as whether the advertisement was informative, or whether it was memorable. A jury test can also be used where a panel of consumers view the advertisements and they then rate it according to how attractive and informative it was and how successfully it caught their attention. Sometimes major problems regarding cultural interpretation can be circumvented in the pre-testing stage.

Launch the advertising campaign

The advertising campaign is planned with a certain due date in mind. If a new product is launched, close co-ordination between the manufacturing and marketing sections are needed to ensure that the organisation can fulfil the demand created by the advertising campaign.

Co-ordinate the advertising campaign

The advertising campaign must be co-ordinated via an internal marketing campaign so that all the employees are aware of what the message states and what is expected of them.

Review the campaign

The problem with advertisements is that it is difficult to ascertain if the advertising campaign reached the stated objectives. Questions such as: 'Did we get 10% more people buying the product?' must be answered. Usually marketing research needs to be done to ascertain if the stated objectives were reached.

The following types of post tests can be used:[14]

- **Aided recall**. Consumers are shown an advertisement and then asked certain questions, for example 'Where have you seen it in the past?' and 'Was it something you read, heard or saw?'
- **Unaided recall**. Consumers are asked what advertisements they saw recently, for example 'What is the most outstanding television advertisement you have seen in the last month?'
- **Attitude tests**. These tests measure how effective an advertisement is in creating favourable attitudes towards a product, service or company. Consumers can be asked to rate a company and its products and services relative to competitors.
- **Inquiry tests**. These tests determine how an advertisement affects consumers' buying behaviour. Coupons, samples or a telephone number to phone to get free information are included in the advertisement and the number of enquiries that result is used to determine the effectiveness of the advertisement.
- **Sales tests**. These tests are done to determine how the advertisement has influenced sales. Marketers can for instance compare the sales reached with the old advertising campaign with the sales reached with the new advertising campaign.

The results of the post-test can be used to revise the advertising campaign. If for instance the tests show that the advertising message was misunderstood by a large percentage of the target market, the advertisement should be changed.

Direct marketing

Direct marketing is another of the communication alternatives that can be used. Direct marketing is defined as a two-way process that uses one or more advertising options (e.g. direct mail, telephone or Internet) to obtain a measurable reply from the customer.[15] Analysing the definition, we can describe the focus of direct marketing as follows:

- **Two-way process**. Direct marketing is an interactive process, that is, there are two parties involved, namely a supplier and a customer.
- **Measurable reply**. Direct marketing aims at customers to react to a proposal, for example, to send in order forms by mail or by means of the Internet or by making phone calls in response to invitations and offers.
- **Databases**. Databases are constructed to keep records of all the active clients.
- **Overall strategy**. Direct marketing must be seen as part of an overall marketing communications strategy.

Some of the best examples of direct marketers in South Africa are Verimark and Glomail. Both these institutions have developed a long-term, sustainable competitive advantage with direct marketing being the cornerstone of their activities.

Verimark – Direct marketing's success story in South Africa[16]

Verimark started out in 1977. Its aim is to source the best products in the houseware, health and fitness, do-it-yourself, automotive and cosmetic ranges. The business model of Verimark works in the following way:

1. **Direct marketing especially Direct Response Television (DRTV)**. Verimark is one of the largest buyers of airtime on television in southern Africa. These advertisements can usually be seen late at night and early in the mornings, with Saturdays and Sundays the best days to see these advertisements.
2. **Stocking products in the retail sector's chain stores**. Verimark's products are placed on special shelves, so that a shop-within-a-shop is created. Hyperama, Game and Pick n Pay have these products in their stores.
3. **Company-owned and franchised stores**. There are currently 65 'As seen on TV' stores in shopping centres in South Africa.
4. Verimark participates in **international consumer and trade shows** to broaden their exposure to the market.
5. Verimark also uses **Internet and database marketing** aimed at a specific target market which they have on their database.

The benefits of direct marketing for the customer can be seen in that customers can do business from the comfort of their homes, therefore resulting in greater shopping convenience and getting a higher quality of service, which is an advantage for people afraid of the possibility of crime. Furthermore, it helps to encourage a cashless society, since debit and credit cards are used.

The benefits for the direct marketer are found in the fact that a long-term relationship can be built with the customer, the message can be directed at a specific customer, a database can be developed and results can be precisely measured. There are various direct marketing methods that can be used. Figure 9.6 summarises the alternatives.

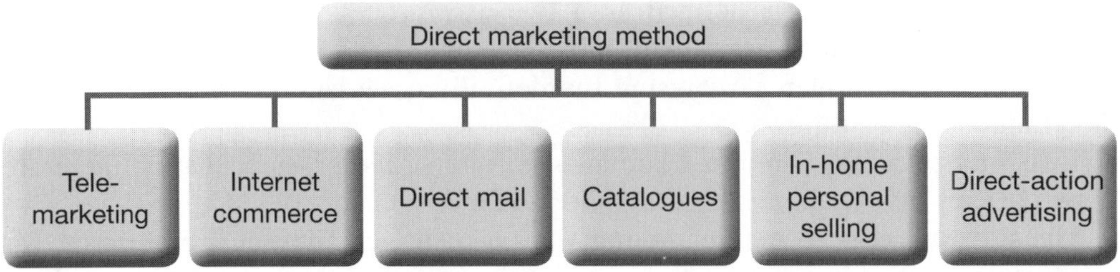

Figure 9.6 *Direct marketing methods*

- **Telemarketing** is marketing done via the telephone. Inbound telemarketing occurs when the customer makes the call in response to the direct marketer's advertisement on television. Outbound telemarketing originates from the marketer where the operator calls the customer. Cell phone and time-share companies often make use of this method.
- **Direct mail** makes use of the postal service or private delivery organisations to deliver the product or message to the customer. It usually contains a specially designed despatch envelope, a letter, a brochure, a response aid (coupon or reply-paid envelope) and an incentive to respond quickly.
- **The catalogue** is one of the older direct marketing techniques. A wide range of products can be ordered from catalogues. Today, many companies also display their catalogues on the Internet.
- **Direct-action/response advertising** is used extensively by Verimark. Mass media is used (e.g. television and newspapers) and customers react by phoning a toll-free number. More recent variations are shows, direct mail and direct sales points inside chain stores and self-standing stores.
- **Internet commerce** is a newer form of interactive electronic media. Every computer terminal that is linked can be used and payment is done by using a debit or credit card. Plane tickets, Internet banking and the purchase of almost any product is possible through the Internet.
- **In-home personal selling** is also in the declining phase of its life cycle. One of the best examples is the so-called Tupperware parties that are held at a person's home, where friends and neighbours are invited to attend. Miglio and Honey jewellery is also sold in this way.

Personal selling

Personal selling can be described as one-to-one personal communication between the organisation (through its representatives) and the customer, so as to convince the customer to purchase the product or service of the organisation.

Looking at this description, we can identify the following key aspects:

- Personal selling is face-to-face communication.
- There are higher costs involved in reaching the customer than with some of the other communication media.
- There is usually a greater impact on the customer since the customer is directly confronted by the salesperson selling the product or service.
- There is flexible communication in that the salesperson can adjust his message to provide additional information and/or to overcome objections of the customer.
- Certain products, such as expensive durable products (e.g. a car or furniture) actually require the services of a salesperson to secure the sale.

Types of salespeople

Three types of salespeople can be identified, namely:

- **Order-getters** who prospect for new customers. To illustrate this we can look at the sales representative of a paint company in Gauteng. He will visit new hardware shops in order to try and get the owner to buy paint from the company. By performing this activity, the salesperson generates new orders.
- **Order takers** are salespeople that, to use the paint example again, visit existing customers (hardware shops) in order to see if they want to purchase another order of paint from the company. These salespeople are interested in repeat sales from the existing customers.
- **Support personnel** are salespeople who supply administrative support to the order-getters and order-takers. Still using the paint example, we may classify the technical person that provides advice on the toll-free number to retailers and to the final customers as an example of support personnel.

Steps in the personal selling process

There are six basic steps that can be identified in the personal selling process.

1. **Prospecting for customers**. The focus is to identify new customers/organisations or existing customers that are on the customer database. Salespeople should use as many leads as possible. They can get referrals from other customers or use referral sources such as suppliers or dealers. They can also get the names from newspapers or directories. Once the salespeople have identified the leads, they should qualify them, in other words identify the good ones and eliminate the poor ones. Qualifying factors to consider include financial ability, location, possibilities for growth, etcetera.
2. **Preparation for the sale**. Before the salesperson will go on to visit the customer, he or she must first obtain enough information about the customer/organisation and its buyers in order to understand the needs of the customer. Doing this will enhance the chances of the salesperson to make a sale.
3. **Presentation**. The salesperson should know how to greet the buyer and get the relationship off to a good start. The appearance of the salesperson is also very important. The presentation is the foundation of the sale. The salesperson must stimulate interest. He or she may use the technique of being a problem solver – for instance, by concentrating on the needs of the do-it-yourself

market. The salesperson may demonstrate to the hardware owner ways to clean rollers and paint brushes, which would make it easier to sell the new non-toxic thinners product that he or she is marketing. This can be done by a physical demonstration of the product. When buyers can see or handle the product, they remember it better.

4. **Handling objections**. There are usually objections raised by the prospective buyer, and salepersons need to be trained with regard to handling objections. A generic objection, for instance, is that the price of the product is too high. A good salesperson will anticipate this type of objection and counter the objection by referring to the new revolutionary benefits of the product, for example, non-toxic, no-fumes and so on.
5. **Closing the sale**. It is important that the customers are reassured that they are making the right decision in buying the product. The paint salesperson may for instance close the sale by asking for a delivery date. If the answer is positive and a delivery date is agreed upon, the sales transaction is closed. There are many other methods to close a sale, for instance the salesperson can ask for the order, offer to help write up the order, ask which particular model the buyer would like or indicate that the buyer will lose out if he or she does not buy now.
6. **Follow-up**. The importance of following up on a sale cannot be over-emphasised. The salesperson must ensure that the customer is happy with the product. This can be done, for instance, by phoning or calling on the customer after a few weeks to enquire whether the customer is satisfied with the performance of the product. This will increase goodwill towards the company and provide an opportunity to prevent major dissatisfaction, which could destroy the long-term relationship with the customer. Following up helps to maintain customer loyalty, generate repeat sales and also helps to sell additional products or services to the same customer.

Sales promotion

Sales promotion can be defined as: The direct encouragement or incentive to the sales force of the organisation, the distribution channel members or the consumer, with the objective of ultimately creating an immediate sale.[17] From this definition we can identify certain key elements, namely:

- Sales promotion is a **short-term communication** tool to help promote the organisation's products and services. Sales promotions can therefore not change the customer's buying behaviour over the long term.
- Sales promotions work in a **complementary** way to the other marketing communication tools such as advertising and personal selling, to get customers to buy the product or service. Sales promotion on its own will not be able to obtain the overall promotion objectives of the organisation.
- Sales promotions generally create a **positive customer attitude** because the perception is created that the customer gets a present. One of the best examples of sales promotions is the discount coupon that you receive, e.g. the Edgars voucher which states that you will get R150 discount on sales of at least R500.

Types of sales promotions

There are three different types of sales promotions, namely:

- Sales promotions aimed at the final customer.
- Sales promotions aimed at the distribution channel members, also called trade promotions.
- Sales-force promotions aimed at the salespeople of the organisation doing the personal selling.

The different types and examples of each are depicted in fig. 9.7.

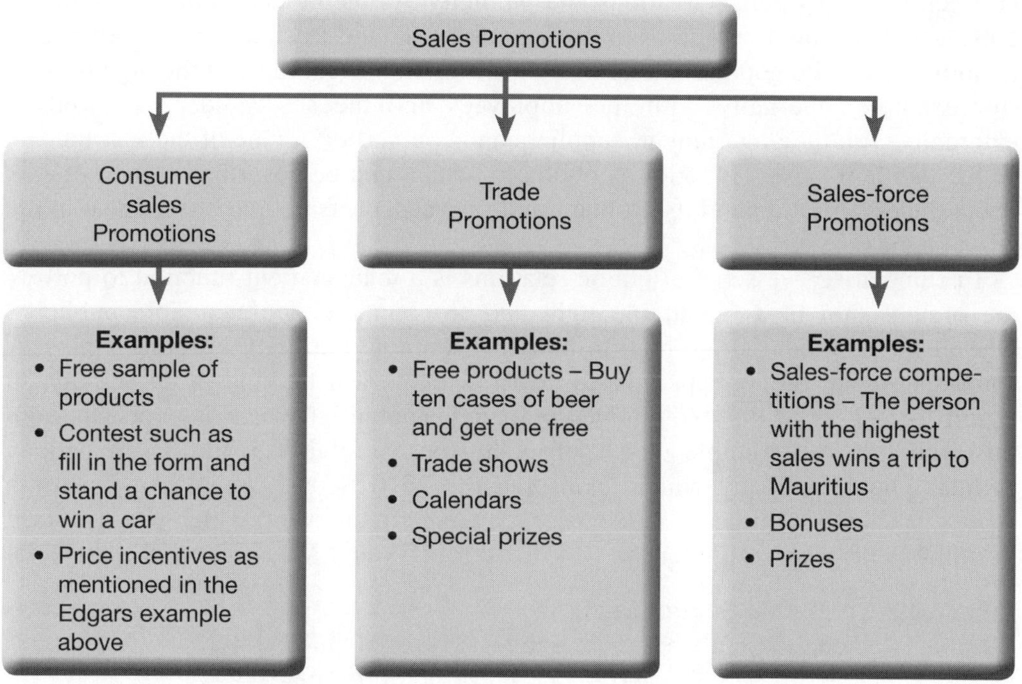

***Figure 9.7** The three types of sales promotions*

- **Consumer sales promotions** are seen as an aid to getting a specific response from the customer, for instance, getting them to buy a certain brand of washing powder. It can also help to counteract promotion campaigns of the competition. If the competition advertises strongly on television that their brand is the cheapest, your organisation may react by launching a sales promotion campaign in which you hand out free samples of your product to show people how good your product is.
- **Trade promotions** are used to get the distribution channel members, for instance, the wholesalers and retailers, to buy large quantities and to sell these products to the customers. A sales contest can be launched aimed at the different retailers selling the product, where the first prize is a trip to Mauritius for the store manager whose store sells most of the product.
- **Sales-force promotions** are aimed at the salespeople of the organisation as a means of encouraging them to sell more of the organisation's product to

the intermediaries and the final customer. Sales conventions are held where salespeople are motivated to sell more. This is further linked to a contest to determine the salesperson who sold the most during the previous financial year. Prizes could be overseas holidays, financial incentives and awards.

Public relations and publicity

The public relations function of a business is a separate function that is sometimes confused with the marketing function. However, there is a place for both of these functions in the organisation. It is necessary also to explain the differences between the terms public relations and publicity. As mentioned, public relations is a management function similar to that of marketing and finance. The aim of public relations is to build good relations with the different stakeholders of the organisation (for example, internally with the employees and the shareholders, as well as externally with the government, suppliers and competitors). One of the instruments of the public relations function is publicity, which can be described as news items about the organisation and its products and services, or its people, that appear in the mass media.[18]

To summarise, we see that public relations is a management function to portray the organisation in a favourable light and to counteract unfavourable publicity. One of the methods with which to obtain favourable publicity is sponsorships. A sponsorship can be described as an investment of cash or kind in an activity, in return for access to the exploitable commercial potential which is expected from this activity.[19] An example of a sponsorship is that of MTN, the South African cellular phone company which sponsored the 2010 Soccer World Cup in South Africa, spending millions of rands to get coverage in an event, which was televised to millions of people all over the world. Both FIFA and MTN received a financial

Publicity: Cadbury's School Games[20]

Cadbury's launched the Cadbury's School Games initiative in 2007. The project is aimed at encouraging the youth of South Africa to get active in sport. The Department of Sport and Recreation became a partner in the project because it tied in with their objective of re-introducing physical education at school level in order to ultimately build a 'healthier nation'.

The project is aimed at identifying and nurturing athletic talent among high school students, and it involves 18 000 high schools throughout South Africa. The campaign culminated in the Cadbury School Games at the end of the year, with exceptional athletes being recognised with bursaries to further their education and build their athletic talents in order to become the stars of tomorrow.

The coverage received for the campaign was very well-balanced, ranging from fast moving consumer goods publications, to business publications, to lifestyle publications, to trade publications and also youth publications. All this exposure ensured that massive awareness and interest was created about the initiative, which reinforced Cadbury's positioning as a responsible corporate citizen.

return. The beneficiary (FIFA and the SA Bid Committee) received funds directly while the sponsor (MTN) expected to gain a favourable change in the consumer behaviour of customers.

From the above it is clear that the public relations function has a wide range of audiences that it is targeting while the marketing function concentrates more on the direct customer or potential customer.

Some basic public relations activities are summarised in table 9.3.

***Table 9.3** Examples of public relations activities*

Open-house policy and fairs	The value of a plant tour, if you are the manufacturer of a product, cannot be underestimated. Visits by ordinary people create a feeling of transparency and goodwill. Guided tours are done by organisations such as Amalgamated Beverage Industries (ABI), Toyota, BMW and South African Breweries (SAB) in South Africa.
Exhibitions and shows	Exhibitions at shows such as the Pretoria Show or the Rand Easter Show raise the exposure of organisations and their ranges of products or services.
Organised social activities	An organisation's yearly golf day is an example of an organised social activity that is used to project a favourable image of the organisation. It also provides an opportunity for networking with the organisation's external stakeholders.
Lobbying	Lobbyists are used by certain organisations to lobby with stakeholders such as governmental institutions. The alcohol and tobacco organisations in South Africa are using lobbyists to communicate with and hopefully influence decision-makers.
Press news releases	Newsworthy information is provided to the press for publication.
Special events	A special event is organised to attract attention to a new holiday destination and can be promoted by inviting journalists to a free weekend with the expectation that it will bring favourable publicity.
Sponsorships	Sport sponsorships in South Africa represent a major method to obtain publicity. Sasol is the major sponsor for South African Rugby. The *Cape Argus* and the Pick n Pay cycle tours are other examples of sponsorships.

Ethical marketing communication

Ethical issues are of extreme importance in marketing communication. When companies do not adhere to ethical standards, a lot of negative and damaging publicity can result. Marketing communication is often criticised as untruthful or deceptive, offensive or as exploiting certain target markets.

In direct marketing for instance, the pictures provided are often unrealistic, misleading or deceptive. Consumers order products such as diamond earrings from pictures, only to receive earrings that are much smaller than the 'real size' portrayed in the photos.

Ethical considerations are also important in advertising. Companies should guard against advertisements that are viewed by consumers as offensive and in bad taste. Many consumers object to advertisements that show products such as contraceptives and personal hygiene factors, women as sex objects, nudity, sex scenes and advertisements that shock. Advertisements that are viewed as exploiting a certain target group such as children should also be avoided.

Unethical marketing communication can negatively influence the product sales and profitability of a company and marketers should do thorough research into ethical issues before a marketing communication campaign is developed.

The offensive Nando's advertisement[21]

Nando's enraged the African National Congress Youth League (ANCYL) just before the general elections in 2009 by flighting an advertisement that mocked the ANCYL leader's demand for change. The advertisement depicted Julius Malema as a ventriloquist's puppet, wearing a '100% Julius' badge, saying: "You order a quarter peri-peri chicken with chips and a cool drink for R33.95. You pay with R40, you get R6.05 change, but if you pay with R100, you get R66.05 change. That's more change than you paid for the meal in the first place.'

Julius Malema and the ANCYL were of the opinion that it was a racist advertisement that was disgusting, ridiculous and disrespectful to African leaders. The ANCYL also threatened Nando's with militant action should they not withdraw the advertisement.

Although Nando's defended the advertisement by saying that they did not want to poke fun at Malema, but merely wanted to bring light heartedness during the serious time of the elections, the ANCYL did not feel the same way, and Nando's had to withdraw the advertisement.

Summary

In this chapter external communication and more specifically marketing communication was addressed as a way in which an organisation communicates with its target audience. The basic functions of marketing communications were discussed, namely to inform, persuade and remind. It was mentioned that an integrated marketing communications campaign is used by organisations and fig. 9.1 depicted the functioning of the IMC campaign. This figure is the key to understanding this chapter.

The various marketing communication alternatives were then discussed, namely advertising, direct marketing, personal selling, sales promotions, public relations and publicity. It must be remembered that these communication alternatives are discussed in isolation, but that in practice all the options could be used to develop an integrated marketing communications campaign which adheres to ethical principles.

Case study: The Player 23 Campaign[22]

In February 2009 Vodacom embarked on a new marketing communication campaign to leverage its sponsorship investment in South African rugby. The campaign was designed to create a lasting emotional bond with enthusiastic rugby fans in South Africa. The campaign features a rugby fan called Jan, the 23rd player, who is following his daily routine, but with the team following him around and trying to be exactly like him. Jan is an integral part of the team and knows all of the players and their strengths and weaknesses. The advertisement also features the well-known Afrikaans singer Robbie Wessels singing a song.

Besides the television and print advertisements, a critical driver of the interactive element of the campaign is the website (www.player23.co.za) where fans can download their own lockers and personalise them by adding their names, pictures and favourite teams. Fans can also download all the latest news on the Super 14 and other rugby mobile content to personalise their phones via the mobile element.

A pared-down version of the website, a mobi site, was also developed. Both make photographs taken of fans enjoying the matches around the country available for download, e-mailing or MMS. There is also a Rugby Blog where users can share their views about upcoming matches, a 'Kick-it to Win-it' game, a Super Bru Match prediction tool, and fixtures, logs and results are available immediately after each game.

In a follow-up to the first advertisement, a second advertisement was introduced. As in the first one, this advertisement features Robbie Wessels, but a new element is added, namely a rivalry between Jan and a new rugby fan, Elton. At the end of the advertisement Jan and Elton realise that they are both on the same side and both wear the number 23 on their backs.

The overriding message is that it is not about rivalry, it is about getting behind the Springboks as a nation, and that all supporters are Player 23s.

Exercise

1. What is the objective of the Vodacom Player 23 marketing communication campaign?
2. Which target audience did Vodacom select for the campaign?
3. Which media types did Vodacom use for the campaign?
4. What type of approach to the message has been used in the advertisements?

CHAPTER 10

Developing a marketing mix for service products

Learning outcomes

After studying this chapter you should be able to:

- clearly distinguish between a service product and a physical product;
- classify the different types of services that can be provided;
- explain the distinguishing features that are unique to the service product;
- describe the components of the service product; and
- combine the elements of the expanded marketing mix for services into appropriate marketing programmes.

Introduction

Michelle and Michael decide that they are in need of a holiday. They visit a travel agent to gather information on the various destinations that they can visit. After carefully considering their options and looking through numerous brochures of the different destinations, they decide to go on a holiday to Mauritius. The travel agent books their airline tickets and hotel accommodation for them and helps them to arrange their visas. Michelle uses her credit card, issued to her by her bank to pay for the trip. She also arranges to purchase traveller's cheques, as well as additional travel insurance, from the bank. Shortly before they go on their trip, Michael uses the telephone in their home to confirm their flight arrangements with the travel agent. Michelle and Michael make use of a local shuttle service to take them to the airport where they pay a porter to carry their luggage to the check-in counters. Whilst waiting for their flight they relax and have a hamburger in one of the restaurants in the terminal building.

The previous paragraph shows that we encounter numerous services in our lives. Services are everywhere and we make use of them every day of our lives. From banking to surfing the Internet, we are dependent on the availability of services to add to our value of life. There is an important difference between a service product and customer service. Service companies primarily provide a service product, for example travel bookings or entertainment. Service (or client service) is something that needs to be provided by those businesses offering a service product, as well as those businesses offering a physical product like a car or a television. Client service is offered in support of the core product or service. This chapter focuses solely on the concept of service businesses. Please note that in the case of service businesses, customers are referred to as clients, so that term is used throughout this chapter.

In previous chapters in this book you have heard about the marketing mix consisting of 4 Ps – product, price, place (distribution) and promotion. These traditional 4 Ps relate mainly to the development of marketing programmes for physical goods like a car or a bar of soap. When dealing with the marketing of services, like travel or entertainment, there are another three important factors which bring the total number of Ps to seven.

What is a service?

The main difference, and the most obvious difference between goods and services is that goods are physically **produced** and services are **performed**. Consider the difference between buying a tin of paint (physical product) to paint a bedroom and hiring a painter to paint a room (service to be performed). The complex nature and diversity of service products has given rise to different definitions of services.

Definitions of services

- 'Services are deeds, processes and performances'... 'Services include all economic activities whose output is not a physical product or construction, is generally consumed at the time it is produced, and provides added value in forms that are essentially intangible concerns of its first purchaser.'[1]
- 'Services are the production of an essentially intangible benefit, either in its own right or as a significant element of a tangible product, which through some form of exchange, satisfies an identified need.'[2]
- 'A service is an act or performance offered by one party to another. Although the process may be tied to a physical product, the performance is essentially intangible and does not normally result in ownership of any of the factors of production.'... 'Services are economic activities that create value and provide benefits for clients at specific times and places as a result of bringing about a desired change in – or on behalf of – the recipient of the service.'[3]

Two points are clear: 1) services are performances of a task and; 2) the client does not take possession of the service, but simply makes use of it at a point in time. We can illustrate these two points by means of a few examples. When you purchase an airline ticket you do not purchase the aircraft but simply the right to occupy a seat on the aircraft for the duration of the flight. When you invest money in a bank you do not own the bank but are merely using them to invest your money. The service that they provide is to invest your money and try to provide a satisfactory return on the investment for you.

Different services have varying degrees of tangibility and intangibility attached to them. Tangibility, in the services marketing context, refers to the extent to which a product can be held. Let us look at these differing degrees of tangibility.

Tangibility spectrum

Products and services have varying degrees of tangibility attached to them. Fig. 10.1 identifies these differing degrees of tangibility for products and services on a continuum starting with pure goods on the extreme left of the figure through to pure services on the extreme right side of the figure.

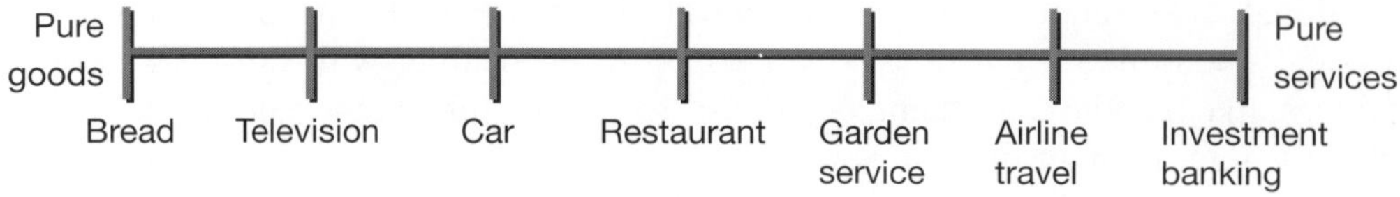

Figure 10.1 *The tangibility of goods and services continuum*

It should be quite apparent that physical goods have a service component attached to them (e.g. cars in the form of financing arrangements or the servicing of the car itself) and service products have a tangible component to them (e.g. restaurants and the food that is served there). Services are generally speaking those that are found to have a dominant intangible component to them, that is, those 'products' found to the right of the continuum.

Phillip Kotler, the so-called father of marketing, proposes five categories that explain the different degrees of tangibility:[4]

- **Pure tangible goods**. The product that is produced is entirely tangible with no accompanying services. A pen or a bottle of shampoo can be classified as a purely tangible product that has no service element.
- **Tangible goods with accompanying services**. A tangible product is provided with services that add overall value to the tangible product. For example, when a computer is purchased (tangible goods), a technician might help you install the product and support is also provided should any difficulties be experienced.
- **Hybrid offers**. In this case, the tangible and intangible components of the product are virtually equal. Restaurants, for example, offer tangible goods for sale in terms of the food and drink but also have an intangible component in that they cook the food for you, bring it to your table and in some cases entertainment is provided in the form of music.
- **Major services with accompanying minor goods and services**. The bulk of the offering is intangible in nature but there are some tangible elements that are offered to support the main service. A hotel is an example. The main offering is accommodation, which is intangible. Supporting the main service are tangible items like meals and drinks, as well as other supporting services like room service and laundry services.
- **Pure services**. The offering here is purely a service with no accompanying tangible elements. Consulting services, doctors, dentists and investment advisers fall into this category.

The focus of the discussion in this chapter relates to those services and offerings that tend to fall towards the right hand side of the continuum, that is, pure services.

Unique characteristics of service products

Taking the definitions of services and the degrees of tangibility into account, it can be seen that there are distinct differences between service products and physical products. These differences need to be considered by the marketing manager when developing marketing programmes for a service product. Over the years five main characteristics of services that distinguish services from physical products have emerged. These are namely intangibility, inseparability, perishability, heterogeneity and ownership.[5]

- **Intangibility**. When purchasing a service you cannot touch it, see it, smell it, test it or taste it prior to the purchase. This makes it more difficult and more risky for the client when deciding whether to purchase the product or not. The service provider has to overcome this perceived risk and try to make the service seem more 'tangible'. Evidence of the service and its quality needs to be given to the client.
- **Inseparability**. The production of the service normally occurs at the same time that the client consumes it. What this implies is that the client forms an integral part of the production of the service by the service provider and in many cases requires the active participation of the client in the process. This leaves little room for error on the part of the service provider. If a mistake is made or an error occurs, the client is immediately aware of it and experiences it as it occurs. In the case of a physical product, on the other hand, if an error occurs during manufacturing then the necessary corrective measures can be taken to ensure that the client is not exposed to the error, or a defective item can be replaced.
- **Perishability**. A service cannot be stored like a tangible product. This means that a service product cannot be produced a week in advance and then stored until it is needed. It has to be produced and utilised when demanded. Take for example an airline seat: if there are ten unoccupied seats on a scheduled flight then the potential income on that particular flight for those particular seats is lost. They cannot be carried over to the next flight; they can never be sold. As a result of this characteristic, the marketer has added pressure to try to manage supply and demand.
- **Heterogeneity**. The service provided on Monday might be slightly different from the service provided on Tuesday. The fact that human beings are involved in the delivery of a service product results in unavoidable variations in the service that is delivered to individual clients. Each client might receive a different service depending on the time of the day, the mood of the service delivery person and/or numerous other influences that affect the circumstances at the time the service is performed. Quality control and employee training play an important role for the service provider.
- **Ownership**. When you purchase a physical product you take ownership of the product. When you purchase a service product you do not take ownership of anything tangible. You purchase the right to temporarily access something or the temporary use of something but you have no claim to ownership. If you watch a movie in a cinema, you purchase the right to watch the movie and to sit in the allocated seat. You do not own the seat or the movie after the movie is finished.

A massage at the day spa

You decide to go to the Chicama day spa for a massage treatment. A massage is intangible; you cannot hold it or take it home with you once it is finished. Production and consumption takes place at the same time. The client has to be present for the service to be rendered. The client will experience the service immediately and will immediately be aware if the masseuse is doing a good or bad job. For Chicama, if they have no bookings for one of the sessions during the day then the potential revenue that could have been generated from the massage room is lost forever. It cannot be carried over to the next day. Heterogeneity is clearly a key issue here.

Even through essentially the same service is being delivered (a back massage for example) a client on Monday might have a better experience than a client on Tuesday because a more experienced masseuse is working on the Monday and not the Tuesday. The experience could be affected by a whole range of factors – perhaps the air conditioning is set too cold on the Tuesday resulting in a negative experience compared to the experience they might have received on the previous day when the air conditioning was set just right. Finally, once the massage is over, the client does not own the massage table, the massage oils or the masseuse. The client only has the temporary use of the facilities and services of the masseuse.

Classification of services

No perfect classification of services exists. Different authors have developed different classification schemes. Some classify services based on the type of service that is provided, e.g. healthcare services, financial services, professional services or communication services. Others look at whether the service provided is people or equipment-based, the degree of dependence on the presence of the client and whether the service is destined for personal or business use. In this section we will look at ways of classifying services identified by Christopher Lovelock.[6]

- The **degree of tangibility or intangibility** of service processes. In this case we must identify whether the service being provided contains a physical element, like providing food, or whether it is a pure service with no tangible components.
- **Who or what is the direct recipient** of the service process? Is the service performed on the client himself or herself or on something that belongs to the client? When watching a movie in a cinema the client is the direct recipient. Jewellery repair is performed on an object, with or without the client being present.
- **The place and time of service delivery**. In this instance we need to identify whether the service provided needs to be taken to the client or whether the client has to go to the provider to receive the service. In many cases the client has to go to a place designated by the service provider. The client has to go to the airport to catch a flight or to the cinema to watch a movie. To repair a washing machine it might be necessary for the service provider to go to the client's home. Banking services were previously only provided in a bank; now they can be done on the Internet or over the phone.

- **Customisation versus standardisation**. Do all clients receive the same standard of service or is the service offering tailored to individual client requirements? Financial services like household insurance through and insurer like Alexander Forbes might be tailored to an individual's specific needs. In terms of standardisation all clients receive the same standard of service delivered in an identical fashion. Studying a course in marketing for example where everyone receives the same book, same study guides, same assignments and same examination. Many services might follow a standard procedure but deliver a customised output.
- **Nature of the relationship with the clients**. Here we look at whether a personal relationship is developed with the client, as in the case of private banking or your doctor, or whether the service encounter is a once-off impersonal transaction, for example a bus ride or the purchase of a ticket at Computicket.
- **Extent to which demand and supply are in balance**. The tourism industry is in most cases seasonal and there are extreme variations in demand, which places pressure on supply. The marketer must try to balance demand and supply by either adjusting capacity or by implementing marketing strategies that will smooth consumer demand.
- **Extent to which facilities, equipment and people are part of the service experience**. Some services rely heavily on physical facilities, equipment and people. An airline is very equipment (aeroplane) and people (cabin crew) intensive. An insurance salesperson might need only a car to travel to a client's home or may even be able to provide the service over the phone or by e-mail.

The services marketing triangle

The unique characteristics associated with services and the various classifications that can be identified present the marketer with a set of challenges different from those encountered by a marketer of a physically tangible product. Any services marketer who wants to be successful will have to carefully consider the issues that are associated with services marketing. In this regard we will look at the make-up of the services marketing triangle, the elements of the traditional marketing mix (4 Ps), as well as the expanded marketing mix for services.

The services marketing triangle identifies three key players that are essential to ensure the success of a service offering. Fig. 10.2 identifies the three key players as (1) company, (2) providers and (3) clients. Positive interaction among these three players is essential to ensure that a quality service is delivered. For success to be achieved it is essential that three types of marketing are carried out. Fig. 10.2 identifies these three types of marketing as external marketing, internal marketing and interactive marketing.

External marketing: Making promises

External marketing involves communication from the company to the consumer to offer its services and establish expectations about the service level that the client can expect from the company. This communication may be in the form of a television advertisement, a magazine advertisement or personal selling. In services marketing,

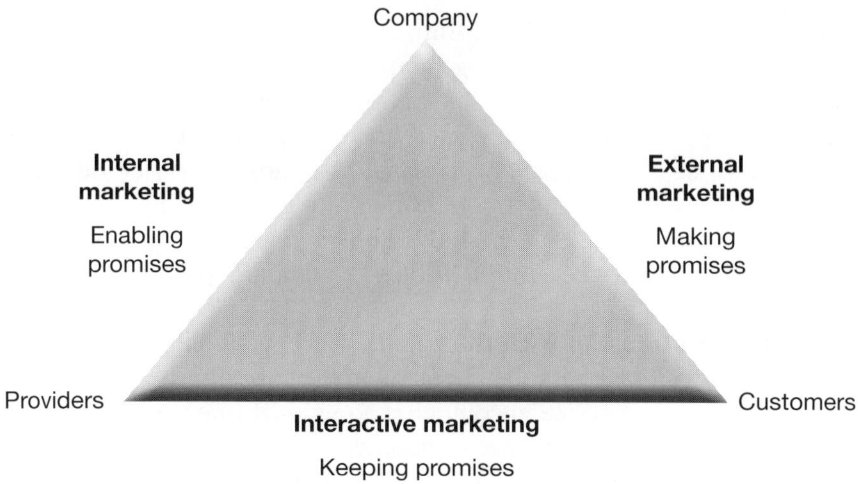

***Figure 10.2** The services marketing triangle*[7]

as will be seen later in the chapter, physical evidence such as the appearance of the place of business and the appearance of staff also play a role in communicating the quality of service offered by the service business. The primary focus of this arm of the services marketing triangle is to make promises. It goes without saying that the business is under considerable pressure to ensure that these promises are kept.

Interactive marketing: Keeping promises

Interactive marketing occurs between the client and the service delivery personnel. This interactive marketing occurs at the time when the client and service delivery staff members come into contact and the service is performed. Every effort needs to be made by the client contact staff to ensure that the service that is delivered to the client is of the highest quality and value.

Internal marketing – enabling promises

Internal marketing is something that· is being taken seriously by many businesses. Quite simply it means training your employees and giving them the necessary tools and skills to perform the jobs at the highest level so that the client is satisfied with the service that is delivered or performed. Without this internal marketing, the danger exists that the client will not receive the expected service; with the result that the client takes his/her business elsewhere and possibly spreads negative word-of-mouth to friends and family.

The services marketing mix

Chapters 6 to 9 in this book address the components of the marketing mix - **product**, **price**, **promotion** and **place**. These four elements are also important and relevant for services products although there are naturally some adaptations that have to be made and other points that have to be considered. The intangible nature of the services product and the fact that production and consumption occur simultaneously lead to the identification of three additional elements to the traditional marketing mix in an attempt to accommodate these unique characteristics. These three additional elements (additional three P's) are **people**, **processes** and **physical evidence**.

Each of the traditional 4 P's and the additional three P's are discussed in the following sections. For more detailed discussions on the traditional 4 P's, refer back to Chapters 6 to 9 to refresh your memory.

The service product

If you remember, a product was defined in Chapter 6 as being a physical object, an intangible service, an idea, programme or a personality that can be offered to a market for attention, use, acquisition or consumption so that a consumer's needs can be satisfied. In the case of the services product you are offering an intangible product to the client. When developing this service product it is important for the marketer to remember that the client purchases the product because of the benefits it will offer him/her and the accompanying satisfaction. With the service product, a certain service level is expected. The level of service provided determines a client's level of satisfaction or dissatisfaction.

The services marketer needs to pay attention to four service product levels: the core service, the expected service, the desired service and the unexpected service (fig. 10.3).[8]

- **Core service**. This is the basic service offered to the client and must be performed to deliver any form of satisfaction. The core service is the reason the organisation is in business. The Gautrain offers as its core service transport from point A to point B.
- **Expected service**. This is the minimum level of service expected by the client and must be present if any level of satisfaction is to be experienced by the client. The expected service is the level of service expected by the client by any provider of a similar service in a specific industry. When taking a car for a service, apart from checking the mechanical functioning of the car, most people expect that their car

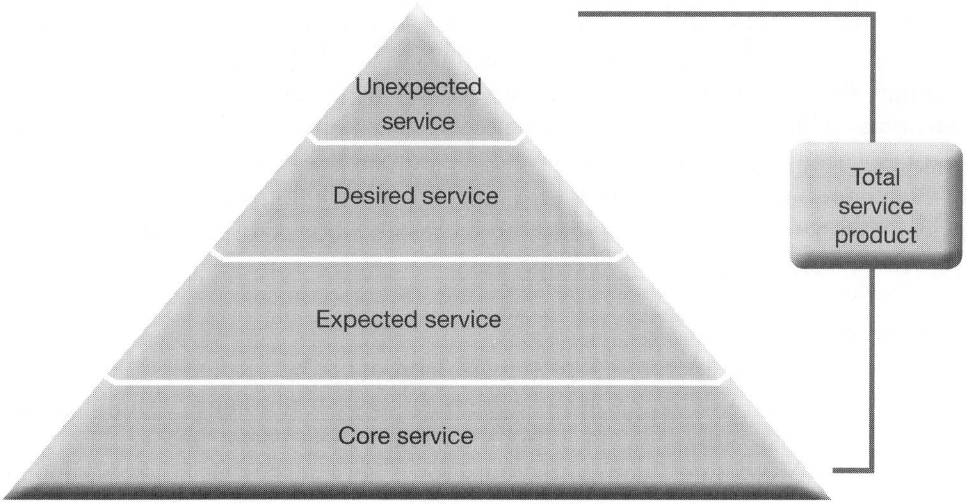

***Figure 10.3** The four service product levels*

will also be washed before it is returned. If it is not washed, most clients will be dissatisfied even though the car wash does not form a part of the core service.

- **Desired service**. This level of service represents a client's ideal service but it is over and above the expected service level. A business that can offer the client these desired levels of service is creating a point of differentiation for themselves from competitors. The client does not expect this level of service, but is impressed when he or she receives it. A gym that offers its clients personalised training programmes, as well as advice from personal trainers while the person is training, is looking to distinguish itself from competitors and offer its clients a service that adds value to their gym experience.
- **Unexpected service**. This level of service exceeds a client's expectations and desired level of service. The unexpected service comes as a real surprise to the client and adds significant value to the service in the eyes of the client. It is a strong differentiating point from competitors. An example is a medical aid scheme that offers mothers-to-be special discounts on expensive items such as nappies and car seats, and also provides a help line for any pregnancy-related questions. These added offerings are an unexpected service that is not offered by the majority of the other competing medical aid schemes.

When designing the service product, the marketer must ensure that all the core and expected elements are present. The features of the service must be carefully considered and adapted to the unique nature and market of the service in question. Careful analysis of competing services must lead to a service offering being developed that gives the company a competitive advantage over its competitors. Remember: 'No Competitive Advantage, No Cash Advantage'.

Positioning is referred to in Chapter 5 as finding a niche (gap) for the product in the minds of the client in order to create a unique place for the product in the market place. When developing the positioning strategy it is essential that the marketer positions the service from the perspective of the consumer. In other words, consider how the consumer perceives the service offering and not how you as the marketer perceive the service offering. Make sure that you focus on the client's determinant attributes and not simply the important attributes of the service when positioning the service.

Positioning plays a crucial role in the development of a service product. By effectively positioning the service product, you can add a degree of tangibility to the service product which will reduce the perceived risk to the client when deciding between competing service providers. If successful, this will provide a significant competitive advantage over any competitors.

Promotion of services

A key element in the marketing of physical products or service products is that you should be able to deliver what you promise in your marketing communication efforts. If you cannot keep your promises, you will create a bad reputation for your business. Marketing communications for a service business are particularly important because of the intangible nature of the service product. The increased role played by the staff, particularly the front-line staff, in terms of direct client contact also heightens the importance of marketing communications for services.

Definitions of attributes

- **Important attributes** are attributes such as safety, image and convenience that the consumer considers important when deciding between competing services.
- **Determinant attributes** are those attributes that actually determine the buyer's final choice of service. A determinant attribute does not have to be the most important attribute, but it is the attribute that the consumer uses to ultimately distinguish one service offering from another.[9]
- **The difference between important and determinant attributes**: When considering which airline to use on a trip from Cape Town to Johannesburg the consumer might view safety, cleanliness of aircraft, friendliness of cabin crew and comfort as being important attributes. However, whilst safety, cleanliness of aircraft and friendliness of cabin crew are important attributes, any normal passenger might expect that these attributes are present with each competing airline and thus not use them to determine their final choice. Pricing of the ticket, however, might be a key issue to the client and is the attribute upon which the final decision is made. Price in this case is therefore the determinant attribute and not the other important attributes that have been mentioned.

Marketing communication

We saw in Chapter 9 that the main objectives of marketing communication are to inform, persuade and remind. In the case of services this means you must first let consumers know about the service that you are offering and where to find it; convince consumers that your service will provide the best package of benefits, and then remind them to take action and use the service whenever they require any similar service.

As you know by now, there are distinct differences between services and goods. These differences have implications for the marketing communications developed by the services marketer.[10]

- **Intangible nature of services**. Through visual representations and other promotional devices, efforts can be made to add a tangible element to the service product. When advertising their businesses, many restaurants show their venue, the ambiance as well as plates of their food being enjoyed by their patrons.
- **Client-contact personnel's involvement in service production**. You will notice that in many advertisements for service products there is an image of the contact staff. These people are always smiling and shown as being very helpful. It is essential that this visual representation be carried through in reality. In other words, what is shown and promised in the advertisements must be communicated to the employees and delivered to the client.
- **Client involvement in production**. Communications can be used to educate consumers on what to expect in the service delivery process and what their role in that process is. Should there be any changes in the way that the service is delivered, communications should inform clients of this change so that they perform their role appropriately when they next make use of the service. In order

to ensure that people enjoyed watching the matches played during the FIFA Soccer World Cup, many communications were released advising people of the best ways of getting to the stadium on time.

- **Incorrectly targeted communications**. If a message reaches an untargeted market for physical goods such as running shoes, the results would not be serious. The untargeted persons would simply not purchase the running shoes and there would be no impact on the target market. The situation is different in the case of some services. In the case of service products, the untargeted audience could influence the experience of the targeted audience. Opera appeals to a select audience of people. If a group of people (incorrectly targeted) with no interest in opera attend the performance, they may talk and fidget during the performance, thereby reducing the enjoyment of those who do enjoy opera.
- **Balancing supply and demand**. As has been mentioned already, service products cannot be stored. Marketing communications can play a crucial role in stimulating short-term demand in periods of low demand and smoothing out demand during high-demand periods. Many hotels offer mid-week breaks at short notice to increase occupancy rates during these sluggish periods.

The elements of the marketing communication mix were explained in Chapter 9.

This next section will briefly outline some specific points that relate to each element with regard to services marketing.

Advertising

Advertising is very good at reaching a large audience very quickly. For many service products, advertising is the first point of contact with the client. It sets the scene for service expectations and establishes an image in the minds of consumers. Five roles can be identified for services advertising.[11]

1. Introduce the service to the consumer and create a general awareness of the service.
2. Develop a personality for the service that matches the requirements of consumers.
3. Match the values and capabilities of the service business with those of the client.
4. Set the scene of what clients can expect from the service and motivate employees to live up to the expectations created in the advertisement.
5. Form a foundation for sales representatives so that the clients they call on already have a favourable impression of the service business and know what to expect.

It is extremely important that the expectations created in the advertisements can be delivered to the consumer, otherwise there will be dissatisfaction and the consumer will look elsewhere.

Sales promotion

Sales promotions are short-term incentives used to stimulate buying. They can be particularly useful in stimulating demand during periods of low demand or to create additional awareness of a service being introduced to the market. The various sales promotion tools that are available to the services marketer, as well as examples of each, are highlighted in Table 10.1.

Table 10.1 *Sales promotion tools that could be used to market services*

Tool	Description	Example
Sampling	The client has the opportunity to use the service free for a limited period of time	A free week trial period at a gym before signing a longer term contract
Coupons	Used to stimulate sales in the short term. Client receives a voucher that entitles him or her to a prescribed discount on the service provided	Some car service centres place coupons in newspapers and offer the client a 10% reduction for the servicing of their car on presentation of the coupon
Gift premiums	Free services or merchandise offered when a particular service is utilised	Many fast food outlets (like Steers or McDonald's) offer free toys for children when a particular product is purchased
Competitions	Help to stimulate trial of a service. The client is persuaded to try the service through the possibility of winning a desirable prize after using the service	Many banks offer the client the chance of winning their home loan free if they apply for a mortgage with the bank
Price discounts	The price charged for a service is reduced for a limited period in order to stimulate interest in a service offering with the hope that the customer becomes a loyal user over time	Airlines might, in order to increase demand and thus fill more seats, reduce their prices on certain flights at certain times during the year or during times when demand is low
Loyalty programmes	These programmes are long term in nature and focus on building loyalty over time. The more you make use of a particular service the more rewards you can receive	South African Airways Voyager programme. The more you fly with the airline, the more Voyager miles you earn. Once you have accumulated a certain amount of miles you can claim 'free' flights

Specialities	These are give-away items that a service provider gives to its clients in order to continuously remind you of the services that they offer	An insurance salesperson might give you a pen with his or her contact details on it. Many businesses give their client calendars or desk-pads which have contact details printed on them
Sign-up rebates	In order to persuade consumers to sign up or make use of a service the initial sign-up fees are waived	In order to encourage people to sign up with DSTV, free installation of the dish might be offered

A well-designed sales promotion strategy can effectively complement an advertising strategy and create a sustainable competitive advantage for the service business.

Personal selling

The very nature of the service product means that great emphasis is placed on personal selling activities. Advertising creates an awareness of the service business, whilst personal selling facilitates the transaction and brings in revenue. Front-office personnel can be considered to be performing a selling function. Sales representatives, agents and other company representatives involved in selling the company's services play a crucial role in developing relationships with clients, which is crucial for long-term loyalty. Once again the unique characteristics of the service product mean that personal selling for service products can be more complex. Eight differences between selling goods and selling services can be identified.[12]

1. From a consumer perspective, the purchase of a service product entails more risk (particularly due to the intangible nature of the service).
2. The purchase of a service product is viewed as being less predictable than for goods due to the perceived risks and the unknowns.
3. The mental image that the client has of the service business is an important consideration when deciding on the purchase of the service.
4. The intangible nature of the service product means that the client places a great deal of importance on the service provided by the salesperson.
5. Consumers place greater importance on personal recommendations when deciding on the purchase of the service product.
6. Fewer price comparisons are made for service product purchases.
7. Clients are involved to a larger extent in the purchase of a service product than for a physical good.
8. The sales personnel of a service business must be good listeners and be experts in their jobs in order to provide clients with sufficient information on the service to reduce any fears or uncertainties that they may have.

Direct marketing

Direct marketing, as described in Chapter 9, is a two-way communication process that requires an action or response from the consumer. Direct marketing offers the advantage that it can be personalised to each individual client and in this way a relationship can be developed. As you already know, relationships are important in the services marketing context.

The success of direct marketing relies to a large extent on accurate and comprehensive databases. In services marketing, many businesses already have quite comprehensive lists of the client base which serve as a good starting point for marketing. Think of your bank: it already has all of your details on record and of every other client. In order to sell their accident insurance policies, all they have to do is access the information on their internal database and contact the client. The same applies to opticians. If they want to promote a range of prescription sunglasses, they can start by accessing their database of current and past clients.

Public relations

The ultimate aim of public relations is to generate goodwill towards the company from outside interest groups. Public relations are seen as being more credible than other forms of promotion because they come from an impartial source. As a result, a strong positive image for the company can be developed. The following are key tasks for public relations:

- Develop and maintain the image of the service business.
- Give support to other promotional activities of the business.
- Manage problems that may arise with regard to the business and its image in the market.
- Reinforce the positioning of the business and the services that are offered.
- Influence the various publics that have an interest in the business and its activities.
- Help with the launching of new services into the market.
- Become involved in community projects.

The various publics to which public relations are directed, as well as the tools that can be used in public relations, are all described in Chapter 9.

Distribution of services

Chapter 7 deals with marketing distribution decisions. Distribution for services relates to the availability and accessibility of a service to clients. Availability means the service is available to the client whenever he or she wants it. Accessibility refers to the relative ease with which the client can conduct a transaction with the service provider.

The nature of the service being provided will go a long way to determining the location of the service provider, as well as the extent of the facilities that will be required. In this regard, attention needs to be given to the types of interactions that are involved between the client and the service provider. Three types of interactions are of interest to us.

- **The client goes to the service provider's premises**. An example is when you go and watch a movie or you go to the local gym. For the service provider the choice of a good location that creates the appropriate image is important as the client comes into contact with the provider's facilities. These facilities serve as a quality cue for the client and will influence the client's level of satisfaction.
- **The service provider goes to the client**. In this case an insurance salesperson will visit the client at home or the washing machine repairperson will make a house call. Location and image of physical facilities do not play an important role in this case because the consumer does not see the service provider's premises.
- **No contact at all between the service provider and the client**. Internet banking involves no physical contact between the provider and the client. Telkom provides a telephone line service where the service is provided to the client without any need for contact with the service provider. Even complaints related to the service can be handled without direct contact.

As with the distribution of physical goods, a number of channel options are available to the services marketer when deciding how best to make their services available to consumers. The very nature of the service product (intangibility and inseparability of production and consumption in particular) generally means that the distribution channel is shorter for service products than for physical goods. The various options that are available include direct channels, indirect channels and multi-channels (fig. 10.4).[13]

- **Direct channels**. This simply entails the service provider providing the service directly to clients. For example, a client goes to a restaurant and the service provider serves a meal to the client.
- **Indirect channels**. In this case there are intermediaries between the client and the service provider that ensure that the desired service offering is delivered to the client. A service provider, such as computicket or ticketweb, acts as an intermediary between the client and a service provider, for example a particular theatre that sells tickets to a play through Computicket.
- **Multi-channels**. The service marketer might decide that more than one of the channels, as identified in fig. 10.4, is needed to reach the selected target market. A theatre might sell tickets to its performances from the theatre itself (direct channel) and also make use of an intermediary like ticketweb (indirect channel).

The choice of channel and the number of channels utilised are important decisions for the services marketer. It should not be too difficult for clients to receive the service or have to inconvenience themselves too much. This is not always possible (think of the time and effort it requires to catch a flight) but the service provider should manage the inconvenience. Inefficient distribution channels are likely to result in clients seeking alternative service providers for future purchases.

Pricing the service product

Refer back to Chapter 8 to refresh your memory on pricing decisions. Price is one element that a consumer can use to distinguish between competing services. It

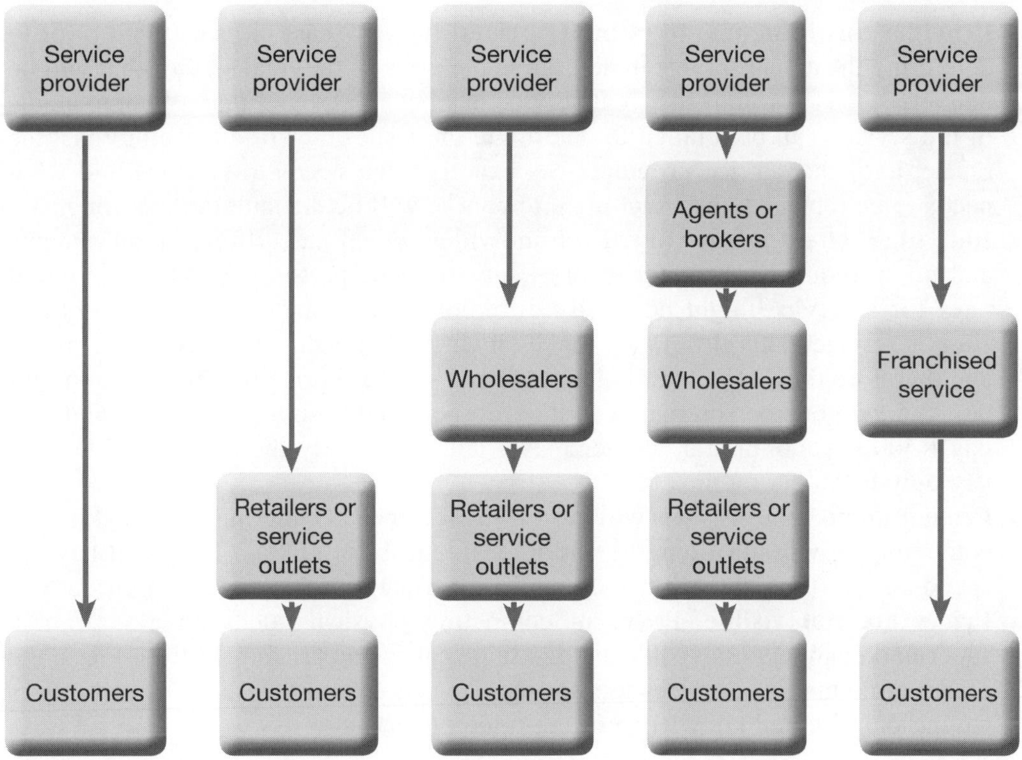

Figure 10.4 *Distribution channels for services*

can also be used to evaluate the quality of the service that is being offered. In the context of services, pricing can be a complex issue. The unique characteristics of the service product could mean that ten people could each pay a different price for the same service. Marketing managers need to approach pricing of service products cautiously to ensure that they attract clients whilst maximising yield and capacity.

Zeithaml and Bitner identify three key aspects relating to consumer perceptions of services that need to be kept in mind by the services marketer when looking at pricing their offerings. These are: client knowledge of prices, the role of non-monetary costs and price as an indicator of quality.[14]

Client knowledge of prices

For the client this is relatively limited except for those services that are utilised frequently. Even then that is no guarantee. There are a number of reasons for this relative lack of knowledge.

- **Service heterogeneity limits knowledge**. Because each service delivered to each client could be different, it is difficult to set one standard price that will be levied to the client. Even with an individual client, the price charged today might be different tomorrow due to differing circumstances or slight variations to the overall service requested. A doctor might give you a flu injection one week and then the next week, treat a broken leg. The medical bill will be different for these two services.

- **Provider unwillingness to estimate prices**. In many cases it is difficult prior to delivering the actual service to determine the price of the final service that will be delivered. It is not until the final service has been delivered that all components of the service can be totalled to determine the final bill. For a washing machine repair, until the service provider sees exactly what needs to be done and what needs to be replaced, the exact price to charge will be difficult to determine.
- **Individual client needs vary**. Each individual client has different requirements and might require a different level of service to be performed. What one client pays for a service might be totally different to what another client pays for a similar service. This difference makes it difficult for clients to compare prices and therefore they do not really know what a standard price for the service might be. At a gym one person may want the full personal training experience and will pay R400 per month and another may want to use only the basic facilities and pay only R250 per month.
- **Price information is overwhelming in services**. Gathering information on competing services is a lengthy and intensive task for clients. They will have to spend a lot of time and effort looking for information for comparison purposes.
- **Prices are not visible**. Prices of competing physical goods on a shelf in a supermarket are readily visible and facilitate easy comparisons. With services, the prices of competing services are not readily visible and this leads to consumers having only limited knowledge of the price of services.

The role of non-monetary costs

These are costs to the consumer that do not involve an actual monetary cost but involve other forms of perceived risks. A consumer will, either consciously or subconsciously, evaluate these non-monetary costs when deciding to make use of a particular service. The non-monetary costs are time, search, convenience costs and psychological costs.

- **Time costs**. As previously mentioned, the client in most cases is directly involved in the performance of the service. This requires that clients have to give up some of their valuable time in order to take 'delivery' of the service. In many cases the length of time to deliver the service cannot be specifically determined and therefore a period of waiting is required. Think of the number of times you have had an appointment with the doctor for 10:00 am and have had to wait for an hour before you actually saw him or her.
- **Search costs**. Much effort is required when searching for the preferred service provider. The consumer has to expend a lot of effort in order to gather information on the different service providers and the prices of the different services. This task is made even more difficult because the different service providers do not provide exactly the same service.
- **Convenience costs**. Whether the client goes to the service provider or the service provider comes to the client, the client still has to arrange time in his or her schedule for the appointment which can sometimes be very difficult. In some cases a lot of preparation may be needed to prepare for the service to be provided. Distance learning institutions are more convenient than residential institutions in

that students do not have to go to classes on a daily basis but can study according to their own schedule. In this case an element of inconvenience is eliminated (although the comparison between the two types of institutions is more complex than this).

- **Psychological costs**. With all the factors that need to be considered, especially the client's lack of knowledge of the service being provided, it is not surprising that clients have a number of fears that affect them when considering the purchase of service products. These fears can also be as a result of previous bad experiences with a particular service. Anyone who has built a house or had a root canal treatment at a dentist can attest to this.

Price as an indicator of quality

Service marketers must carefully consider the messages that they send to the client through the prices they set for their services. In situations where the risk of purchase is high to the client, where there is little information available or where it is difficult to compare the quality of different service providers, clients will use the price of the service as an indicator of quality. If the price is too low it might be perceived as being of lower quality. Conversely, if the price is too high, a client may have unrealistic expectations of the service that will be provided.

As can be seen from the points above about pricing, it is an extremely important issue that needs close attention from the service marketer. Lovelock sums up the pricing issue by identifying seven key questions that the services marketer needs to keep in mind when deciding on how to price their offerings.[15] These seven questions are summed up in Table 10.2.

Physical evidence

We have seen that service products are essentially intangible. In order to add an element of tangibility, the service marketer will make use of physical evidence to create an atmosphere and image for the business. This so-called physical evidence gives the client an indication of the quality of the service provided and gives him or her the reassurance that the service purchased will meet expectations.

> **Definition**
> Physical evidence is defined as 'all aspects of the organisation's physical facility, as well as other forms of tangible communication'.[16]

In other words, it is what the offices of the business look like, what their vehicles look like, what their stationery looks like, and what the feel or atmosphere of their business premises is. Table 10.3 identifies the main elements of physical evidence.[17] The combination of these three elements forms an image in the minds of clients. Marketers should ensure that the correct image is created in order to attract the desired target audience.

Table 10.2 *Seven questions to be addressed when pricing a service*

Question	Underlying issues
How much should be charged for this service?	What costs is the business trying to recover? Is the business trying to achieve a specific profit margin or return on investment by selling this product? How sensitive are customers to different prices? What prices are competitors charging? Should discounts be offered from the basic prices? Are psychological pricing points used?
What should be the basis of pricing?	Execution of a specific task? Admission to a service facility? Units of time? Percentage commission on the value of the transaction? Physical resources consumed? Geographic distance covered? Weight or size of object serviced? Should each service element be billed independently? Should a single price be charged for a bundled package?
Who should collect payment?	The business that provides the service? A specialist intermediary (agent, bank, etc.)? How should the intermediary be compensated for the work – flat fee or commission?
Where should payment be made?	The location at which the service is delivered? A convenient retail outlet or financial intermediary? The purchaser's home?
When should payment be made?	Before or after delivery of the service? At which times of the day? On which days of the week?
How should payment be made?	Cash? Token? Stored value card? Cheque? Electronic funds transfer? Credit or debit card? Credit account with service provider? Vouchers? Third party payment?
How should prices be communicated to the market?	Through what communication medium (advertising, sales people, promotions, etc.)? What message content (what role should price play in these communications?)

Table 10.3 The main elements of physical evidence

Servicescape	Other tangibles
Facility exterior • exterior design • signage • parking • landscape • surrounding environment	• business cards • stationery • billing statements • reports • employee dress • uniforms • brochures • Internet and web pages
Facility interior • interior design • equipment • signage • lay-out	
Ambient factors • air quality • air temperature • music and other sounds • noise • lighting	

Servicescape

The concept of servicescape is introduced in Table 10.3. It is a very important concept in the context of services marketing. Servicescape refers to the appearance of the physical surroundings (interior and exterior) where the interaction between the client and the service takes place. This includes the atmospherics or ambient factors of the surroundings, for example smells and sounds.

- **Exterior design**. The design of the service location should match the image created in the consumer's mind. Banks, for example, should give an impression of security and trustworthiness. A plumber's premises do not need to look like those of a bank because the consumer has different expectations of a plumber. Signage is an important aspect in all businesses. They should clearly identify the business and inform potential clients where to go, times of operations and the services offered. Signage also includes the logos on the trucks or vans used by the business when contact personnel travel to the homes of clients to perform a service.
- **Interior design**. The reception area of a business is normally the first thing a client sees when entering the premises. It immediately communicates a message to the client and can have a lasting effect. Once again, the design of the interior should match the client's expectations and should complement the exterior design. Interior design also includes items such as the furniture in the reception area, the use of pot plants, the placement of equipment, the colour of the paint on the walls and the general neatness of the interior. The availability of forms

to be filled in if necessary (such as deposit slips in a bank) is also an important consideration.

- **Ambient factors**. This term refers to the general feel of the building of the business and the atmosphere. The various ambient factors (or atmospherics) include smells and aromas, sounds and music, and the light and temperature. The impact of these and their importance are quite obvious. The aromas in a restaurant must make clients feel hungry and must make them want to eat their food. Just imagine what your reaction would be if you could smell burnt food. Would you want to eat there? People respond differently to different styles of music. Certain restaurants, such as the Spur steak ranches, play pop music or commercial music to create a family atmosphere. Other more sophisticated restaurants that serve speciality foods to upmarket clients might play classical music which enhances the feeling of exclusivity.

Sounds also help create a certain image and atmosphere. In a Spur steak ranch you can hear the food sizzling on the grills, the waiters carrying glasses and other customers talking throughout the restaurant. In a restaurant that wants to create a more upmarket, exclusive feel, there is a lot less noise and the entire atmosphere is far more sedate. Temperature is also important: if a building is too hot or stuffy, then it forms a negative impression in the client's mind. Added to this, lighting can be very effectively used to create an atmosphere or mood for a service business. Lighting can be used to highlight certain features or set a tone of exclusivity: bright lights seem to indicate a vibrant atmosphere whilst duller and focused lighting creates a more exclusive image.

Other tangible elements

As can be seen from Table 10.3, other tangible elements include items such as business cards, business stationery, statements, appearance of staff and the design of the service's website. Each of these elements serves to provide clients with an element of tangibility that makes it easier for them to evaluate the service they are purchasing. This serves to reduce the perceived risk associated with the purchase of the service. As a simple example, think of your monthly bank statement. If it arrived scribbled on the back of an old piece of paper you would not be impressed or have a high opinion of the way the bank does business. On the other hand if it comes to you neatly laid out with the company logo you would have a higher opinion of them. The same applies to a service provider's website. If it is neat, easy to use and is attractive it will create a better impression than one that is dull, poorly structured and provides insufficient information. It is very important that services marketers fully understand the services that they are marketing and the image that they want to portray. This image must be incorporated into the design of the physical evidence that the client will encounter when visiting the service providers' premises or when the service provider visits the client's home to perform the service. Providing an element of tangibility to an otherwise intangible service is crucial in assuring the client of the quality of the service that will be provided.

Processes

In producing the service product there are a number of steps that are followed to deliver each component of the service. Viewed from a managerial perspective, we can say that delivering the service product is a process.

> **Definition**
> A process includes the actual procedures, mechanisms and flow of activities by which the service is delivered – the service delivery and operating systems.[18]

Some service businesses have relatively simple products and therefore relatively simple processes for the delivery of their service (think of a washing machine repairs service or a dry cleaning service). Others have services that are a lot more complex and therefore require carefully planned and managed strategies (think of banks and hospitals, for example).

The importance of managing these processes cannot be underestimated. If the process does not run smoothly then there will obviously be delays or problems will arise. Problems at any stage of the process can create a negative impression. Even worse is that a small problem at the beginning of the process can snowball at successive stages and create a seemingly never-ending string of delays. This will result in unhappy clients and a negative image of your business. It is therefore essential that all aspects within the business function smoothly to ensure that an appropriate level of service is delivered to the client.

Two very important concepts are particularly valuable to the services marketer in managing the service delivery process: critical incidents and service blueprinting.

> **Definitions**
> - **Critical incidents** are specific interactions between the client and the service provider that are especially satisfying or dissatisfying.[19]
> - A **service blueprint** is a graphic representation of the essential components of the service performance. It identifies the service personnel, the points of interaction between clients and service providers, the contact points between workers and other workers, and the frontstage evidence and the backstage processes or activities.[20]

Simply stated, a critical incident refers to particular points of contact during the service delivery process between the client and the service provider. Each point of contact has a significant bearing on the satisfaction or the perceived quality of the service delivered. See fig. 10.5 for an illustration of the various critical incidents in a dental appointment.

Service blueprinting is a visual representation of the activities that are essential in the process of delivering a requested service. A clear distinction is made between those activities that occur in view of the client and those that occur behind the scenes and are not seen by the client. As can be seen in fig. 10.5, activities that occur in view of the client are referred to as frontstage activities and those that occur out of the client's sight are termed backstage activities.

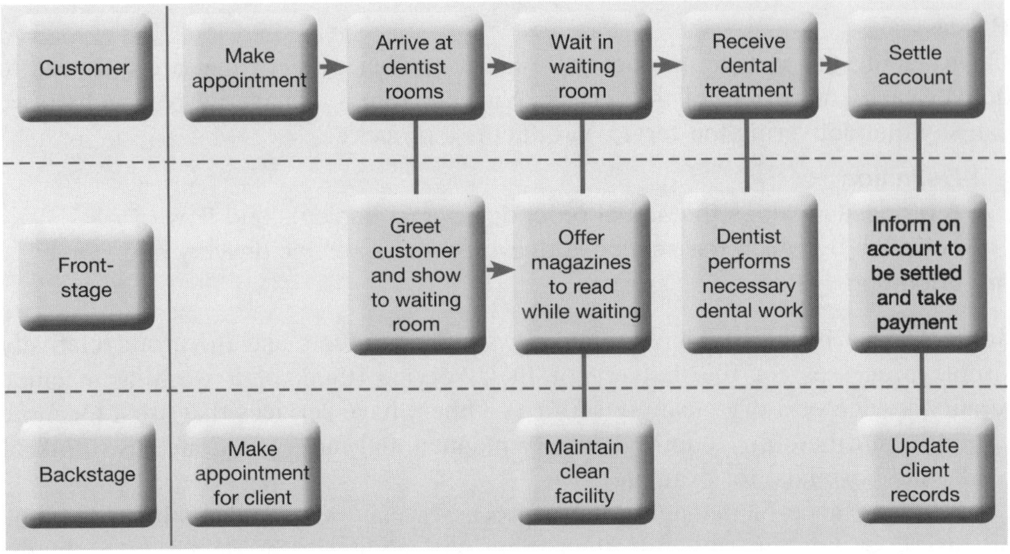

Figure 10.5 *Service blueprint for a dental appointment*

People

As you have probably realised, services rely heavily on people – people to deliver the service to people, people to provide people with information, people to handle reception activities and people to manage the entire process. In this section we will look briefly at three specific areas: Employees as part of the service product, clients as part of the service process and the client-employee contact situation.

Employees

Employees have an important role to play in the delivery of the service product. They play a role in the production of the product, the marketing of the product and in many cases form part of the service product. A hairdresser would be a good example of this. With this in mind, it should be clear to the reader that a lot of attention needs to be given to the employees to ensure that they are properly recruited, trained and motivated to deliver a quality service to the clients.

The concept of internal marketing arose from the need to ensure that internal staff members understand and accept the marketing plans being implemented by the business. The concept is quite logical: inform your employees of the products being offered to the market and give them training on how to sell and support the product. Three different situations can be identified where internal marketing is most appropriate [21]

- **Developing a service culture**. In this case the employees are informed of the business strategies of the business and the directions that are being taken. Also, positive relationships are developed and employees are taught service skills and how to communicate with clients.
- **Maintaining a service culture**. This situation logically builds on the previous situation. The main focus is to maintain and further develop the relationships

that have been built internally and to ensure that the desired image is perceived by clients. It is extremely important that the employee perceives management's support in this situation.
- **Introducing new goods, services, marketing activities and campaigns**. The focus here is on gaining employee acceptance of new products and marketing campaigns that are being launched. Also of importance is informing employees (and gaining their acceptance) of any new systems or processes that are being introduced and how their actions need to be modified to continue providing a superior service to clients.

The key to the success of any internal marketing programme is the support of all interest groups; top management through to the client-contact and support personnel.

To effectively and efficiently serve clients, the right people need to be recruited. This, however, is much easier said than done. Careful consideration needs to be given to the nature of the service being offered and then an appropriate job description needs to be developed. Naturally, certain characteristics are more desirable for front-line staff than are necessary for back-room staff. Every effort must be made to identify those candidates who have the charisma and energy to deal with clients on a daily basis. Training can overcome certain shortcomings in personnel, but it is no substitute for appointing the correct candidate from the outset. The core focus of training and development is to provide employees with the necessary knowledge and skills to ensure that they operate optimally in their job. Staff development is concerned with providing employees with additional skills and knowledge that are necessary for any new activities that the business may engage in.

Two important concepts when dealing with employees are empowerment and enabling.

- **Empowerment** refers to giving your client-contact personnel the authority to make decisions and take action in problem-solving situations that may arise. Naturally there are limits to the amount of authority that can be given to these employees due to a number of legal and financial implications that may exist.
- **Enabling** refers to providing the employees with the necessary support and structures so that they are able to make the independent decisions that are permissible because of empowerment. For enabling to be effective there needs to be management support, knowledge support and technical support. Without this support there is no empowerment.[22]

Empowerment and enabling of employees is important because it means that client contact personnel are able to provide a quicker response or solution to clients, which ultimately helps build client loyalty.

Clients

We have mentioned on many occasions that clients are heavily involved in the production of the service product. You may remember that we highlighted one of the unique characteristics of services marketing as being inseparability. This related to the simultaneous production and consumption of the service, which means that client contact personnel are particularly important. How a client experiences this service production process and his or her feelings during this activity, have a huge impact on the overall satisfaction with the service. As a result, the service provider must ensure that the service that is delivered is delivered in a controlled and well-managed manner.

When developing a system to manage clients in the service-delivery process, it is important to understand the needs and expectations of clients. Refer to Chapter 3 to refresh your knowledge on consumer behaviour. It is important, however, to realise that there are certain levels of consumer expectations, each of which needs to be understood in order to meet the client's expectations. These levels include:

- **Ideal service**. In a perfect world this is the service the client receives where there are no problems and everything goes according to plan.
- **Desired service**. This is the service the client would ideally like to receive. This expectation is based on previous experiences and is more realistic than the ideal service level expectation.
- **Adequate service**. This refers to the minimum level of service that the client is willing to accept. Anything below this level will lead to dissatisfaction.
- **Predicted service**. Based on previous experience, the client will have an idea of the service level to expect. The higher the predicted service level, the higher the adequate service level.
- **Unanticipated service**. This represents the unexpected additional services or items that a client receives that were not expected but that add significant levels of satisfaction and value to the client's experience.
- **Zone of tolerance**. Between the adequate service level and the desired service level is a zone of tolerance. In this zone the client will accept the service level that is delivered, without complaining, and without being particularly satisfied.

The obvious goal of the service provider would be to provide a service that is as close as possible to, or even exceeds, the desired service-level expectations of your clients. There are three areas that need to be addressed to effectively manage clients.

- **The management of client waiting periods**. Most readers will probably have had many bad experiences with regard to waiting. The queues at the Department of Home Affairs are well known and are a source of frustration for many people because of the amount of time that is wasted, the heat, the crowdedness and the boredom. It is essential that a service business implement a system to reduce client waiting time. This can be done by implementing reservation systems, better management of capacity and providing alternatives for making use of the particular service. Each service operation, depending on the nature of the service that is provided, will have to design its own waiting management system to accommodate the unique nature of their product.
- **The management of client participation**. It is possible to involve clients in the delivery of the service product to a greater extent. This involves an element of self-service. For relatively simple service products, this is a good option because the client is able to perform the task without the risk of making a costly mistake. For example, purchasing concert tickets over the Internet or selecting your own

brochures in a travel agency are relatively simple tasks and hold minimal risk for the client and the service provider. On the other hand, more complex services are more risky as a client would have little knowledge of the service and therefore self-service would be less of an option. Just imagine if your medical doctor told you to look through some of his medical books to perform your own diagnosis! It is a trial and error process for the service provider to identify which aspects are suitable for self-service and which are not.

- **Handling difficult clients**. Most people will have had to deal with, or seen difficult clients in a shop. It is important to realise that no matter what the complaint or how angry or calm the client is, a complaint needs to be handled decisively and professionally. Angry and complaining clients can be very destructive and can result in your business gaining a bad name (fairly or unfairly). Suffice it to say, a strategy needs to be in place to effectively handle any complaints that may arise in the course of doing business.

Client-employee contact

The nature of the service product means that client contact personnel and clients come into contact with one another. Each one has his or her own objectives and instructions. Individual employees and clients will respond in different ways to different situations. It is important for the service provider to realise this and to work out the necessary strategies. Many of the difficult situations that arise have to do with control or perceived control. Clients want to feel in control of the process because they are the ones paying the money. Client contact personnel want to feel in control because they are the ones delivering the service. The management of a service business wants to feel in control of its employees because they are the ones who direct the employees' performance and ultimately by implication, the performance of the business.

Management must balance this so-called fight for control. Strategies must be developed to ensure that service personnel feel that they have sufficient control over the service delivery to ensure that they can deliver a quality service. Strategies must also be developed to make clients feel that they have some form of control over the process and make them feel more involved in the service that is being produced for them. This can be achieved by making them feel that they have a say in the service that is produced or by providing them with information or knowledge about the service in question. Knowledge is power, as the saying goes. The more information a client has of the service being provided, the more in control he or she feels.

Summary

This chapter focuses on the key issue of services marketing and the application of the elements of the extended marketing mix to the services environment. We clearly saw that service products are different from physical goods. The marketing mix for services was explored in depth. It is important to note that, in addition to the traditional 4 Ps of the marketing mix for physical goods, there are three additional marketing mix elements for the marketing of service products, namely processes, people and physical evidence.

Case study: kulula's 'Flying 101' plane design achieves global fame[23]

Johannesburg, 8 February 2010. Kulula's latest plane design has been a worldwide hit after being seen by plane-spotters en-route to South Africa. Photos of the new livery dubbed 'Flying 101' have since been viewed by millions having appeared on some of the world's leading blogs, spurring a frenzy of online comments. All this before it even touched down in South Africa.

The design covers the plane's exterior in a tongue-in-cheek guide to the various parts of the planes interior, such as the 'Mile-high initiation chamber'. The plane is just one of a fleet expansion of eight state-of-the-art Boeing 737-800s (each with unique livery). As these planes will be replacing the 737-400s currently used in kulula's fleet, South Africans can look forward to spotting the new 800s during this year.

"The 'Flying 101' was conceptualised and designed by kulula's in-house design department. This branding idea is a result of our 2010 strategy to demystify air travel for our fans," comments Nadine Damen, kulula Marketing Manager.

"Initially spotted by plane-spotters across the globe, our 'Flying 101' plane has become famous on the world wide web before touching South African soil," continues Damen. "We've been amazed by the number of blogs that have posted 'Flying 101' images as well as the large number of people talking about the new branding on Twitter."

The first Boeing branded with the 'Flying 101' landed in Johannesburg on Monday 8 February 2010 and started operating from 13 February 2010. The second Boeing underwent its transformation and appeared to kulula fans much like an oversized container box, with the words 'this way up' printed on its side and was launched on the 8 February 2010.

Exercises

1. Kulula has taken a bold and humorous approach in branding its aircraft. Discuss this innovative painting of their plane in terms of the physical evidence element of the marketing mix.
2. Discuss how the unique characteristics of services apply to a service provider like kulula.com.
3. Explain the concept of the total service product in terms of kulula.com and the service it provides.
4. The unique design of the plane identified in the case study forms a key part of kulula's product strategy and marketing communication. What message is being sent and how is it addressing the unique characteristics of services that need to be overcome by the marketer?
5. Develop a basic service blueprint for kulula where you map out the service process and identify the relevant critical incidents.

CHAPTER 11

Integrated marketing

Learning outcomes

After studying this chapter you should be able to:

- explain how the marketing concept relates to the critical marketing decisions;
- explain how marketing information can be obtained through the marketing information system (MIS);
- explain the effect of the environment on the design of the marketing mix;
- discuss how the determinants of consumer behaviour influence marketing decision making;
- identify how the choice of target market determines the design of the market offering;
- discuss the decisions made for each of the marketing mix elements;
- explain what changes have been made to the marketing mix in terms of a service product; and
- discuss the effect of marketing ethics on a business.

Introduction

The previous chapters have established the core analysis and information sources that need to be identified, researched and discussed before any marketing decisions can be made. These core information areas form the basis for designing an informed and effective market offering. There is a strong tendency to discuss solutions or to prepare answers before the problem has been identified! The preceding chapters also highlighted the decisions and processes in the two major areas of a marketing strategy namely choosing a target market (segmenting, targeting and positioning) and designing the marketing mix. In this chapter, we review how each of the previous chapters affect the decisions made by marketers in terms of offering a product or service to the marketplace. We will now try to integrate the chapters by establishing the link between these core information areas and the market decisions.

The marketing process

Traditionally there have been four major areas about which marketing management must make decisions. Once the target market is chosen, the marketer must make decisions about what to offer (the product), the place where the product is to be sold or delivered to the customer (distribution of the product), how the customer will be informed about the product (marketing communications), and the price of the product, which should reflect the value of the product to the customer. The four variables combine to represent the market offering which the marketer develops in order to meet and satisfy the needs of the customer. These four traditional marketing variables (also known as the 4 Ps) are known as the marketing mix.

Fig. 11.1 shows how the core analysis and topics discussed in the previous chapters interact in the marketing process to facilitate the achievement of the objective of an organisation. Once the target market is chosen and its needs properly understood through research, the marketing mix can be developed in order to meet the market needs. If this is done successfully, the marketer can contribute to the main objective of any business, namely the maximisation of profitability in the long term. This occurs within the context of a dynamic marketing environment.

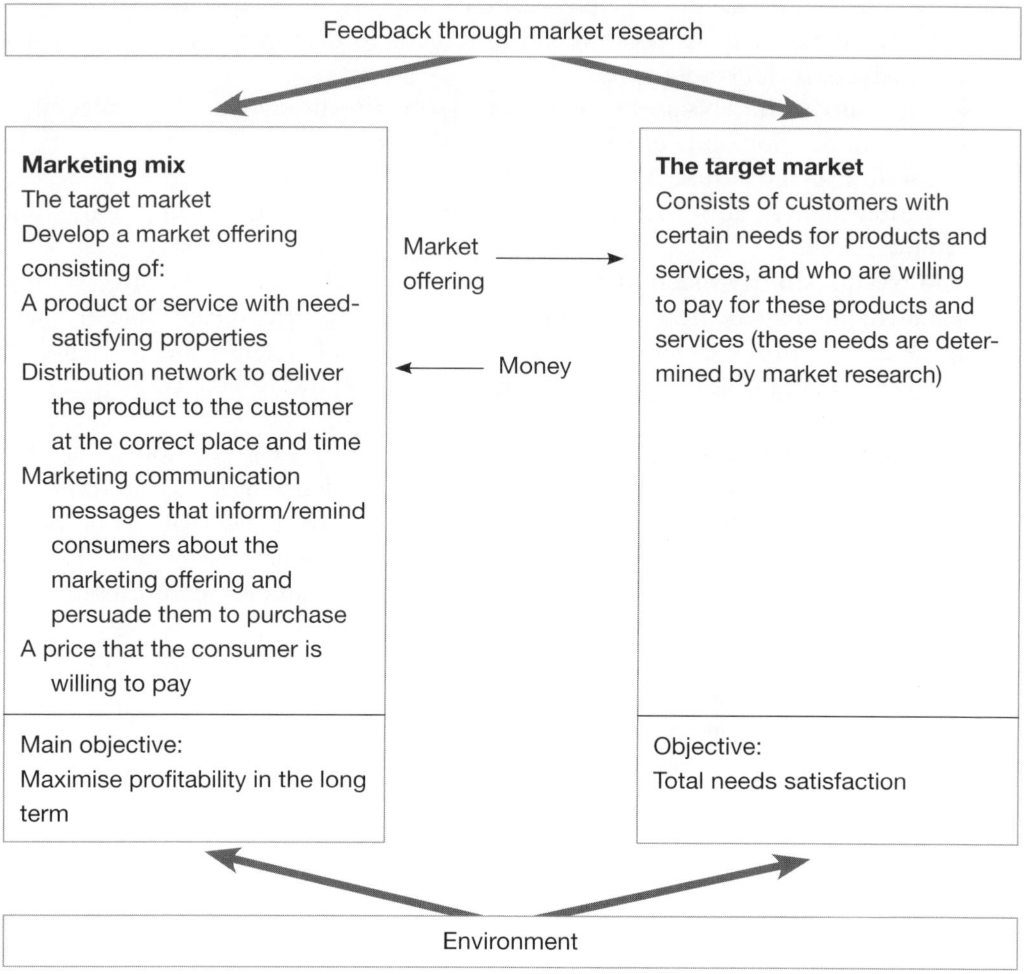

Figure 11.1 *The marketing process (Adapted from Strydom et al. 2006.* Marketing management, *5th edition. Cape Town: Juta, p 21.)*

The fact that many businesses now have a large service component in their value proposition aimed at specific target markets means that the traditional marketing mix (the 4 Ps) is not adequate for marketing service products – an issue covered in detail in the previous chapter. The three elements added to the traditional mix to form this expanded mix are:

- **Customer service**. This helps marketing management to differentiate the business and helps to build closer relationships with customers.
- **People**. The staff members form an integral part of the product, especially those employees who are involved in high levels of contact with customers.
- **Processes**. The policies and procedures of the business influence how a product or service is created or delivered to customers.

Market orientation

An organisation with a marketing orientation, and following the well-known marketing concept has four important characteristics:

- **Customer focus**. This refers to the efforts made to discover customer needs so that satisfaction can be delivered.
- **A team approach**. This means using cross-functional teams and an integrated approach to develop and deliver customer solutions.
- **Competitor orientation**. This refers to the continuous recognition of where competitors have an advantage, their competitive position and marketing strategies.
- **Social responsibility orientation**. This means that all of the above three factors must be implemented within the scope of acting in a socially responsible manner. All the actions of the organisation must be checked off against this prerequisite to ensure the organisation protects its 'licence to operate' in society.

These four key characteristics lead to a business being in a position to deliver satisfaction to its customers. If this is measured and if the business performs in delivering satisfaction to the customer effectively, the profitability of the business can be enhanced through better customer retention and increased loyalty. This is evidenced by a number of benefits that a loyal customer can provide for a business over a period of time:[1]

- increased purchases;
- reduced operating costs;
- referrals to other potential customers; and
- the ability to justify a price premium to differentiate the product from those offered by competitors.

When this marketing orientation is coupled to effectiveness in the marketplace, the profitability of the business is reinforced. Peter Drucker, a famous management expert, is credited with the statement that an organisation has two main tasks: acquiring customers, and innovation. The ultimate goal of a strong marketing orientation is to develop and implement marketing strategies that attract, satisfy and retain target-market customers. This is done through the marketing strategy, which includes the target market and the marketing mix, as shown in fig. 11.2.

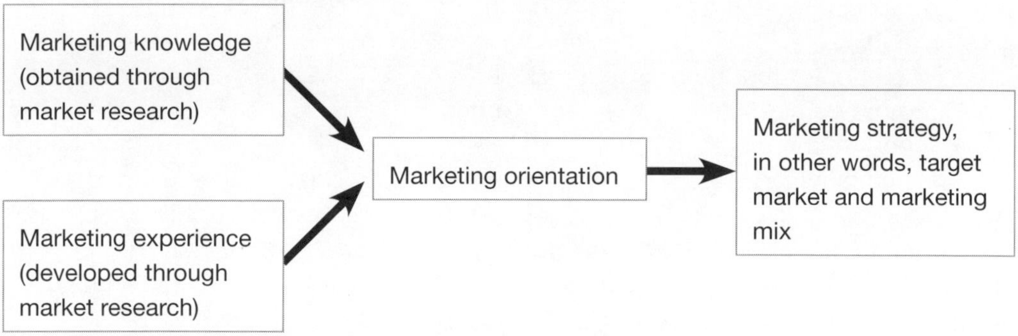

Figure 11.2 *How marketing orientation shapes marketing decisions*

Philip Kotler, a well-known marketing academic, feels that the trends in the environment have led to the recognition that a more comprehensive, interdependent integrated approach is needed to take this environmental volatility into account in the marketing concept. This 'holistic marketing concept' has four broad components:[2]

- **Relationship marketing**. The aim is to build win-win relationships with key constituents like customers, employees, marketing partners, and members of the financial community. This network, if built up successfully, can facilitate the achievement of the organisation's objectives.
- **Integrated marketing**. The marketing mix is the combination of marketing activities and tools needed to meet the customer's needs. They should work together to deliver value to the customer. They should work together to provide a synergistic effect, that is, the effective management and design of the mix must maximise the joint effect of all the activities in the mix. The focal point should be the delivery of benefits for the customer.
- **Internal marketing**. This makes sure everyone working in the business embraces and supports the marketing effort by co-ordinating the functions and efforts of the staff. The place to start is making sure all the marketing functions like marketing and sales work together, then making sure that every department and level of management is aligned to the same marketing view.
- **Performance marketing**. This incorporates operating in a socially responsible manner, as well as understanding the marketing metrics and scorecards that impact on the financial performance of the business. The relationship of marketing activities to profits has received much attention in the last few years, and the marketing function in a business has the responsibility of ensuring that the company's actions are seen to be measurable and based on sound business principles.

Environmental change and marketing mix adaptation

In the late 1990s the impact of inflation, advancing technology and deteriorating exchange rates, among other factors, meant that Toyota SA had to reconsider its model range and the entry price of the lowest priced model in its range. The market was looking for economical entry-level cars and Toyota found that there was a gap between its lowest priced offering and that of other competitive car marques. During the decade that began in 2000, Toyota had to change its approach.

While continuing to offer value-based products, in 2001, they expanded its product range by launching a hybrid petrol-electric car called the Prius. By 2004, there was a 6-month waiting list for the model, so the company decided to roll out hybrids throughout its product range. This new positioning of the global Toyota brand is a clear response to the market's broader awareness of key environmental challenges facing the world. The company has changed its advertising pay-off line to 'Lead the way', reflecting its new focus on energy efficient 'green' cars. It is emphasising the environmentally friendly features of its products, such as advanced technology for fuel efficiency and lower carbon emissions, and is continuing to research and develop these aspects of its offering.

The marketing environment

It has already been established that the marketing environment of a company is dynamic and made up of a number of sub-environments which interact with one another. As discussed in detail in chapter 2, changes in the macro-environment (economic, political, social and technological) fall outside the control of the organisation.

Marketing managers need to understand the wider business environment (macro-environment), but they should concentrate on those aspects that can be influenced, such as the controllable variables of product, price, communication and distribution. This is illustrated in fig. 11.3.

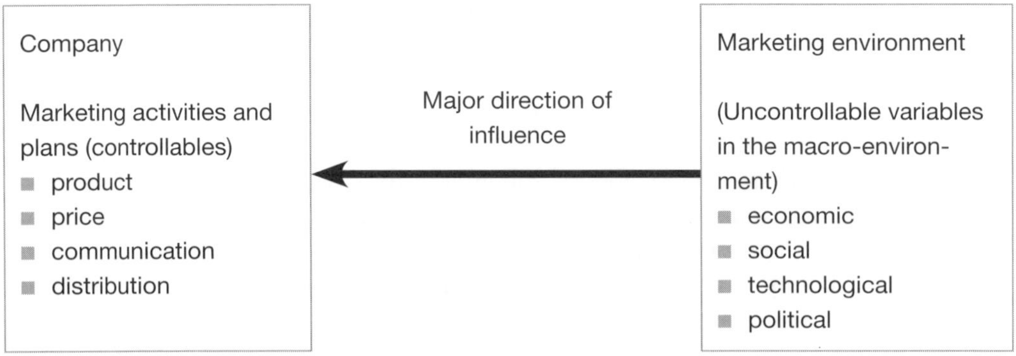

***Figure 11.3** Environmental influences and marketing management (Adapted from Strydom et al. 2006.* Marketing management, *5th edition. Cape Town: Juta, p 21.)*

The effectiveness of marketing will be determined by how well it can match the offerings of the organisation to the requirements of the marketplace. Marketers therefore need to develop an 'outside-in' orientation – being led by the market. This can be seen as the strategic role of the marketing function in the organisation. This is no easy task, as evidenced by the many organisations that no longer exist, or have lost market share to competitors. There is a tendency for organisations to become preoccupied with their daily operational problems (often termed fire-fighting), which leads to a loss of contact with the needs of customers and changes in the environment. Small changes may well be the precursors of more significant changes, so marketers must continually monitor what is going on and be willing to respond. Fig. 11.4 illustrates a framework for environmental monitoring and adaption.[3] Environmental monitoring identifies short-run changes and long-term trends. These are classified as opportunities, threats or inconsequential events. If adaptation is required, it can only take place within the controllable aspects of the marketing mix.

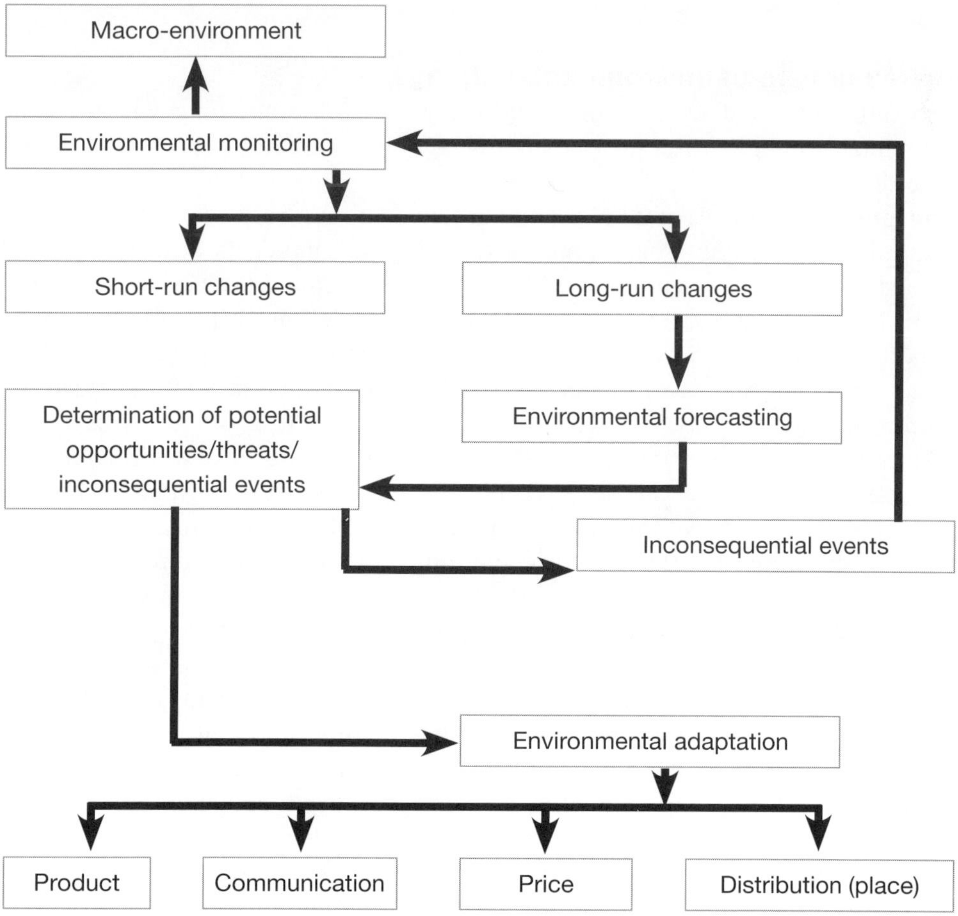

Figure 11.4 *Environmental adaptation and monitoring*

Winds of change

One of the most significant changes in today's marketing world is how consumers research and buy products. The Internet has been a major catalyst for this shift. In many product categories such as electronics, health care, and financial services, consumers are ignoring traditional marketing communication methods and using the Internet to research products and decide what to buy. Over half of all USA electronics consumers use the web to narrow down the choice of brands. In 2005 almost half of all customers who bought insurance researched it online before talking to an agent, and this is expected to rise to 80%. More consumers are visiting consumer-generated sites and blogs, as they trust these third-party sources more than corporate communication efforts.

Source: Adapted from Court, D. 2007. The evolving role of the CMO. *The McKinsey Quarterly*, no. 3, pp 29–39.

Four key drivers of environmental change

We are all aware that we are in an 'information age', something which requires fundamental strategic responses from management to four important drivers of change drivers.[4]

- **The globalisation of markets**. Changes in communication and transportation mean that any business can launch a website and market its offerings globally, as easily as if it was marketing to customers just around the corner. Companies like Microsoft, Intel, Merck and McDonald's are selling in key global markets. Smaller companies must be innovative and flexible to compete on the global stage – visit the www.stormkoek.co.za site to see how one South African wine producer is using innovative ways of selling its wares to a global market.
- **Changing industrial structures**. Old traditional markets have declined and new markets have emerged. These markets offer good profit opportunities for those marketers that can move fast enough to capitalise. Many economies are shifting to being information-based, with corresponding shifts in the structures and ways of distributing products and services. Visit the www.amazon.com to see how many products are available for delivery as a download, rather than a physical item like a book or CD.
- **The information revolution**. The Internet and broadband networks have created an explosion in connectivity that has revolutionised almost every aspect of business. Intranets have changed the way a business can operate, making it possible to facilitate cross-functional teams working together through informal networks to produce and support products. Levi's has an ongoing information feed from its retailers on the sizes and styles of its jeans being sold, which enables it to ensure that an order for fabric from its supplier Miliken Company can be placed for immediate delivery. Miliken responds by ordering more fibre from its supplier Du Pont. In this way costs have been reduced, service and delivery speeded up, and response time to consumer demand improved.

- **Rising customer expectations**. These three trends above have led to a rise in customer expectations. Market segmentation was the initial response to meeting customer needs. Companies made an increasing number of variants to meet customer needs – e.g. Nike had 347 different types of running shoes. This high level of the number of variants led to higher costs and limited effectiveness. The information advances led to a new strategy – mass customisation, where media and products could be tailored and made to order for the individual customer! The explosion in information meant that companies could gather information on a customer from many sources and store it, using it to gain insights into individual customers to be able to better meet the specific needs of that customer and communicate directly with individual customers. For example, Dell computers could deliver a customised computer solution to a customer's door within 48 hours of the order being received.

Obtaining and using marketing information

It is imperative for a marketing organisation to have an effective marketing information system (MIS) – see the discussion in chapter 4. Such a system helps to integrate all the different types of marketing information and makes this information available to the decision makers in a useful and timely form, as illustrated in fig. 11.5.

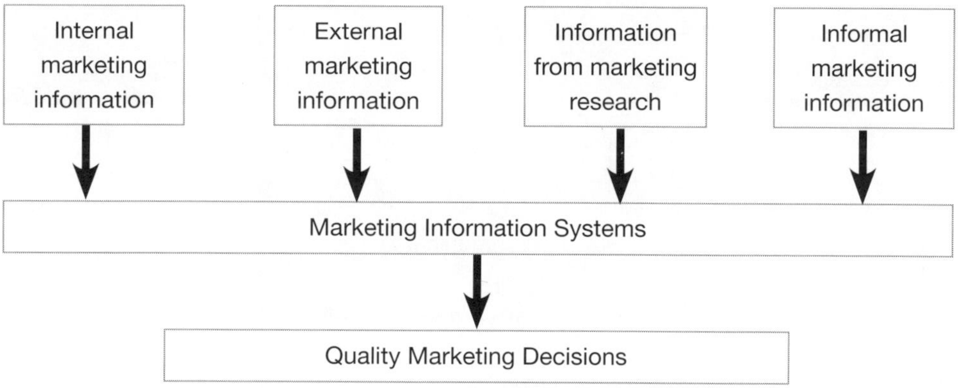

Figure 11.5 *Sources of information for an MIS (Adapted from Cant, M. 2010.* Essentials of marketing. *Cape Town: Juta, p 65.)*

The purpose of the MIS is to collect, analyse and evaluate all the information that is likely to be of value when making marketing and other decisions.[5] The idea is to uncover customer insights that can be used to develop a value proposition that meets the customer's needs and provides differential advantage against competitive offerings. The information system is therefore the interface between marketers making decisions and the marketing environment. The MIS provides key information for every other function within the organisation, including, but not limited to production, operations, and research and development (R+D). Many large organisations have formal MIS structures. Some small businesses do not have a formal system but very effectively use informal channels to keep in touch with the market.

Fig. 11.6 shows the connection between the information gathered and marketing decisions. Any responses to the environment are then monitored and evaluated to determine whether they are succeeding in better aligning the organisation to the market.

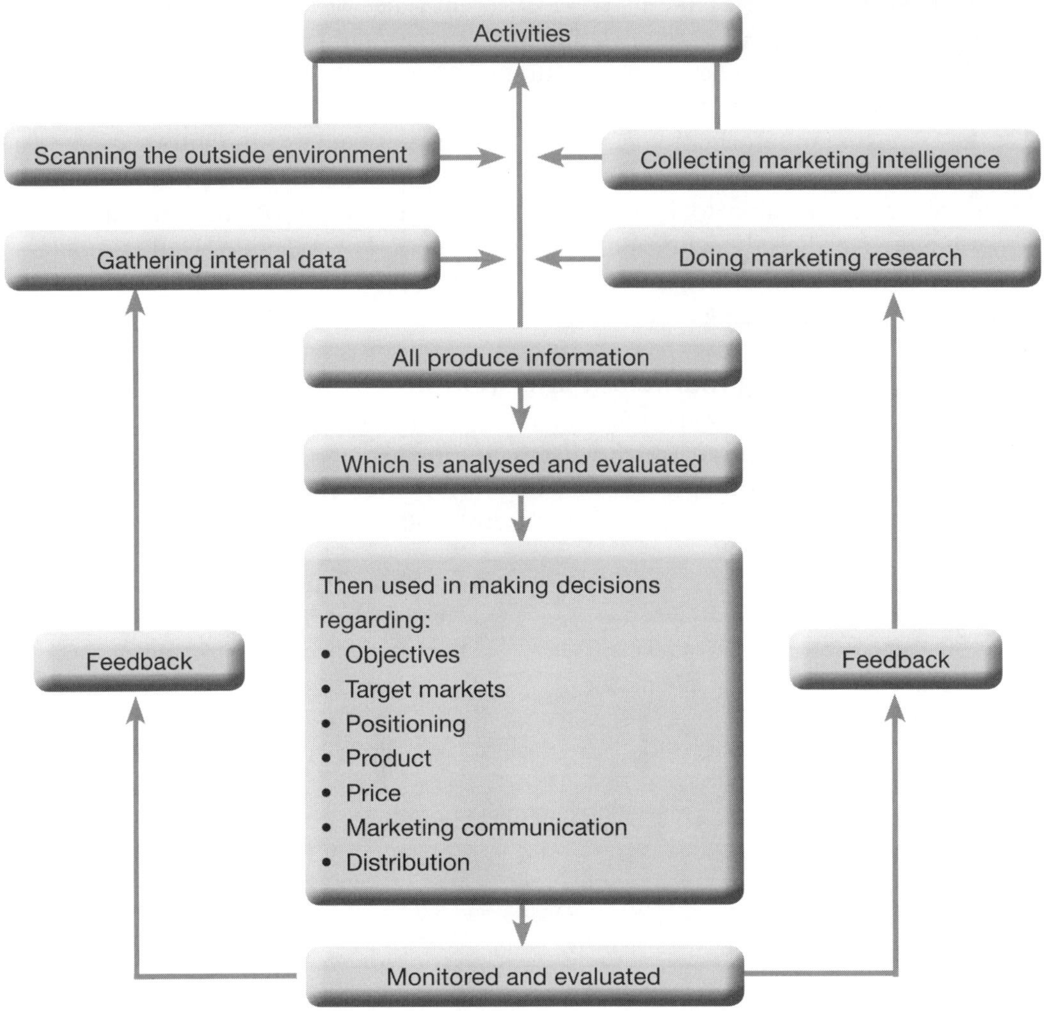

Figure 11.6 *MIS and Marketing decision making (Adapted from Strydom, J. et al. 2006* Marketing management. *6th edition. Cape Town: Juta. p150.)*

Perspectives on consumer behaviour

One of the basic premises of marketing is that by understanding consumers and their purchasing habits, marketers can design an effective offering to help them achieve their objectives. This topic is covered in detail in chapter 3.

There are many basic questions that any marketer must be able to answer about the market, such as who the consumers are and why they buy. This information is critical because marketing is supposed to be the link between the customers and the organisation. Fig. 11.7 illustrates the relationship between the environment, the marketer and the consumer.

The case of Encyclopedia Britannica

The Encyclopedia Britannica brand was one of the strongest and well-known brands of encyclopaedias in the world for over two centuries. The evolution of the information age and home computing, however, led to declining sales. Parents' behaviour had changed, so they bought computers for their children, and connectivity, rather than printed encyclopaedias. The cost of producing a printed set of the Britannica encyclopaedia was about £250, and sold for £1 300–£2 200 in the UK. It still marketed through expensive direct marketing channels. Microsoft and other companies launched CD-ROM versions of their reference publications which cost about £1 to make and sold for £50 but more often were given away or bundled with computer or software sales. Also, they were easier to use, had sophisticated electronic features, including advanced search capability. They also included sounds, music, images and films.

Britannica saw the threat finally, but when it launched its own CD-ROM, it charged £755, to avoid undercutting the sales personnel selling the physical product. Only in 1997 was the decision taken to abandon the sales force, and the product placed on the Internet to salvage its eroding market position. It now offers the print, DVD and online versions, but other sites such as Wikipedia are still effectively challenging its position.

Britannica's management had failed to recognise the implications of the environmental trends, or that its sales force had become an expensive liability, and that the real competitor was the computer and the Internet.

Source: Adapted from Boyle, P. 2008. *Value-based marketing*. Chichester, West Sussex: Wiley, pp 8–9.

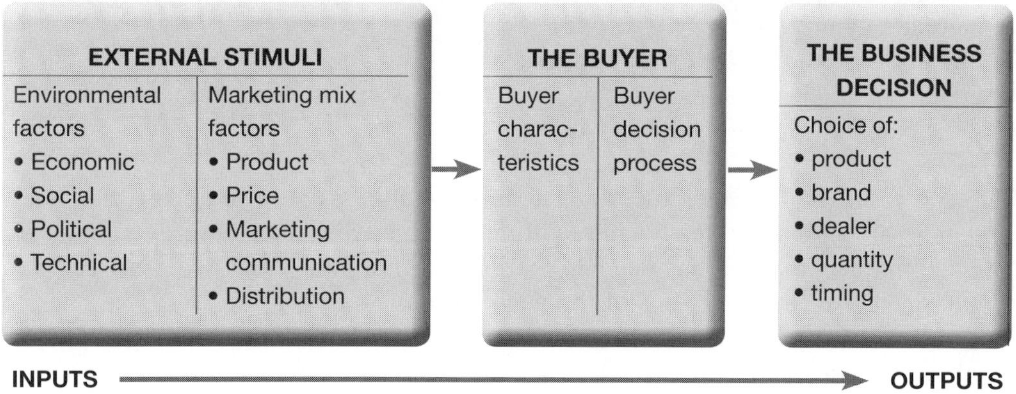

***Figure 11.7** A simple model of buyer behaviour (Source: Adapted from Wilson, RMS & Gilligan, C. 2009.* Strategic marketing management, *2nd edition. Oxford: Butterworth-Heinemann, p 199.)*

The environmental variables under which all market players operate also have an influence on the consumer. Likewise, the marketing mix designed by the marketer should also have an impact on the consumer. These two aspects are external stimuli to the customer. There are also internal stimuli that affect the decisions made by the consumer. The buyer's own characteristics, for example, will affect his or her decisions. Different consumers will have different perceptions and expectations, and the manner in which the buyer proceeds through the decision-making process will also affect the purchasing decision. Each consumer may have different individual or group influences, and no two consumers are exactly alike. The level of involvement of the buyer with the product will determine how seriously and systematically he or she proceeds through the steps in the decision-making process. Lastly, the buyer will make a number of decisions. The marketer's job, through the marketing mix, is to persuade the buyer to buy the marketer's products, and to deliver the need satisfaction that will hopefully ensure that the buyer will remain a loyal consumer.

Just as the marketing environment is constantly changing, consumers are also affected by changes in the environment, and their needs will also change. Any business must be aware of the changing characteristics and needs of its consumer base. These could be significant changes, which the business will have to address through its marketing activities.

Wilson and Gilligan have identified a number of characteristics which are associated with what they term the 'new' consumer:[6]

- the development of new value systems;
- greater emphasis on value for money;
- higher levels of price awareness and price sensitivity;
- an increased demand for and a willingness to accept more and exciting new products;
- less fear of technology;
- lower levels of brand and supplier loyalty;
- greater willingness to experiment with new products, ideas and delivery systems;
- a greater cynicism;
- higher levels of environmental awareness;
- greater scepticism about politicians, big business and traditional institutions; and
- the changing roles of men and women.

The end result is that consumers are more demanding, more aware of offers, less brand loyal, and more ready and willing to complain than before. The recent passage into law of the Consumer Protection Act in South Africa will only serve to emphasise these characteristics of the new consumer.

The core of any marketing strategy is a commitment to understanding consumer needs and problems – see fig. 11.8.

In fig. 11.8, we see that an organisation must monitor the changing consumer needs and the changing ways in which the consumer uses the product. These two factors will affect the benefits which the consumer is seeking. The business responds to these through changes in some aspect of the marketing mix. By successfully meeting these consumer needs and delivering the benefits desired, the business can satisfy its consumers, increasing the likelihood of success. Note that the consumers determine what value they receive from a business by weighing up the benefits which they perceive as being delivered to them against the cost of the product or service.

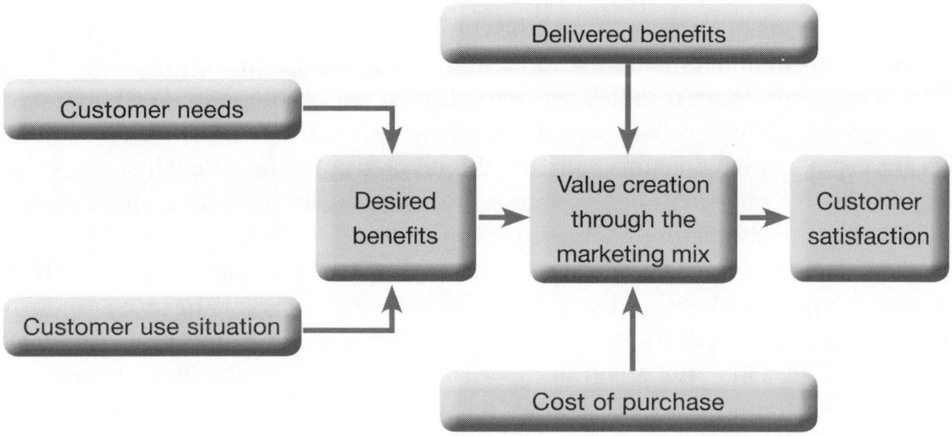

Figure 11.8 *Consumer analysis and the marketing mix (Source: Adapted from Walters, D & Lancaster, G. 2000, Implementing value strategy through the value chain.* Management Decision, *38(3), pp 160–178.)*

Marketers must therefore ensure that their customers believe that they are receiving value for money compared to what is available from competing companies.

Applying customer insights to marketing and sales efforts

Tesco, a leading UK retailer, looked at its loyalty card data in combination with survey data on what customers were not buying. It found that in some of its store formats young mothers bought fewer baby products in its stores because they trusted pharmacies more. Tesco launched BabyClub to provide expert advice and also targeted coupons to specific customers. Its share of baby product sales in the UK grew from 16% in 2000 to 24% in 2003.

Best Buy, the leading consumer electronics retailer in the USA, integrated shopper research, point-of-sale data, and demographic analysis to see what shopper segments were over-represented or under-represented in specific areas and then varied its store formats and product assortments accordingly. Stores located near large concentrations of affluent male professionals offered more high-end home theatre equipment, specialised financing, and same-day delivery. Stores closer to moms with families featured softer colours, personal shopping assistants, and child-oriented technology products. After the stores changed to the new formats, sales surged by 7% and the gross profit rate jumped significantly.

Source: Adapted from Forsyth, JE, Galante, N & Guild,T. 2006. Capitalising on customer insights. *The McKinsey Quarterly*, no. 3, pp 43–53.

Target-market selection and positioning

The importance of target-market selection and positioning is best understood in terms of the phenomenon of fragmentation,[7] whereby technology and cultural differences contribute to the splintering of the market into diverse groups. These are environmental aspects, many of which work together. In selecting a target market, marketers need to understand how to recognise the various groups that make up the total market. This process relies on marketing research (chapter 4), which assists the marketer to find the best way to segment the market. (chapter 5). Once the different segments have been identified the market potential of each segment must be established. Again, market research is instrumental in the selection of segments that will help the company to achieve its objectives.

Having decided on a specific target market or markets, the marketer will have to determine how to position the product in the target market. In order to do this, further market research in terms of the competitor positions and need satisfaction may be required. Once the positioning strategy has been established the marketing mix must be tailored to meet consumer needs effectively. If correctly designed, the marketing mix is how the marketer will meet the needs of the consumers in such a way that the consumer's perception of the product matches the positioning strategy selected by the marketer.

Note that there are continuous changes in the market, so the environment must be monitored continuously to determine whether repositioning is needed. Fig. 11.9 shows the segmenting, targeting, positioning and designing progression when developing the marketing mix.

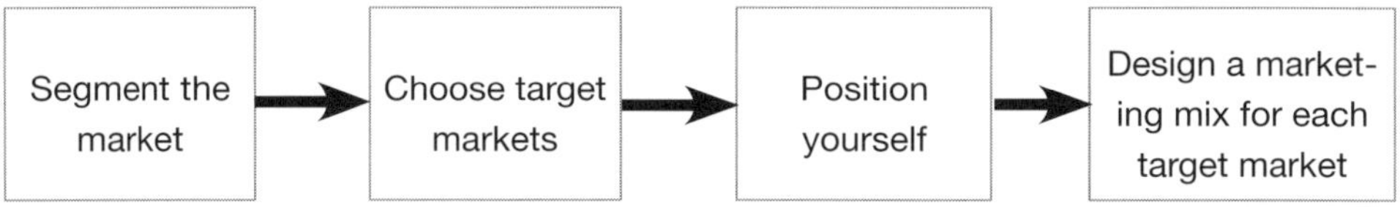

Figure 11.9 *Progression for pinpointing the market (Adapted from Venter, P & Jansen van Rensburg, M. 2009.* Strategic marketing: Theory and applications for competitive advantage. *Cape Town: Oxford University Press, p 143.)*

The marketing mix

The previous sections of this chapter formed the basis for an information base from which marketing decisions can be made. These are the building blocks upon which any effective marketing campaign is based. The care and attention to detail exercised by the marketer with these building blocks will help make key decisions in respect of target market and the marketing mix that is required to address that market.

The traditional marketing mix is a combination of marketing decisions designed to influence customers to buy the enterprise's products and/or services, the well known 4 Ps described in detail in chapter 6 (product), chapter 7 (distribution or place), chapter 8 (price) and chapter 9 (promotion). This is shown in fig. 11.10.

Product decisions

The marketer must determine what the actual product offers, as well as the need-satisfying benefits which should be included. The marketer needs to make decisions regarding the range of different types of product and/or service to make and offer. This is called the product mix.

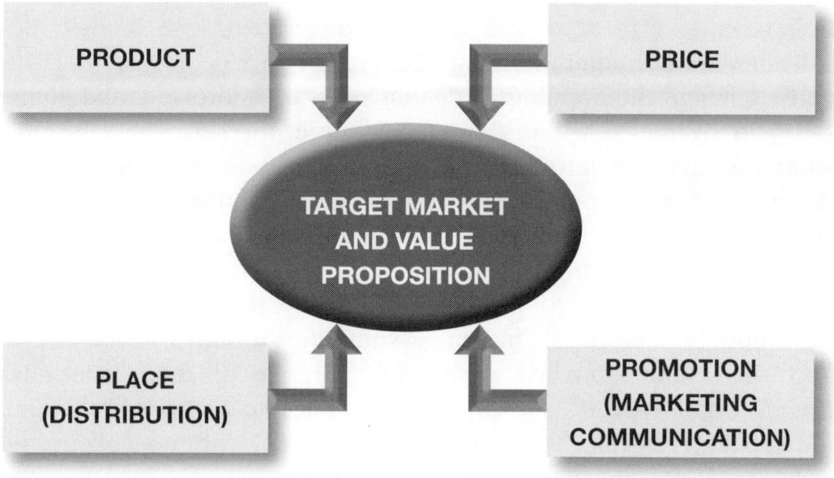

Figure 11.10 *The marketing mix*

Harley Davidson and the 4 Ps

Harley Davidson used the 4 Ps of marketing to position its motorcycles to a new customer segment: the baby boomer generation in the United States. The product was changed by introducing a new engine, but retaining the 'heavy metal' look. The promotional strategy was changed by shifting the advertising to promote a softer image. It featured celebrities such as Elizabeth Taylor on a Harley. The objective was to attract the high-income segment. It changed its distribution strategy by cleaning up the dealerships so that they did not look so dark and so that they were more customer-friendly. Harley Davidson expanded its product range to include motorcycle fashion accessories displayed in a clean, bright atmosphere. They priced their motorcycles to reflect the value that the high-income earners place on living out their fantasies on a Harley Davidson motorcycle. (The upper end of the motorcycle range often runs into the $20 000 price range.) The company has established a group called the Harley Owners' Group (HOG) that offers networking benefits and rides to special events. It has also established an extensive website devoted to the Group with accessories, information and events. All these components demonstrate a well-co-ordinated marketing mix targeted to a specific segment of the market.

Source: Adapted from Kotler, P & Keller, KL. 2009. *Marketing management, 13th edition*. Upper Saddle River, NJ: Prentice-Hall, p 180.

Specific product strategies must be established: whether the product mix will be extended through product diversification; whether it will be reduced for more specialisation; whether to standardise the product range; how to differentiate or distinguish the product from other competitive products; and decisions on how to manage possible obsolescence of the product. A plan for the development and commercialisation of the products must be developed. The product design and package design are an important component of product decisions. The whole issue of a brand name and the branding decisions must be addressed, and plans made to establish brand awareness within the selected target markets.

Although product is usually the first component of the marketing mix addressed by marketing, the development and design of the product offering and package are totally dependent on input from the environmental analysis and consumer analyses. Without researching these two areas, the marketer cannot effectively design a product offering to meet the needs of the consumer. For example, changing economic conditions may necessitate developing a lower-priced product item. Mercedes-Benz launched its A and B range of models and BMW SA developed its 1 and 3 series as a response to economic changes in the marketplace that required entry-level motorcar offerings. Evolving use of products may necessitate packaging design changes. Both of these could lead to new product opportunities and/or brand extensions.

Pricing decisions

Price is important because it is the only element in the marketing mix that generates revenue. It is also important because it affects the enterprise in a direct way, namely the profitability of the business. The marketer will need to establish the price sensitivity of the target customers, and will then need to establish the basic price. This can be done on the basis of costs, on the basis of the demand for a product, or on the basis of competitive pricing structures. All three of these factors will influence the setting of a price. The marketer must also establish flexibility in the pricing structure through the use of adjustments. These factors could include different types of discounts and the geographic location of the customers.

We have referred to the effect of the environment on pricing by noting that economic conditions could lead a marketer to develop a lower-priced alternative. The marketer must monitor the environment to analyse the effect of the environmental factors on pricing. New developments in materials and processes can have significant impact on the bottom line of a business as a result of its impact in pricing and margins. Technology, in particular, has provided significant threats to many businesses by its accelerating rate of change, yet it also provides opportunities to improve bottom-line performance by improving profitability. Developments such as just-in-time, materials management systems and e-commerce have had a significant impact on the profit margins of motorcar manufacturers. Many cars are now sold over the Internet, with significant impact on promotion and distribution costs and therefore on pricing. Marketers must also carefully research and monitor the target market's sensitivity to its pricing strategy. Marlboro is the leading cigarette brand in the world, yet it had to implement a significant price decrease a few years ago, when research revealed that it was losing market share because smokers were switching to lower-priced or generic cigarettes. The price decrease, although unusual in terms of traditional marketing strategy, succeeded in regaining lost market share.

Distribution decisions

The marketer will have to establish the intensity of distribution needed to meet the market's needs and expectations. This could be intensive, selective or exclusive distribution intensity. The marketer will also have to decide on the type of distribution channel through which to deliver the product or service to the final consumers. There are many options to consider here, from direct channels through to those that utilise intermediaries such as retailers, wholesalers and agents. The effect of the physical position of the marketer's own business could be included here, as the location of a business is often the most critical determinant of possible success.

Distribution decisions and distribution channel design are areas where rapid changes are occurring in terms of the marketing mix. The use of the Internet for direct sales is revolutionising the way many firms reach their customers. Dell computers recently overtook Compaq as the leading personal computer seller in the USA, and Dell has a completely different distribution strategy to Compaq. While Compaq distributes through the traditional computer retailer channels, Dell uses a direct channel by selling to customers over the Internet. This innovation has led to significant reductions in distribution costs and has also had a direct effect on its pricing policy. It is critical for marketers to monitor both changes in the environment and consumer expectations of where they want to purchase products. In so doing, they will always be able to meet consumer needs by providing the right product at the right time.

Promotion decisions

It is essential for marketers to inform current and potential consumers in the marketplace about their products and their marketing activities. This communication can be done by using marketing communication tools such as advertising, sales promotion, personal selling and publicity.

It is clear that a number of decisions are associated with the use of these communication tools, such as what message to deliver, what media to use, what size budget is required, and what promotional support activities to implement. All of these must be implemented, co-ordinated and evaluated. The marketer must also communicate internally throughout the organisation to ensure that the employees and staff are aware of what the expectations are in the marketplace and what message the organisation is delivering to its target audiences.

Media choices are an area to which marketers must pay particular attention. The growing number of media choices (Internet, hot air balloons, travelling billboards, SMS, new magazines and new television stations such as satellite television and e-tv) means that marketers have to pay particular attention to making the correct choices for communicating with the target markets effectively. This requires systematic research of the consumer base to monitor trends in terms of media as well as advertising campaign impact. Nando's, for example, has been particularly effective in designing campaigns that are related to current events in South Africa. Its success is as a result of monitoring the environment for opportunities.

Adaptation of the traditional marketing mix

At the beginning of this chapter it was said that the traditional view of the marketing mix has been expanded to seven elements (7 Ps) to take into account the growing importance of people, process and physical evidence in the marketing of service products).[8]

- **People**. This includes all the people who play a part in the delivery of service and influence the buyer's perception – the staff, the customer, and the front-line service personnel.
- **Process**. This includes the actual procedures and activity flows through which service is delivered, including the organisation's operating system and service delivery system.
- **Physical evidence**. This is the environment in which the service is delivered as well as the interface between the company and the customer. It also includes the tangible aspects of delivering the service or communicating the service.

  Table 11.1 provides more detail.

Table 11.1 *The expanded marketing mix elements for service products*

People	Process	Physical evidence
Employees	Activity flow	Facility design
Customer interaction	Standardisation	Atmosphere
Internal marketing	Customisation	Equipment
Capabilities	Service delivery	Signage
Effectiveness	Database management	Employee dress
Availability	Technology	Literature
Selection		
Training		
Motivation		

The importance of people in the marketing mix

All of the people involved in the delivery of service to the customer will affect how the consumer perceives the service itself. These perceptions are influenced by many factors, such as how the people are dressed, their personal appearance, their attitude and their behaviour. The actual person providing the service, who we will call the contact person, is probably the most important person in terms of the consumer's perceptions. These people are the focal point of the service encounter and they have a tremendous influence on how a consumer perceives the total service experience. We only have to think of our own experience of people doing this kind of work (e.g. bank tellers, waiters, counter clerks, retail salespeople) to become aware of how critical they are to the organisation.

This implies that there are serious considerations for an organisation in terms of staff productivity and training. The staff must have the ability to cope with all types of customer, they have to deliver service reliably, and they have to help present a consistent image to the consumers. One way of helping to ensure that this occurs is by means of internal marketing. Internal marketing is marketing to your employees so that they are informed, committed and motivated to deliver the required standard of service on a consistent basis.

The marketer of a service product has to carefully plan this 'people' factor of the expanded marketing mix. He or she has to clearly spell out exactly what is expected from all staff in their interactions with customers. All parts of the human resources function must be included in marketing decision making to ensure a favourable impact on the customer.

These activities include the recruitment, training, motivating and rewarding of staff. Disney World in Orlando, USA is well known for the excellent service culture it has developed. Many South African organisations, such as Pick n Pay, have sent their own staff to Disney World to attend courses in service and people management skills.

Process in the marketing mix

Process includes the flow of activities by which the service is delivered. These activities can be illustrated by the service delivery system and the operations system. The actual way in which the service is delivered to a consumer is used as a means by which consumers judge whether the service is satisfactory or not. This means that the production of the service – the process – is an important part of marketing. The aim is for smooth, efficient, customer-friendly procedures designed with the consumer's satisfaction in mind. The delivery process must therefore be designed as if from the customer's point of view. Many procedures and processes may be useful to the organisation, but from the customer point of view, may simply be seen as bureaucracy, and may be detrimental to good customer service.

Types of process activities

A number of different types of process activities have been identified.[9] One type is those that have been established in support of the service encounter. These could include administrative systems, data-processing systems, consumer tracking and database management systems. Other processes are not visible to the customer but help to ensure that the service delivery proceeds smoothly. This includes organising and planning activities. Planning is important to ensure that the consumer experiences the service with the least inconvenience. This would be reflected in the design of forms, the information requested from customers, the payment procedures, the credit procedures, and the design of queuing systems. Some organisations cause consumer frustration because of complicated bureaucratic procedures and policies that they follow. These may appear to be unreasonable or illogical.

A related aspect is whether the service process is a standardised process or whether it is customised to each consumer. McDonald's, for example, is renowned for the process design that allows it to provide a quality meal very quickly in a consistent manner. Other competitors, such as Burger King, advertise the fact that customers can have it their own way, as they will prepare the burger the way the customer wants it. Another example of this concept is a comparison of two successful airline companies, Southwest in the United States and Singapore Airlines. Southwest is a no-frills, no exceptions, low-priced airline that offers frequent, relatively short-length domestic flights. All of the evidence that it provides is consistent with its vision and market position. Singapore Airlines, on the other hand, focuses on the business traveller and is concerned with meeting individual traveller needs. Thus, its processes are customised to the individual, and employees are empowered to provide non-standard service, when needed. In South Africa we have British Airways and kulula.com, which are run by the same company yet follow very different models for delivering a travel experience.

Physical evidence in the marketing mix

It is often said that 'seeing is believing', yet one of the characteristics of service is that service is intangible to consumers. This means that they cannot see it, hear it or touch it. The fact that a consumer cannot see service before it is actually consumed means that the risks of purchasing a service are greater than purchasing a traditional physical product. You cannot, for example, see a haircut on the shelf before deciding whether you would like your hair cut. This means that it is extremely important for the marketer to give the consumer tangible evidence of the nature or quality of the service so that the consumer's risk perception is reduced.

Physical evidence can be explained as the tangible elements that support the service delivery, and that help to give clues about the positioning of the service product. It also gives the consumer evidence that symbolises the intangible benefits that they may have received. A consumer looking at a travel package could be provided with a brochure that describes the highlights of the tour and gives colour photographs of the hotels and sights that the customer is likely to see. The more glossy and detailed the brochure, the more evidence is provided to the consumer as to the value of the trip. Other examples of physical evidence include letterheads, business cards, report formats, signage and equipment. When the service product is such that consumers do not have much with which to judge the actual quality, they will look for these clues as a basis for judging the quality. Bear in mind that people and processes also provide clues to the consumer. Physical evidence gives a business an ideal opportunity to indicate to consumers the level of service that they will receive.

Types of physical evidence

There are two different types of physical evidence, namely essential evidence and peripheral evidence.[10]

Essential evidence is critical to the service, and contributes significantly to the consumer's purchase decision. For example, a tour bus operator could provide essential evidence through the type, appearance and newness of the buses it runs. For a university, the library and computer facilities could be considered essential. The actual lecture venues and their equipment would also be essential.

Peripheral evidence is not as important to the service delivery and usually consists of things that the consumer can keep or use. There are many examples of this. Banks provide chequebook and credit card holders. Hairdressers or medical professionals provide appointment cards. Hotels make available a range of toiletries (such as soap, shampoo and bath gel) for their guests to use and take with them. These items enhance the service and make its delivery easier, and may add value to the service in small ways that the consumer appreciates.

Marketing ethics

The whole issue of ethical behaviour in business is gaining more momentum because of the importance of sustainability in the governance and operations of a business. Ethics are the public's perception of an organisation's standards of behaviour. Marketing ethics would then be the public's perceptions of the organisation's marketing actions, and involves the moral judgement of the consequences of what the organisation does and says in relation to marketing activities.[11] Although we would like to believe that all marketing actions are integrated within an ethical and moral system guiding all business, it is clear that many times this is not the case. See chapter 1 for more information on ethics in marketing.

Some issues around marketing ethics

Research done in 2000 identified some of the pressing issues facing marketing ethics at the time. These included bribery, fairness, honesty, pricing, products, personnel, confidentiality, advertising, data manipulation, and purchasing.

Source: Adapted from Venter & Van Rensburg. 2009 *Strategies Marketing*, p. 346.

Products

Consumers satisfy their needs and wants through products and services. One of the long debated ethical issues around products is product safety. Consumers use products every day believing that they or their friends and families will not be harmed or injured. It is very difficult, however, for a consumer to have the knowledge and expertise to judge whether a product is safe or not, so society relies on business to consciously develop safe products and promote the safe usage of those products. The principle of due care says that the manufacturer has more knowledge and expertise than the consumer, so the manufacturer or service provider has an obligation, above and beyond any possible contract, to make sure that the consumers are safe from being injured by defective products and service.

The recent case of defective accelerators in Toyota motor vehicles (see chapter 2) is a perfect example of the problems that can arise from this issue. Toyota was severely criticised for its lack of action around a problem which, in some cases, may have led to loss of life. The actions of management in hiding the reports of malfunction and denying the problem led to senior managers being required to account for this in front of US lawmakers and global impact on the brand. The lawsuits themselves have yet to be sorted out, and the share price of Toyota suffered as a result. In South Africa, Toyota SA handled the issue better, and made a concerted attempt to recall all cars possibly affected. As a result the brand has not suffered as much damage here. Even service providers need to be careful, as shown by the well-known case of McDonald's being successfully sued by a customer who burned herself because the coffee she spilled on herself was too hot. The courts held that McDonald's had not taken enough care with the temperature and the processes it used to avoid the accident.[12]

Product quality

Bottled water sales are booming, but who is responsible for assuring the quality of that water and the authenticity of its claimed source of origin – a spring? Consumers have a right to get what they pay for, so business has a general responsibility to make sure the quality matches the claims that it is making about the product. Warranties are a method of ensuring compliance with this notion.[13] Express warranties are those that the seller explicitly state about the product's character, durability, and in the packaging, labelling and advertising of the product. Many 'low-fat' products are under consumer watchdog eyes because of the vagueness of the claim on the packaging that does not reflect the authentic qualities or contents of the product. Implied warranties revolve around the claim, implicit in a sale, that the product is fit for the intended use or application it is usually used for. This does not mean the product has to be perfect, rather that it is suitable for what it is ordinarily used for. Another issue is the willingness of the company to deliver on a warranty. Many car owners claim that car manufacturers have denied valid warranty claims or made the process very difficult to reduce the likelihood of having to pay out on the warranty.

Pricing

Pricing has often been an ethical minefield for retailers and marketers. In South Africa, the passage into law of the National Credit Act helped strengthen the position of the consumer against unscrupulous retailers and manufacturers. Retailers often use '**bait and switch**' pricing tactics. This involves advertising an item at low price, but stocking so few units that the item is quickly sold out. This is done to give sales staff an opportunity to try to convince consumers to buy a more expensive item.

One of the big ethical issues in pricing is that of pricing that hides the true cost – or **hidden pricing**. Interest, surcharges and other '**stealth fees**' like insurance can increase the price of a product significantly beyond the advertised price. Another form of this tactic is to **reduce the quality or quantity** of a product. **Promotional pricing** may be misleading, e.g. when a retailer sells a product 'on special' but on an inflated markup. **Rebates** that consumers have to claim is another problem area, because businesses know that many consumers will not send in the necessary documentation.

Price fixing has been in the news regularly in South Africa, with companies like Sasol, Pioneer Foods, and PPC Cement suffering reputation damage through the actions of some of its managers. (See chapter 1 for several examples.) Horizontal price fixing is when competitors agree to collude on pricing. Vertical price fixing is when manufacturers and retailers agree to set prices. SABMiller is fighting accusations by the Competition Board that it uses its market power to force retailers to sell at certain prices. **Price gouging** is when a seller exploits a short-term situation where buyers have little option for a product by raising prices substantially. During the 2010 Soccer World Cup tournament, some fan parks were selling South African beers at R40 a bottle, compared to a normal price of between R13 and R20 a bottle. In the travel industry, the high-season, low-season use of **price discrimination** is often a bone of contention for most consumers.

Labelling and packaging

These methods are where consumers get their primary information, yet often they don't tell consumers the right information or what they need to know. The information, even if correct, can be hard to understand or misleading, such as products that claim to be 'low fat' but in fact are not. Unscrupulous marketers look for loopholes to exploit. New symbols on packaging are also confusing, such as the carbon footprint-neutral symbol and 'green' claims. This has led to the term 'greenwashing' – the communication of a misleading environmentally friendly claim by a marketer. Packages can also be misleading through their shape and size – for example, a large package may contain an inappropriately small item. Ethical marketing is based on the idea is that marketers have a moral obligation to provide usable information and packaging that is truthful. The Advertising Standards Authority (ASA) website provides information on many cases where misleading labelling and packaging claims were allegedly made, and the ASA rulings on those cases (www.asasa.org.za).

Invasion of privacy

The ill-considered use of telesales by many South African marketers has highlighted the ethical aspects related to this form of direct marketing. The South African consumer landscape is being increasingly regulated, and the Consumer Protection Act and National Credit Act, among other laws, will make it necessary for marketers to be very careful about compliance or face legal repercussions. Internet spam (junk e-mail) and the use of Internet 'cookies' (feedback software downloaded to a user's computer without permission) are two of the more controversial current issues in electronic media.

Advertising

The concern with advertising to children has always been a major ethical issue, and much work has been done to legislate what is allowed or not. The goals of advertising are to inform, persuade and remind consumers about a product or service, so as to influence the purchasing decisions of consumers. Although much legislation exists on managing this, there are still areas of concern. The delivery of clear, truthful information is thought of as the basis for advertising, but many marketers use deceptive techniques to achieve their aims.[14]

- **Ambiguity**. An advertisement may be vague enough to be understood in two or more ways. A well-known food marketer promoted 'light' desserts, implying these had fewer calories than its other desserts. When challenged, the company responded by saying the word 'light' referred to the texture of the product.
- **Concealment of facts**. Here the marketer suppresses facts that may not be advantageous to their product, or purposefully avoids saying anything that would

make the product less attractive. For example, Bayer aspirin advertised that it had 'the ingredient that doctors recommend most', without saying the ingredient was aspirin.

- **Exaggeration**. This is when the marketer makes claims that are not supported by evidence. In a recent ASA ruling, the ASA Directorate held that Supreme Slim's weight loss and appetite suppressant claims, as well as the product name (Supreme Slim) created an unsubstantiated impression that using this product would result in weight loss. The advertisement appeared on www.supremeslim.co.za, and promoted the respondent's slimming product with claims which included 'Appetite Suppressant • Suitable for men & women • Accelerates Metabolism • Non Addictive • No Chemicals • Get results without exercise • Increases energy levels • Body Detoxification • Fat Burner • Healthy eating plan included'. The marketer was instructed to withdraw the name 'Supreme Slim' and the claims with immediate effect and not to use them again in future.
- **Psychological appeals**. This is an appeal using primarily emotion, not reason as its basis. These appeals would include power, sex, masculinity, aspiration, and the like to sell, and can raise serious moral issues. The advertisements for brands such as Calvin Klein and Axe Deodorant are examples of adverts using blatant sex appeal. Recent complaints have been levelled at advertisers making use of photography editing software to severely alter the appearance of models in their images, creating an unrealistic idea of what constitutes beauty. Dove Soap has responded to this theme by launching its 'real beauty' campaign using 'real women' to promote its products.

Summary

In this chapter, we have established how the topics covered in the previous chapters help to shape the decisions made by marketers in terms of the marketing mix. In fact, a number of analyses were needed in order to accomplish this.

Firstly, the marketing orientation of the business was analysed to ensure that the company culture is correct and proactive. Secondly, the marketing environment and its effect in all the decision-making areas of marketing were highlighted. Thirdly, we emphasised the importance of marketing research in order to align the market offering with the marketing environment and to meet customer needs. This all entails a thorough understanding of the customer and the characteristics that affect the decisions made in terms of purchasing. Lastly, target market selection and positioning are critical, as all the decisions made by marketing are made as a result of selection and positioning. These are the main considerations for all marketing decisions and the development of the marketing mix to meet the needs of the chosen target market. Fig. 11.11 presents a visual diagram of this viewpoint. Nick Smith, the MD of Accenture's Marketing Transformation group, identifies four characteristics that will define the marketing leaders of the future:

- A foundation built on a well-tuned integrated marketing operation that is central to all functions in the business and helps produce and take advantage of innovation and growth.

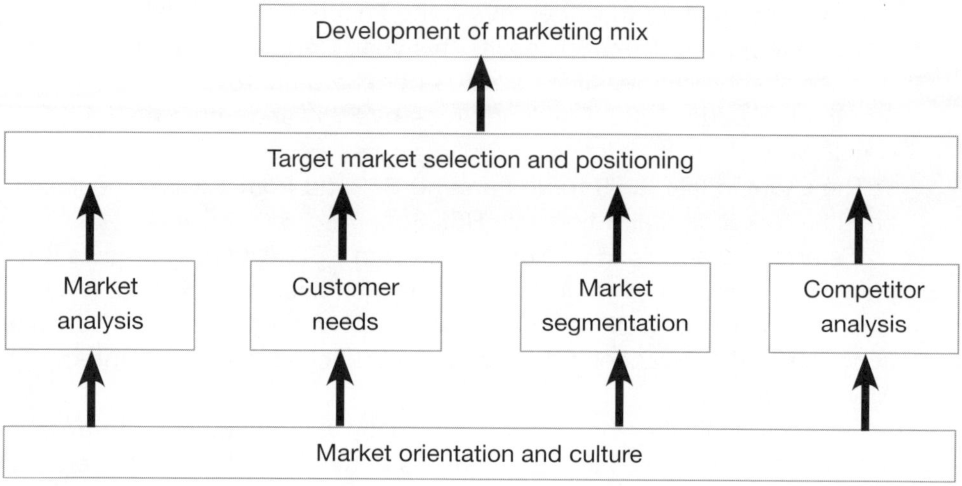

Figure 11.11 Core analysis for marketing decisions

- The capability to generate data-driven insights into customer preferences and behaviours, and to act on them.
- The use of the insights to develop relevant, innovative, differentiated value propositions and offers and design meaningful interaction with targeted customers.
- The ability to facilitate customer engagement by creating opportunities for ongoing dialogue with customers.

As Smith highlights in the points above, the company that is willing to look for growth strategies led by the customer (a customer-centric company) will create its own favourable future.

Case study: Capitec

Capitec CE Riaan Stassen loves the thrills of racing – whether it's in business or satisfying his personal interests. When he went on holiday a few weeks ago, he flew to São Paulo to attend the Brazilian Formula One Grand Prix.

Formula One motor racing and Capitec's innovative banking business may seem far apart but there are common threads, including a competitive culture and ability to achieve results through operational excellence and teamwork. These are key ingredients in Capitec's growth and its success in executing an innovative strategy.

The company is still a minnow compared with the big four banking groups, but it is making many traditional bankers sit up and take notice. It is also attracting new customers fast. It now has an active customer base of 2.1 m, up by 74% in the past two years.

Capitec was founded in March 2001 and listed in February 2002, just nine days after Saambou collapsed, triggering a crisis for the small banks sector. It successfully weathered that crisis and, so far, has survived the present recession.

It in fact has more than weathered the financial crisis. While all the listed have reported weaker results this year, Capitec boasted a strong balance sheet, with headline earnings per share up 48% for the six months to August 2009. Dividends rose by 83% and return on equity was 28%.

The share in late 2009 traded around R62, up from 120c at the listing, and its market capitalisation was R5.23bn.

It started by acquiring a microlender from PSG Group. That gave it a platform from which it could quickly establish itself and expand. It has since transformed itself into a general retail bank, offering loans, savings accounts and transactions done through branches, cards, the Internet, ATMs or partners.

How is it achieving this growth, especially in a downturn? There are two main reasons. First, its founders understand their customers' needs, particularly in the mass market and low-income sector. Second, they developed an innovative strategy and business model aimed at addressing those needs better than the established players. They have executed that strategy well. The second aspect is important because their main market insights were not necessarily original.

They recognised that though the SA banking sector is highly sophisticated, much of the population has no or limited banking facilities. Many people find banking products and services difficult to understand and expensive. Often they can't easily get the credit they need. They distrust banks. They mostly – or entirely – use cash rather than bank products. Whatever the cause, it resulted in procedures that are complex, cumbersome and inconvenient for the average customer.

This is where Stassen has turned the tables for Capitec. He may not have been the initial brains behind Capitec's business strategy, but he is certainly the brains behind making it a successful banking model.

He is different from the traditional banker – he says he is nonhierarchical, consultative and often informal in his approach. Because he is not a natural reader, he says he learns a lot from observation and personal contact with the market and Capitec branches. There is no township in SA he has not visited, and he wants to visit at least half the branches every year. So, any slowdown in the company's growth rate is unlikely to be caused by a lack of personal contact with the market.

Capitec chairman Michiel le Roux attests to this: "Riaan's genius is that he has been able to understand the needs of customers in the market we identified and match them with the bank's business model and systems. He runs the business in a way that enables that model to work. I saw the gap in the market in terms of focusing on a segment, but not how to do it [make it work]."

Capitec's distinctive approach is linked to the unusual backgrounds of its founders. Most top bankers have spent all – or most – of their careers in the banking industry. At SA's big four banks – Absa, Standard, Nedbank and First National Bank – the usual route to the top is to move up through the ranks. Much of the training takes place internally, and managers become steeped in the traditional banking culture. Innovative thinking, and ability to carry it out, is unusual, partly because the big groups are stuck with costly technology and branch networks established over years.

Stassen has been in banking for more than a decade, but it's his second career. He was educated in Stellenbosch at the 143-year-old Paul Roos Gymnasium, then completed a BCom at Stellenbosch University and qualified as a chartered accountant.

After a spell as audit manager at accountancy firm Coopers & Lybrand, he joined Distillers, which later merged with Stellenbosch Farmers Wineries (SFW) to form Distell, as operations manager.

At Distillers, part of the Rembrandt Group, Stassen was exposed to a culture closely attuned to marketing and what customers want. He recalls that Rembrandt founder Anton Rupert took a keen interest. "In those days Rupert personally approved all the labels and brands, and attended most of the quarterly marketing meetings," says Stassen.

In that environment there was a strong awareness of the value of driving the brands and understanding the market, adds Capitec marketing & corporate affairs executive Carl Fischer, who was at SFW at the time. In the mid-1990s, Le Roux left as Distillers CE to start a banking venture backed by investor and entrepreneur Christo Wiese, who controlled Pep Stores, a retail chain pitched mainly at the mass market. They launched Pep Bank, which was linked to Pep Stores.

Soon afterwards, Wiese acquired control of Boland Bank. The new Pep Bank was merged into it, with Le Roux taking over as CE of the merged operation. He asked Stassen to join him.

Boland was then an unfocused, rural bank, trying to be everything to everyone, says Stassen. Its new management team sharpened its focus and increased its exposure to the mass market, a sector they understood well because of their background in the liquor industry. "From day one, Riaan's attitude has been to have absolute focus on a clearly defined market segment," says Fischer.

Experiences gained at Boland influenced the birth of Capitec in other ways, too. Boland was the first bank to build a significant microlending book. It grew to R1 bn, which in the late 1990s was considerable exposure to a new and risky market. That book was later sold to African Bank Investments (Abil), a specialist in microlending.

Boland merged with two other medium-sized banks, the Natal Building Society and Board of Executors (BoE). Le Roux remained CE and he and Stassen were joined by several others from the beverages industry. At Boland they were part of a team that refined the thinking behind the Capitec strategy.

Later, after BoE had been merged with Nedbank, they took the idea to PSG Group, where Mouton and PSG director Chris Otto helped develop the thinking. Le Roux says it was PSG's backing that got the idea off the ground. "Without their support, it would all have remained just a dream," he says.

Several of the old Boland team are still involved in Capitec's senior management or board. Alongside Le Roux, Stassen and Fischer are business development manager Andre Olivier; operations head Gerrie Fourie, who was previously at SFW; IT head Christiaan Oosthuizen, who was IT head at Boland; and risk management head and company secretary Christian van Schalkwyk, who ran risk and legal at Boland.

"Together we developed interesting concepts, such as taking the bank to the customer instead of the other way round," says Stassen.

"The fact that our people came in from another industry has been an advantage," adds Le Roux. "It may be an advantage to grow up in an industry but there is also a danger that you can't see the wood for the trees."

An example Le Roux cites is the limited banking hours the big groups have retained for decades, though the retail industry has moved to longer hours, seven days a week. Capitec says they offer "extended banking hours beyond 8 am and 5 pm".

But what really sets them apart from the rest of the banking herd? Among other things, there's still the strong liquor connection. Experience in the liquor industry influenced the way Capitec views its market. Stassen recalls that in the 1980s and early 1990s, there were strict liquor laws in SA. The middle class was much narrower than now. Yet 80% of liquor sold in the domestic market was consumed by blacks, many of them in the mass or low-income market.

Capitec targets the mass market (though not exclusively), as it has geared its business to volumes. But it defines its market by customer needs rather than income. "I prefer not to look at the market in terms of income or wealth. That's very traditional marketing. That's a lesson I learnt in the liquor industry," says Stassen. "I hate the idea of labelling people in terms of their income. We want to be status-neutral."

The company has recognised that many customers have similar needs and concerns about banks. With that insight, it's expanding its client base into the middle market – to affluent locations, such as Rosebank in Johannesburg. "If you go into a traditional bank at the end of the month, there is always a big queue at the inquiries counter. You have to ask why," says Stassen. "People want to be in control of their finances. The fact that so many people withdraw their cash from banks tells us they don't feel in control."

Capitec's business is built around four core principles:

Affordability: fees and interest rates charged on its products are significantly lower than at other banks;

Accessibility: achieved mainly through the branch network;

Convenience: cash can be withdrawn, and purchases made, at retail partners such as Shoprite, Pick n Pay and Pep, or from ATMs; and

Simplicity: transactions are quick and simple, with no paperwork.

Capitec's 371 branches are central to its strategy. The moment you walk into one of these branches, you know they are different from a typical bank branch. They are relatively small, at 180-200 m^2, but are carefully positioned and low-cost. Branch costs are minimised, as none of the transactions other than deposits involves cash.

When customers deposit cash at the branches, it goes straight into a drop safe. Cash can be withdrawn at ATMs or at the partner retailers but not over the counter in the branches.

As branch staff don't have to worry about looking after cash, they can give customers more personal attention. It also reduces security needs and costs. There is no armoured glass in front of counters, so customers have direct contact with trained consultants.

Transactions are simple as customers never fill in forms; the branches are paperless. Customers use a single card and pin number, and are identified biometrically with cameras and fingerprints. And things happen quickly. The company says a deposit should not take longer than 60 seconds.

As the branches are relatively small and inexpensive, they can be targeted more precisely. In Bellville near Cape Town, there are two branches within 300 m of each other. One has a client profile in the middle-income market. The other, near the station, has clients mainly in the mass market.

At all the branches, processes are designed to give customers more control, while keeping costs down. Management noticed that when most people go to an ATM, the first thing they do is check their balance. Capitec's ATMs now give account balances automatically – at no charge.

It avoids pricing products on sliding scales, or offering different products for different markets. It also does not quote figures such as effective interest rates, which need explanations.

It also offers cheaper options than the "big four" on a transactional account – far higher interest rates and lower transactional fees (between R2.50 and R3.50 for withdrawals or transfers). Online banking is free. In a basic transactional account, Capitec pays 7% interest on balances of less than R10 000. That is remarkably high, but drops to 6.25% for balances of more than R10 000 (presumably Capitec does this to lower concentration risk in its deposit base: better to have a widely spread deposit base so chances of large-scale withdrawals are lower). The big four banks offer interest rates of less than 1% on most of their transactional accounts.

One of its biggest advantages, says Stassen, is that it offers a single, standardised product range that's relatively narrow. Most of the bank's loan book is short-term, though it has started offering 36-month loans.

Management has resisted the temptation to use the branches to sell other financial services. The bank provides free credit life insurance on six- to 36-month loans. It has also avoided going into products such as home loans, though that could develop later.

"Riaan is very disciplined. When you have a branch network, it is easy to get seduced by other opportunities and start diluting your focus. That hasn't happened. We prefer to offer fewer things and do them well," says Le Roux.

Much of the focus is on operational efficiency. All staff activities are managed on budgeted production time. When customers enter a branch looking for a loan, they are expected to be able to leave within 15 minutes, with the transaction completed. Transactions are closely monitored. "I can go to a computer now and tell you the hourly turnover for the bank and for each branch and consultant," says Stassen.

Le Roux adds that all Capitec's staff are trained in all of its products, which is not true of the bigger banks. Stassen says he likes working to an agreed methodology, in a disciplined organisation.

Overall, Capitec has shown considerable success at tapping into a large market that has not been well served by the traditional banking sector. Personal contact with clients and staff, innovation, delivering products that clients want and efficiency are all important parts of a formula that has so far worked well for the company and investors.

Its ability to continue the growth will depend partly on how well management maintains the focus and efficiencies. Capitec's performance may not yet have reached the standards shown by Ferrari's Formula One team, but Stassen does seem to be racing in that direction.

Source: Adapted from McNulty, A. November 6, 2009. In the fast lane: behind Capitec's successful model. *Financial Mail*, pp-34–41.

Exercises

1. What where the environmental factors that impacted on the creation and development of the Capitec brand?
2. Identify how the behaviour and attitudes of consumers affected the development and evolution of the Capitec value proposition.
3. Explain the actions that Capitec took in terms of both the traditional marketing mix and the expanded marketing mix elements to be able to deliver its value proposition to its target markets.

CHAPTER 12

Marketing and the Internet

Learning outcomes

After studying this chapter you should be able to:

- define the concepts of the Internet and the World Wide Web (WWW);
- identify the benefits of the Internet;
- describe the virtual environment in which the Internet operates; and
- identify areas in which the Internet can create value for the marketer.

Introduction

We have all heard of the Internet and the Web and many of us have probably used it in one way or another. The same is true of most businesses. Many organisations are already using the Internet to a greater or lesser extent. Others, while they probably know about the Internet, are still biding their time before they 'climb on board'. They might even question why they need to consider the Internet at all. Looking at the statistics as depicted in table 12.1 it might be prudent for business still harboring doubts regarding the Internet, to reconsider:

***Table 12.1** Internet statistics*

Number of Internet users in 2009	1.73 billion (18% increase from 2008)[1]
Number of websites in 2009	234 million
Number of Internet users in South Africa in 2009	5.3 million (15% increase from 2008)[2]

According to the World Wide Worx a similar growth rate is expected for South Africa for 2010, reaching the 6 million user mark. There are a number of reasons for the accelerated growth in the number of users in South Africa. One being the varied range of application services and social networking platforms such as Facebook available to local users. We will look at social networking later in this chapter. Looking at these statistics South African organisations must carefully consider their Internet strategy. When applied well, the Internet could be a powerful tool in the marketing arsenal.

Businesses are using the Internet in many different ways, including to advertise their goods, generate publicity, transact sales online, communicate with customers, suppliers and business partners, provide customer support, procure goods, automate their business functions, integrate their business activities with those of their partners in the value chain, send electronic invoices, make and receive electronic payments, and much more. This chapter specifically looks at Internet marketing – the marketing concept in a virtual world, the marketing mix, and the role of the Internet in enabling marketing activities such as customer relationship marketing.

What is the Internet?

The Internet can generally be defined as a world-wide interconnected network of computer networks.[3] The Internet enables a computer or network in one part of the world to communicate with a computer or network located somewhere else in the world using either an ordinary telephone line or a special dedicated data line.

Put another way, the Internet is little more than the global networking infrastructure that enables computer networks around the world to communicate with each other. The Internet Protocol (IP) represents a set of standards that allows different types of computers with different operating systems and different applications to communicate with each other and share data. Thus the Internet is the underlying infrastructure, while the IP is the 'language' that the computers on the Internet use to 'talk' to each other.[4] Each computer on the Internet is represented by an exclusive unique number known as an IP address.[5] Fig. 12.1 provides a depiction of the reach of the global Internet.

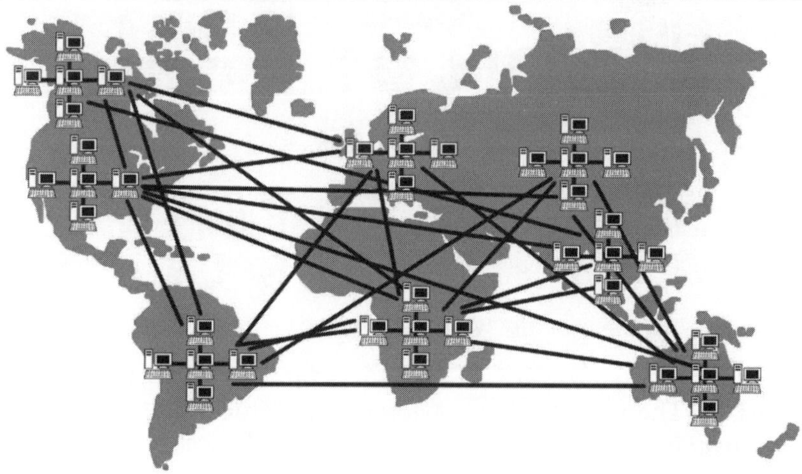

Figure 12.1 *The Internet – a network of computer networks*[6]

The power of this global system of interconnected computer networks comes from the fact that: (a) it provides an easy-to-use communications channel for millions of individual and corporate Internet users; (b) the information available on all of these computer networks is now available to everyone; and (c) the Internet infrastructure facilitates the conducting of various business activities such as advertising, publicity, procurement, account payment, data-sharing and sales transactions. Previously only users on a specific network had access to the information on that particular network.

Of course, much of the information is still proprietary and thus password-protected. Nevertheless, there remains gigabyte upon gigabyte of information freely available via the Internet, bringing about an information explosion where everybody with Internet access has virtually unlimited information and knowledge about almost any topic.

The World Wide Web

The terms 'Internet' and 'World Wide Web' (WWW or Web) are often used interchangeably, but do not quite mean the same thing. The Web can be defined as the system of connected documents on the Internet, which often contain colour pictures, video and sound, and can be searched for information about a particular subject.[7] It is a subset of the Internet, comprising billions of web pages on hundreds of millions of websites. These pages contain clickable links (hyperlinks) to other parts of the same website, or to a document on the site, or to another website or document. This is schematically represented in fig. 12.2.

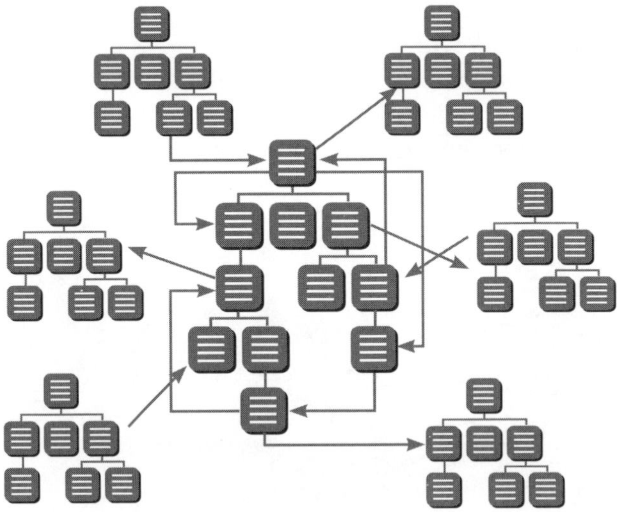

***Figure 12.2** Interlinked pages on the World Wide Web*[8]

The Web was created in 1989 at CERN, Switzerland's nuclear research facility, by Tim Berners-Lee. The term 'web' was coined by Berners-Lee in 1990 to describe information spanning the planet like a giant spider's web, with threads linking knowledge and information from all over the globe, making it available to a worldwide audience.[9] The actual tool that you use to view website pages is a software program called a web browser. There are many programs, but the most popular could be said to be Microsoft Internet Explorer, Mozilla Firefox and Google Chrome.

There have been few developments in the modern world that have grabbed the imagination of people across the globe in quite the same way as the World Wide Web. In a complex world of technology, the Web is easy to use and incorporates pictures, sounds, animations, photographs, video and other multimedia features, adding to its attraction and intuitiveness.

Advantages of the Internet for business:[10]

- Large amounts of information can easily be stored and updated on the Internet and are accessible to anyone connected to the Internet.
- Information that was previously only available as paper-based documents to a limited audience because of the cost involved in wider distribution, can now be made available quickly and easily to all interested parties and to a much wider, international, audience.
- Any information published on the Internet is immediately available to a global audience.
- The information can be presented in multimedia form, including text, sound, video, photographs and animations, making it very user-friendly.
- The information is interactive. The user can complete a reply or order form, or send an e-mail message to the company concerned and can also navigate between sites located at the opposite sides of the globe or around the corner.
- A web-based document and its contents can be electronically linked to a wealth of supporting documentation all over the world.
- Information is available 24 hours a day and 365 days a year.
- The medium is intuitive.
- A website is an affordable environment to use for both the user and supplier of information and services.
- The Web allows you reach the masses – a market of over 600 million users at present, expected to rise to one billion in the next few years.
- The Web allows you to customise your information to meet the needs of each individual customer (often referred to as mass customisation).
- You can transact sales directly on the Web.
- Using Internet-based technology, firms can integrate, automate and synchronise their businesses with those of their suppliers, customers and partner organisations.

The Internet is now being linked to other information and communication technologies such as cell phones, thereby extending its capability and reach. It is, for example, possible to send an SMS from a cell phones to a web user and vice versa.

Marketing and the Internet

Definition

Internet marketing can be defined as: 'the application of the Internet and related digital technologies in conjunction with traditional communication to achieve marketing objectives.'[11]

An important point is that the Internet does not change the fundamentals of marketing. However, it provides an important new distribution channel for businesses to reach their customers. It may well require a new approach to marketing, but the core elements of the marketing concept discussed at the beginning of this book remain the same. There is still a customer whose needs must be satisfied (customer orientation); the business still strives to make money (profit orientation); and it is still necessary to make effective and efficient use of all of the resources available to the business in order to satisfy customer needs (systems orientation).

In addition, the business must still deal with the micro-, market- and macro-environments discussed earlier and it still has control over the four main variables that comprise the marketing mix, namely the product, as well as its price, promotion and distribution. All of these elements remain in place. Perhaps one significant difference between traditional marketing and Internet marketing is that an additional environment comes into play, namely the virtual environment.

The virtual environment

The virtual environment is made up of the digital 'bits and bytes space' found in the world of microchips, computers and electronic networks. The fact that you, as a marketer, now have to consider the implications of working in a virtual world brings another dimension to marketing. The virtual environment has its own peculiarities and requires a different approach by marketers.

In the case of the Internet, the virtual environment is represented by your computer screen and all interactions happen in that display. The virtual environment crosses the other three environments, namely, the micro-, market- and macro-environments, as depicted in fig. 12.3.

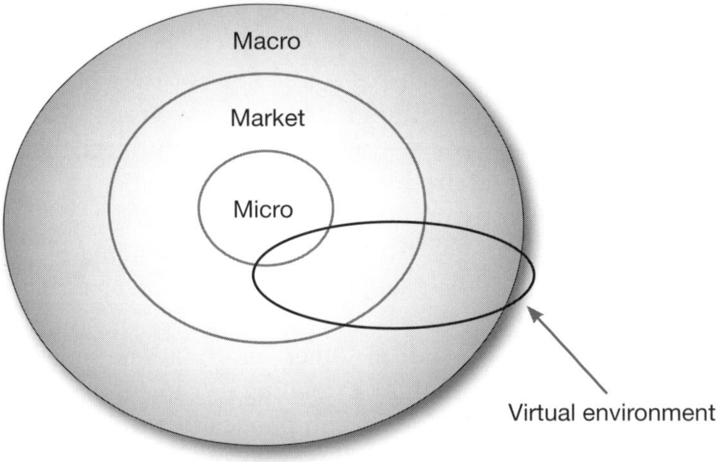

Figure 12.3 *The virtual environment comprises all environments on a single interface*

For example, in the case of the micro-environment, a company's intranet (an internal Internet-based network, accessible only to staff) places company information and online communication channels at the disposal of staff. In the case of the market environment, the firm's website can be accessed by (and even integrated with) those of suppliers, customers and business partners. Finally, in the case of the macro-environment, the business can use the Internet to access and keep track of (or 'tune in to') macro information and developments.

The marketspace versus the marketplace

As early as 1994, Rayport and Sviokla wrote in the *Harvard Business Review* that the Internet has brought with it a virtual realm which they termed the 'marketspace', with which organisations in all spheres of business and of all sizes need to come to terms.[12] The marketspace, they pointed out, is a virtual world where products and services exist as digital information and where transactions and interactions occur electronically. This new world, they said, requires new and innovative ways of marketing products and providing value-added services to customers. The marketspace is very different to the physical world or 'marketplace' that marketers are familiar with, where interactions occur between physical buyers and sellers at actual locations.

This idea of a marketspace is very similar to the idea of a 'virtual environment'. The concept of an 'environment', however, fits in with the more traditional marketing view of the micro-, market- and macro-environments.

Marketing activities and the Internet

Notwithstanding the myriad ways in which companies are already putting the Internet to work, there are still a number of key marketing areas where this medium can be of use in business. The Internet and the Web can help the marketing activities of a business by:

- enhancing marketing communications;
- facilitating the marketing mix of the business;
- undertaking marketing research;
- disseminating information;
- transacting sales; and
- facilitating customer service and support.

Marketing communications

The Internet provides a global standard for information exchange. Spanning the world, the open standard of the Internet represents an extensive and powerful communications network, improving inter- and intra-organisational communications. This is achieved through various means, including through the use of:

- websites;
- e-mail marketing;
- e-newsletters;
- e-zines;
- e-forms;
- autoresponders;
- usenet newsgroups;
- frequently asked questions;
- discussion forums;
- advertising;
- search engine marketing and search engine optimisation (SEO);
- viral media; and
- social media.

These online 'tools' are used extensively by businesses to communicate marketing messages to customers and potential customers.

Websites

Websites are considered a form of communication in their own right, as they contain information in the form of text, sound, video, graphics and animations available to any visitor (see fig. 12.4 for examples). At the same time, in addition to facilitating this outgoing form of communicating, websites make it possible to create reciprocal communication channels by enabling customers to send information to the owner of the site. This is achieved by way of reply forms and/or questionnaires that customers must complete in order to obtain additional information, to make enquiries, or to supply data for further processing.

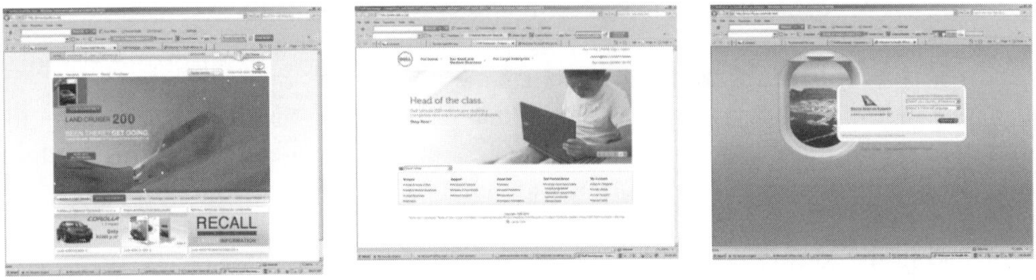

www.toyota.co.za www.dell.co.za www.flysaa.com

Figure 12.4 *Examples of corporate websites in South Africa*

Stokes identifies three fundamental aspects of a successful website: good design, good search engine visibility, and a high level of usability.[13]

Design

A website needs to have the user or customer in mind and must have clearly set goals. A site might sell products and services to the user, or request the user to submit information, sign-up for e-mail newsletters, or the user may need to download information from the site. The website should be credible and one of the means of doing this is by good design. Easy-to-find contact information, believable testimonials, credible third party references and fresh content that is updated regularly all add to the credibility of a website.

Search engine visibility and optimisation

Internet users most commonly use search engines such as Google, Yahoo, Ask Jeeves and Overture. Once a search criterion has been entered a number of pages emerge from the search, usually a great many, known as a search engine results page (SERP).[14] Swanepoel notes that users most commonly only pay attention to the first 10–50 sites listed on the results page (depending on the search engine or preference settings). A large amount of traffic (measured by the number of visits to a website) is crucial for any website to be successful and is one of the criteria that is most commonly used by search engines to rank results.[15] Without website traffic the marketing goals for the website might not be reached. In order to optimise the number of visitors from search engine searches, marketers should take the following into consideration:

- A website should have a **search engine-friendly structure**, free from technical barriers and errors.

- Users search by means of **keywords**. Marketers should research the most common words customers/users will use in order to find the information, products or services they are looking for, and ensure the company uses the same terms to describe its own offerings. The aim is to get as many users as possible to visit the company's site first, before considering visiting those of competitors.
- The **content** of the site is the most important part of any website, and it should obviously relate to the keywords that have been chosen. The content should be targeted at specific search keywords and key phrases.
- The more **links** to your website from a search engine or another website, the more relevant and important your website is perceived to be. Marketers can stimulate the creation of links by writing valuable relevant content that people would like to read. Creating tools and documents other users/customers would like to use might be to the benefit of the website.
- Lastly, marketers need to ensure that users **return**, repeatedly visiting the site and spending time to see what it has to offer. Valuable and relevant sites develop higher search engine rankings, thus ensuring more visits to company sites.

Usability

Usability refers to how easy users/customers find it to complete a task on a website, whether it be searching for information, purchasing a product or signing up for a newsletter. The better a website functions, the better the impression.

E-mail marketing

Electronic mail, better known as e-mail, is a method of sending an electronic message in the form of a computer text file from one computer to another. It is one of the most important services available on the Internet, as well as being one of its earliest applications. E-mail competes directly with both the land-based postal system, as well as with telephone and fax services, but offers a number of unique benefits over these traditional forms of communications.

- **Affordability** – e-mail is considerably cheaper than the telephone, fax or post.
- **Attachments** – one of the most powerful advantages of e-mail is the ability to attach additional computer files, such as word-processing documents, spreadsheets, graphics, presentations and engineering drawings.
- **Place** – the recipient does not have to go to a particular physical place to receive e-mail as is the case with physical post or faxes. E-mail can be downloaded anywhere in the world.
- **Format** – e-mail is a digital format which allows the recipient to cut and paste content without having to retype it; it can be forwarded to others; it can be electronically filed; and it can also be printed if necessary.
- **Avoiding gatekeepers** – telephone calls, faxes and post are often channelled through a third person, e.g. a personal assistant; managers often still access their own e-mail, enabling direct communication with them.
- **Communication processing** – recipients can decide when and if they want to read a particular message.

- **Mailing lists** – e-mail allows you to create mailing lists and to send a standard communication to a number of people at the same time (batch processing).
- **Interactivity** – e-mail provides a degree of interactivity which may include multimedia elements and links to websites.
- **Management** – filing, storing and finding e-mail messages is easy and efficient as everything is in electronic format. Follow-up correspondence is also more efficient as old messages can be re-accessed from appropriate file folders and replied to at a convenient time, knowing that the correct address and original correspondence is embedded in the message.
- **Critical mass** – e-mail is fast becoming the preferred means of communication.

A word of caution when considering e-mail marketing: marketers need to be aware that due to the large number of e-mails customers receive, many mails are simply ignored. An e-mail marketing campaign needs to be ingenious, fresh and deliver useful e-mails that customers/users would want to read. One of the problems with e-mail is its ease of use. With an increasing number of companies and individuals using e-mail, the numbers of e-mail messages being sent and received over the Internet is increasing exponentially (see table 12.2). Handling large volumes of e-mails is a problem most companies already have to face. Marketers also need to be aware that their e-mails might be marked as spam by web servers and not delivered. Spam (junk e-mail) is an e-mail sent without the user requesting it. It is usually sent in bulk without proper targeting having been done.

Table 12.2 *Growth in the use of e-mail in the world*[16]

The number of e-mails sent on the Internet in 2009	90 trillion
Average number of e-mail messages per day	247 billion
The number of e-mail users worldwide	1.4 billion
New e-mail users since the year before	100 million
The percentage of e-mails that were spam	81%
Increase in spam since 2008	24%
The number of spam e-mails per day (assuming 81% are spam)	200 billion

E-newsletters

An electronic newsletter (or e-newsletter) uses the same technology as e-mail. The difference is that e-mail is usually a short, specific and directed message, and an e-newsletter is more 'newsy' in nature. Newsletters are usually focused around a particular topic, may consist of several sub-topics and pages, and they are sent to a number of readers simultaneously, usually to the members of an e-mail mailing list (such as your customer database). E-newsletters can be very powerful marketing tools if they address a topic of interest to their readers (see fig. 12.5 for an example).

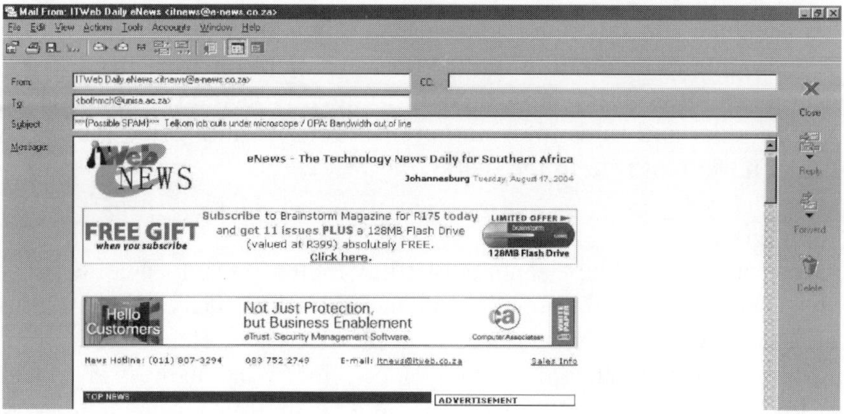

Figure 12.5 *The ITWeb newsletter*

E-zines

An electronic magazine (or e-zine) is similar in concept to an e-mail newsletter. E-zines are usually web-based rather than e-mail-based (although e-mail-based e-zines do exist) and they are much more graphic, involving multimedia features; they more closely mimic their physical magazine counterparts. E-zines may appear as highly dynamic and newsy websites.

E-forms

Electronic forms (or e-forms for short) are extremely popular in the online world and are used for gathering information for a wide variety of purposes, from registering for seminars or to receive e-newsletters, to business order forms, questionnaires and database query forms. Forms represent an important design element in web pages. They bring with them a degree of interactivity, they open up a communications channel between the customer and the company, and they are dynamic in nature.

Equally important to the company is the fact that forms represent a valuable marketing tool. The data they gather can be added to the company's marketing and customer database, which, in turn, can be used for database-marketing purposes. In addition, developing an in-depth understanding of the wants and needs of a customer is a prelude to developing a closer relationship with that customer.

Autoresponders

Autoresponders, also referred to as mailbots, are becoming critical tools in the marketing activities of many modern businesses. An autoresponder is software that filters incoming e-mails and then sends automated responses to the sender based on the information contained in the originating e-mail. Autoresponders also range from very expensive, sophisticated programs using artificial intelligence to cheaper, less powerful ones (indeed, your e-mail program probably has an autoresponse facility built in). For a company receiving thousands of e-mails every day, an autoresponder is as important as a call-centre handling thousands of telephone calls daily.

In a world where some companies are receiving tens of thousands of e-mails daily, autoresponders ensure that every customer is immediately dealt with and helps enhance the customer experience. They help in sending back instant acknowledgements, channelling enquiries, pre-empting the need for human-generated replies by pointing customers to frequently asked questions (FAQs), and forwarding product and sales information or articles to interested parties. As such, they fulfil an important role in the marketing process.

Usenet newsgroups

Newsgroups form part of the Usenet network, which represents a collection of some 50 000 discussion groups that function on an e-mail-like basis where users post and read messages covering a wide range of topics. It is an electronic bulletin board used to discuss a particular topic such as sport, hobby or business area.[17] Usenet is a service that can be accessed by users using an e-mail program such as Microsoft Outlook Express. Generally, however, users will need to log in to a dedicated Usenet news server, generally hosted by their Internet service providers (ISPs). Once logged in, they can subscribe to a newsgroup of interest to them (even though they are subscribing, there is no cost) and can read what the participants are saying. Alternatively, users can access newsgroups via Google's 'News' facility, which provides web-based access to the Usenet network (see fig. 12.6).

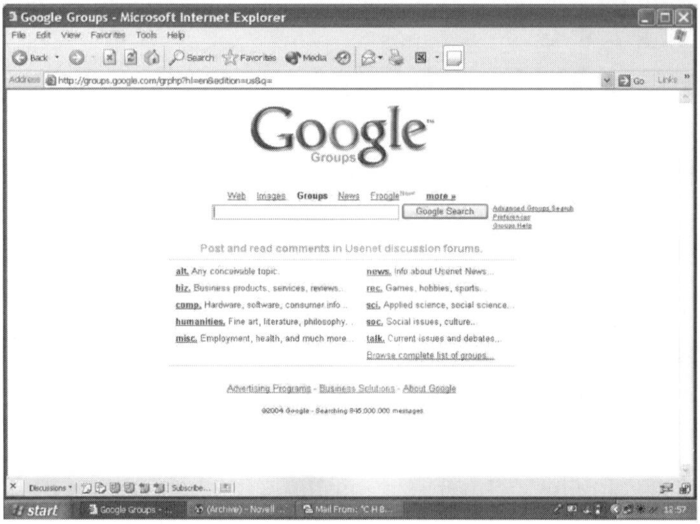

Figure 12.6 *Google's News facility*

There are newsgroups for every conceivable topic, as well as for many business topics (such as importing, exporting, advertising, customer service, local events, exhibitions and marketing). Usenet and newsgroups can serve as a useful tool in communicating with and marketing to both customers and potential customers, and a lot of valuable information is shared on the Usenet network. The problem with Usenet is the 'noise'. A lot of spam can be found in these newsgroups and users may need to wade through a lot of articles before finding those relevant to them. Nevertheless, many companies put considerable effort into marketing on the Usenet service and achieve quite a bit of success through this medium.

Frequently asked questions (FAQs)

FAQs, while somewhat static, are powerful tools with which to assist the customer. An FAQ consists of a commonly asked question and a corresponding reply. The reply may not only provide the required answer, but may contain links to a wealth of supporting information, perhaps highlighting other services and products available from your company, and so helps in the important tasks of up-selling and cross-selling. An FAQ list is important because it helps overcome common problems your customers may be experiencing. Providing a swift answer to a problem helps bring the customer closer to the organisation and contributes to a positive customer experience.

Discussion forums

Discussion forums are online services where a user can post a message that can be viewed by other users. Readers of these (generally) text-based messages can then post a reply to the original message. Subsequent readers can then either post replies to the original message or to the replies (known as 'threads'). Discussion forums are very similar to newsgroups but the main difference is that they are run by a specific organisation for that organisation's benefit. They are also asynchronous in nature (i.e. the individuals are not 'talking' to each other at the same moment in time – one person posts a comment and someone else may reply several hours, days or even weeks later).

Discussion forums are useful in the case where a strong community exists, such as between programmers that use a particular programming language, where members may want to share ideas and discuss issues among themselves.

Online advertising

Online advertising refers to advertising on the Internet. It includes adverts on search engine results (known as pay per click or PPC advertising) as well as adverts placed everywhere else on the Internet. PPC advertising will be discussed at the end of this section. Online advertising has two main goals: namely to build a brand or to promote sales.

The benefit of advertising on the Internet is that it is an interactive medium. Instead of the business sending out a one-way message, the customer now comes to the website of the business and can choose to interact with the advertisement and with the website, or not. There is thus a move away from supplier-push advertising to customer-pull advertising. In fact, this is indicative generally of marketing on the Web, not only of advertising.

Some of the most common online advertising methods include:

- interstitial banners;
- pop-ups and pop-unders;
- map adverts;
- floating adverts;
- wallpaper adverts; and
- banner adverts.

Advantages of advertising online

There are a number of advantages of advertising on the Web.[18]

- **Rapid presentation**. You can get a web advertisement online or an e-mail sent out in a few hours, versus a few days or weeks (even months) in the case of newspaper or magazine print, or television, or radio. What is more, it is immediately available to a global audience.
- **Easy modification**. Changing a television advertisement can prove to be extremely expensive. Even a newspaper advertisement is costly to revamp. A website, on the other hand, can be updated or modified relatively quickly and cheaply.
- **Affordability**. Given the relatively low cost of a website and e-mail, and their potential reach, the cost per viewer is considerably lower compared with other forms of advertising.
- **No space or time limits**. A television advertisement can only be screened a few times per month and a newspaper advertisement only lasts as long as the newspaper is current, which is probably no longer than a day or so. In addition, television, radio, the print media and other advertising media such as billboards are all limited in terms of space. The Internet, however, has no such limits. The advertisement is always available to the viewing public, 24 hours per day, 365 days per year and there is no limit to the amount of information that can be made available via the Internet. The advertisement can also be changed and corrected at any time because users will only see the current version when they visit the website.
- **Multimedia elements**. The power of the Internet comes from the fact that it is a multimedia environment. It can deliver not only text, graphics, animations and photographs, but stereo sound and video as well. Indeed, the Internet combines the widest range of media to impact on the viewer. It is possible, therefore, to demonstrate aspects of the product in a way and in such depth that cannot be achieved with other advertising media.
- **Buyer involvement**. The Internet is an interactive medium. Customers can be encouraged to interact with the advertisement by filling in forms, leaving messages, completing questionnaires, asking questions, pushing buttons, or requesting more information. What is more, visitors to a website can choose what they want to view. They can explore the advertisement in greater detail or depth or only scan those parts of the advertisement they are interested in. Although some of the other media also offer a degree of interactivity, there is no other advertising medium that is as interactive as the Web.
- **Measurability and data gathering**. This is perhaps the largest benefit of banner advertising – it is measurable. Marketers can get an exact measure of the number of users responding to their advertisement, by means of electronically counting the click-through rate. A click-through rate refers to the number of clicks on the advertised link divided by the number of times the link was exposed. This is usually given as a percentage. Marketers can determine the success of their banner adverts and adjust the advertisment accordingly.

- **The advertising benefit of e-mail and e-newsletters**. Besides the more traditional advertising opportunities offered by the Web and websites, simple e-mail programs available as a standard on most computers can be used in conjunction with lists of addresses (also called 'address books' or 'distribution lists') to send out e-mail with an advertising slant. The use of e-mail for advertising is growing steadily. Innovative companies should also consider creating e-newsletters that offer value-added information that would be useful to a select group of prospects. The e-mail newsletter can be promoted on the company's website, encouraging visitors to subscribe to the newsletter with the promise that they will be receiving useful information related to the topic in question. In this way, the viewer initiates the contact and the e-mail newsletter is not being forced on the viewer. The advertising benefit comes from the fact that the business that produces the newsletter (a) becomes associated with the newsletter and, as long as it is a good newsletter, this association should have a positive impact on the business; and (b) within the newsletter, the business can unobtrusively advertise its products and services.

Online marketing communication models

Traditionally, marketing communication has been seen as a one-to-many communications model. This means that the business creates an advertising message that it then 'pushes' to customers using mass media such as the radio, television, newspaper or magazines. Alternatively, in the case of direct marketing (such as with direct mail), the model is a one-to-one model. In this instance, the business creates a personalised advertising message that it sends to its individual customers. The Internet, however, offers various communications models (see fig. 12.7).

- **One-to-one** – as with direct mail in the physical world, it is possible to create highly personalised marketing communications messages and to direct these to individual customers using the Internet (with the added advantage that the customer can immediately reply or respond to the communication).
- **One-to-many** – once again, the Internet can serve as a one-to-many communications medium and most corporate websites and mass e-mail marketing campaigns fall in this category (they have a fixed message that is communicated to all).
- **Many-to-many** – in this case, through the use of third-party websites (called 'portals'), it is possible to facilitate two-way marketing interactions and communications between many different organisations and customers (in this model, it is even possible for customers to communicate with other customers).

Advertising using third-party websites

In addition to the advertising options we have discussed so far, it is also possible for businesses to advertise on other third-party websites. Such websites would usually be well-known and popular websites that generate a lot of visitor traffic, e.g. the M-Web website.

In this instance, it is common to make use of banner advertisements. These are advertisement-like banners or strips that appear at the top, bottom or side of a web page and which, if you click on the banner, will take you to the advertisers' web page. Banner advertisements have generally been limited with their success, except in the case where the third-party website in question has a very large and highly targeted audience.

Take ITWeb in South Africa for example. This is one of the premier portals focusing on news and information about the information technology (IT) industry. Because ITWeb has a very large and loyal audience, if you wanted to target people in the IT industry, placing a banner advertisement on ITWeb would most likely prove very successful.

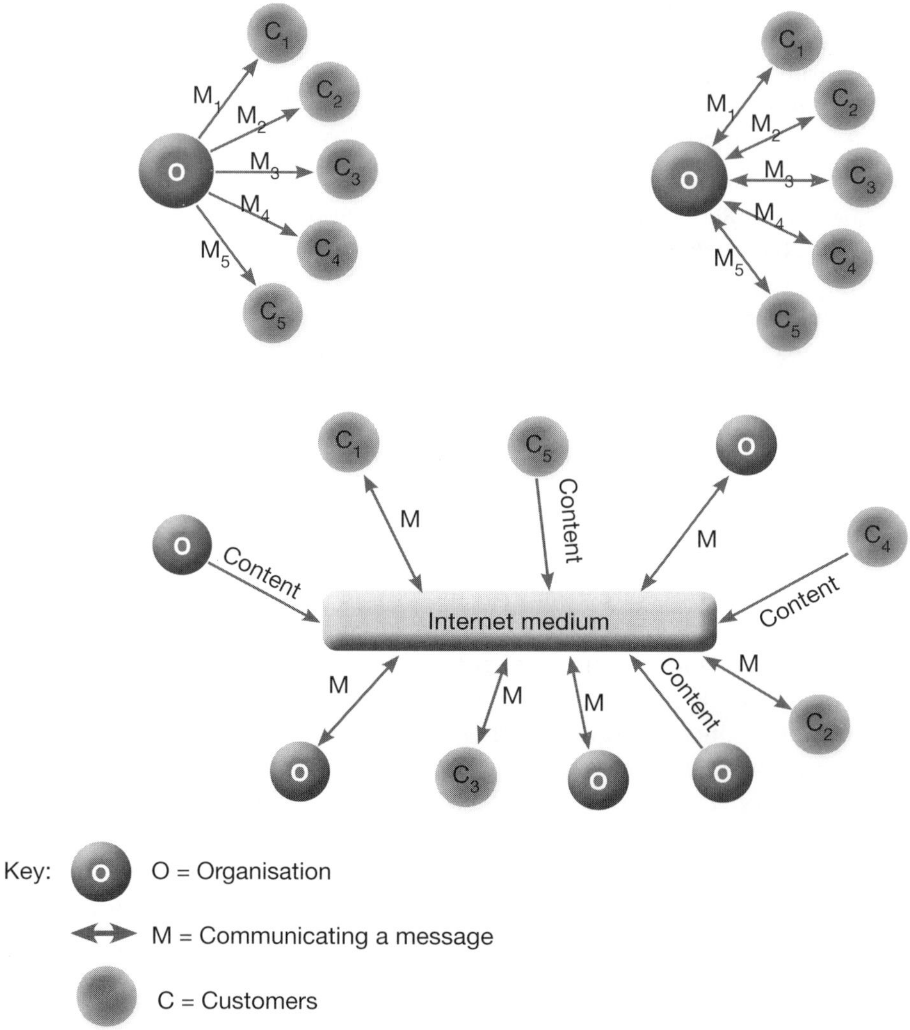

Figure 12.7 *Various Internet-based marketing communications models*[19]

Most advertisements are sold on the number of page views, measured in thousands and referred to as a 'cost per thousand' or 'cpm'. Thus a R250 cpm means that it will cost you R250 to get 1 000 visitors to view (but not necessarily click through to) your banner advertisement. Other ways of negotiating online advertising would be to sponsor a web page for a flat fee (probably the best arrangement if you are not sure of how many visitors the website is getting), or to arrange some kind of affiliate relationship. An affiliate programme operates by creating a partnership between two online organisations in such a way that the one organisation pays the other for the referrals generated by hosting a link (usually in the form of a button) on the latter organisation's website that points to the first organisation's website.[20]

Pay per click (PPC) or paid search advertising

As the name suggests, pay per click (PPC) or paid search advertising is an advertising system where the advertiser only pays for each click on their advert. It is most often used on search engines or banner advertising. Here the advertiser pays for number of clicks on the advertisement instead of the number of times the advertisement is viewed.

Google generates most of its income from advertising. In the first quarter of 2010, Google's revenue increased by 23% to a total of US$6.77 billion at the end of March 2010.[21] PPC adverts are usually listed as sponsored links. See fig. 12.8 for an example.

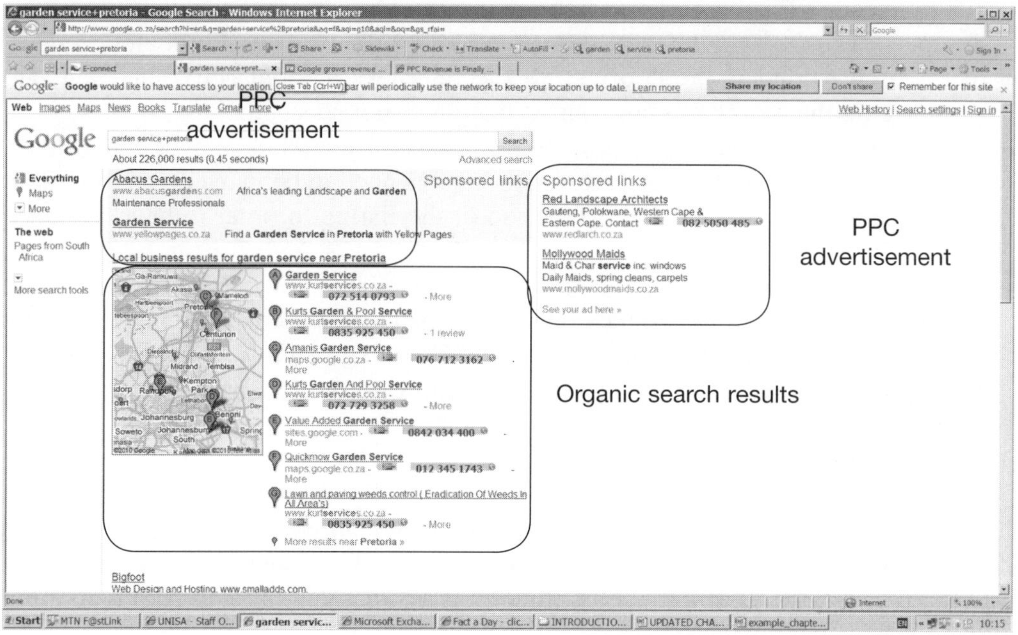

Figure 12.8 *Pay per click advertising and organic search results on Google*

PPC advertisements are also keyword-based, and the benefit of this is that the user shows intent, by means of their search. In other words, the customer is already in the process of buying or looking for information. The benefits of PPC adverts are the same for general online advertisements, but with the added benefit that it costs very little to set up and a marketer can track every cent spent on the advert on keyword level. This will let the marketer know what works and what does not. PPC and search engine optimisation – as discussed above – should lead to an effective search engine marketing strategy.

Search engine marketing

When a user enters their search criteria in a search engine, the results shown are referred to as the search engine results page (SERP). These results are usually shown on the left hand side of the search engine. These results are not influenced by any financial gain for the search engine and are thus referred to as organic listing or organic search results. Fig. 12.8 shows where organic search results are found on the SERP of the Google search engine. The relevance of the results of the search engine over time will determine the success of the search engine. Search engine optimisation (SEO) focuses on the improvement of the ranks of the organic search results. Search engine optimisation is something that marketers can increase by ensuring that their websites are search-engine friendly, relevant and up to date.

Successful search engine marketing not only focuses on the SEO of websites, but also on the PPC advertising of a website. Internet marketers need to know that search engine marketing (SEO and PPC advertising) is important to any website and therefore to the company for a number of reasons.[22]

- The customer/user is the driver of the search. They find what they are looking for by means of a search. A search engine search drives a customer/user to the company website, which leads to awareness, information and, ultimately, sales.
- The search engine is the doorway to the Internet. Without active and relevant presence on the search engine your website will not succeed.
- The number of Google searches alone per day is estimated to be over 200 million. In order to be part of the search results, websites need to be listed on major search engines and also close enough to the top of the listing in order to have a chance of a click-through.
- Users trust organic search results more than PPC results, but a PPC strategy could create enough interest while the company website increases its organic listing by means of search engine optimisation. A PPC strategy should not be used alone, but rather in combination with an organic search strategy (SEO).

Viral marketing (buzz marketing)

Should you receive e-mails from friends, think of the number of times you might have forwarded a catchy advertisement, silly video or song featuring a brand. It happens every day. Viral or buzz marketing is the electronic version or word-of-mouth. Stokes splits viral marketing into two types, namely organic viral marketing and controlled viral marketing.[23]

Organic viral marketing

This refers to a campaign which is not planned nor has any input by the marketer. If this is successful, a brand's equity can be boosted at very little cost. The communication takes place between consumers without any influence from the marketer. An organic viral campaign can be beneficial to a company should the message be positive, but it can have a detrimental effect should the message be negative.

Controlled viral marketing

Controlled viral marketing campaigns are strategically planned and have defined goals for the brand being marketed. For a viral marketing campaign to be successful, a number of aspects should be considered.[24]

- **Use tactics to build awareness and trial.** The goal with a viral campaign is not only to create awareness of a brand, but also for customers to try out the brand or product. Viral marketers need to set the scene for this to happen. Customers should want, and not be forced, to tell others about their experience with a product encouraging others to try it as well.
- **No acquisition without identification**. Marketers need to know whether their campaign has had any effect on sales or further recommendations. They need to put measures in place in order to capture details of consumers to determine the effect of the viral campaign such as collecting an e-mail address, signing up the customer for an opt-in newsletter programme or tracking offer redemption.
- **Look beyond the transaction**. Once a customer has been exposed to the viral campaign and marketers have recorded details, it is up to the marketer to keep in contact with the customer. What is strived for is a long-term advocacy role by the customer to the company, product or brand. Passing on an e-mail or application does not mean that the customer is loyal to the organisation or brand. Marketers could use their valued customers to participate in special events and forums to make them feel more active and closer to the brand.
- **Connect your advocates to product development**. Viral marketing should allow customers to give suggestions or vote on an idea. This will allow the customer to feel part of the brand and will lead to customers becoming brand advocates. American Express (Amex) has also exploited this trend with its viral Members Project campaign. Anyone can register to suggest a charitable project for Amex to fund – and Membership Rewards members can vote to pick the winning idea, which Amex has undertaken to fund up to the value of $5 million. It is the type of viral campaign that will funnel identifiable prospects into the Amex marketing stream and engage current cardholders on a deeply emotional level. It is a textbook example of how to generate and leverage buzz. Simba had a recent 'What's your lekker flavour' competition campaign calling on customers to suggest uniquely South African flavours for a new chips range. The reward for the winning flavour is R200 000 and 1% of all future sales. A fast-selling flavour could mean earning up to R500 000 each year forever for the winner of the best flavour.

Although viral marketing can be very unpredictable, if planned well, it can be immensely beneficial. Viral marketing most often than not is linked to social media.

Social media

There are currently more than 400 million Facebook users worldwide, and 50% of the active users log on to Facebook on any given day. In South Africa, Facebook has 2.5 million users. The average Facebook user has 130 friends. People spend over 500 billion minutes per month on Facebook. There are more than 100 million active users currently accessing Facebook through their mobile devices.[25] Nearly 75 million users logged onto Twitter in January 2010.[26] The number of Twitter users increases by 300 000 every day.[27] With these statistics in mind it becomes obvious that marketers should understand the workings of social media and embrace the opportunities they present. In the past, the objective of an online marketing campaign might have been to get users or customers to click through to the company's website, now it is to create sustained engagement with customers.[28]

Social media is media created, published and shared by individuals on the Internet.[29] It includes images, video, general posts and a lot more. Social networking sites include MySpace, Facebook, Twitter and an example of a business networking site is LinkedIn. Users use Blogs to record their opinions and feelings on topics and receive comments in turn on their posts. Users share Podcasts and share information by means of collaborative sites like Wikipedia. Social media allows users to constantly be in touch with their world. Vollmer refers to this as being 'always on' and therefore a very viable communication target.[30] The Internet is now the number one media source of media for consumers at work and second place at home. Furthermore, many consumers see social media as a more trustworthy source of information about products and services than corporate communication.[31]

Blogs

A blog is a condensed word for 'web log' and is typically a website that allows users (bloggers) to post entries on different topics and allows readers to comment on posts.[32] In 2009 there were 126 million blogs.[33] Blogs could have anything on them, including links, text, video, audio and images, anybody can start a blog, and anyone can write anything on their blog. This allows individuals and companies alike the opportunity to publish and share ideas and invite responses. See figs. 12.9 and 12.10 for two entirely different blogs.

Corporate blogging is an excellent way for staff, investors and prospective customers to communicate. Blogging assists in the fostering of a community around a brand. In order for a corporate blog to be successful it is important for staff to be well informed. Transparency and honesty is key, but there should be a clear stipulation about which information is sensitive and off-limits to bloggers.

Blogs can be extremely powerful as a marketing tool because consumers place a lot of trust in them. The views they express are available long after they were posted. To marketers, blogs give a momentary view of a brand or product. It allows marketers to see how people really feel about it. Blogs work extremely well with a viral campaign as it gets people talking, forwarding information and linking people to a company website. This leads to brand awareness.

Twitter is a microblogging site which allows users to publish short updates (limited to 140 characters). There are about 75 million Twitter accounts, although only 15 million users are active on Twitter.[34] Of the active users, 55 000 are from South Africa, with most of the users being in Cape Town, followed by Johannesburg.[35] As with ordinary blogs, microblogging can add tremendously to a viral campaign. It allows users to send links of viral videos and other viral marketing links.

Figure 12.9 *Seth Godin's blog (http://sethgodin.typepad.com/seths_blog)*

Figure 12.10 *Dooce.com (Heather B Armstrong's Blog www.dooce.com/)*

Social networking sites

The most popular social networking sites are MySpace, Facebook and LinkedIn. On these sites, users create a profile and can interact with their connections, by means of sharing updates, links and multimedia. Social network sites are usually free to members and generate revenue from advertising. They gather demographic information from members which in turn can be used by advertisers to target their adverts at a particular audience. Marketers can also create pages and have customers become 'fans' of their page. It allows marketers the platform to interact and communicate with customers, while also allowing customers the opportunity to voice any issues they might have with the brand, product or company. This has the potential to lead building of customer relationships. See fig. 12.11 for a view of a Facebook page for a small business named PixelPro. Pixelpro is a professional photography service provider situated in Pretoria. It posts updates every day, which

***Figure 12.11** PixelPro's Facebook page (www.facebook.com)*

include product offerings, comments from customers, promotions, as well as general information.

Podcasts

A podcast is a method of publishing audio programmes via the Internet. Users can create their own self-published radio shows. Podcasting became very popular with the availability of iTunes. Radio stations have jumped on the bandwagon and realised that podcasting allows listeners to listen to their programmes over the Internet at a convenient time. In South Africa nearly all radio stations offer podcasts (see fig. 12.12 for an example). Universities and other education institutions have realised that podcasting is a powerful tool to provide students with additional tuition or assist students who are unable to attend lectures.

Podcasts could be a marketer's dream because they are relatively inexpensive, and the content can reach a niche market, making it extremely targetable. Marketers can also see exactly how many users download a podcast. The content is controlled by the marketer. Marketers can have a blog that works side by side with the podcast which allows users to respond to the podcast, which provides feedback for marketers to do it better next time. For podcasts to be successful, marketers need to ensure that the content is of a high quality with relevant content, which is real (and not an audio format of the corporate brochure).

Video and knowledge sharing

YouTube is perhaps the best known website for users to upload, view and share videos. These videos range from music, amateur videos, video logs, jokes, information programmes and advertisements. A total of 12.2 billion videos were seen on YouTube during the month of November 2009. Close to 82% of all blogs have YouTube videos embedded on them.[36] The South African equivalent of sites

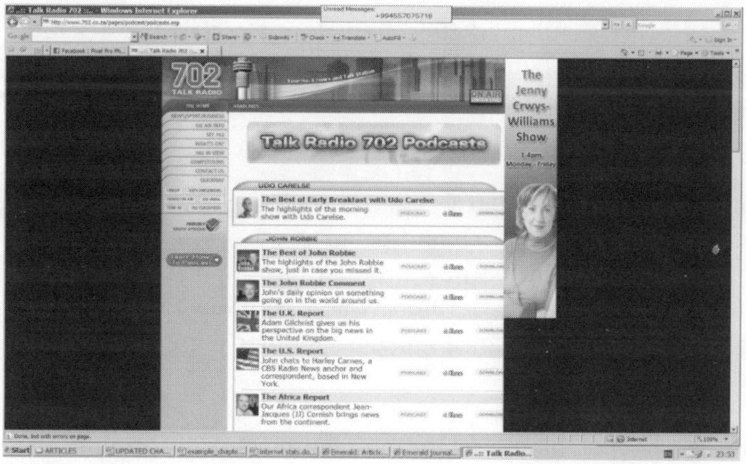

Figure 12.12 *Podcasts of Talk Radio 702 (www.702.co.za/pages/podcast/podcasts.asp)*

like YouTube are Zoopy and MyVideo. Marketers realised that there is no time limit for an online advertisement as is the case with television. This allows marketers to extend their creativity and message to users. It all comes down to the content of the video. If the content is relevant and worth watching there will be viewers.

Knowledge sharing occurs mainly though a web page named a wiki. This type of web page allows readers to add, edit and update its content without the need for much technical knowledge. The page provides readers with tools to easily monitor the changing state of the wiki. Users can discuss the issues around the content until a consensus can be reached. Possibly the most well used and known wiki is Wikipedia.

It is apparent from the discussion above that with social media the user or customer is in charge of the communication message, not the marketer. This can be unfamiliar or uncomfortable territory for marketers who are used to being at the helm of any and every marketing message. So how should a marketer proceed using this new medium? The answer lies in the integration of the online communication tools with the off-line communication tools. Internet marketing will not be successful if not followed through with off-line methods. The bottom line to successful marketing with social media is to listen to the customer when providing feedback, and make the customer part of the marketing campaign instead of only the target.

In this 'always on' environment, turning off is what people do when faced with a poor marketing campaign. It is important for marketers not to lose focus of their core marketing activities as set out in the previous sections of this book. We have discussed the marketing mix at length in the previous chapters of this book. Let us recap how the Internet can be used with the marketing mix.

The Internet and the marketing mix

The unique features of the Internet, such as its multimedia environment, permanent availability, global reach, affordability, ease of use, ability to store vast amounts of information, speed interactivity, ability to reach a mass market, ability to customise information for individual users, as well as its ability to transact sales, makes the Internet a very powerful marketing tool. If we revisit the 4 Ps marketing mix discussed earlier in this book in the context of the online world, we will have a better idea of how the Internet impacts on each of these elements.

Product

If we look at the product, the Internet can be used to gather market information that will help shape how the product should be adapted to meet customer needs (which is important, for instance, in the new product development process). The Internet can also be used to keep product developers abreast of up-to-date information on the latest product and technology developments in other companies and in other parts of the world.

The Internet is also being used very successfully to procure production materials and other, often cheaper inputs to the production process, online. By integrating the firm's online customer relationship management activities (discussed later in this chapter) with the organisation's production and supply-chain management activities, information gathered from customers can translate into faster, or even real-time inputs to the production department and production engineers. If a change in consumer demand or consumer tastes or if an extraordinary number of complaints are received, this data can immediately be fed through the system to the production department, where engineers will take whatever action is necessary. This action might be to increase or decrease production or to fix a production problem which is causing the errors. The Internet can also be used to gather information on competitive products to see how your product compares with others (i.e. benchmarking).

Price

The Internet can impact on price by helping to save costs on the one hand, and by keeping the organisation in tune with competitive prices. Searching the Internet will quickly reveal what prices your competitors are charging. Also, you can use the Internet to communicate your prices to your customers and you can make your online price lists easily changeable to keep up with changing circumstances.

From a cost point of view, the Internet serves as an extremely affordable marketing and advertising tool allowing you to reach a global audience at a fraction of the old cost. As a communications tool, e-mail is cheap compared with other communication media such as the telephone and fax. Add to this the fact that the Internet allows you to target and transact directly with the customer, thereby by-passing the many intermediaries in traditional marketing channels. This process is referred to as disintermediation. In some instances, the Internet can even be used as an extremely cheap distribution medium for electronic products, such as books, designs and software.

These factors, either individually or in combination, allow a business to achieve quite considerable savings, which can be translated into lower prices for customers, or greater margins for the business. It also enables the business to be more flexible with its pricing policies.

Promotion

This is perhaps where the Internet is at its most powerful. The multimedia nature of the Internet, combined with its capacity to deliver huge amounts of information to users, means that it is the perfect medium for advertising and promoting products.

Businesses can now not only publicise their companies over the Internet, but can also advertise their products and services to a global audience at a fraction of cost of traditional advertising. Internet advertising is easy to update and easy to expand – there is no real limit on how much information can be made available. Furthermore, the business can focus in on the product, providing video footage, audio clips, detailed graphics, photographs and animations, in addition to text. This enables the business to provide a level of detail not possible with other advertising media.

Traditional advertising and promotion is often out of the league of all but the largest companies. The Internet has changed this. Combined with e-mail, e-newsletters and e-zines, even the smallest business is now able to advertise and promote its products very effectively to a global audience at a very affordable cost.

What is more, any intermediaries the business may be using, including its sales staff, agents, distributors and even the customers themselves, can be kept informed of new price lists, new product introductions, product updates and of other related information, via the Internet. And another area where the Internet can prove valuable is in sales promotion. Marketing, after all, ends in selling and the Internet offers one of the most affordable ways of reaching an audience and enabling that audience to transact with you. We discuss Internet advertising and online sales transaction again later in this chapter.

Distribution

Although not appropriate for most products, the Internet has been used quite successfully as a distribution medium for products and service offerings such as software, books, magazines, certain consulting services, engineering drawings, language translations and graphic design, or any other type of product or service that can be transmitted in electronic form. Indeed, many software companies have tapped into markets around the world very effectively by advertising and distributing their programs over the Internet. Many users today would rather download the latest software off the Internet than go to the local computer store to buy an often more expensive copy of the software. At least off the Internet you are likely to get the software at a cheaper rate, faster, as well as the latest version of it.

In other instances where physical products need to be packed and sent by ship, air or parcel post, the Internet can serve a valuable role in putting all the appropriate distribution information at the customer's disposal. It also allows a business to identify and compare transport companies and freight forwarders, and puts customs duties, freight rates, exchange rates and other relevant information at your fingertips in real time.

Today, parcel delivery companies such as DHL, FedEx, UPS and Dawn Wing allow customers to track their parcel(s) via their websites, ensuring that the customer is always in control of where his or her package is. The Internet has become integral to their operations and a part of their customers' service expectations.

Mobile tracking technology manages courier company growth[37]
Advances in mobile tracking technology have enabled courier and logistics company Dawn Wing DPD to cope with the substantial growth in the movement of parcels. The courier has also become part of other organisations' supply chains. Dawn Wing's business-to-counter consumer deliveries have grown by about 40% in recent years.

The company's logistics system makes use of hand-held GPRSMMT devices that communicate through South Africa's cellular phone network. Dawn Wing functions locally and can tailor its service offering, and subsequently its logistics system, to what is needed in the South African market, without having to follow an international organisation's business structure.

In addition to couriers making deliveries as promised, clients also want real time access to information about the delivery process – they want to see how quickly their parcels are moving along the delivery supply chain. GPRSMMT-based logistics software enables Dawn Wing to provide a visible supply chain and constantly updated information to clients in real time. The system informs clients that their parcels have been delivered within minutes after actual delivery.

The Dawn Wing logistics system makes fetching and delivering orders placed over the Internet much faster and easier. The Internet provides an opportunity to order goods in real time, at any time of the day or night. A delivery system should also be in real time if is to efficiently meet the demands placed on it by an Internet ordering service.

The Internet and marketing research
Marketing research is the task of locating or gathering information that will gain the company a business advantage. Online market research is the practice of using online surveys and information sources to conduct market research. The Internet is nothing less than the largest library of information in the world, and information can be found on virtually any subject. Marketers can:
- conduct desk research on the Web;
- conduct surveys on the Web; and
- send out questionnaires using e-mail.

Using the Internet, it is possible to gather information about markets, industries, competitors, countries and even individual customers. Most of this information is already available on the Internet and the amount of information available is growing daily, as is the quality of the information. This information is published by companies, industry bodies, trade associations, governments, research houses, chambers of commerce and other similar organisations.

Conducting online desk research is about browsing or searching the Internet for the information you want. This involves learning how to use the many search engines and keeping record of useful websites that serve as a 'springboard' to other relevant information. This is not an easy task, but the marketer who makes an effort to regularly search the Internet for marketing information will undoubtedly reap the rewards.

What is more, businesses are increasingly using the Internet to send out questionnaires and to conduct online surveys. These surveys range from surveys of individual to online group surveys (such as conducting an online focus group, which Internet technology now makes possible). Some surveys are simply posted on the Web, with the request that visitors to the website complete the survey (which usually comprises a number of questions linked to several checkboxes). With other surveys, the questionnaire is sent to respondents by e-mail, with the request that they complete the questionnaire, returning it to the researcher with the click of a button. On the researcher's side, the system can be programmed to automatically analyse the incoming information.

In the case of Web-based surveys, one drawback is that you only reach those persons who visit the website. As only about a fifth of the South African population has access to the Internet and of those, only a small percentage may visit the site in question, the survey is likely to be somewhat biased. E-mail-based surveys are usually better, as a far greater percentage of the population have access to e-mail, but there are still portions of the population who will be excluded because of lack of access to the technology concerned. Nevertheless, online research is gaining in popularity because it is one of the easiest ways to launch a survey and the results can also be quickly and automatically analysed.

The Internet and information dissemination

Companies often store useful information (for example, detailed product specifications) that they would like to distribute to their customers, except that this can be very expensive in the physical world. In addition, television and radio advertisements are restricted in the amount of space or time they have available. Even product brochures are expensive to produce and again, they can only contain a limited amount of information.

By contrast, the Internet it is a very cheap way to disseminate information. For many businesses the Internet serves as a means of getting useful information that would otherwise only be stored away in filing cabinets to customers and to interested stakeholders (e.g. shareholders and staff). It is also a useful way of getting breaking news and other critical marketing or public relations information to the marketplace quickly. An announcement of some impending development (a take-over bid, for example) can be disseminated to shareholders within the hour using the Internet.

The Internet and corporate publicity

Positive publicity can be a powerful weapon in bringing awareness, acceptance and desirability to a business. In this regard the Internet is a useful medium for promoting and publicising a business and its activities. The Internet is a lot like the grapevine – it is the rich soil in which the seed of a publicity message can germinate very quickly, especially when using social media, such as corporate blogs. It is an environment where people eager for information come to share ideas, information, interests and news. The key to successful publicity is to listen to customers, respond to others and to build a voice for the company by means of an online presence.

An online presence could start with a website. A creative, trendy website can bring a lot of positive publicity towards an innovative business (e.g. the Nando's site www.nandos.co.za). An online presence goes further than a website alone, of course. Public relations practitioners are encouraged to use Internet marketing communication tools to increase the reach of the entire marketing strategy.

Publicising and branding the activities of your business on the Web are certainly a lot faster than the more traditional publicity machinery such as mail-shots and press releases, and you also have more control over the message, whereas a magazine editor may cut your public relations message to fit a particular page. In addition, as more and more people in a growing number of industries turn to the Web for relevant market and industry information, so the Internet grows in its effectiveness as a means of promoting the company and its activities. It is also relatively cheap.

Figure 12.13 *Nandos – A public relations website (www.nandos.co.za)*

Transacting sales online

Seventy-seven percent of South Africans with Internet access are shopping online. The most frequent purchases are music, movies and airline tickets.[38] While many individuals and businesses believe the Internet should be used simply to maximise sales, this strategy is flawed, argues Tom Vassos, author of Strategic Internet Marketing.[39] The ultimate goal of marketing is to maximise profitability. Therefore a comprehensive Internet marketing plan should focus on three objectives, namely increasing sales, decreasing the cost of doing business, and improving communications with all stakeholders, the last of which should help achieve the first two objectives.

To date, the Web does not conclusively prove to increase sales, but it does have a proven track record at decreasing costs and improving stakeholder communications.

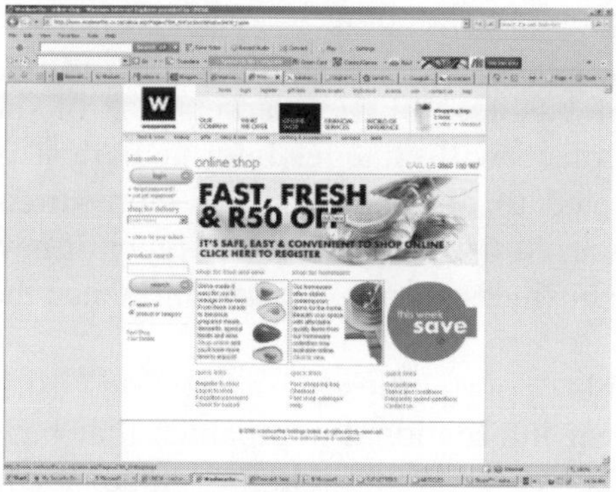

www.woolworths.co.za

www.pnponline.co.za

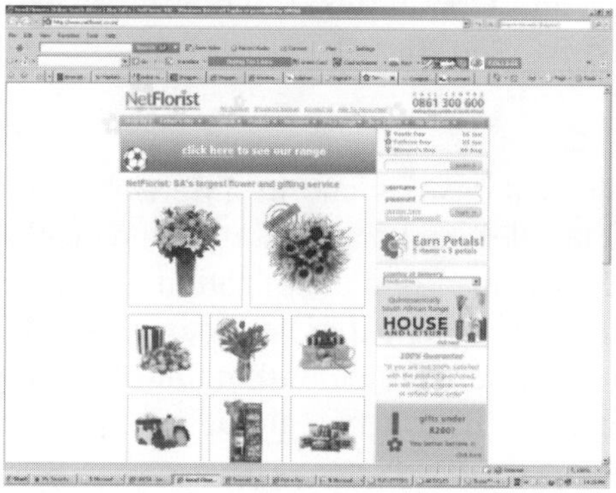

www.netflorist.co.za

www.computicket.com

Figure 12.14 *Popular transaction websites in South Africa*

The situation is changing, however, as the Internet reaches its critical mass.

There are several reasons why the Web has not yet proved highly successful at increasing sales. The first hurdle is the question of payment. Users have been reluctant to give credit card and other banking details over the Internet for the fear of these being compromised. This situation is being remedied with powerful encryption programs being developed. Most South African banks are now advertising the fact that clients can undertake a broad base of banking activities using the Internet. For many buyers (and sellers) dealing with distant, unknown clients, buyer insecurity can represent a very real stumbling block.

Finally, this is a new phenomenon and users also need to get used to it. There will always be those who will buy over the Internet and those who will not, just as some people readily buy from direct-mail companies and others do not. As the Internet reaches a greater portion of the population, so the number of Internet shoppers will increase. Increasing pressure on individual leisure time will encourage people to shop online from the comfort of their homes, rather than using their free time to jostle with other shoppers for a limited selection of products and services in packed outlets.

From a business perspective, as interest in online shopping increases, so it will become more viable and attractive to use the Internet as a business medium. It can be expected, however, that the nature of business in the marketspace of the Internet versus that in the traditional marketplace will change. Intermediaries, in the traditional sense, for example, are expected to disappear with a more direct producer-to-customer channel taking their place. At the same time, a number of new cybermediaries are expected to come onto the business scene soon and influence the way business is done.

Nevertheless, the Web does offer considerable opportunities for facilitating virtual transactions. There are number of well-known international companies that have been extremely successful selling their products on the Web, including Amazon and Dell. In South Africa, we have a large number of online retailers. Some retailers have a physical presence, such as Woolworths and Computicket, while other exist mainly online, such as Kalahari.net and Netflorist. See fig. 12.15.

Customer service and support

Customer service takes different forms in different industries and in different foreign markets. In some cases, the support is targeted at resellers and distributors, while in other instances, the support may be aimed at the final consumer, or a combination of both.

The idea of the support is to help your customers or distributors receive as much value-added benefit from your products. This customer service will include not only customer support but also training, customer help-lines, news about new product developments, price changes, etc.

Benefits of online support services

- **Automate routine procedures**. It is possible, using Web technology, to automate responses to customer enquiries. For example, should a customer lodge a query, file a complaint, or request certain information, the company's website will automatically respond with an e-mail, acknowledging receipt of the query which should generate positive customer response (this is called an autoresponse, discussed above). Alternatively, the company may post answers to FAQs, so that when a customer has a question, he or she may well find an answer already posted on the FAQ section.
- **Offer 24-hour support**. The Internet is available 24 hours a day, 365 days per year. This means that the customer can log on to the website any time of the day and request information or assistance, or look up product information. With the ability to automatically respond to an enquiry, it is also possible to arrange that an acknowledgement be e-mailed automatically to the customer (as discussed above). Thus, the customer can lodge an enquiry at 02h00 in the morning and receive an initial reply almost immediately!
- **Keep technical information accurate and up-to-date**. Using the enormous space available on the Web, product catalogues, technical manuals and data, as well as price lists, can now be made available online. In addition, this information can easily be updated. This makes it possible to keep customers fully informed,

with the option to access whatever information they require without having to first interact with a company representative.

- **Slash hard-copy distribution costs**. The distribution of printed marketing material is often one of the undesirable expenses incurred by many businesses, especially when distributing overseas. This can have the effect of reducing the amount of material that is distributed to customers in order to keep costs down. Using the Web, however, there is virtually no cost attached to distributing large amounts of information and so greater amounts of information and material can be made available on a more regular basis.
- **Give the customer more control**. With a website, the customer has control. Customers decide when to get the information they want, as well as what information they want. There is no need to play 'telephone tag' with sales representatives or technicians (leave messages which may not receive a response at a convenient time). They can also choose to subscribe to the company e-newsletter to receive selected news of interest to them.
- **Get closer to the customer**. By inviting the customer to respond to customer surveys and by giving the customer greater control over the product information, the purchase decision and follow-up support, the company is able get closer to the customer. This is a prelude to developing an on-going and long-term relationship with the customer.
- **Turn paper manuals into digital documents**. Too often a business generates vast amounts of paper-based information. This information inevitably lies on desks and in filing cabinets and is seldom distributed, even though it could be of value to customers, distributors, suppliers, staff and other stakeholders. However, with the Web this information can now easily, cheaply and quickly be turned into online information sources for all to see, regardless of where in the world they are.
- **Develop a relationship with the customer**. We have already said that the Web is most powerful at developing relationships between businesses and customers. Relationship-building goes beyond drawing the business and customer closer together. It is about sharing a common interest, where the customer proactively seeks out the business and its products. Locking customers into the value proposition of your business through the integration of their systems with your own makes it less likely that a customer would want to move to your competitors. Forging a closer relationship with customers adds considerable weight to the marketing efforts of your business and ultimately helps reduce risk.

Customer relationship management (CRM)

The Web is accelerating the process in which selling products becomes more a matter of establishing an ongoing relationship than of performing a single isolated transaction. In an environment where your competitor is a click away, it is essential to create an online environment that locks the customer into your business. This will only happen if you succeed in providing the customer with business value and a pleasant online experience. The two go hand in hand. Business value in an unpleasant online environment will not hold customers, but at the same time customers are not there just to enjoy their online experiences – they are looking for business opportunities and value.

It is important to bear in mind that business value can be provided on three fronts. Firstly, the online environment can be developed in such a way that it adds value to the customer in its own right. An adaptive, intelligent customer front end can go a long way in personalising the online experience for the customer. Secondly, and perhaps most importantly, the product or service that the business sells must add value in itself. It's no use having a great website with lots of useful features and that is easy and fun to navigate, but the product that is being sold is undesirable. Finally, the staff and physical business processes (e.g. distribution logistics) of a business must be geared towards enhancing the customer's experience with the business. Remember that the Internet is but one way of interacting with the customer.

Behind the scenes, however, it is important that the front end of the business and underlying systems facilitate customer interaction and two-way communication at any time or place. Every suitable communications channel – from e-mail to discussion forums – should be used to this end. The system should be able to track customers and their preferences, habits and buying patterns, and to remember them when they return. This knowledge must be actionable and repeatable. The front end and content will be customised or personalised based on the knowledge that has been gathered about each customer, and presented when he or she visits the site again. The broad objectives behind implementing an online CRM system include the following:[40]

- segmenting customers into different value and profile groups;
- improving two-way, any-time, any-place communication with customers;
- involving customers in improving the service levels of the business by soliciting constant feedback from them;
- ensuring that customers receive consistent service;
- reducing the cost of getting customers, particularly the second time round;
- ensuring that customers stay with you over a lifetime;
- increasing your share of customers;
- reducing the prospect-to-sale cycle time;
- leveraging value from cross-selling and up-selling; and
- enabling a business to harness value of its customers as an actionable, durable asset.

Perhaps the most important aspect of successful customer relationship management online is that it leads to improved customer loyalty.[41] It is a well-known fact that it costs a company more to attract a new customer than it does to implement a retention strategy. Using the Internet is another means to ensure a level of customer loyalty that benefits the company as a whole.

Ethics and Internet marketing

Privacy, trust and honesty are issues that exist not only in the physical word, but in the virtual word of the Internet as well. Not so long ago customers were very concerned for the safety of the credit card information on transaction websites, so much so that it prohibited potential customers from using the Internet for online shopping. Sites have to continuously assure their customers that their information is safe when doing transaction. Companies need to ensure that their Internet security is continuously updated to keep the information of their customers safe. A further measure is to inform customers of any possible irregularity which might occur; Banks providing Internet Banking for example, provide customers with regular warnings and additional information on their websites of possible scams which might do rounds. Another feature marketers could implement online is to provide customers with options to increase their privacy. Marketers could also give customers the option to receive further marketing information, giving the customer the power to decide whether future marketing should be targeted to him/her.

Another ethical issue which concerns marketers is the fact that Internet users are not always who they say they are. A user may be a child using his or her parents' computer or an Internet café. The issue is not so much that the material a company places on the web might be harmful to a child, but rather that it is unethical to market to a child. Companies need to put measures in place which will help them determine whether the person receiving online marketing messages is indeed an adult.

Customers should be able to trust a website, for not only the products or services it sells, but also for what the company represents by means of its online presence. This requires a level or transparency and honesty. Companies need to have a united marketing approach which is supported online as well as offline.

Summary

We began the chapter by looking at what the Internet is; examined the link between the Internet and the World Wide Web; and highlighted the benefits of the Internet and the World Wide Web. We went on to relate the marketing concept to the virtual world; discussed the marketing mix in the context of the online realm, and identified the characteristics of a new environment that marketers need to come to terms with, namely the virtual environment or marketspace.

Finally, we identified several areas within the marketing activities of a business where the Internet can be put to work. These include marketing research, the marketing mix, advertising, customer service and support, corporate publicity, sales transactions and export marketing. Some of these areas will be more relevant for some businesses than for others. We suggested that marketers need to consider their business activities very carefully to see where and how the Internet might play a role.

The Baby Sense website

Baby Sense is a company which originated from the writing of a book by the same name in 2004. The company has grown to be a very successful business. Baby Sense authors appear regularly on the Great Expectations television show on e-tv. They also have regular seminars held in the major city centres for pregnant moms and dads. Today Baby

Sense is much more than a range of successful books and products. Baby Sense, based in Cape Town, has embraced the Internet and uses it successfully as part of its marketing strategy.

Visitors to www.babysense.co.za will notice that this site provides parents and about-to-be-parents with a lot of information. This website attracts around 5 000 South African visitors per month, but has around 600 000 hits per month. The website provides information on the range of products which can be purchased online or in stores, a directory of other service providers, workshop/talk information and links to other sites. The Baby Sense online presence has gone a lot further than just a website. The authors provide a regular blog and newsletter, which reaches around 8 000 readers. Their Facebook community has over 3 300 members and they have over 135 regular followers on Twitter. Visit the website and explore what the site has to offer, then answer the questions that follow.

Exercise

1. Which further online marketing tools would you suggest to Baby Sense?
2. How could Baby Sense apply social networking even better?
3. Discuss the Baby Sense website in the context of the 4 Ps of the marketing mix.
4. How would you suggest Baby Sense builds an online relationship with their customers?
5. Which ethical issues do you think Baby Sense should be aware of?

Terminology

Above, at or below competitors' prices A competition-based approach to pricing where the price is set at a level that aims to meet or beat competitors' prices.

Adoption process The stages through which an individual consumer passes in arriving at a decision to try, or not try a new product.

Advertising Non-personal promotion of a product or organisation through paid channels in the mass media.

Advertising campaign The advertising plan of an organisation for a specific period, indicating the media to be used, the messages and images to be conveyed, and the scheduling of activities to be performed.

Advertising objectives These are more specific than the promotion objectives and relate only to the advertising part of the promotion campaign. Themes for these objectives are, among others, awareness, recall, comprehension and believability.

Affective component The component of attitude that has to do with a person's feelings.

Affiliates Arrangements between websites in which a website which helps to generate traffic for another is paid for doing so.

Allowances A pricing method to encourage intermediaries and final users to buy a product, for example a trade-in allowance and a promotional allowance.

Associative groups Groups to which a person aspires to belong.

Assortment gap The gap between the range of products a customer wants to buy and what is actually available at a particular business.

Attitude A learned predisposition to behave in a consistently favourable or unfavourable way toward market-related objects, events or situations.

Automatic groups Groups to which a person belongs as a result of age and gender.

Autoresponder Software that can automatically send a response to an incoming e-mail depending on the occurrence of certain words in the mail.

Auxiliary activities Activities such as the supply of information, storing, risk taking and grading.

Auxiliary businesses Businesses that are not directly involved in the transfer of title, but provide support services for the selling process.

Banner advertisements Advertisements on websites, typically graphic in nature, that invite users to click through to another website.

Barter A form of payment in kind in which products or services are exchanged without any money changing hands.

Behavioural component Represents the outcome of the cognitive and affective components of the decision to buy or not to buy.

Belongingness or social motives The desire for love, friendship and group acceptance.

Brand A name, term, sign, symbol or design, or a combination of these which uniquely identify the product.

Breadth of product mix The number of product lines a specific organisation manufactures or markets. *See also* Depth of product mix.

Budget A plan expressed in money terms, indicating the marketing activities for a specific future period.

Business objective/Short-term objective These are usually set by functional managers for a period, usually one to three years.

Business products Products such as raw materials, machinery, cleaning materials, computers and motor vehicles that are bought by an organisation to use in its own operations to deliver another product or service.

Business-to-business markets *See* industrial markets.

Cash discounts A form of discount in which the customer is encouraged to pay in cash, helping the cash flow of the organisation. For example, a customer may be offered a 10% discount for paying an account within 15 days.

Cash-and-carry wholesaler A type of wholesaler located outside the central business area, usually close to a highway. Customers must pay cash for purchases and generally no packaging is provided.

Causal research Marketing research to test hypotheses about cause-and-effect relationships.

Census Data about every member of the population of interest to a marketer. This is different to a representative sample, in which generalisations are made about the whole population of interest, based on data obtained from a sample of individuals.

Chain store A branded retailer with many branches falling under a head office, for example, Shoprite Checkers or Edgars.

Channel captain The leader in a specific distribution channel for certain products.

Channel leadership *See* channel captain.

Channel management In distribution two decisions must be taken: 1) which is the best channel to use to get the product to the customer (also called the transaction decision), and 2) the physical distribution management decision. Channel management refers to the management of both the transaction flow of the product being sold and decision making about physical distribution.

Cherry pickers Consumers who are extremely sensitive to price and go from store to store to pick the best-priced items.

Child-dominant families Families in which children have a strong influence on family buying decisions.

Click through The number of times visitors to a particular page on a website have clicked onto a particular banner advertisement to visit the website the banner points to. This is usually measured in click-throughs per thousand visits to a particular page.

Client expectations The pre-trial beliefs that a client has about the performance of a service and the reference against which the service performance will be measured.

Client loyalty A deeply held commitment to keep buying a particular product or service which is resistant to situational influences and marketing efforts to cause the client to switch preferences.

Client service The service offered in support of the core product or service.

Cognitive component This refers to a person's knowledge and perceptions of a product that may be acquired by direct experience of that product.

Cognitive dissonance An uncomfortable feeling caused by holding conflicting ideas simultaneously. In the context of this book, people who have bought a product or service may regret having made that decision, even if there is nothing wrong with the product, service or price.

Communication process The flow of information from the communicator (marketer) to the recipient (target audience) and back.

Competition-based methods of pricing Setting prices at a level that aims to meet or beat competitors' prices.

Competitive intelligence (CI) The collection of information about competitors.

Competitor A business that offers similar products or services and is competing for the same market.

Consumer A person who consumes, especially one who acquires goods or services for direct use or ownership rather than for resale or use in production and manufacturing. In this book the word customer and consumer are used interchangeably.

Consumer analysis Inquiry into the needs of consumers in order to better deliver what they want.

Consumer behaviour The behaviour patterns of decision units (individuals and families) in respect of buying products and services.

Consumer market Individuals and households buying goods and services for personal consumption.

Consumer products Products aimed at individual consumers at the bottom of the value chain, which are usually sold through retailers.

Consumer promotion Promotion activities aimed at the final consumer of the product, usually an individual person, for such consumer products as clothing, groceries, furniture and holidays.

Convenience products Products that are fairly cheap and readily available and which require little effort or preparation by consumers, such as bread and milk.

Convenience sampling A research sample based on the easiest population members from which to obtain information.

Convenience store Retailers that are open for extended periods of time or do not close at all.

Corporate culture The sum total of the values, symbols and traditions of a business and the style of leadership applied by top management in motivating, communicating, exercising authority and managing conflict.

Cost-based methods of pricing Setting prices based on the cost of manufacturing a product or delivering a service.

Cost-plus pricing Pricing a product or service based on calculating the cost and adding set percentage (e.g. 50%) as the profit margin.

Critical incidents Specific interactions between the client and the service provider that are especially satisfying or dissatisfying.

Culture A pattern of behaviour common to members of a society, or of a group within that society.

Customary pricing Price based on what is the custom, e.g. a standard vending machine price for an item.

Customer orientation A focus on meeting the needs of the target market, based on establishing client satisfaction standards, monitoring customer satisfaction, and taking corrective action where necessary.

Customer satisfaction index (CSI) A survey that measures the overall satisfaction of a consumer with a product or service and ranks the results. For example, new car owners may be asked after a year about their experience with the company that sold them the car. This could form the basis of a ranking of dealers, from best to worst.

Customised process A selling process that is geared towards meeting the individual needs and requirements of every consumer.

Data A collection of facts from which conclusions may be drawn, e.g. statistics, opinions, facts or forecasts about a particular product or service.

Demand-backward pricing Using market research to determine the price a consumer would be willing to pay for a particular product or service, and then determining what it would cost to produce that product or service.

Demand-based methods One of the four methods to determine the approximate price level for a product or service, in this instance based on the demand for the product.

Department store A single store that has identifiable departments, e.g. men's clothing, women's clothing, tableware and cosmetics, e.g. Stuttafords.

Depth of product mix The variety of options offered in a particular product line, e.g. many different brands of razor blades. *See also* Breadth of product mix.

Descriptive research Marketing research to better describe marketing problems, situations, or markets, such as the market potential for a product or the demographics and attitudes of potential consumers.

Desired service The consumer's ideal level of service; above the expected level of service.

Determinant attributes Those attributes that actually determine a consumer's final buying choice of product or service.

Differentiated marketing Designing offerings for specifically identified target market segments or niches.

Direct channel A distribution channel where the manufacturer or producer of a product sells the product directly to the final consumer.

Direct mail Direct marketing through single mailings, which includes letters, e-mails, samples, brochures, pamphlets, catalogues and small gifts.

Direct marketing The use of different media to persuade the target audience to buy a product or service at any location. Also called database marketing.

Discount house Retailers that sell a range of products at a discount, based on a low markup and the expectation of high turnover. Some of the best-known discount houses in South Africa are Dion and Game.

Distribution The process through which products and services are moved from the manufacturer to the customer.

Distribution channel A channel for the manufacturer of a product or service to deliver the product to the customer. This may include wholesalers and retailers.

Durable products Products that are used repeatedly without losing their functionality, e.g. stoves and washing machines.

Early adopters Consumers who buy new technology before most other people do. *See also* Innovators, Laggards, Late majority *and* Early majority.

Early majority Consumers who will adopt a product or service after it has proven successful with others. *See also* Early adopters, Innovators, Laggards *and* Late majority.

Economic environment The economic forces that shape consumer behaviour, e.g. interest rates, the business cycle, the rate of unemployment and the amount of disposable income.

E-form A form that is filled in electronically, typically on the Internet.

Emotional motives Motives that involve emotions; these correspond with Maslow's social and esteem motives.

Esteem motives The desire to feel important in the eyes of others and to see oneself in a positive light. These motives include self-esteem, self-respect and the desire for status, superiority and prestige.

Ethical pricing considerations When the price of a product is partially determined by questions of right and wrong. For example, the price of a life-saving drug would partly be determined by the means of the people who need it. If the majority of people who need it are poor, the price will probably be set at a low level.

Exchange marketing activities The buying and selling of goods and services.

Exclusive distribution One of the three different types of intensity of distribution: intensive, selective and exclusive. Exclusive distribution means that only one intermediary sells a specific product, e.g. Porsche dealers have an exclusive distribution channel to sell those cars.

Executive summary A short summary of the main objectives, decisions and recommendations of a marketing plan. Generally, it briefly describes the marketing plans, the product or service on offer, the target markets, competitors, and the level of expected sales.

Expanded marketing mix (also called the 7 Ps) Expanding the 4 Ps of the traditional marketing mix (product, place [distribution], pricing and promotion [marketing communication]) to include people, processes and physical evidence.

Expected service The minimum level of service expected by the consumer that must be present for the client to experience any level of satisfaction.

Experience effect The reduction in per-unit cost of a product as the volume of output increases and the experience of a worker improves.

Experimental research The testing of data in controlled conditions.

Exploratory research Marketing research to gather preliminary information that will help to better define problems and suggest hypotheses for how to solve them.

Extended decision maker The person who takes the final decision from whatever alternatives there may be.

External marketing Communication by the company to the consumer.

External stimuli Environmental and marketing influences on the decisions made by a consumer.

Family In the marketing context, the term 'family' includes grandparents or other relatives who live under the same roof as a nuclear family (also known as extended family).

Fire-fighting When a business is preoccupied by day-to-day operational problems.

Fixed-cost (FC) Cost that remains the same for a business regardless of changes in the volume of products sold.

Focus groups Groups of 8 to 12 participants led by a moderator in an in-depth discussion on a particular topic.

Four-link chain A situation where three intermediaries and the manufacturer are involved in distributing the product to the customer.

Fragmentation The splintering of the market into many diverse groups.

Franchising A business arrangement where the franchisor (the company) grants the independent party (the franchisee) the right to sell the products or services to the customer. Examples of a franchise are McDonald's and KFC.

Frequently asked questions (FAQs) A website page that lists commonly asked questions with answers to those questions.

Functional objectives Short-term objectives within a functional area such as marketing.

Gatekeepers People who control the flow of information from one person to another.

General dealer A very old form of retailing that sells a wide range of products, usually found in the rural areas of South Africa.

Geographical adjustments Changes in price that depend on the distance from the point of manufacture.

Group factors Also known as external determinants and include the cultural group, reference groups, the family and the social class system.

Habitual decision making When a consumer buys the same brand without thinking about it.

Halo effect The positive or negative impact that the reputation of a business or its product may have on another entity. For example, when Daimler Benz started to manufacture the Colt bakkie, Colt experienced a positive halo effect.

Husband-dominant families Families where the husband decides what should be bought.

Hybrid channels A situation where more than one distribution channel is used to sell products to the customers. For example, Coca-Cola is sold in cafés, convenience stores, supermarkets, hypermarkets and discount stores. Also called multiple channels. *See also* Intensive distribution.

Hyperlink An electronic clickable link between websites, or pages on the same website, or to a file stored on a website.

Hypermarket The largest retail outlets, usually located near highways and in the outer suburbs of a city.

Important attributes The key factors (e.g. safety, image and convenience) that consumers consider to be significant when choosing between competing products and services.

Impulse decision making/buying Buying decisions made on the spur of the moment, or immediately when they become aware of a want or need. Retailers put certain products in checkout queues to promote last-minute impulse buying.

Individual factors Also known as internal determinants or basic determinants, these determine a consumer's decisions and behaviour. These include a consumer's needs, motives, attitudes, perception, personality and learning abilities.

Industrial markets Entities that buy goods and services to be used in the process of manufacturing other products.

Influencer Influences the final decision in the sense that his/her suggestions and wishes are reflected in the family's decision.

Information Data that is relevant for decision making.

Information gap The gap between what a consumer knows about a product and what might prompt him or her to buy it.

Initiator The first person to suggest that a specific product or service be bought.

Innovators The small minority of consumers who are the first ones to buy new technology. *See also* Early adopters, Early majority, Late majority *and* Laggards.

Intangible products Non-physical products like an insurance policy or a service.

Intensity of distribution The level of availability of a particular product, determined by factors such as production capacity, the preferences and location of consumers, and expected level of demand.

Intensive distribution Using all available outlets to sell a product such as milk and bread. *See also* Hybrid channel.

Interactive marketing Marketing that is very responsive to individual customer preferences.

Intermediaries or resellers Entities that sell on goods and services for a profit, acting as a link in a chain, e.g. retailers that procure goods from producers and sell these consumers, or wholesalers that procure goods from producers and sell these on to retailers.

Internal marketing The efforts of an organisation to communicate with, and motivate its employees make their contribution to the goal of improving customer satisfaction. Internal marketing may include training employees and giving them the necessary tools and skills to perform the jobs at the highest level so that the client receives a satisfactory service.

Internal stimuli Personal characteristics of the consumer that could affect buying decisions.

Internet marketing Using website and related digital technologies to achieve marketing objectives.

Internet retailer Retailers that sell products over the Internet, also called e-tailers, e.g. picknpay.co.za and woolworths.co.za.

Internet service providers (ISPs) Companies that provide individuals and firms with access to the Internet.

Inventory The amount of stock in a company, that is, merchandise, raw materials, and finished and unfinished products which have not yet been sold.

Judgement sampling Non-probability samples in which the selection criteria are based on personal judgement that the element is representative of the population under study.

Just-in-time (JIT) manufacturing A system to increase the return on investment by reducing in-process inventory, so that only as much of a particular raw material, product or product part as is required is in stock, 'just in time' for it to be used when needed.

Labelling A marketing tool that ranges from a single tag attached to a product to complex graphical designs, aimed at creating a brand identity, grading and describing the product.

Laggards Consumers who are the last to adopt new technology. *See also* Early adopters, Early majority, Late majority *and* Innovators.

Late majority Consumers who tend to buy technology towards the end of the product life cycle. *See also* Early adopters, Early majority, Innovators *and* Laggards.

Learning The process by that individual consumers acquire the knowledge and experience they apply to future-related buying decisions.

Lifestyle The unique pattern of living that influences and reflects an individual's consumption behaviour.

List price The price that is charged for the product, i.e. the selling price, before making any adjustments.

List server A computer program that manages subscription requests for a mailing list, and distributes new messages and postings, and distributes messages from individual members of the list to all the members on the list.

Living Standard Measure (LSM) A South African model that provides data for marketers to segment the market based on such aspects as monthly household income, urbanisation, access to services and ownership of cars and major appliances.

Long-term objective The position an organisation wants to be in over some future period, usually three to five years.

Loss-leader pricing A competition-based method of pricing where a product is priced below or at cost to attract customers who may buy other items while they are buying the loss leader. *See also* Cherry pickers.

Macro-environment The large-scale external forces outside the control of a business that may affect its operations, such as the economy, politics and technology.

Mail-order store A type of retailer that sells products by mail, e.g. by circulating a catalogue or placing an advertisement to obtain orders, and then shipping items by mail.

Manufacturer franchise When a manufacturer provides a franchise to a franchisee to sell its range of products.

Manufacturer to wholesaler franchise A franchise operation where the wholesaler receives a franchise from the manufacturer to sell its range of products in a certain geographic area.

Market environment The forces outside the control of a business (e.g. the actions of customers and competitors) that may directly affect its operations.

Market offering The product or service developed by a marketer to meet and satisfy the needs of the consumer.

Market orientation A focus on meeting the needs of the target market, based on establishing client satisfaction standards, monitoring customer satisfaction, and taking corrective action where necessary; a strong awareness of competitors and their offerings in order to remain competitive.

Market segmentation The process of dividing a total market into market segments or target markets of consumers with common needs or characteristics, and selecting one or more segments to target with a distinct marketing mix.

Marketing The process whereby a company offers its market something of value in order to facilitate an exchange that is satisfactory to both the organisation and the individual. For this process to be judged successful, the objectives of both parties must be met.

Marketing activities Those activities that must be performed during the transfer of goods and services to ensure customer satisfaction and stimulate demand.

Marketing audit A comprehensive, systematic, independent and periodic examination of a company's marketing environment, objectives, strategies and activities, with a view to determining problem areas and opportunities, and recommending a plan of action to improve the company's market performance.

Marketing concept A managerial philosophy that holds that the business must be customer-oriented, follow an integrated approach, make a profit and meet its social responsibilities. *See also* Customer orientation.

Marketing control The continuous process of measuring and evaluating the results of marketing strategies and plans, and taking corrective action to ensure that marketing objectives are attained and competitors beaten.

Marketing cost analysis An examination of the sources of marketing cost, including why they are incurred, how large or small they are, and how they change over time.

Marketing decision support system (MDSS) A computer-based system that helps a marketing decision maker to confront problems by means of direct interaction with databases and analytical software programs.

Marketing environment The environment in which a business operates, made up of a number of sub-environments.

Marketing information system (MIS) A formalised set of procedures for generating, analysing, storing and distributing an ongoing flow of pertinent information to marketing decision makers.

Marketing instrument There are four classic marketing instruments, namely the *product*, the *place* (distribution channel), the *promotion* being used, and the *price* charged for a product. A unique combination of these four instruments plus the target market constitute the marketing strategy. They are referred to as the 4 Ps.

Marketing mix The variables under the control of marketing management which must be used to meet the needs of the consumers. These variables traditionally include the 4 Ps – product decisions, pricing decisions, promotion decisions and distribution decisions (place).

Marketing objective A marketing objective is what you want to achieve through your marketing during the time frame of the plan.

Marketing plan A written document containing the guidelines for a business unit's marketing programmes and allocations over the planning period. All relevant quantitative and qualitative details must be mentioned in the marketing plan and it must be specific.

Marketspace The virtual world where products and services exist as digital information and where transactions and interactions occur electronically.

Maslow's hierarchy of motives Abraham Maslow identified five basic needs which form the basis of human motivation, and classified them in a hierarchy of importance. Lower order needs such as the need for food and shelter must be satisfied before human behaviour starts to become motivated by higher order needs, such as the need for love, esteem and self-actualisation at the top.

Mass customisation Website technologies that make it possible for companies to use the information they have about individual customers to create unique online offerings tailored to that person's perceived needs every time he or she visits the website.

Mass marketing Producing mass consumer goods, and using mass distribution and mass promotion methods to address the mass market.

Media The 'vehicles' through which a message is sent to the target audience. Many media exist within each element of the marketing mix.

Meeting a competitor's prices A status-quo objective meaning that your price is the same as that of your competitor.

Membership groups These are groups to which a person has obtained membership, for example a social club.

Micro-environment This refers to the functional areas and everything else inside the business that can be controlled by a business.

Micro-marketing The practice of tailoring products and marketing programmes to suit the tastes of specific individuals and locations, including local marketing and individual marketing.

Mission This defines the fundamental, unique purpose of a business and identifies its products or services and customers. It is a declaration of the core reason why a business exists.

Modified rebuy When a buyer wants to regularly modify product specifications, prices, and terms of business with suppliers.

Motivation The driving force within individuals that impels them to action.

Multiple channels Also called hybrid channels.

Need Can be defined as any human requirement or ability upon which human performance and efficiency depends.

Negative groups Groups with which a person does not wish to be associated.

New product development process The steps taken to identify a new product idea, translating it into a real product, testing it, and launching it in the market.

New-task buying The first-time purchase of a major product.

Niche marketing Marketing to sub-groups within the market segments.

Non-durable products Products that are consumed in one or a few applications and that have to be replenished.

Non-price competition A status quo objective where the business wants to add value to its product rather than compete on price.

Non-probability sampling Sampling for market research that relies on the personal judgement of the researcher, so there is a chance that not every item in a population will be included. *See also* Probability sampling.

Non-profit organisation An organisation established for a purpose other than to make a profit, e.g. a development objective. It therefore seeks to cover costs from donors and perhaps generate a surplus.

Norms Social norms are the expected behaviours for members of a group.

Nuclear family Comprises a father, a mother and children.

Objective The desired outcome that a business is aiming for.

Observational research The systematic process of recording the behavioural patterns of people, objects and occurrences without questioning or communicating with them.

Odd-even pricing A demand-based method of using prices that end in odd numbers, e.g. R9.99 instead of R10.

One-link chain A distribution channel where a manufacturer/producer sells directly to the customer, also called the direct channel.

Opinion leader This is a reference person to whom other consumers will look when forming opinions and taking buying decisions.

Output standards Norms used in evaluating marketing results. Sales, measured in income or physical units, are probably the most important marketing output standard.

Outstanding marketing activities A range of activities performed by the manufacturer/reseller in order to sell its goods.

Ownership gap The gap between a consumer wanting something and owning it. This gap may be filled by extending credit to the consumer.

Packaging The activities involved in designing and manufacturing the container or wrapper for a product. From a marketing point of view, the focus is on how it could contribute to the value of the product and how it could assist in marketing the product.

Page views The number of times a particular page on a website has been viewed.

Payment in kind Payment in which no money is transferred between buyer and seller, but something else of value is exchanged. (See also **Barter**.)

Penetration pricing The opposite of price skimming. A demand-based method of pricing where a product is introduced at a very low price to increase sales.

People In the marketing context, this refers to the people who play a part in the delivery of service, and are part of the expanded marketing mix (the 7 Ps).

Perception Can be defined as the entire process by which an individual becomes aware of the environment and interprets it so that it will fit into his or her own frame of reference.

Peripheral evidence This is evidence that is not as important to service delivery as physical evidence.

Personal selling The selling of the products of an organisation face to face by a sales representative.

Personality Inner psychological characteristics that both determine and reflect how a person responds to his or her environment.

Physical distribution management The aspect of distribution that involves the management of physically transporting products to customers and customer outlets.

Physical evidence Tangible aspects of how successfully the service or product has been delivered or communicated in the expanded marketing mix (the 7 Ps).

Physiological motives In Maslow's hierarchy of needs, the obvious needs for human survival, including the need for food, water, sleep and sex.

Planning The process of a company setting goals, developing strategies, and outlining tasks and schedules to accomplish its goals, taking into account its strengths, weaknesses and the opportunities and threats it faces in the market.

Political environment Government and the laws and regulations that regulate businesses.

Positioning Finding a niche (gap) for the product in the minds of customers in order to create a unique place for the product in the market place.

Positioning statement Clearly identifies the target market, benefits offered to it by the product, and the way in which the product is differentiated from its competitors.

Predictive research Research conducted to forecast future values such as market shares or sales income.

Prestige pricing A demand-based method to differentiate the product by means of a high price to impress the customer.

Price The amount charged for a product or the value that the customer exchanges for having a product.

Price follower A price objective to follow price changes of competitors.

Price leader A price objective to be ahead of competitors with regard to price changes.

Price lining A demand-based method where price lines are identified and the price differs per price line.

Price sensitivity How responsive consumers are to the price of a product.

Price skimming The opposite of penetration pricing – a demand-based method where a new product is launched at a premium price.

Pricing constraints Factor that will influence the decision regarding the price of a product.

Pricing objectives The objectives that the organisation wants to attain with its price strategy, e.g. a R5 million profit.

Primary data Information collected for the specific purpose at hand.

Primary marketing activities For example, the transporting of goods by the manufacturers to the reseller or end customer.

Probability sample In this type of sampling, each item in a population has a known chance of being included through strict statistical procedures.

Process The actual procedures, mechanisms and flow of activities by which the service is delivered – the service delivery and operating systems.

Product concept A perspective of the main dimensions of a product, namely the core, tangible and augmented product and the product image.

Product life cycle (PLC) The time a product spends in the marketplace, from its inception until it is withdrawn from the market.

Product line A number of related products to meet identified consumer needs through specific mixture of technological and/or product features.

Product mix The range of product items manufactured or sold by an organisation.

Profit orientation Ensuring that the needs of customers are met, sales targets are met, and a certain return on investment is made.

Profit-based methods of pricing One type of pricing objective is to attain a certain profit or to maximise profits.

Promotion management All the activities performed and decisions taken regarding the promotion campaign of the organisation.

Promotion mix A combination of a number of promotion elements that are roughly categorised into six groups: advertising, direct marketing, sales promotion, personal selling, public relations and the Internet.

Promotion objectives The targets set before the promotion campaign is finalised to aid the development of the campaign and later to serve as a baseline against which to measure the success of the campaign.

Promotion process The steps taken to develop and implement a promotion campaign for a specific period.

Promotional allowance Payments made by the manufacturer or reductions made to intermediaries for providing promotional services such as advertising.

Public relations Managing the relationship between the organisation and its internal and external shareholders in order to maintain and improve the image of the organisation.

Publics Various interest groups that have a direct or indirect relationship with the organisation, such as labour unions, creditors, investors, suppliers, the labour force, channel and retail partners, and government.

Pulling a product through the channel A situation where marketing communication is focused on customers in order to determine what their product demands are.

Pushing a product through the channel A situation where the manufacturer promotes a product to an intermediary such as a wholesaler, who promotes the product to retailers, and so on.

Quality Quality could be defined as a product that is produced to a consistently high set of standards, or a service delivered to a consistently high set of standards that satisfies specific customer requirements. Ultimately quality refers to giving the customer what he or she expects.

Quality gap The gap between what the manufacturer sees as acceptable and what the customer sees as acceptable.

Quantity discounts Giving a customer some product or service free for buying a certain quantity, e.g. customers who buy ten dozen eggs get a dozen free.

Rack-jobber A specific type of wholesaler who manages shelf space in a retail store that stocks a wide range of products. He or she obtains an income from this management function while the retailer who provides the shelf space receives a return on sales.

Rate of return on total assets (ROA) The return that the business gets on its invested capital. For a comparison, investing R100 000 in an interest-bearing bank account at a certain time might earn interest of 7% per annum. A business investing R100 000 would expect to earn an ROA of more than 7%, or it might as well put the money in the bank.

Receiver The recipient of the message, called the target audience. Many people who receive a promotional message are not part of the organisation's target audience.

Reference groups One or more people that a consumer uses as a basis for his or her forming responses and performing behaviour.

Relationship marketing Efforts to build long-term relationships with customers.

Repositioning The process whereby the original personality of a brand is altered to appeal to a different market segment.

Research design A framework or blueprint for conducting a marketing research project.

Research objectives The precise information needed to solve a research problem.

Reseller markets Organisations that buy goods and services for resale at a profit.

Resellers Intermediaries who buy a product from the manufacturer (take title or take the product on consignment) in order to resell it at a profit.

Retailers Intermediaries who sell directly to customers (usually the last distribution line of products to customers). According to the formal definition, retailers sell more than 50% of their products to the final customer.

Safety motives These include the need for safety, health and security.

Sales analysis A comparison of current sales with post-sales, industry sales, sales by competitors, and forecast sales as a method of evaluating the performance of a business.

Sales budget The sales budget is an output standard with which the marketing results can be compared. A sales budget consists of a forecast of possible sales in rand value and/or physical units and a forecast of the sales cost incurred to realise these sales within a specific future period.

Sales concept The recognition that consumers will not buy enough of a company's products unless a special promotion and selling effort is made.

Salesforce promotion Incentives for sales representatives to improve their inputs in terms of sales, winning new accounts, realising trade support, pushing 'slow' products and introducing new products. Incentive schemes could include prizes, such as a trip overseas or special bonuses.

Sales forecast The estimated sales of the products of a business in all its target markets, expressed in rand value and/or physical units, for a specific period.

Sales intermediaries Agents who do not take title to the products they sell; their task is to bring the buyer and seller together. They work mainly on a commission basis.

Sales-oriented objectives These are price objectives aimed at increasing sales of the product of the organisation.

Sales promotion Communication tools that offer incentives to consumers to buy and trade audiences to sell the product.

Sales quotas Quantitative targets that have to be reached in a specific period; these can be established by regional offices, branch offices, sales departments and individual sales representatives to direct the sales activities of these units.

Sample A segment of the population selected to represent the population as a whole.

Sample size This refers to the number of people in a survey.

Sample units A single element or group of elements subject to selection in a sample.

Sampling frame This refers to a list that the researcher assembles of all eligible sampling units.

Satisfaction This is the client's fulfilment response. It is a judgement that a product or service feature, or the products or service, provided (or is providing) a pleasurable level of consumption-related fulfilment, including levels of under- or over-fulfilment.

Seasonal discounts Discounts given during a certain season, for example Easter or Christmas.

Secondary data Information that already exists somewhere, having been collected for another purpose.

Segment marketing Dividing the market into broad segments and adapting marketing offerings to match the needs of those segments.

Selective attention The recognition that people do not pay the same amount of attention to all marketing messages, they are selective about what they take in.

Selective distribution Distribution where only a limited number of outlets (intermediaries) are selected to sell a product, usually a shopping product.

Selective exposure Deliberately selecting the stimuli to which an individual is exposed.

Selective interpretation Consumers interpreting information on the basis of their own attitudes, beliefs, motives and experiences.

Selective recall The tendency of consumers to forget the marketing message.

Self-actualisation In Maslow's hierarchy of needs, this is the desire for self-fulfilment; to become all that one is capable of becoming.

Sender The source of the message being sent to the target audience; in this context, the marketer.

Service blueprint An accurate picture or map of the service system so that the different people involved in providing service can understand it, and their role in it.

Service recovery A planned process/strategy for returning a dissatisfied client to a state of satisfaction with the company.

Service sponsor franchise A type of franchise where the service provider franchises its selling operations to independent salespeople. Fast-food chain operations usually follow the route of a service sponsor franchise.

Services Support to customers selecting, purchasing, and maintaining a product or service, possibly including online or telephone support, offering a return policy, or having a warranty.

Servicescape The appearance and ambience of the physical surroundings (interior and exterior) where the interaction between the customer and service provider takes place.

Shopping products Products that consumers compare with one another, seek additional information about, and are prepared to shop around for.

Simple random sample Probability sampling in which the sample is selected in such a way that every member of the population has a known and equal chance of selection.

Social classes Groups with more or less the same income and status in society.

Social responsibility The idea that businesses are part of the larger society in which they exist.

Socio-cultural environment The social and cultural trends and changes in which an organisation operates.

Space gaps This refers to the gap between the place of manufacture and the place of consumption.

Spam Unsolicited and inappropriate e-mail (also referred to as junk mail).

Spaza shop An informal type of convenience store (retailer) that operates mostly in disadvantaged areas in South Africa.

Speciality products Products for which consumers have a specific brand preference or would spend time and effort to gather information about before making a choice. The products are expensive or are relatively expensive in their product class.

Speciality store A type of retailer selling a limited variety of product lines but a wide variety in the lines that it stocks.

Standardised process Trying to set standard procedures so that activities are performed the same way, thus getting service consistency.

Status-quo objectives Maintaining prices for a business while keeping abreast of what competitors are doing – a 'don't rock the boat' approach to pricing.

Straight rebuy A routine, low involvement purchase with minimal information needs.

Strengths Areas in which a business does well and that set it apart from competitors.

Supermarket A large self-service retailer mostly selling groceries.

Survey research The gathering of primary data by asking people questions about their knowledge, attitudes, preferences and buying behaviour.

SWOT analysis An analysis of strengths and weaknesses (which relate to the organisation's internal environment), as well as opportunities and threats (which relate to the external environment) so that an organisation can more effectively market its products.

Syncratic families These are families where decisions are made jointly by the father and the mother.

Systematic sampling A probability sampling technique in which the sample is chosen by selecting a random starting point and then choosing every nth element in succession.

Systems orientation When all sections and departments in an organisation work together to meet the needs of the organisation.

Tangibility Something that has actual form and substance, that can be touched.

Tangible products Products with real physical form and substance that constitute the main part of the total product package.

Target audience The people at which a specific promotion mix element is aimed. The target audience is highly related to the target market, but not necessarily the same.

Target market Consumers who have the needs or characteristics that the organisation decides to serve.

Target population The first step in the sampling process where the complete set of elements is identified for investigation.

Targeting The process whereby a marketing mix is tailored to fit some specific target customers.

Technological environment Refers to changes in all aspects of technology and its effect on business.

Telemarketing Using the telephone to sell directly to customers or inform them about a product or new incentive scheme.

Test marketing Launching a prototype product in a limited market (normally geographically limited), supported by a very focused marketing campaign, to determine whether it is likely to be successful in the wider market.

Three-link chain A distribution channel that comprises the manufacturer, a wholesaler and a retailer.

Time gap The gap between when the product is produced and when it is consumed.

Total cost (TC) The total expenses incurred by the business in manufacturing or marketing a product.

Trade discounts A discount given to an intermediary for performing marketing services.

Trade promotion Promotion tools aimed at the distribution and retail partners in the channel to entice them to market the organisation's new and existing products more forcefully.

Transaction flow That part of the distribution decision that involves the buying and selling of the product through the distribution channel.

Truck-jobber A wholesaler who delivers perishable products to a retailer.

Two-link chain A distribution channel where the manufacturer sells to one other intermediary, usually a retailer.

Undifferentiated marketing Organisations that target the whole market with a single product.

Unsought products Products that consumers would rather ignore but are forced to consider, like a funeral policy and insurance policies.

Value groups Broad groups of customers with similar values, attitudes and motivations.

Variable costs (VC) Costs that change in a business in direct relation to the volume sold or manufactured (within given parameters).

Warehouse Storage for unsold products (also called inventory).

Wholesalers A business that sells more than 50% of its products to another intermediary, such as a retailer.

Wife-dominant families Refers to a family where the wife is dominant in buying decisions.

Yield management The process of allocating the right type of capacity to the right type of client at the right price so as to maximise yield or revenue.

Zone of tolerance A service level that is adequate, that the client will accept, even if it is less than what the client would like.

References

Chapter 1

1. Kotler, P & Armstrong, G. 2010. *Principles of marketing, 13th edition*. New York: Pearson, p 16.
2. McDaniel, C, Lamb, CW & Hair, JF. 2006. *Introduction to marketing, 8th edition*. London: Thomson South-Western, p 6.
3. Kotler & Armstrong, Op cit., p 570.
4. Pride, WM & Ferrell, OC. 2010. *Marketing, 15th edition*. London: South-Western CENGAGE Learning, p 14.
5. Adapted from www.customerthink.com.
6. Du Plessis, F, Van Heerden, N & Cook, G. 2010. *Integrated marketing communication, 3rd edition*. Pretoria: Van Schaik, p 375.
7. Adapted from Donna Fluss, searchcrm.techtarget.com.
8. Ibid.
9. Comment on www.customerthink.com by Dr Francis Buttle, www.buttleassociates.com, francis@buttleassociates.com).
10. American Marketing Association (www.marketpower.com); Kotler, P. 2003. *Marketing management, 11th edition*. Upper Saddle River, NJ: Prentice-Hall, p 9; Kotler & Armstrong, Op cit., p 18; Dibb, S, Simkin, L, Pride, WM & Ferrel, OC. 2006. *Marketing: Concept and strategies, 5th edition*. New York: Houghton Mifflin, p 7; Pride, WM & Ferrell, OC. 2006. *Marketing*. Boston MA: Houghton Mifflin, p 4; Pride & Ferrell 2010, Op cit., p 5; Lamb, CW, Hair, JF, McDaniel, C, Boshoff, C & Terblanche, N. 2009. *Marketing, 3rd edition*. Cape Town: Oxford South Africa, p 4.; McDaniel et al., Op cit., p 6.
11. Kotler & Armstrong, Op cit., p 31.
12. McDaniel et al., Op cit., p 11.
13. Based on Du Plessis, PJ, Jooste, CJ & Strydom, JW. 2001. *Applied strategic marketing*. Johannesburg: Heinemann, pp 67–68.
14. Kotler, P. 2000. *Marketing management: The Millennium edition*. Upper Saddle River, NJ: Prentice-Hall, p 37.
15. Du Plessis et al. 2001, Op cit., p 67.
16. Du Plessis et al. 2001, Op cit., p 68.
17. McDaniel et al., Op cit., p 6.
18. Kotler, P, Armstrong, G, Tait, M et al. 2008. *Principles of marketing*. Cape Town: Pearson Education; Kotler et al., Op cit., p 34.
19. Based on Du Plessis in Du Plessis et al. 2001, Op cit., pp. 67–68.
20. Ibid, p 68.
21. Kotler et al., Op. cit. 2008, p 33.
22. Jones, TO & Sasser, WE. 1995. Why satisfied customers defect. *Harvard Business Review*, November–December, pp 88–99.
23. Ibid.
24. Reichheld, FR. 2000. Loyalty-based management. *Harvard Business Review*, March–April, pp 64–73.

25. Lamb et al. 2009, Op cit., p 11.
26. Pride & Ferrell. 2010, Op cit., p 15.
27. *Marketing Mix*. 1999. It's business and it's personal. (August).
28. Abramson, NR. 1998. Practising relationship marketing in Southeast Asia: Reducing uncertainty and improving performance. *Management International Review*, 38, p 113.
29. Kotler & Armstrong 2010, Op cit., p 79.
30. McDaniel et al., Op cit., p. 6.
31. Kotler & Armstrong. 2010, Op cit., p 62.
32. Pride & Ferrell, Op cit., p 15.
33. Kotler & Armstrong. 2010, Op cit., p 62.
34. Ibid., p 77.
35. Lamb et al. 2009, Op cit., pp 19 and 23.
36. Dibb et al. 2006, Op cit., p 49.
37. Lamb et al. 2009, Op cit., p 24.
38. Dibb et al. 2006, Op cit., p 47.
39. Kotler & Armstrong. 2010, Op cit., p 79.
40. Dibb et al. 2006, Op cit., p 47.
41. Kotler & Armstrong. 2010, Op cit., p 77.
42. Ibid., p 79.
43. Ibid., p 80.
44. Ibid., p 43.
45. Based on Du Plessis in Du Plessis et al. 2010, Op cit., pp 15–16.
46. Competition Commission, South Africa. 2009. *Annual Report 2008–2009*. www.compcom.co.za/assets/Files/annual-report-2008-2009.pdf, accessed 2 July 2010.
47. Ibid.
48. Ibid.
49. Creamer, T. 2009. Sasol agrees to higher R250m fine after more fertiliser breaches are unearth*edition*. *Engineering News*, 19 May. www.engineeringnews.co.za/article/sasol-agrees-to-higher-r250m-fine-after-more-fertiliser-breaches-are-unearthed-2009-05-19, accessed 2 July 2010.
50. Competition Commission, Op. cit.
51. Cokayne, R. 2006. BMW dealers fined R8m for fixing prices. *Business Report*. www.busrep.co.za/index.php?fArticleId=3093187, accessed 2 July 2010.
52. Chauke, A. 2010. Sky-high air ticket prices under fire. *Times Live*. www.timeslive.co.za/news/article282195.ece, accessed 2 July 2010.
53. Van der Merwe, C. 2008. Competition authorities raid steel companies' offices in new price probe. *Engineering News*, 23 June. www.engineeringnews.co.za/article/competition-authorities-raid-steel-companies-offices-in-new-price-probe-2008-06-23, accessed 2 July 2010.
54. Carroll, AB. 1996. *Business and society: Ethics and stakeholder management, 3rd edition*. Cincinnati, OH: South-Western College Publishing, p 111.
55. Boatright, JR. 2000. Globalisation and the ethics of business. *Business Ethics Quarterly*, 10(1), pp 1–6.

56. Martin in Laczniak, GR & Murphy, PE. 1985. *Marketing ethics*. Lexington, MA: Lexington Books, p 1.
57. Du Plessis in Du Plessis et al. 2010, pp 15–17.
58. Duncan, TR & Caywood, C. 1996. The concept, process and evolution of integrated marketing communication, in *Integrated communication: Synergy of persuasive voices*, edited by Esther Thorson & Jeri Moore. Mahwah NJ: Lawrence Erlbaum Associates, p 264.
59. Shimp, TA. 2000. *Advertising promotion: Supplemental aspects of integrated marketing communications*, 5th *edition*. Fort Worth TX: Dryden Press, p 66.
60. Duncan & Caywood, Op. cit., p 265.
61. Ibid., p 674.
62. Ibid., p 675.
63. Ibid., p 676.
64. Nantel, J & Weeks, WA. 1996. Marketing ethics: Is there more to it than the utilitarian approach? *European Journal of Marketing*, 30(5), p 10.
65. Chonko, LB. 1995. *Ethical decision making in marketing*. London: Sage, p 3.
66. Moerdyk, C. 2005. Advantage (January), p 32.
67. http://ec.europa.eu/enterprise/policies/sustainable-business/corporate-social-responsibility/index_en.htm, accessed 8 October 2010.
68. Pride & Ferrell. 2010, Op cit., p 11.
69. Kotler & Armstrong. 2010, Op cit., p 51.
70. www.sanlam.co.za/wps/wcm/connect/sanlam_en/sanlam/search/search+results, accessed 8 October 2010.
71. SAB Miller year report 2010. www.sablimit*edition*.co.za/sablimited/content/en/sab-overview, accessed 23 August 2010.

Chapter 2

1. International Trade Administration Commission of South Africa. 2006. *Import control guidelines for the importation of used or second-hand vehicles*. www.itac.org.za/import_guidelines.htm, accessed 14 June 2010.
2. Ibid.
3. O'Sullivan, A & Shiffrin, S. 2003. *Economics: Principles in action*. Upper Saddle River, NJ: Prentice-Hall, p 387.
4. South African Broadcasting Corporation (SABC) News. *BRT services running smoothly after attacks*. www.sabcnews.com/portal/site/SABCNews/menuitem.5c4f8fe7ee929f602ea12ea1674daeb9/?vgnextoid=ecb93e3b3fc58210VgnVCM10000077d4ea9bRCRD&vgnextfmt=default, accessed 24 June 2010.
5. Statistics South Africa. 2009. *Statistical release P0302: Mid-year population estimates*. Pretoria: Statistics South Africa.
6. Schiffman, L & Kanuk, L. 2009. *Consumer behaviour, 9th edition*. Upper Saddle River, NJ: Prentice Hall, p 394.
7. Humpries, M. 2010. *Twitter and Facebook generated $9 million for Dell last year*. www.pcpro.co.uk/news/enterprise/356044/twitter-earned-dell-9-million, accessed 4 July 2010.

8. Competition Tribunal South Africa. 2010. The Competition Commission and Pioneer Foods (Pty) Ltd. www.comptrib.co.za/list_judgement.asp?jid=1120, accessed 4 July 2010.
9. Competition – Pioneer Foods. *Business Day*, 3 November 2010. http://www.businessday.co.za/Articles/Content.aspx?id=125692, accessed 4 November 2010.
10. *Oxford Pocket Dictionary of Current English.*
11. Woolworths. n.d. *Our company: The environment.* www.woolworths.co.za/Caissa.asp?Page=ITB4_RHConText&Post=CO-Environment, accessed 4 July 2010.
12. Optical Energy. 2009. Frequently asked questions: When will Joulie be available? www.optimalenergy.co.za/faq/general.php, accessed 4 July 2010.
13. Marais, H. 2009. *Impact of the global recession on South Africa.* www.amandlapublishers.co.za/home-menu-item/156-the-impact-of-the-global-recession-on-south-africa, accessed 24 June 2010.
14. Kotler, P & Armstrong, G. 1996. *Principles of marketing, 7th edition.* Englewood Cliffs NJ: Prentice Hall, p 71.
15. Toyota. 2010. *Customer FAQ regarding the sticking accelerator pedal and floor mat pedal entrapment recalls.* http://pressroom.toyota.com/pr/tms/customer-faqs-regarding-the-sticking-153495.aspx#link%201, accessed 22 June 2010.
16. Kotler, P & Armstrong, G, Op cit., p 289.
17. Porter, M. 1985. *Competitive advantage: Creating and sustaining superior performance*, as quoted in Hitt, M, Hoskinsson, R & Ireland, R. 2009. *Management of strategy, 9th edition.* Cincinnati OH: South-Western, p 97.
18. Institute of Marketing Management Graduate School of Marketing. 2010. *Mission and vision.* www.imm.co.za/about/about_mission.php, accessed 27 June 2010.
19. South African Revenue Service. 2010. *About SARS.* www.sars.gov.za/home.asp?pid=201, accessed 27 June 2010.
20. Drucker, P. 1968. *The practice of management.* Bungay, Suffolk: Pan, pp 85–108.
21. Strydom, J. 2004. *Introduction to marketing, 3rd edition.* Cape Town: Juta, p 32.
22. Machado, R. 1996. *Marketing for small business.* Cape Town: Juta, p 163.
23. Ibid.

Chapter 3

1. Radder, L, Li, Y, Pietersen, JJ. 2006. Decision-making styles of young Chinese, Motswana and Caucasian consumers in South Africa: An exploratory study. *Journal of Family Ecology and Consumer Sciences*, 34, p 20–31
2. American Marketing Association online dictionary, www.marketingpower.com/_layouts/Dictionary.aspx?dLetter=C, accessed 11 October 2010.
3. Adapted from Brassington, F & Pettitt, S. 2006. *Principles of marketing, 4th edition.* Harlow, Essex: Pearson Education.

4. Brassington, & Pettitt, Op. cit., p 101.
5. Kotler, P & Keller, KL. 2007. *A framework for marketing management, 3rd edition*. Upper-Saddle River, NJ: Prentice-Hall, p 95.
6. Brassington, & Pettitt, Op. cit.
7. Armstrong, G, Kotler, P, Harker, M & Brennan, R. 2009. *Marketing: An introduction, 8th edition*. Harlow, Essex: Pearson Education, p 159.
8. Du Toit, GS, Erasmus, BJ & Strydom, JW. 2010. *Introduction to business management, 8th edition*. Cape Town: Oxford, p 377.
9. Cannon, J, Perrault Jr, WD & McCarthy, EJ. 2008. *Basic marketing: A global managerial approach, 16th edition*. Singapore: McGraw-Hill.
10. Murphy, PE & Staples, WA. 1979. A modernized family life cycle. *Journal of Consumer Research*, 6, pp 12–22.
11. Armstrong, G, Kotler, P, Harker, M & Brennan, R. 2009. *Marketing: An introduction, 8th edition*. Harlow, Essex: Pearson Education, p 159.
12. Kotler, P. 2000. *Marketing management, Millennium Edition*. Upper Saddle River, NJ: Prentice-Hall.

Chapter 4

1 Zikmund, WG. 2000. *Exploring marketing research, 7th edition*. Orlando, FL: Dryden Press, p 28.
2. Ibid.
3. Op cit., p 29.
4. Churchill, GA & Larobucci, D. 2002. *Marketing research: Methodological foundations*. Cinncinatti, OH: South-Western/Thomson Learning, p 29.
5. National Department of Agriculture. n.d. Agricultural Marketing Information System. http://www.agis.agric.za/mis/, accessed 23 March 2010.
6. Burkhardt Research Services. n.d. *Competitive intelligence case study*. www.burkhardtresearch.com/ci_study.html, accessed 26 March 2010; AuroraWDC.com Competitive Intelligence. n.d. What is competitive intelligence? www.aurorawdc.com/whatisci.htm, accessed 23 March 2010; Viviers, W. 2002. Mededingende intelligensie: Jy kan dit nie meer ignoreer nie. *Finansies & Tegniek*, 14 June: 46.
7. Zikmund, Op cit., p 25.
8. Churchill, GA. 2001. *Basic marketing research, 4th edition*. Orlando FL: Dryden Press, p 25.
9. Armstrong, G, Kotler, P, Harker, M & Brennan, R. 2009. *Marketing: An introduction*. Upper Saddle River, New Jersey: Prentice Hall, p 117.
10. www.bday.co.za/content/direct, 29 April 2002.
11. Adapted from Scarborough, NW & Zimmerer, TW. 1998. *Effective small business management*. Columbus OH: Merrill, p 483.
12. Ibid.
13. Cant, MC, Strydom, JW & Jooste, CJ. 1999. *Essentials of marketing*. Cape Town: Juta, p 74.
14. Op cit., p 90.
15. Op cit., p 91.

16. Adapted from Strydom JW, Jooste, CJ & Cant, MC (eds). 2000. *Marketing management, 4th edition*. Cape Town: Juta, pp 149–165.
17. Churchill, Op. cit., p 72.
18. Hair, JF, Bush, RP & Ortinau, DJ. 2000. *Marketing research: A practical approach for the new millennium*. Singapore: McGraw Hill, p 36.
19. Cant et al., Op. cit., p 99.
20. Bothma, CH & Bothma, M. 2002. *Power searching for online business*. Pretoria: University of South Africa study guide, pp 50–51.
21. Zikmund, Op. cit., p 40.
22. Bothma & Bothma, Op. cit., p 30.
23. Hair et al., Op. cit., p 126.
24. Bothma & Bothma, Op. cit., pp 16–18.
25. 23 South Africa Search engines. www.philb.com/cse/southafrica.htm, accessed 31 March 2010.
26. Internet World Stats. 2010. World Internet usage and population statistic (as at 30 June 2010). http://www.Internetworldstats.com/stats.htm, accessed 11 November 2010.
27. Zikmund, Op. cit., p 286.
28. Churchill, Op. cit., p 111.
29. Cant et al., Op. cit., p 107.
30. Armstrong et al., Op. cit., p 125.
31. Hair et al., Op. cit., pp 263–265.
32. Armstrong et al., Op. cit., p 126.
33. Cant et al, Op. cit., p 114.
34. Ibid.
35. Adapted from Churchill, Op. cit. p 449.
36. Zikmund, Op. cit., p 470.
37. Salkind, NJ. 2009. *Exploring research, 7th edition*. Upper Saddle River, NJ: Pearson Prentice-Hall, p 98.
38. Zikmund, Op. cit., p 71.
39. www.marketingweb.co.za/marketingweb/view/marketingweb/en/page71644?oid=. 11668, accessed 31 March 2010

Chapter 5

1. Jobber, D. 2010. *Principles and practices of marketing, 6th edition*. Maidenhead, Berkshire: McGraw-Hill, p 260.
2. Brassington, F & Pettitt, S. 2000. *Principles of Marketing, 2nd edition*. Harlow, Essex: Pearson Education.
3. Cannon, J, Perrault Jr., WD & McCarthy, EJ. 2008. *Basic marketing: A global managerial approach, 16th edition*. Singapore: McGraw-Hill.
4. Cant, MC, Strydom, JW, Jooste, CJ & Du Plessis, PJ (editors). 2006. *Marketing management, 5th edition*. Cape Town: Juta.
5. Strydom, JW, Cant, MC & Jooste, CJ. 2000. *Marketing management, 4th edition*. Cape Town: Juta.

6. Statistics South Africa. n.d. *Census 2001 at a glance*. www.statssa.gov.za/census01/html/default.asp, accessed 28 October 2010.
7. Nations Online Countries of the World. n.d. *Provinces of the Republic of South Africa*. www.nationsonline.org/oneworld/south_africa_provinces.htm, accessed 28 October 2010.
8. Statistics South Africa, Op. cit.,
9. Statistics South Africa. 2009. *Mid-year population estimates*. www.statssa.gov.za/publications/P0302/P03022009.pdf, accessed 28 April 2010.
10. South African Advertising Research Foundation. n.d. *Living Standards Measure*. www.saarf.co.za, accessed 28 April 2010.
11. South African Advertising Research Foundation. 2010. *Living Standards Measures May 2010 presentation*. www.saarf.co.za, accessed 28 April 2010.
12. Kotler, P. 2000. *Marketing management: The Millennium edition*. Upper Saddle River, NJ: Prentice-Hall.
13. BizCommunity. 2010. *Capitec named Brand of Tomorrow*. www.bizcommunity.com/Article/196/82/45534.html, accessed 19 October 2010; Bolin, L. 2004. *Capitec in solid performance post-unbundling*. www.capitecbank.co.za/pdf/mediaReleases/Capitec%20FOCUS%20interview%2021Jan04.pdf, accessed 19 October 2010; Capitec Bank. 2010. *Annual report*. www.capitecbank.co.za/annualReport_2010/Capitec_Group_AR_2010.pdf, accessed 19 October 2010; Adapted from inputs by C Nel as per email dated 25 October 2010.

Chapter 6

1. Partly based on Armstrong, G, Kotler, P, Harker, M & Brennan, R. 2009. *Marketing: An introduction*. Harlow, Essex: Pearson Education, pp 247–249.
2. Nickels, WG & Wood, MB. 1997. *Marketing relationships, quality, value*. New York: Worth Publishers, p 236.
3. Kotler, P & Amstrong, G. 1993 *Marketing: an introduction. 3rd edition*. Englewood Cliffs: Prentice-Hall, p 221.
4. Gerzema, J & Lebar, E. 2009. The trouble with brands. *Strategy + Business*, Issue 5 Summer, pp 1–2.
5. Based on Van der Walt, A, Strydom, JW, Marx, S & Jooste, CJ 1996. *Marketing Management, 3rd edition*. Cape Town: Juta, p 200.
6. Pretoria Portland Cement green strategy pays off. *BDFM Insights*, 10 March 2010.
7. Kortler & Armstrong, Op. cit., p 258
8. Adapted from Assael, H. 1993. *Marketing: Principles and strategy*. Fort Worth TX: Dryden, p 374.
9. Assael, Op. cit., p 734.
10. BizCommunity.com. 2008. 'Amaizing' sandwich packaging ditches plastic, becomes tray. www.bizcommunity.com/Article/196/87/28514.html, accessed 19 April 2010; Grant, L. 2008. Woolworths to launch Earth friendly cleaning products, www.treevolution.co.za/2008/09/woolworths-to-launch-earth-friendly-cleaning-products, accessed: 19 April 2010; Various information

from Woolworths website www.woolworths.co.za/caissa.asp?Page=ITB4_RHContext&Post=Home, accessed: 19 April 2010.

Chapter 7

1. Handfield, RB, Monczka, RM, Guinipero, LC, Paterson, JL. 2009. *Sourcing and supply chain management, 4th edition*. London: Thomson South-Western, p 13.
2. Cant, MC, Strydom, JW, Jooste, CJ & Du Plessis, F. 2006. *Marketing management, 5th edition*. Cape Town: Juta, p 402.
3. Adapted from Cant et al., Op. cit, p 406.
4. Adapted from Cant et al., Ibid.
5. Coelho, F, Easingwood, C & Coelho, A. 2003. Exploratory evidence of channel performance in single vs multiple channel strategies. *International Journal of Retail & Distribution Management*, 31(11), pp 561–573.
6. Webb, KL, & Hogan, JE. 2002. Hybrid channel conflict: Causes and effects on channel performance. *Journal of Business & Industrial Marketing*, 17(5), pp 338–356.
7. Ibid.
8 Ibid.
9. Rix, P. 2004. *Marketing: A practical approach, 5th edition*. Boston, IL: Mcgraw-Hill, pp 335–336.
10. Adapted from Strydom, JW (ed). 2002. *Distribution management*. Pretoria: Van Schaik, p 93.
11. Webb & Hogan, Op. cit.,
12. Adapted from Ferrell, OC & Hartline, MD. 2008. *Marketing strategy, 8th edition*. Mason, OH: Thomson South Western, pp 266–267.
13. Adapted from Cant et al, Op cit., pp 404–405.
14. Based on Strydom, JW, Jooste, CJ & Cant MC (eds). 2000. Marketing *management, 4th edition*. Cape Town: Juta, pp 296–299.
15. Based on Sullivan, M & Adcock, D. 2002. *Retail marketing*. London: Thompson, pp 12–13.
16. Based on the Financial Year Report of the Shoprite Group, 2009, pp 1–36.

Chapter 8

1. Anon. 2008. The art of drug pricing. www.thebody.com/contents/art13514.html, accessed 4 February 2010.
2. Armstrong, GC & Kotler, P. 2000. *Marketing: An introduction, 5th edition*. Upper Saddle River, NJ: Prentice-Hall, p 289.
3. Indounas, C & Avlonites, GJ. 2009. Pricing objectives and their antecedents in the services sector. *Journal of Service Management*, 20(3), pp 342–374.
4. Pick n Pay website. n.d. www.pickandpay.co.za/ccinvestigation/, accessed 24 January 2010.
5. *Business Report*. 2010. Crises leave arms spending unscath*edition*. www.busrep.co.za/generalprintaricle.php?articleid=5338365& SeetanId=5, accessed 24 January 2010.

6. Based on the definitions supplied in Mansfield, E & Yohe, G. 2000. *Microeconomics: theory/applications, 10th edition*. New York: Norton, pp A1–A12.
7. Da Silva, IS. 2010. 2010 overpricing undermines tourism business. SA Tourism website, accessed 22 January 2010.
8. Skinner, SJ. 1994. *Marketing, 2nd edition*. Boston, MA: Houghton Mifflin, pp 423–432.
9. Newmark, Z. 2009. VW will cost 900 euros to build – estimate. www.worldcarfans.com/109070320269/vw-up-will-cost-900-euros-to-build-report, accessed 16 February 2010.
10. Taylor, A. 2010. Hyundai smokes the competition. *Fortune*, 161(1), p 39.
11. *Business Day*, 31 July 2001.
12. Anon. 2009. Understanding Apple's positioning: Part 1 – a premium brand at a premium price. www.switchtoamac.com/site/understanding-apples-positioning-part-1-a-premium-brand-at-a-premium-price.html, accessed 27 January 2010.
13. Indounas & Avlonitis, Op. cit., p 349.
14. Van der Walt, A, Strydom, JW. Marx, S & Jooste, CJ (eds). 1996. *Marketing management, 3rd edition*. Cape Town: Juta, pp 447–452.
15. Hinterhuber, A. 2008. Customer value based pricing strategies: Why companies resist. *Journal of Business Strategy*, 29(4), p 4.
16. Hinterhuber, Op. cit., p 42.
17. Strydom, JW, Jooste, CJ, Cant, MC. (eds). 2000. *Marketing management, 4th edition*. Cape Town: Juta, pp 458–463.
18. Hoch, SJ & Fox, EJ. 2004. Cherry picking: The weapon of choice for price-conscious consumers. Consumers.Knowledge@Wharton, 14 January 2004.
19. Crotty, A. 2010. Tribunal pioneers R200m fine. *Business Report*. www.busrep.co.za/generic/print-article?articleIID=5338372&FSeetanID=8, accessed 4 February 2010.
20. Competition – Pioneer Foods. *Business Day*, 3 November 2010. http://www.businessday.co.za/Articles/Content.aspx?id=125692, accessed 4 November 2010.

Chapter 9

1. Adapted from McDaniel, C, Lamb, CW & Hair, JF. 2008. *Introduction to marketing, 9th edition*. Cincinatti, OH: South Western, p 440.
2. Kitchen, PJ. 2004. *Marketing communications: Principles and practice*. London: Thomson, p 93.
3. Kotler, P & Armstrong, G. 1997. *Marketing: An introduction*. Upper Saddle River, NJ: Prentice-Hall, p 429.
4. Du Plessis, F. 2003. *Integrated marketing communication*. Cape Town: New Africa Books, p 49–53.
5. Armstrong, G, Kotler, P, Harker, M & Brennan, R. 2009. *Marketing: An introduction*. Upper Saddle River, NJ: Prentice-Hall, p 403.
6. Armstrong et al., Op. cit., p 404.

7. Jain, SC. 2000. *Marketing planning and strategy*. Cincinnati, OH: South Western, p 489.
8. McDaniel et al., Op. cit., p 456.
9. Armstrong et al., Op. cit., pp 414–415, 418.
10. McDaniel et al., Op. cit., p 484.
11. Belch, GE & Belch, MA. 2009. *Advertising and promotion: An integrated marketing communications perspective*. New York: Irwin McGraw-Hill, p 344.
12. McDaniel et al., Op. cit., pp 486–487.
13. Churchill, GA & Peter, JP. 1998. *Marketing: Creating value for customers*. New York: Irwin McGraw-Hill, p 482.
14. Ibid.
15. Belch & Belch, Op. cit., p 738.
16. www.verimark.co.za, accessed 24 July 2006.
17. Kitchen, PJ. 2004. *Marketing communications: Principles and practice*. London: Thompson, p 291.
18. Belch & Belch, Op. cit., p 574.
19. Kitchen, Op cit., p 362.
20. www.redcube.co.za/index.php/campaigns/info-case_studies/cadbury_games/, accessed 24 February, 2010.
21. www.timeslive.co.za/sundaytimes/article63833.ece, accessed 8 March 2010; http://blogs.dispatch.co.za/dispatchnow/2009/04/21/nandos-julius-malema-ad-disgusting-ancyl/, accessed 8 March, 2010; www.iol.co.za/index.php?set_id=1&click_id=3095&art_id=vn20090425063801637C202606, accessed 8 March, 2010.
22. www.themarketingsite.com/live/content.php?Item_ID=8706, accessed 3 March 2010; www.clickthinking.com/our_work/vodacom.php, accessed 3 March 2010; http://bizcommunity.com/Article/196/12/36746.html, accessed 3 March 2010.

Chapter 10

1. Wilson, A, Zeithaml, VA, Bitner, MJ & Gremler, DD. 2008. *Services marketing: Integrating customer focus across the firm, European edition*. Boston MA: Irwin McGraw-Hill, p 5.
2. Palmer, A. 2004. *Principles of services marketing, 5th edition*. Berkshire: McGraw Hill, p 5.
3. Lovelock, C. 2001. *Services marketing: People, technology, strategy, 2nd edition*. Upper Saddle River, NJ: Prentice-Hall, p 3.
4. Kotler, P. 2003. *Marketing management, 11th edition*. Upper Saddle River NJ: Prentice-Hall/Pearson Education International, p 445.
5. Hoffman, KD, Bateson, J, Wood, E & Kenyon, AJ. 2009. *Services marketing: Concepts, strategies and cases*. London: Cengage Learning, pp 26–51.
6. Lovelock, Op. cit., p 35.

7. Gronroos, C. 2000. *Service management and marketing: A customer relationship management approach, 2nd edition*. Chichester: John Wiley, pp 54 & 373.
8. Jordaan, Y & Prinsloo, M. 2004. *Grasping service marketing, 2nd edition*. Pretoria: The Authors, pp 84–87.
9. Lovelock, Op. cit., p 199.
10. Lovelock, Op. cit., p 288.
11. Jordaan & Prinsloo, Op. cit., p 241.
12. Jordaan & Prinsloo, Op. cit., p 251.
13. Strydom, J & Theron, DP. 2009. *Managing and marketing services*. Helderkruin: Red Peppers, p 163.
14. Wilson et al., Op cit., p 429.
15. Lovelock, Op. cit., p 278.
16. Hoffman et al., Op. cit., p 264.
17. Wilson et al., Op cit., p 242.
18. Johnson, R & Clark, G. 2005. *Service operations management: Improving service delivery, 2nd edition*. Harlow: Prentice Hall-Financial Times, p 172.
19. Palmer, Op. cit., p 115.
20. Palmer, Op. cit., p 97.
21. Gronroos, Op. cit., p 336.
22. Gronroos, Op. cit., p 347.
23. Jordaan & Prinsloo, Op. cit., p 155.
24. kulula.com. 2010. *Press release, 8 February 2010: kulula's 'Flying 101' plane design achieves global fame*. www.kulula.com/info/pressreleases2010.aspx, accessed 2 October 2010.

Chapter 11

1. Adapted from Brink, A & Berndt, A. 2008. *Relationship marketing and customer relationship management*. Juta: Cape Town, p 43.
2. Kotler, P & Keller, KL 2009. *Marketing Management, 13th edition*. Pearson: Upper Saddle River, p 610.
3. Adapted from Busch, PS & Houston, MJ. 1985. *Marketing: Strategic foundations*. Homewood, IL: Irwin, p 82.
4. Adapted from Doyle, P. 2008. *Value-based marketing*. Chichester, West Sussex: Wiley, pp 4–10.
5. Cant, M. 2010. *Essentials of marketing*. Cape Town: Juta, p 64.
6. Wilson, RMS & Gilligan, C. 2009. *Strategic marketing management, 2nd edition*. Oxford: Butterworth-Heinemann, p 201.
7. Adapted from Kotler, P & Keller, KL. 2009. *Marketing management, 13th edition*. Upper Saddle River, NJ: Pearson, pp 59–68.
8. Venter, P & Jansen van Rensburg, M. 2009. *Strategic marketing: Theory and applications for competitive advantage*. Cape Town: Oxford University Press, p 263.

9. Zeithaml, VA, Bittner, MJ & Gremler, DD. 2009. *Services marketing, 5th edition*. New York: McGraw-Hill, pp 265–267.
10. Smith, N. 2010. How Chief Marketing Officers can drive a new growth agenda, *Outlook: Point of View*, 1, March.
11. Adapted from Rensburg, R & Cant, M. 2009. *Public relations: African perspectives*. Heinemann: Johannesburg, p 252.
12. Both of these cases can be Googled easily for more information.
13. Adapted from Shaw, WH. 2011. *Business ethics, 7th edition*. Boston, MA: Wadsworth, p 226.
14. Shaw, Op cit., pp 235–241.

Chapter 12

1. Internet World Stats. n.d. *World Internet usage and population statistics*. www.Internetworldstats.com/stats.htm, accessed 5 May 2010.
2. World Wide Worx. 2010. *SA Internet growth accelerates, (18 January 2010)*. www.worldwideworx.com/archives/234, accessed 5 May 2010.
3. *Cambridge Advanced Learner's Dictionary*. 2010. http://dictionary.cambridge.org/dictionary/british/the-Internet, accessed 5 May 2010.
4. Computer Hope. n.d. *IP*. www.computerhope.com/jargon/i/ip.htm, accessed 5 May 2010.
5. Bothma, CH. 2000. *E-commerce for South African managers*. Pretoria: Interactive Reality.
6. Ibid.
7. Cambridge Advanced Learner's Dictionary. 2010. http://dictionary.cambridge.org/dictionary/british/the-world-wide-web#the-world-wide-web__3, accessed 5 May 2010.
8. Bothma, Op. cit.,
9. W3C. 2003. *People of the W3C*. www.w3c.org/, accessed 31 May 2010.
10. Bothma, Op. cit.,
11. Chaffey, D, Ellis-Chadwick, F, Johnston, K & Mayer, R. 2006. *Internet marketing: Strategy, implementation and practice*. Harlow, Essex: Pearson Education, p 523.
12. Rayport, JF & Sviokla, JJ. 1994. Managing in the marketplace. *Harvard Business Review*, (November-December), pp 141–150.
13. Stokes, R. 2008. *eMarketing: The essential guide to online marketing*. Johannesburg: Quirk eMarketing, pp 73–91; 197–218.
14. Swanepoel, J. 2007. *The e of marketing*. Cape Town: Juta, p 41.
15. Stokes, Op. cit.,
16. Royal Pingdom. 2010. *Internet 2009 in numbers, 22 January 2010*. http://royal.pingdom.com/2010/01/22/Internet-2009-in-numbers, accessed 5 May 2010.
17. Chaffey et al., Op. cit., p 532.
18. Keeler, L. 1995. Cyber marketing. New York: AMACOM (American Management Association).
19. Chaffey et al., Op. cit., p 351.

20. Coupey, E. 2001. *Marketing and the Internet: Conceptual foundations*. Upper Saddle River, NJ: Prentice-Hall.
21. Perez, JC. 2010. Google grows revenue 23 percent in Q1. *Bloomberg Buisnessweek* www.businessweek.com/idg/2010-04-15/google-grows-revenue-23-percent-in-q1.html, accessed 26 May 2010.
22. Melissa. 2009. *Paid search vs. organic search, 23 December 2009*. Optimum7.com. www.optimum7.com/Internet-marketing/paid-search/paid-search-vs-organic-search.html, accessed 26 May 2010.
23. Stokes, Op cit., p 50.
24. Ferguson, R. 2008. Word of mouth and viral marketing: Taking the temperature of the hottest trends in marketing. *Journal of Consumer Marketing*, 25(3), pp 179–182.
25. Facebook Press Room. n.d. *Statistics*. www.facebook.com/press/info.php?statistics, accessed 26 May 2010.
26. Schonfeld, E. 2010. Nearly 75 million people visited Twitter's site in January (16 February 2010). *Techcrunch*. http://techcrunch.com/2010/02/16/twitter-75-million-people-january/, accessed 26 May 2010.
27. Twitter. 2010. *Website monitoring, April 2010*. http://twitter.com/monitoringblog, accessed 26 May 2010.
28. Harris, L & Rae, A. 2009. Social networks: the future of marketing for small business. *Journal of Business Strategy*, 30(5), pp 24–31.
29. Stokes, Op cit., p 272.
30. Vollmer, C. 2008. *Always on: Advertising, marketing and media in an era of consumer control*. New York: McGraw-Hill.
31. Strategic Direction. 2010. Getting the social media on your side: Marketing specialists must embrace the world of technology. *Strategic Direction*, 2010 pp 6–9.
32. Stokes, Op cit., p 260.
33. Royal Pingdom, Op. cit.,
34. Wilhelm, A. 2010. Are there only 15 million active Twitter users? (26 January 2010.) *THW Social Media*. http://thenextweb.com/socialmedia/2010/01/26/15-million-active-twitter-users, accessed 27 May 2010.
35. Fuseware: Strategic Social Media Integration. 2010. *SA twitter report 2010 (April)*. http://www.fuseware.net/reports/sa-twitter-2010/, accessed 27 May 2010.
36. Royal Pingdom, Op. cit.,
37. Morrison, L. 2008. Mobile tracking technology manages courier company growth. *Engineering News*, 14 November. www.engineeringnews.co.za/article/mobile-tracking-technology-manages-courier-company-growth-2008-11-14, accessed 28 May 2010.
38. Media Update. 2010. *South Africans continue to shop online: MasterCard survey, 23 March 2010*. www.mediaupdate.co.za/default.aspx?IDStory=23919, accessed 27 May 2010.
39. Vassos, T. 1996. *Strategic Internet marketing*. Indianapolis, IN: Que Corporation.

40. Internet Solutions, 2000. *What is CRM?* www/is.co.za/solution/e-commerce/whatiscrm.html, accessed 27 May 2010.
41. Lee-Kelly, L, Gilbert, D & Mannicom, R. 2003. How e-CRM can enhance customer loyalty. *Marketing Intelligence & Planning*, 21(4/5), pp 239–248.

Index

Entries are listed in letter-by-letter alphabetical order. Page references in *italic* indicate where a figure or table relating to the index entry term can be found.